THE WORLD ENCYCLOPEDIA OF BUTTERFLIES & MOTHS

A NATURAL HISTORY AND IDENTIFICATION GUIDE TO OVER 565 VARIETIES AROUND THE GLOBE

SALLY MORGAN

LORENZ BOOKS

This edition is published by Lorenz Books,
an imprint of Anness Publishing Ltd, info@anness.com

www.lorenzbooks.com; www.annesspublishing.com

If you like the images in this book and would like to investigate using them for publishing, promotions or advertising, please visit our website www.practicalpictures.com for more information.

© Anness Publishing Ltd 2024

A CIP catalogue record for this book is available from the British Library.

Publisher: Joanna Lorenz
Editorial Director: Helen Sudell
Special Photography: Robert Pickett
Illustrators: Penny Brown, Peter Bull, Stuart Jackson-Carter, Felicity Cole, Joanne Glover, Jonathan Latimer, Carol Mullin, Fiona Osbaldstone and Denys Ovenden.
Book and Cover design: Nigel Partridge
Production Controller: Ben Worley

PUBLISHER'S NOTE
Although the advice and information in this book are believed to be accurate and true at the time of going to press, neither the authors nor the publisher can accept any legal responsibility or liability for any errors or omissions that may have been made.

In memory of Nicola Tovey, a wonderful friend who is greatly missed.

CONTENTS

THE WORLD ENCYCLOPEDIA OF
BUTTERFLIES
&MOTHS

INTRODUCTION

Among the most colourful of the insects are the butterflies and moths. These insects make up the Lepidoptera – the scale wing insects, so named because their wings are covered in tiny scales. It is the structure of the scales and the pigments within them that create the huge variety in wing colours.

Identifying the world's most beautiful butterfly is a much debated question, but among the contenders must be the glossy swallowtails and iridescent morphos. Size, as well as beauty, is another aspect much discussed among butterfly and moth lovers, and they do range in size considerably. The largest moth is the Atlas moth (*Attacus atlas*), so large that it is easily mistaken for a bat when it flies, and the Queen Alexandra's Birdwing (*Ornithoptera alexandrae*) butterfly, which is found in the rainforests of New Guinea. The smallest moth is the tiny Nepticulid moth, with wings just a few millimetres wide, while the smallest butterfly is the North American Pygmy Blue (*Brephidium exilis*), which has a wingspan of less than 20mm (0.79in). Within this varied group are more than 180,000 named species in 127 families and 46 superfamilies. This number is likely to increase as more species are discovered in remote rainforests and other habitats.

Insects

Butterflies and moths are insects and they belong to the phylum *arthropoda*, a huge phylum that contains three out of every four species of animal. Spiders, crabs and millipedes are all Arthropods, which are animals with segmented bodies that are covered in an exoskeleton and have jointed appendages. The insects are the largest class within the arthropods. This highly successful and diverse group has adapted well to life on land, and is one of just three groups that has taken to the skies. Of the three, it was the insects that first evolved the power of flight more than 100 million years ago, followed later by birds and bats. Flight has enabled them to colonize an enormous range of habitats.

Another characteristic feature of insects is their life cycle, which involves metamorphosis. Some insects have larvae that when growing, go through a series of moults in which their appearance becomes more like

*Above: The Red Postman (*Heliconius erato*) is one of the many butterflies found in the world's tropical rainforests.*

that of the adult. This is an incomplete metamorphosis. Butterflies and moths exhibit complete metamorphosis – the larva is totally transformed into an adult during the pupal stage.

Geographical range

Butterflies and moths are dependent on plants as a source of food for both the adult and the caterpillar. As a result,

Below: Lepidopterans have a basic body plan of a head, thorax and abdomen with three pairs of legs and two pairs of wings.

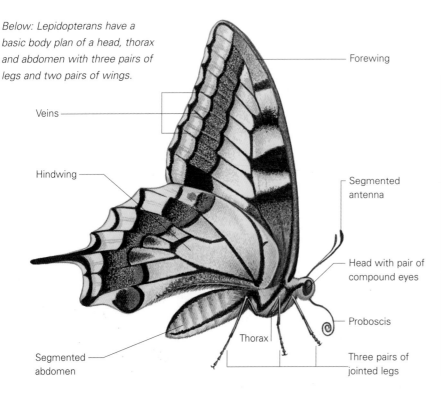

Forewing

Veins

Hindwing

Segmented antenna

Head with pair of compound eyes

Proboscis

Thorax

Three pairs of jointed legs

Segmented abdomen

*Below: Lepidopteran caterpillars vary in form and colour. One of the more striking is this Chinese Owl silkmoth (*Brahmaea hearsayi*).*

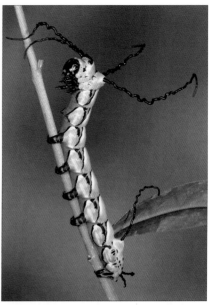

they can be found in a wide variety of habitats, from the tropical rainforests to mountain slopes, from arid grasslands to Arctic tundra. The only places from which both are absent are the polar regions and some of the world's deserts. Some migratory species, such as the Painted Lady (*Cynthia cardui*) and the Monarch (*Danaus plexippus*) have a wide distribution, occurring across several continents while others occur within very specific localities. For example, the Avalon Hairstreak (*Strymon avalona*) occurs only on Santa Catalina Island off the Californian coast.

More than 500 species of butterfly and moth are featured in this book, from the widespread and common, such as the Small Tortoiseshell (*Aglais urticae*) and Large White (*Pieris brassicae*), to the rare and unusual, such as the Giant African Swallowtail (*Papilio antimachus*) and Elsa Sphinx moth (*Sagenosoma elsa*). Sadly, butterflies and moths are coming increasingly under threat as habitat destruction continues at an ever-increasing pace. Additional threats come from collectors, who target the larger and more beautiful species, and

of course from global warming. Habitat preservation is critical for the survival of these wonderful insects, since without healthy habitats the battle for their future cannot be won.

*Above: The two pairs of a butterfly's wings are held together during flight, so that they move as one. This Emperor Swallowtail (*Papilio ophidocephalus*) comes from southern Africa.*

Butterfly or moth?

Many people perceive butterflies as being different from moths, but this distinction is not really that clear. Often, the moth has a larger, more feathery looking antenna, although this is lacking in many. Butterflies usually have a club-ended antenna. Moths tend to be active at night, but there are day-flying moths. Moths are considered to be more drab, and lack colourful scales, but again there are examples of brilliantly coloured moths such as the Uraniidae. To add to the confusion, the group of butterflies called skippers shares many features in common with moths and are now no longer included within the butterfly families, while some butterflies have more in common with caddis flies.

*Right: The red wing spots of the daytime Burnet moth (*Zygaena filipendulae*) warn predators that it is poisonous.*

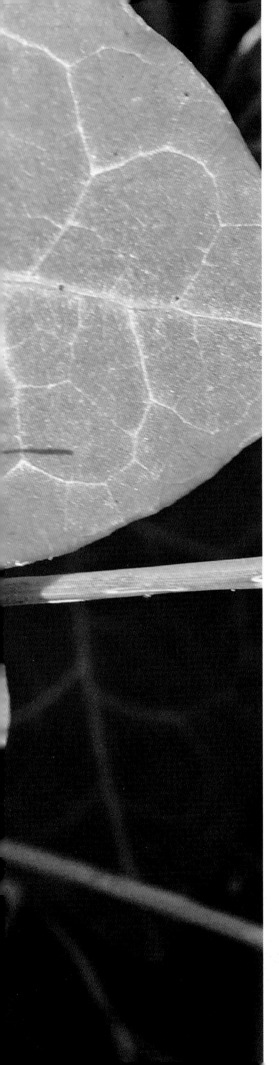

LEPIDOPTERANS

Butterflies and moths are typical insects in that they have three body parts: a head, a thorax and an abdomen. The body is covered by an exoskeleton, which consists of a series of hard plates, called sclerites, which are joined to each other by membranes. This arrangement gives flexibility to an otherwise inflexible body covering. The head bears some remarkable organs; a pair of compound eyes, a pair of segmented antennae and highly modified mouthparts. Attached to the thorax are two pairs of wings and three pairs of jointed legs. Insects have developed longer legs than are seen in more primitive arthropods such as the Myriapods (millipedes and centipedes), in order to permit faster movement. By reducing the number of their legs to six, they have gained speed at the same time as retaining balance. Butterflies and moths have two pairs of wings, which are mostly large, membranous, and covered in scales.

One of the best known features of butterflies and moths is their transformation from caterpillar to adult, the metamorphosis. Lepidopterans exhibit complete metamorphosis, and they pass through four distinct stages in their life cycle: egg, larva, pupa and adult. The appearance of the larva is completely different to that of the adult.

Lepidopterans have very short lives, with most living less than a couple of weeks. During this time they have to find a mate and lay fertile eggs. To make this process easier, butterflies and moths release scents to lure members of the other sex. The female moths, for example, release chemicals known as pheromones which drift on the wind to be detected by the male moths. Many male butterflies rest in conspicuous places such as hilltops, where they watch for a female, while others sit by the pupa of a female and wait for her to emerge. The female maximises the chances of her caterpillars surviving by laying her eggs on or near the food plant. The caterpillars emerge and start eating straightaway. This is the growth stage of the life cycle, and the caterpillars continue to feed until they are ready to pupate. Metamorphosis takes place in the pupa and the adult emerges and the cycle starts again.

*Left: The Speckled Wood butterfly (*Pararge aegaria*) is just one of the many butterflies that are found along hedgerows and the edge of woodlands.*

EXTERNAL ANATOMY

The external appearance of butterflies and moths is surprisingly uniform. All have a segmented body divided into three body parts, together with wings and long legs in the adult. However, the size and shape of the wings varies considerably, and there are some species that only have two pairs of functional legs.

The basic segmented body plan consists of a section with a dorsal sclerite called the tergum, which is joined to the ventral sclerite, the sternum, by the lateral membranes called the pleura.

Head

The head is joined to the thorax by a flexible membrane, the neck. The head carries the mouthparts, the sense organs including a pair of compound eyes, and a pair of antennae.

In adults, the mouthparts have been modified for sucking so that liquid can be drawn up a tube. The sucking apparatus, the proboscis, is used to suck nectar from flowers and fruits. It is formed from the galeae of the maxillae, the two grooved halves being joined together to form a long tube.

The proboscis

The longest proboscis, up to 30cm (12in) long, is found in hawkmoths. A few lepidopterans have a much shorter proboscis, which is better adapted for piercing soft fruits. In several families, the mouthparts are either reduced or absent. For example, silkmoths, eggars,

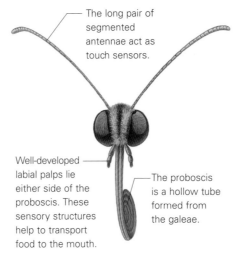

The long pair of segmented antennae act as touch sensors.

Well-developed labial palps lie either side of the proboscis. These sensory structures help to transport food to the mouth.

The proboscis is a hollow tube formed from the galeae.

Above: The structure of the head of a typical butterfly, with its compound eyes, antennae and sucking mouthparts.

emperors and goat moths do not feed at all as adults. Instead, they rely upon food stores that are built up during the larval stage. These moths are short-lived, surviving only long enough to mate and lay eggs. Both larval stages of butterflies and moths, together with the primitive superfamily, Micropterigidae, have retained a pair of chewing mandibles.

Above: The compound eyes are placed to the side of the head to give all-round vision. The eyes are very sensitive to movement.

The compound eye

Each compound eye comprises a number of ommatidia that work together. Each ommatidium consists of a light-gathering part and a sensory part where the light is detected and an electrical signal sent to the brain. The compound eye works in such a way that each ommatidium produces a series of spots of light of differing intensities, and it is these spots that are combined to give an overall view of the object.

Adult lepidopterans have a pair of compound eyes that provide a wide field of vision. The eye detects movement, differentiates between wavelengths of light, detects polarized light and distinguishes a simple image. The positioning of the two eyes, with their wide field of view, gives an insect the ability to judge distances, which is important for avoiding objects when flying and for enabling the insect to land safely. Typically, caterpillars have three ocelli, which are primitive eyes.

Left: At rest, the tube-like proboscis is coiled up under the head. It is extended for feeding. A muscular pump, formed from enlarged muscles in the pharynx, draws up liquid through the proboscis.

Butterfly and moth antenna

Antenna shape is surprisingly variable, both between both butterflies and moths, between males and females and between Lepidopteran families. Most butterflies have long, thin but stiff antennae that end in small knobs or clubs. Moths tend to have either pectinate (comb-like and feathery) or filiform (thread-like) antennae. Pectinate antennae occur in the geometrids, eggars, tussocks and some noctuid moths, while the most extreme filiform antennae are found in the Adelidae, in which the males have antennae that are up to five times longer than their wings. There are, however, numerous exceptions to this general observation, such as skippers that have antennae with angled tips rather than club-ended antennae.

Among moths, there are some with club-ended antennae, namely the Castiniidae. Male antennae tend to be larger and, in moths, pectinate in shape. This is because the males rely on their sense of smell to locate females, using their antennae to detect pheromones.

Above: This male Giant Comet moth has a long pair of pectinate antennae.

Below: Most butterflies have antennae that are club-shaped at the end.

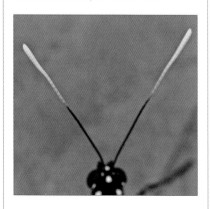

Above: The wings are attached to the second and third segments of the thorax. The abdomen is formed from 10 segments and has no appendages.

The ocelli do not produce a detailed image, but are able to detect changes in light levels.

Antenna

The head bears a pair of segmented antennae, each with a basal scape, a pedicel and a flagellum. The main function of the antenna is as a touch sensor. Within the second segment of the antennae lies the Johnston's organ, which responds to different stimuli. For example, it acts as a proprioceptor by detecting movement in the antenna. The Johnston's organ has been found to be critical in moths where it has an important role in maintaining flight stability, with loss of control being observed in moths in which the flagellum was removed.

Thorax

The thorax is sub-divided into three segments, pro-, meso- and meta-thorax with a pair of legs attached to each. Each leg consists of six segments, which articulate with each other by membraneous joints. The coxa articulates with the thorax, then come the trochanter, femur, tibia, tarsus and

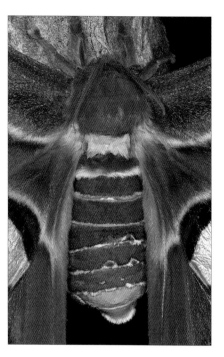

Above: The upper surface of the exoskeleton covering each segment is called the tergum, seen here on an Atlas moth (Attacus atlas).

finally pretarsus that forms a pair of claws. In the nymphalids, the number of legs has been reduced to four, with the forelegs being compressed against the thorax. In males, this redundant leg lacks the tarsus and the pretarsus, while the females have all six segments but they are very short. Another feature of lepidopteran legs is a lobe called the strigil on the front tibia, which carries a brush of hairs used to clean the antennae and proboscis. The two pairs of wings are attached to the first two segments.

Abdomen

The cylindrical abdomen has a more obviously segmented appearance. There are 10 segments in all, of which only eight are visible. The last two segments are fused together to form the external genitalia. The arrangement of the female genital openings varies, with some groups having a single opening for copulation and ovulation, while other groups have separate openings. The abdomen is covered in scales and hairs. In some groups, tufts of terminal hairs are used to cover the eggs.

WING CHARACTERISTICS

One of the most distinctive features of lepidopterans is their wings. Virtually all butterflies and moths have two pairs of wings, each of which is covered in minute scales. It is the scales that create the wide range of colours and patterns seen on the wings.

Butterflies and moths have two pairs of wings, each made from a double membrane supported by veins. The shape, colour and venation of the wings all provide useful information for identification purposes.

Attachment

The meso- and metathorax segments of the thorax are adapted for the attachment of the wings. The tergum of these two segments is modified with ridges to provide additional strength and support during flight, as it is the distortion of the tergum that is essential to the movement of the wings.

Wing structure

A lepidopteran wing is a thin membrane supported by a network of hollow veins. The membrane is

Above: The two pairs of wings of this Lime Swallowtail (Papilio demoleus) *are joined to the second and third segments of the thorax.*

Below: A diagram of the wings of a butterfly showing the main veins, which are used to help in classification and species identification.

an extension of the cuticle, formed from two layers of cuticle pushed closely together. The veins develop where the two layers remain separate,

and at this point the cuticle becomes thickened to form the vein. The veins form part of the cirulatory system within the body. There is also a nerve and a trachea (for gas exchange) running along each vein.

The pattern of wing veins is significant as it is fixed and is used for the purposes of classification. Both wings usually have the following veins present on both wings: subcostal, radial, median, cubital and anal. On the hind wing there is an elongated area, bound by veins, called the discal cell.

The two pairs of wings are not identical. Generally, the forewings are larger, while the hindwings tend to display more features such as tails and fringes. For example, most swallowtails have hind wings with long tails, while plume moths have narrow wings that are deeply divided into lobes with a fringe of scales. The fringe serves to increase the surface area of the wing. Some butterflies, such as the Comma (*Polygonia c-album*), even have wings with an irregular outline, which is thought to provide camouflage as it disrupts the outline of the butterfly when at rest.

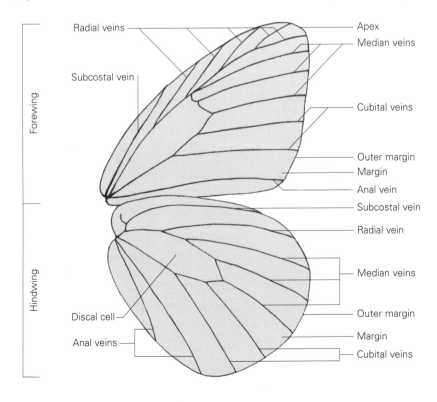

*Above: This Heliconid butterfly (*Heliconius sp.*) keeps its wings raised when at rest.*

*Right: The Grey Pansy (*Precis atlites*), from India, shows a row of striking eyespots on its upperwings when resting with wings open.*

Coupling

During flight, the wings are coupled together to move as one, as this is more efficient and produces greater lift. There are several coupling mechanisms. A simple mechanism involves bristles on the leading edge of the hindwing catching the underside of the forewing, coupling the wings together. This has developed in some species, so that a tuft of long bristles form a frenulum, or wing-coupling structure, that locks with forward pointing bristles on the forewing.

In some butterflies and moths, the frenulum is formed from bristles that have fused together to form a single spine. This locks into a cuticular clasp that sticks down from a vein on the forewing. Swallowtails and skippers lack bristles, and, instead rely on an overlap between the two wings. Some micromoths have a long thin lobe at the base of the forewing that sticks out over the top of the hindwing, catching the frenular bristles.

Wings at rest

Butterflies hold their wings in different positions when at rest, which is another useful feature to help identify a species. Skippers, however, hold their wings in a manner not seen in either butterflies or moths, reinforcing the view that they should not be classified as a butterfly. When skippers land, the hindwings are held out flat, but the forewings are held at an angle of about 45 degrees, giving them a so-called 'fighter jet' appearance. Moths tend to land and hold their wings out flat against the surface on which they are resting. Very often, their hindwing is folded up out of sight under the forewing. For many moths, a tree trunk is a popular resting place and the coloration of their upperwings provides perfect camouflage against bark. The Peppered Moth (*Biston betularia*) is a perfect example. Some butterflies do the same, but others land and hold their wings together in an upright position, like a roof over the abdomen. This hides the often brightly coloured upper surface of the forewings. The underwing of many butterflies is cryptically coloured in a pattern of browns and greens. With raised wings at rest, the cryptic underwing is revealed and the butterfly becomes incredibly difficult to spot on leaves or on the ground. In the Grayling, the position of the wings at rest are carefully oriented so that a minimal shadow is thrown.

*Below: When at rest, the huge wings of the Ailanthus Silkmoth (*Samia cymthia*), spanning up to 14cm (5½ in), can be appreciated.*

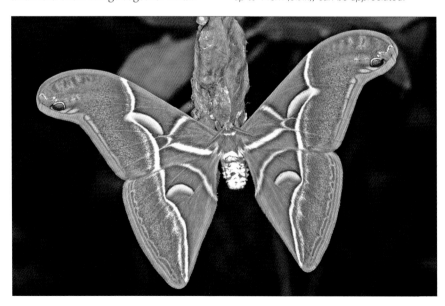

FLIGHT

Insects are one of the three groups of animals that exhibit true flight. It is estimated that this ability dates back some 300 million years, when the first wings developed from a small extension of the cuticle of the thorax. Since then, insects have evolved a remarkable diversity of wings in both size and shape.

Butterflies and moths fly by flapping their wings up and down. Some of the wing movement is produced by thoracic muscles attached to the base of the wings, but most of the movement is generated by changes in the shape of the thorax, using internal muscles.

Within the two segments of the thorax to which the wings are attached are a dorsoventral muscle that runs from the tergum (the upperside of the thorax) to the bottom, a dorsal longitudinal muscle and a basalar muscle (the so-called direct muscle), which runs from the base of the wing insertion to the base of the segment. To move the wing upwards, the dorsoventral muscle contracts, pulling the tergum down and, simultaneously, pulling down the point of attachment of the wing. This distorts the shape of the segment and causes the wing membrane to move upwards. The wing is pulled down when the dorsoventral muscle relaxes, and the longitudinal and the basalar muscles contract.

Below: To fly, Hawkmoths must first beat their wings to raise the temperature of their flight muscles to at least 34°C (93°F).

Moving the wing requires energy, of course, and some of this energy comes from a pad of resilin that forms part of the hinge joint that attaches the wing to the wall of the thorax. Resilin is an elastic material and it is incredibly efficient at storing energy. When the wing moves upward, the pad is stretched and energy is stored. When the wing moves downward, the resilin is released and it snaps back to its original position with the release of energy, energy that is used to move the wing down again.

Wing movement

During the stroke, the wings move at different speeds, the downward stroke being slower than the upward one. The wings do not simply move up and down. Instead they are twisted, tilting backward and forward during the stroke, to provide both lift and forward thrust. This ability to rotate the wing is provided by the direct flight muscle. To fly higher, the insect increases the wing angle by contracting the direct flight muscle. The Cabbage White butterfly (*Pieris brassicae*) is unusual in that, during

take-off, the wings are almost vertical on the upstroke. At the start of the downstroke, the wings are raised high and they 'clap' together and are then flung apart, sucking air into the space between the wings. On the downstroke, the wings are held horizontally and then, at the bottom of the downstroke, they are twisted so that they are in a vertical position ready for the upstroke.

Beats per second

The flight muscles contract as a result of receiving nervous stimuli. In lepidopterans, each nerve impulse produces a single muscle contraction. Hence they have a slow wing beat of between 4 and 40 beats per second. By way of comparison, insects such as the diptera (flies, mosquitoes) and the hymenoptera (bees and wasps) can beat their wings in excess of 200 times per second. This is possible because the nervous stimulation of the muscles is different, with one impulse resulting in up to 10 beats of the wing.

Lepidopteran wings are large, so they are harder to beat quickly. This influences speed and power. The fastest fliers are the Sphingid moths, which have been recorded flying at speeds of nearly 50kph (31mph). Skippers, too, can reach a similar speed.

Below: Heliconius butterflies, such as H. melpomene, have an elongated wing shape and delicate fluttering flight.

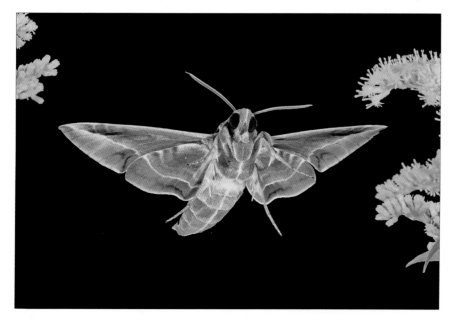

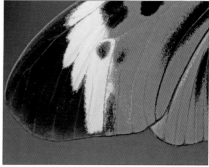

Wing shape

The shape of wing and its role in the speed and style of flight is well studied in animals such as birds, but recent studies of butterflies have shown similar links between their wing shape and flight characteristics. For example, the swallowtail *Troides rhadamantus* is a strong, fast-flying butterfly but it is rarely seen hovering, nor is it particularly manoeuvrable. A related species, *Pachliopta hector,* has a smaller, lighter wing that is elongated in shape. It has a slower flight speed but can hover and it is far more agile. More manoeuvrable still is *Graphium sarpendon,* with an even smaller wing area and a forewing with a narrow

elongated tip and a hindwing lacking a tail. This fast, agile butterfly can twist and turn in its forest habitat, darting quickly from perch to perch.

Skippers are much smaller, with a wing shape that supports a fast flight, giving excellent manoeuvrability and hovering ability. They have stout wing bases and studies have shown that the tips of the wings are deformed during the stroke.

The presence of a tail influences the aerodynamics of the wing. A tailed hindwing serves to smooth the airflow over the wings and helps when gliding. Biologists have also noted that during gliding, the fore- and hindwings separate. This is thought to reduce the

*Above: The wing movement of this Clipper butterfly (*Parthenos sylvia*) in flight can be seen clearly in this time lapse photograph.*

chances of stalling at low speeds or when the wings are tilted at high angles. Gliding is common in the *Papilio* butterflies, which do not have a coupling mechanism joining the wings. In contrast, gliding is not usually seen in moths that have their wings coupled together.

*Below: Swallowtails, such as this Emerald Swallowtail (*Papilio palinurus*), have long tails on their hindwings and strong, swift flight.*

*Below: The Mother of Pearl butterfly (*Salamis parhassus*) has a squared wing with hooked apex. It has a flapping flight.*

*Below: The Atlas moth (*Attacus atlas*) has a wing span approaching 25cm (10in) with a hooked apex on the forewing.*

WING SCALES

Butterfly and moth wings are covered in scales which are variable in structure, each scale being made of cuticle – the flattened extension of a single cell. The scales are responsible for the colour of the wings too, the colour being a result of the reflection of light from the ridged surfaces of the scales.

Left: The Glasswing butterfly (Greta oto) is named after its transparent wing patches, which are created when the scales are lost.

The wing scales of most butterflies and moths are made up of several layers of cuticle, the lower surface being smooth, and the upper surface, ridged. Some are hair-like, while others are plate-like. Scales cover the body too, particularly the abdomen. The scales are set into sockets within the wing membrane, where they are angled to the surface and overlap each other to form a complete covering. In some of the more primitive groups, scales are randomly arranged, but in the Papilionoidae they are arranged in rows. Some species have specialized scales.

Function of scales

Scales have a number of functions. Biologists believe that their primary role is insulation since, while the more primitive species of Lepidoptera have solid scales, most advanced butterflies have scales with air-filled cavities that increase their insulation properties. In addition, the density of scales is much greater, with multiple layers of scales. As well as insulation, the scales help to reduce drag and produce a smooth air flow over the surface of the wing.

Some scales have specialized roles, such as pheromone production. Their most important role, however, is giving colour to the wing. This means that wing scales play a vital role in communication and protection, since colour is involved with camouflage, warning colours and mimicry.

Reflected light

Wing colour is determined by the wavelengths of the light reflected from the surface of the scales. A white appearance is a result of the surface reflecting all wavelengths in equal amounts, whereas black is a result of all the wavelengths of light being absorbed and none being reflected.

In lepidopterans, wing colour is either produced as a result of the refraction of light from the ridged surface of the scales, known as structural or physical colour, or it is produced by the absorption of different wavelengths by pigments in the scales, known as pigmentary colour. Colours such as white, blue or copper together with iridescent tones form as a result of structural colour.

Pigments

There is a range of pigments responsible for wing colour. White can also be produced by white pigments. For example, pigments in the scales of the Cabbage White butterfly (*Pieris brassica*) absorb ultraviolet light and reflect white. The greenish-yellow colour of the Brimstone (*Gonepteryx rhamni*) is produced by a pteridine that absorbs blue light and reflects yellow. This pigment is responsible for intense reds and yellows, such as the orange of the male Orange-Tip. One of the most common pigments is melanin, which produces black and grey, and some yellows and oranges, while carotenoids produce yellows and reds. Carotene cannot be produced by adult insects, so it has to be obtained via the larval food. Green can be produced in two ways. Sometimes it is produced by a carotenoid, but, in the *Papilio* butterflies, it is produced by the overlapping of yellow and black pigmented scales. Also found in *Papilio* butterflies is the unique pigment papiliochrome that produces yellow.

Loss of scales

Lepidopterans lose scales every time they fly, so as they age, more scales are missing from the wings. Scales are lost when they brush against vegetation, or even escape the sticky silk of spider's webs. During windy weather or heavy rain, yet more scales are lost. By the end of its life, a lepidopteran can look quite ragged. Although the insects can fly without their scales or even with parts of the wings missing, the loss affects the aerodynamics and can alter the flight pattern. Flight becomes less efficient and the insect expends more energy when flying.

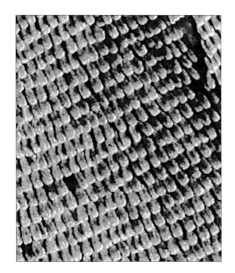

*Above: The scales of the Emerald Swallowtail (*Papilio palinurus*) are arranged in rows, like tiles on a roof. Note some scales are missing.*

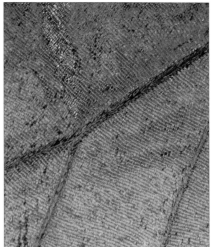

Above: Iridescent blue colour is a result of the diffraction of light from the surface of the tiny scales covering the wing.

Above: Swallowtail butterfly wing colours form when pigments in the scales absorb some light wavelengths and reflect others.

In some, the scales are lost from particular cells of the wing, leading to distinctive wing patterns, such as in the Apollo butterflies (*Parnassius sp.*). In other species, such as the Glasswings, large sections of their wings lack scales, leaving transparent wings. This form of camouflage, often called protective transparency, enables the butterfly to blend in with its background. Transparency is dependent upon none of the tissues absorbing or scattering light. The light must be able to pass through the wing tissue unobstructed.

Glasswings are found in the lower levels of tropical rainforest, where there are patches of dark and light. When they fly they almost disappear from sight, making it difficult for predators to spot them.

Male or female

New research into the structure of scales in the Cabbage White butterfly (*Pieris brassica*) has discovered why the male Cabbage White butterflies in Japan are better at recognizing females than their European counterparts. In Europe, the scales of both the male and female butterfly have pigment grains that reflect ultraviolet light. In Japan, only the male has these pigments. Females lack the pigments, so the ultraviolet light is absorbed rather than reflected, enabling the males to identify females more easily.

Interference and iridescence

Butterflies of the families *Morpho* and *Urania* have spectacular iridescent wings, but these colours are not produced by pigments. Instead, they are a result of the way light bounces off the surface of the scales, a process called interference, giving what is called structural colour. Examination of the surface of these scales under an electron microscope has revealed how the colours are produced.

The *Morpho* scales have an upper surface that is covered in rows of tiny Christmas tree-like structures. Each 'tree' is made up of thin transparent layers of chitin, and they form an array of reflecting surfaces. The colour varies, depending on the angle at which the wing is viewed. When the angle increases, the colour tends to the violet end of the spectrum. The *Urania* moth has a range of iridescent colours. Their scales consist of four thin layers of cuticle, each layer separated by tiny vertical struts of cuticle. By altering the spacing and thickness of the layers, different colours are produced.

*Below: Flashes of blue can be seen when the Blue Morpho (*Morpho menelaus*) flies, but the true beauty of the wings is only revealed when the butterfly settles.*

GENERAL BIOLOGY

Internally, the lepidopterans are little different from other insects. Gas exchange takes place via the tracheal system, they have an open blood circulatory system and Malpighian tubules for excretion. They are ectothermic animals that are dependent mostly on external sources to control their body temperature.

Gas exchange

Insects do not have lungs, but have an internal network of tubes known as the tracheal system. This opens to the air via tiny holes, called spiracles that are found on the thoracic and abdominal segments. They are located laterally, with two pairs on the thorax and six to eight pairs on the abdomen. The spiracular opening leads to a cavity; the atrium and the tracheae arise from this. The spiracles can be opened and closed to regulate water loss occuring from the tracheae and to prevent the entry of dust and other foreign particles. There is a balance between the length of time the spiracles are open to supply oxygen and are closed to reduce water loss.

Tracheae are formed through invaginations of the ectoderm, and each is supported by rings of thickened cuticle which prevent the tubes from collapsing. The tracheae divide into smaller tubes, called tracheoles, just one micron in diameter; they get gradually narrower, to just 0.1 microns. The tracheoles penetrate the muscles and other tissues, making sure that there is a plentiful supply of oxygen to muscles, especially to the flight muscles. If the tracheole system is damaged it can repair itself, and new tracheoles extend into the repaired tissue. When a caterpillar moults, the tracheal system increases in size and new branches of tracheae are formed.

Blood and circulation

These insects have an open blood circulation where the blood, or haemolymph, moves around the main body cavity called the haemocoel. The body organs are suspended in the haemocoel. There is a single, dorsal longitudinal blood vessel with a long tubular heart-like structure. When the muscular walls of the heart contract, a

*Above: A butterfly, such as this Swallowtail (*Papilio ophidocephalus*), regulates its body temperature by altering the angle of its wings.*

wave of blood is pumped forwards into the haemocoel, while blood returns through tiny pores called ostia. Blood also flows along vessels that serve the wings, passing out along anterior veins, through cross veins and returning through the posterior veins. The haemolymph is plasma with blood cells, which are involved in the removal of foreign objects and wound repair, but do not supply oxygen. Since the cells do not contain haemoglobin (a respiratory pigment), the haemolymph is not red. The plasma provides a means of transporting materials, such as glucose or amino acids, around the body.

Excretion

In lepidopterans, as in most insects, the role of excretion is carried out by the Malpighian tubules and the rectum. The Malpighian tubules are long, blind-ended structures that arise from the junction of the mid- and hindgut. Their walls are just one cell thick and they lie in the body cavity. They are moved by circular and longitudinal muscles so that they come into contact with the contents of the haemocoel. This helps the uptake of water, uric acid, salts, and other excretory products from the haemolymph as well as the movement of materials along the

*Below: By beating their wings, moths such as this Oleander Hawkmoth (*Daphnis nerii*) raise their body temperature ready for flight.*

tubules themselves. There, any valuable
materials are absorbed and the rest
is passed by the rectum. Nitrogen is
excreted as uric acid. This is insoluble
and non-toxic, and is excreted with
the minimal use of water, an important
feature in animals that fly and may
live in dry places.

Regulating body temperature

Lepidopterans regulate their body
temperature using mostly behavioural
means. They seek out locations with
suitable temperature, avoiding areas
of extreme high temperature. They aim
to keep their body temperature within
a narrow range so that metabolism can
continue and flight is possible. There
is a minimum temperature below
which the insect is unable to fly.

If the body temperature falls, a
lepidopteran aligns itself at right angles
to the sun to present a larger surface
area to the sun so that more heat is
absorbed and, as the body temperature
approaches 40°C (104°F), it turns to
face the sun to present a smaller area.
Butterflies such as the Fritillaries bask
with the wings open in the sun, and by
varying the degree to which the wings
are opened and aligned with the sun,
the body temperature can be
maintained within a range of 32–37°C
(89.6–98.6°F). If the body temperature
rises further, it holds its wings up to
reduce the surface area or seeks a
shadier position.

When the external temperature falls,
insects become less active and they
seek suitable perches or shelter. In
tropical regions, the higher temperatures
enable butterflies to have much longer
periods of activity, and they are seen
flying well after dusk. If the temperatures
continue to fall, the insect becomes
lethargic and unable to move and,
eventually, it may die. Most insects die
at temperatures below freezing. Those
that survive long periods of cold
weather may produce glycerol in their
haemolymph to act as an antifreeze.

Moths can raise their body
temperature by fluttering their wings,
to generate heat from muscle activity, a
behaviour that is similar to shivering

*Above: The Speckled Wood butterfly
(Pararge aegeria) is often seen basking in a
patch of sunlight first thing in the morning.*

in mammals. In the Saturnia moths,
fanning the wings raises the body
temperature by 8°C (46.4°F) above the
ambient temperature. The amount of
preheating that is required for flight
depends on the ambient temperature.
In a large moth, such as the Tobacco
Hornworm (*Manduca sexta*), this can
take as long as 12 minutes at ambient
temperatures of 15°C (59°F), but just a
minute or so at temperatures of 30°C
(86°F). This ability to raise their
thoracic temperature means that moths
can fly at night.

Internal anatomy

The internal structure of a butterfly,
showing the circulatory, digestive,
excretory and reproductive systems.

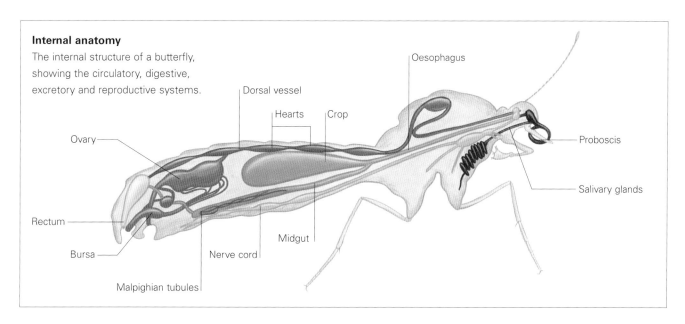

FEEDING

Feeding is an essential part of daily life for most butterflies and moths, the exception being the few adults that lack mouthparts. The adults are seen flitting from flower to flower in their search for sugar-rich nectar, while caterpillars chomp their way through the vegetation.

Most adult lepidopterans are short-lived animals, so all they require by way of food is a supply of energy; this is readily obtained from sugar-rich nectar. The long proboscis can extend deep into the flower to reach the nectaries at the bottom.

Feeding habits

Most species visit a range of nectar-producing flowers, and often there is a cluster of butterflies gathered on particularly good nectar sources such as *Buddleia*. Some species have preferences, for example choosing to visit flowers growing in certain positions, such as at a particular height above the ground, or orientated in a particular direction. Sometimes they visit flowers of a particular colour; for example, hawkmoths tend to show a preference for pale-coloured flowers. A few of the longer-lived adults eat pollen, which supplies the insect with amino acids that may be used in egg production. Moths of the superfamily Micropterigidae are unusual in that they have retained mandibles, which they use for chewing pollen.

Saprophagous species feed on the juices of rotting fruits, dung, urine and sometimes bird droppings. Most wait for the fruits to drop, but the fruit-sucking moths of the genus *Othreis* feed on fruits while they are still attached to the tree; for this reason they are an economically important pest species of orchards. They have a sufficiently strong proboscis that they can use it to pierce the skin of the citrus fruits to suck the juices. Unusually, it is the adult that is the

*Above: The day-flying Hummingbird or Clearwing Hawkmoth (*Hemaris *sp.) extends its long proboscis to reach nectar.*

pest, rather than the caterpillar. Once pierced the fruit ripens more quickly. These moths are also known to be a vector of fungal diseases of fruits.

There are some quite unusual feeding habits among moths. For example, certain moths land on the heads of large mammals such as elephants and buffalo to suck discharge from their eyes. There is even a vampire moth, *Calpe eustrigata*, a Southeastern Asian Noctuid moth, related to the fruit-sucking moths, which uses its very stout proboscis to pierce skin in order to access a vein from which to suck blood.

There are some adults that do not feed at all as they have no functional mouthparts, the Silk Moths (*Bombyx* sp.), for example. The adults emerge with vestigial mouthparts and no digestive system, and so they have to survive on stored fats laid down during the larval stage. Their life span is less than seven days, just long enough to find a mate and lay their eggs.

The caterpillars (larvae) are very different. They are equipped with a pair of powerful serrated-edged mandibles that are used to chew plant matter. Most feed on leaves, fruits and flowers of flowering plants, although a

Digestive system

The alimentary canal consists of the fore-, mid- and hindgut. The foregut consists of the mouth, which leads to the oesophagus and large crop. The pharynx lies behind the mouth and it is particularly well developed with muscular walls into order to pump liquid food into crop, where it is stored. The Micropterigidae lack a crop, while in the Sphingid moths it is particularly large. The midgut consists of the ventriculus and caecae. This is the site of digestion and absorption. The first part of the midgut, the ventriculus, is where much of the digestion takes place. The caecae are small finger-like extensions branching off the ventriculus which increase the surface area for digestion. In adult butterflies and moths, digestion is limited due to the nature of the sugar-rich diet, but its role is far more important during the larval stage. In caterpillars, the epithelium contains goblet cells that are involved with secretion and excretion. The cells store potentially toxic materials and these stores are emptied at the time of moult. The hindgut consists of the ileum, rectum and anus. Taking place here is the uptake of water, salts and amino acids while undigested foods and urine are eliminated.

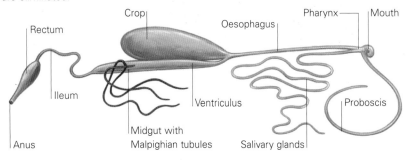

very small number feed on mosses, ferns and even lichens. Some caterpillars feed on a wide range of plants, whereas more specialized feeders are found on only one specific plant species; for example the Monarch caterpillar (*Danaus plexippus*) is found only on milkweed, a plant avoided by most other herbivores. The sap of this plant contains cardiac glycosides, toxic chemicals that cause vomiting and irregular heartbeat in birds and mammals. The Monarch caterpillar has adapted to feeding on this plant by evolving a mechanism to immobilize the toxin. These toxins are then stored in the body of the caterpillar and are passed on to the adult, which thus gains protection from predators.

The food chain

The lepidopterans play a key role in the habitat in which they live. Most butterflies and moths, both adults and larvae, are the primary consumers or herbivores in the food chain. There are a few exceptions to this, such as the saprophagous species and some of the Lycaenidae butterflies. In addition, they are important pollinators of flowering plants. In the case of the yucca, the Yucca moth (*Tegeticula*

*Below: Caterpillars, such as this Common Egg-fly caterpillar (*Hypolimnas bolina*), chew leaves with a pair of toothed mandibles.*

*Above: The European Bee-eater (*Merops apiaster*) feeds on bees, wasps and hornets, but also catches butterflies and moths.*

yuccasella) and a few other related species are the sole pollinators of its flowers, so without this moth the plant would be unable to reproduce.

The role of the Lepidoptera as primary consumers in the ecosystem cannot be underestimated. The caterpillars eat vast quantities – it is estimated that a single caterpillar eats 20 times its weight in plant material. Multiply that by the billions of caterpillars produced each year, and you have a huge amount of green

matter. Caterpillars do not all compete for the same plants, as each species has its own niche within an ecosystem. For example, two species may avoid competition by feeding on different plants, at different levels in the habitat, or emerging at different times of year.

Avoiding predation

The sheer numbers of butterflies, moths and caterpillars makes them an important food source for many predators, especially spiders, insect-eating birds, lizards and small mammals. To combat this, the lepidopterans have evolved a wide range of defensive strategies to avoid predation. Some of the defences are structural, such as caterpillars with irritating hairs. Caterpillars of the Papilionidae have an organ called the osmeterium attached to their thorax that can be everted to spray a liquid at any predator. Others use hearing to evade their predators, for example noctuid moths are hunted by bats. The moths detect the high pitched sounds emitted by bats and react by changing direction or folding their wings and almost dropping out of the sky. Some Arctiid moths go one step better, and emit ultrasounds of their own that warn bats of their distasteful nature.

Visual signs are also important. Many day-flying butterflies and moths that are distasteful have brightly

Above: If disturbed, the Puss Moth caterpillar (Cerura vinula) rears up, pulling in its head to display a bright red ring.

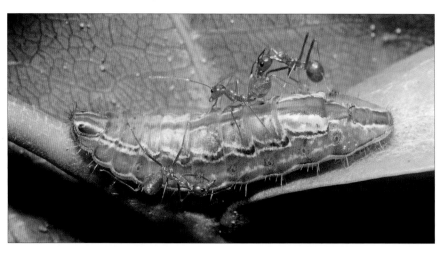

Above: Green tree ants (Oecophylla smaragdina) protect the caterpillar of a Blue butterfly (Narathura sp.).

coloured wings in shades of red, yellow and black that are a warning to predators. Others use startle techniques such as flashing a brightly coloured eyespot to confuse the predator, thereby gaining time to escape. Eyespots and tails on wings may direct any attack away from the head. The Common Tit butterfly (*Hypolycaena erylus*), for example, has a complete false head at the tail end of its hindwing.

Camouflage and disguise

Many predators locate their prey by searching for a particular shape. Lepidopterans evade these predators by using camouflage and disguise to hide their outline. Camouflage can be in the form of patterns that blend with the leaf litter or bark, disruptive patterns that break up the animal's outline, and transparency. Another method is disguise, having a body shape that gives the illusion of being something else, such as leaf or twig.

A pattern of brown and black is the perfect camouflage for moths that rest on tree bark during the day, while a green wing conceals a butterfly among leaves, for example that of the Green Hairstreak (*Callophrys rubi*).

Below: The Polyphemus moth (Antheraea polyphemus) startles predators by revealing two large eyespots on its hindwings.

Some lepidopterans are disguised to look like a twig, leaf or piece of bark, for example, the Buff Tip moth (*Phalera bucephala*) resembles a broken twig of silver birch. Caterpillars are disguised too, those of the genus *Papilio* have the appearance of bird droppings when small, but as they grow and moult they take on bright warning colours. The Dead-Leaf butterflies (genus *Kallima*) have brightly coloured upperwings, but their appearance is transformed when they come to rest on twigs.

The cryptic colours of the moth *Nemoria arizonaria* change during the year. The caterpillars feed on the catkins and young leaves of the oak. The first brood appears in early spring and are yellow, with many small projections. However, this coloration is of little use for the later broods, which

Below: The eye-like markings of the Owl butterfly (Caligo sp.) deter predators such as lizards that hunt by sight.

Above: The twig-like camouflage of the Buff-Tip moth (Phalera bucephala) is achieved when the wings are wrapped around the body.

Above: At rest, the Mother of Pearl butterfly (Salamis parhassus) lifts its wings to reveal its more subdued underside with eyespots.

feed on oak leaves and twigs. Instead, the summer broods are camouflaged as greyish twigs. This alteration in appearance is triggered by diet change.

Disruptive colours break up the outline of the wing. This makes it more difficult for a predator to spot them. Examples include the Angle Shades moth (*Phlogophora meticulosa*) and the Grayling (*Hipparchia semele*). For some species, disruptive colours work best in flight. These butterflies tend to fly slowly and, as they flap their wings, their outline flips from visible to invisible, making it difficult for a predator to follow their flight.

The blue and the ant

Many of the Lycaenidae species have a close relationship with ants, known as myrmecophily. Worker ants usually attack prey animals that they find on their foraging trips. However, when they come across Lycaenidae caterpillars, they do not attack but gather around them to feed on honeydew. The caterpillars are able to appease the ants because of the presence of three organs – the cupola

Right: When folded, the wings of the Indian Leaf butterfly (Kallima inachus) resemble a dead leaf complete with a midrib and veins.

organ, dorsal nectar organ and tentacle organ. When the ants palpate the nectar organ, the caterpillar produces droplets of honeydew, a sugary secretion. In return, the caterpillars get protection from predators and parasites. The caterpillars of some species of Lycaenidae can survive without the attendant ants, but others are obligate myrmecophiles since they cannot survive without them. The caterpillars secrete the droplets whether or not the ants are present, and if the ants are

absent the sugary secretions become infected with fungi. Some of the obligate myrmecophiles are carnivorous and actually feed on their attendants. For example, the mature caterpillars of the Large Blue (*Maculinea arion*) are carried into the nest of the ant *Myrmica sabuleti*. While the attendants feed on the caterpillar's honeydew, the caterpillar feeds on the eggs and larvae of the ants. The caterpillars hibernate over winter, before resuming growth the following spring. They pupate inside the nest from which the newly emerged adult is helped by the ants and protected until it is dry enough to fly.

REPRODUCTION AND LIFE CYCLE

Many adult butterflies and moths only live a few weeks, often just a few days. Their role during this time is one of reproduction. Their ability to fly allows the males and females to find each other, carry out a courtship, mate successfully and allow the female to lay eggs.

When seeking a mate, day-flying butterflies and moths rely mostly on visual recognition. The females tend to be found close to the food plants or on hilltops, so these are obvious places for the males to stake out. Night-flying moths rely on scent.

Pheromones

Many butterflies and moths release pheromones, chemicals that attract or communicate with others. Male butterflies, especially those of the Pieridae, have androconia. These are patches of modified scales on their forewing from which the pheromone evaporates. Others have scent scales on their legs or abdomen. Females also have scent scales, usually located near the tip of the abdomen.

Right: The male Small Copper butterfly (Lycaena phlaeas) *is active in sunlight, defending its territory against other males.*

The pheromone is usually released at certain times of day, to coincide with the activity of the species. For example *Lobesia* sp. males are attracted by the female pheromones, which are released between 9pm and midnight, while those of the genus *Heliothis* release their pheromone between 4am and dawn. Some females only release their pheromone for a short while to attract the male, and once mated, this stops, especially those species in which mating occurs once, for example the silkmoths. However, in species where mating may take place several times, for example *Trichoplusia*,

the pheromone continues to be released for some time. In some species, such as the Zebra butterfly (*Heliconius* sp.), the female releases the pheromone before she has emerged from the pupa, so male butterflies sit beside the pupa awaiting her emergence.

Reproductive system

Female Lepidopterans have two reproductive openings, the vulva, for mating and the ovipore for egg laying. During mating, the male vesica is everted and spermatophores are pumped into the bursa copulatrix. The spermatozoa move along the sperm duct to the spermatheca where they are stored until released for fertilization. The eggs are produced in the ovaries, which are connected to the vagina by oviducts.

The males have a pair of testes, which are connected via the vas deferens to a pair of seminal vesicles and the ejaculatory duct. Spermatozoa are produced in the testes and then packaged into capsules called spermatophores. The penis consists of a tube and the vesica. During mating the vesica is everted into the female's vulva. Externally, the hook-shaped uncus and gnathos are to used to grip the female's abdomen.

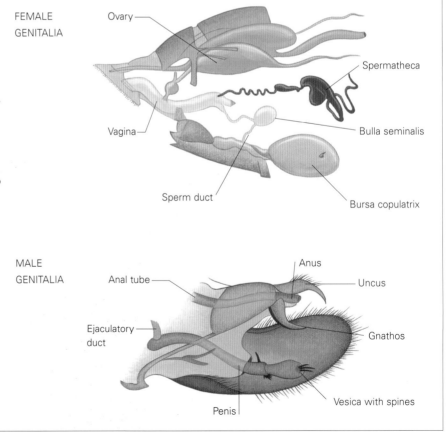

FEMALE GENITALIA — Ovary — Spermatheca — Bulla seminalis — Bursa copulatrix — Sperm duct — Vagina

MALE GENITALIA — Anal tube — Anus — Uncus — Gnathos — Vesica with spines — Penis — Ejaculatory duct

Once the male detects the pheromone he flies upwind, following the trail of the pheromone in the air. Male moths may fly over considerable distances, as far as 11km (7 miles) in the case of the Indian Moon moth (*Actias selene*). These moths have pectinate antennae with a large surface area to detect scents. Interestingly, the pheromone is not always unique to a particular species, but will attract closely related species, so moths within the genus *Saturnia*, *Atheraea*, and *Rothschildia* all react strongly to the same pheromone.

Defending and patrolling

Male butterflies fall into one of two groups when it comes to attracting a female. Some defend territories, areas that the males select because it puts them in an advantageous position to find a female, such as a hilltop, tall tree, or a sunspot on a woodland floor. They do not defend their territory all the time, spending some time perching or feeding. While in territorial mode, they chase away any intruding rival and await the arrival of a female. Their territories are not large and are often transient; for example, the male Speckled Wood (*Pararge aegenia*) seeks out patches of sunlight on woodland floors, while the Black Swallowtail (*Papilio polyxenes*) perches on the tallest plants with views over streams.

*Above: The male Common Lime Swallowtail (*Papilio demoleus*) mates by gripping the female with clasping organs on its abdomen.*

When another male approaches, the first male chases it away in an upwards spiral. The other strategy is patrolling in which males spend much of their time flying up and down a feature in the habitat, such as hedgerows or streams, actively seeking a female.

Courtship

Once the male spots a possible female, he flies down to check that she is of the same species. If she is, courtship can begin. In some species courtship is brief; for example, the male Orange-Barred Sulphur (*Phoebus philea*) knocks the female to the ground within 30 seconds of her flying overhead and mates with her.

*Left: Sexual dimorphism, when males and females have a different appearance, is common in butterflies. Here the male (bottom left) Archduke butterfly (*Lexius dirtea*) has a velvety black upperwing and patches of blue-violet on the hindwing, while the female (top left) has brown upperwings with small yellow spots.*

Other species have a more elaborate courtship. One of the best-studied examples of courtship is that of the Grayling (*Hipparchia semele*). Once the female lands, the male stands in front of her, displaying the uppersides of his forewings so the female's antennae can touch the androconia, picking up his scent to make her receptive. Only then will mating occur. Similarly, in the Clouded Yellow (*Colias philodice*), the male lands in front of the female and beats his wings to release the pheromone.

In the Small Tortoiseshell (*Aglais urticae*) courtship lasts hours. The male follows the female as she flits from bush to bush. When she lands, he walks over her hindwings before she leads him to a sheltered spot to mate.

Other behaviours include the female beating her wings to attract the attention of the male, as with the Silverwash Fritillary (*Argynnis paphia*).

EGGS

The life cycle starts with the eggs, which are laid soon after mating. Egg-laying must take place soon after the eggs have been fertilized. Not only do the eggs differ in shape and size according to the species, but the manner in which they are laid also varies.

Sperm can remain viable in the spermatheca for some time; in some species it may remain viable for many months or even years. However, in most species, egg-laying begins shortly after mating. As the eggs pass down the oviduct, small amounts of sperm are released and fertilization takes place. It is the entry of the sperm that provides the stimulus for the final stage in egg formation. Once the eggs have been fertilized, egg-laying must take place soon after.

Once the eggs are laid, the embryo starts its development. Oxygen uptake increases and energy is released from the breakdown of reserves. The time taken to complete embryonic development varies between species, and is also affected by the ambient temperature. Development will not occur if the temperature falls too low or conditions are too dry, as in a tropical dry season, for example eggs of *Parnassius* and *Lycaena* species. In this case, the egg enters diapause and development is arrested until conditions become suitable.

Egg shape and colour

Butterfly and moth eggs are relatively large compared with the size of the insect and they are full of yolk. The protective shell has pores to allow gas exchange. Often the shell is waxed to reduce water loss. The shape and colour is incredibly variable. Eggs may be tall, round, pitted or ridged. *Pieris* species lay conical eggs with distinct ridges running top to bottom, while moths tend to lay rounded eggs. Colour varies from white and yellow through to blue and brown. In addition, the egg colour may change over time, often getting darker as the embryo develops inside.

Finding food plants

The females always lay their eggs close to, or on, the plant on which the caterpillars depend for food. Her selection is critical, as it affects the survival of the eggs and the availability of food for the caterpillars, since they

Above: The black marks on the round white egg of the Blue Morpho (Morpho menelaus) indicate that the egg has been fertilized.

Below: The yellow eggs of the Zebra Longwing butterfly (Heliconius charithonia) are laid in groups of five to 15.

Above: The sculptured surface of the Monarch butterfly's egg (Danaus plexippus) are laid singly on a plant.

Below: The large white eggs of the Owl butterfly (Caligo sp.) get darker as they develop, and hatch after 12 days.

Above: The Cabbage White butterfly (Pieris brassicae) lays clusters of small, yellow eggs on cabbage leaves.

Below: The female Comet moth (Argema mittrei) typically lays up to 170 smooth, white eggs.

*Above: A female Plain Tiger butterfly (*Danaus chrysippus*) curls her abdomen to lay a single egg on the underside of a leaf.*

singly, or in small groups. Some females have ovipositors that allow them to lay their eggs within the plant tissue, while others, especially those of the Nymphalidae, scatter their eggs while they fly over a suitable location. These species that scatter their eggs tend to lay large numbers of small eggs. In contrast, those that carefully pick the right spot tend to lay smaller numbers of larger eggs. The total number of eggs laid also varies, and in some species 1,000 or more eggs may be laid, for example by the Small Tortoiseshell (*Aglais urticae*).

Some female moths are wingless, for example the female Mottled Umber (*Erannis defoliaria*), and the Vapourer moth (*Orgyia antique*). This anatomical feature ensures that the female lays her eggs on the same plant from which she fed as a caterpillar. The female Vapourer moth lives for just two weeks, just sufficient time to emerge from her cocoon, release some pheromone to attract a male and lay her eggs on the remains of her own cocoon. The female Winter Moth (*Operophtera brumata*) is also wingless. This long-legged moth climbs up the trunks of fruit trees and lays as many as 200 green eggs, either singly or in small clusters near the buds of the tree. The eggs do not develop further until the leaves break in spring.

Despite the great care taken in choosing the right spot for laying the eggs, as many as 99 per cent of lepidopteran eggs are either eaten, parasitized or suffer from disease.

*Below: The female Blue Morpho (*Morpho menelaus*) lays her eggs in clusters on leaves.*

cannot travel far to find suitable food. Finding the right location involves different stimuli including visual, tactile and olfactory ones. Interestingly, the female's ability to respond to colours may vary. Research has shown that female Pierids have a sensitivity to colours of flowers such as red, purple and blue while they are feeding, but when they are ready to lay their eggs, they have a sensitivity to green, thus ensuring they lay their eggs on leaves.

The wax moth (*Achroia* sp.) is attracted by places with a strong smell of beeswax. Once the right location is determined, other stimuli come into play. Chemoreceptors on the antennae,

tarsi and ovipositor make contact with the surface before the eggs are laid. For example, the Cabbage White (*Pieris brassicae*) uses receptors on her tarsi to taste the leaf, looking for the presence of mustard oil. Once found, the female lays her eggs on the underside of cabbage leaves.

Many lepidopterans lay their eggs on the underside of the food plant, a choice of site that provides the eggs with shelter, as it keeps them out of direct sunlight and reduces desiccation. This is also out of sight of predators, as well as providing an immediate source of food for the caterpillars. The eggs are cemented into place by a secretion from one of the accessory glands so that they do not fall off. Some females lay clusters of hundreds of eggs, but the majority lay their eggs

CATERPILLARS

Caterpillar is the common name given to the larval stage of the lepidopteran life cycle. The word 'caterpillar' may date back to the use of the word 'catyrpel' in around 1440, which itself was probably derived from the French word 'chatepelose' meaning hairy cat.

Others believe the origins of the name caterpillar are from two words; 'cate' referring to food, and 'piller' which means pillager or ravager, linking the word to the fact that caterpillars eat large quantities of leaves.

There are usually five stages, or instars, between hatching and pupating, although some tropical Nymphalidae have between four and seven instars. Each instar ends with a moult, when the caterpillar sheds its skin and grows a new, larger one. The skins can also look different, so the appearance of caterpillars can be quite variable between and within species.

Body plan

All caterpillars share the same basic body plan, with a head, a thorax with three segments and an abdomen of ten segments. The head is rounded in shape, with one pair of short antennae and three pairs of ocelli. The mouthparts are very different from the adults, since caterpillars have to chew their food. There is an upper lip (labrum), a pair of toothed mandibles for chewing food, a pair of maxillae with maxillary palps and a lower lip (labium). Attached to the lower lip are two palps and a spinneret for spinning silk.

Above: The developing caterpillar can clearly be seen inside this egg of the Owl Silkmoth (Brahmaea hearseyi).

Above: The caterpillar takes about an hour to chew its way out of the egg, and here it is just emerging.

The thorax of a caterpillar has three pairs of jointed walking legs that end in claws. Caterpillars of the *Papilionidae* family have an osmeterium, a brightly coloured, branched structure that is attached to the front of the thorax. It is usually invaginated out of sight, but when threatened by predators it is everted and releases a defensive pungent liquid.

The abdomen bears appendages called prolegs, which are soft, fleshy outgrowths of the body. Each comprises a base and a planta. The planta usually has some hooks or crochets, which are used for gripping. There are usually four pairs of prolegs

Above: When it is fully hatched, many caterpillars, including the Owl Silkmoth, eat the egg shell.

on segments three to six, and a further pair on the tenth segment, called claspers. As always, there are exceptions. Caterpillars of the Micropterigidae family have eight pairs of prolegs but they are unlike prolegs in other caterpillars in that they lack muscle. The Geometridae have one pair on the sixth segment and another on the tenth. As a consequence this caterpillar has a characteristic looping movement, which involves extending the thorax forward and then pulling up the end of the abdomen. Some of the Noctuidae are semi-loopers, as they have lost the prolegs on segments three and four. Leaf Mining caterpillars (genus *Stigmella*) have fewer prolegs, as do some members of the Adelidae and Incurvariidae.

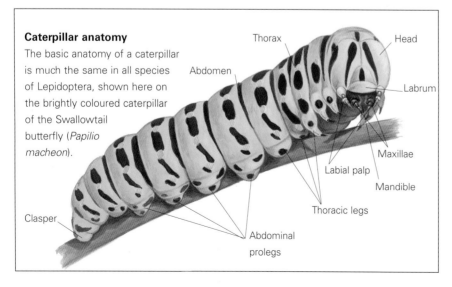

Caterpillar anatomy

The basic anatomy of a caterpillar is much the same in all species of Lepidoptera, shown here on the brightly coloured caterpillar of the Swallowtail butterfly (*Papilio macheon*).

Thorax

Head

Abdomen

Labrum

Maxillae

Labial palp

Mandible

Thoracic legs

Clasper

Abdominal prolegs

*Above: The two-day-old caterpillars of the Zebra Longwing (*Heliconius charithonia*) are golden brown, but as they get older, their colours change to white and black.*

Hairs, bristles and warts

Often the caterpillar is covered in either hairs (setae) or bristles, even warts and tubercules, which bear a tuft of hairs. The hairs of the first instar are called primary setae. These tend to be small and occur in specific places on the body, which assists in the identification of caterpillar species. They are sensory in function. Secondary setae are found on the later instars, especially those that feed in exposed places. These setae vary in shape, number and colour, giving each species of caterpillar its distinctive appearance. They may be long and filamentous, for example, branched, or clustered together in tufts.

Some species have urticating or stinging hairs to deter predators. Some urticating hairs are cylindrical and contain a venom. This is released when contact with another animal breaks off the tip and releases the contents, as, for example, the Cup Moths (Limacodidae) of Australia. Some urticating hairs are simply a contact irritant. They break off easily and can be wafted around. They then create an irritation when they stick to skin, and even penetrate clothing. This type of hair is common in the Tiger, Tussock and Processional moths.

As well as setae, caterpillars may have wart-like tubercles that may or may not bear setae. Some have odd-looking horned or branched processes that are outgrowths from the body. In caterpillars of many Satyrinae and Apaturinae, the tergum on the tenth abdominal segment is extended to form a pair of horns or anal processes. Caterpillars of the Nymphalidae and Hedylidae may have a pair of horns attached to the head.

Spinning silk

Silk glands are important in caterpillars. Silk is made of protein, and when first secreted is liquid, but hardens in the air. The silk is released by the spinneret, which is part of the lower lip. Many caterpillars use their silk to spin a cocoon in which to pupate, while others make protective shelters among the leaves. Some caterpillars evade predators by dropping off a leaf and suspending themselves beneath it on a silk thread.

Instars and moulting

The first instar hatches from the eggs and often its first meal is the eggshell which provides useful nutrients. Then it starts feeding on the food plant, growing quickly. The cuticle of the caterpillar is made from chitin impregnated with sclerotin, which hardens it and makes it inextensible. This means that the caterpillar cannot grow unless it moults its outer covering, and replaces it with a larger one. This process is called ecdysis or moulting. The moulting process is controlled by hormones, the most important ones being ecdysone and juvenile hormone. The role of ecdysone is to initiate rapid cell division in the epidermis, causing it to separate from the old cuticle and form a new one.

*Below: Straight after moulting, the head and legs of the Owl Silkmoth (*Brahmaea hearseyi*) are pale, but darken as the cuticle hardens.*

Above: The Magpie Moth caterpillar (Abraxas grossulariata) moves with a characteristic looping movement.

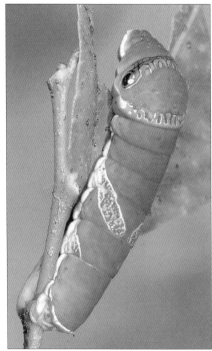

Above: The snake-like caterpillar of the Common Lime Swallowtail butterfly (Papilio demoleus) showing its false eye.

Above: The 4th instar of the Owl Silkmoth caterpillar (Brahmaea hearseyi) has a snake-like appearance, with false eye and scales.

This larger cuticle lies beneath the old one. As the body of the caterpillar expands, the old cuticle splits and drops away, leaving a soft new cuticle which expands as the caterpillar takes in water. This stops once sclerotization has taken place and the new cuticle is no longer flexible.

The role of the juvenile hormone is slightly more complex. It circulates in the haemolymph, and while it is present it ensures that the caterpillar continues to grow and moult. However, in the last instar stage, the

concentration falls and instead of forming a new instar after the moult, the caterpillar pupates.

The time taken to develop from the first to the last instar usually takes between three and six weeks. However, many late summer and autumn caterpillars become dormant in winter, and they resume their development the following spring, when they moult into

Below: Cabbage White (Pieris brassicae) caterpillars accumulate distasteful oils from the leaves they eat, to deter predators.

the next instar and resume feeding. By becoming active early they can take advantage of the warmer weather. Interestingly, in more northerly latitudes and mountain habitats, caterpillars seek out exposed places to overwinter, rather than sheltered spots, because the exposed places are first to thaw in spring. For species found in colder climes, such as the Arctic and tundra, the short summer limits the time available for development. As a result, the caterpillars are dormant for much of the year, and it can take some Arctic moths up to seven summers to complete the larval stage.

Below: The later instars of the Zebra Longwing (Heliconius charithonia) are white with black spines.

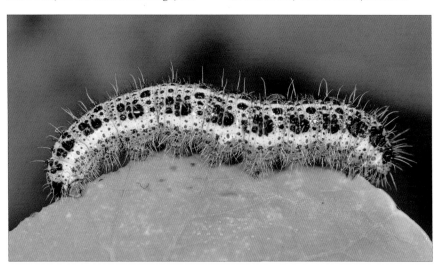

Solitary or gregarious?

Caterpillar behaviour varies between species. Some are solitary but others are gregarious during the first two or three instars. Gregarious species live in large groups, such as caterpillars of the Small Tortoiseshell (*Aglais urticae*) and Cabbage White (*Pieris brassicae*) butterflies and the Gypsy moth (*Lymantria dispar*). They hatch from large clusters of eggs and stay together for several weeks, eating their way through leaves. Some of these gregarious caterpillars use their silk to build a large silken tent that spans across branches of shrubs or trees. They shelter together within these tents, safe from predators. Some lay silken trails from the tent to the food source and they may build a network of silk threads to make it easier to negotiate trees. In the case of the processional caterpillars such as *Thaumetopoae pityocampa*, they move

in single file, head to tails to find food. These are particularly devastating caterpillars as they can completely defoliate a tree, while contact with their urticating setae can cause irritation, rashes and pain. There are benefits and drawbacks to gregarious behaviour. By collaborating it is easier

*Above: The Sycamore Moth (*Acronicta aceris*) caterpillar is covered in tufts of long orange and yellow hairs that deter predators.*

to find food and shelter and gain protection, but living in a group means food supplies are quickly exhausted, and disease spreads more easily.

Instars of the Monarch Butterfly

The Monarch (*Danaus plexippus*) is one of the many caterpillars that change in appearance during the larval stage.

On hatching, the first instar caterpillar is a translucent pale green to grey covered in setae. It feeds in a circular

*Below: The fifth instar of the Monarch (*Danaus plexippus*) attaches itself to a twig and moults for the last time to reveal its pupal case.*

motion, leaving behind a characteristic arc-shaped hole in leaves. When disturbed, it rolls off the leaf and hangs by a silk thread. The characteristic black, yellow and white bands appear in the second instar. There is a distinctive yellow triangle on the head, while the setae are shorter and more abundant. The front and back tentacles are present but short.

The third instar has darker black and yellow bands and tentacles, while the triangular yellow mark on the head has

disappeared. It feeds along the leaf edges and, when disturbed, it drops off the leaf and curls up into a tight ball.

During the fourth instar, bands appear on the thorax, and the front tentacles are much longer.

The mature fifth instar is much larger, plump, with wide, vivid bands and a white dot on each proleg. The front tentacles are much longer. This instar is a wanderer, travelling far in search of somewhere to pupate.

THE PUPA

The third stage in the life cycle of the butterfly or moth is the pupa. It is during this stage that the caterpillar is transformed into an adult. Lepidopteran pupae are very diverse in colour and shape, and some are protected by a silk cocoon.

The pupa of the butterfly is often called a chrysalis, from the Greek word for gold, because of the metallic appearance of many butterfly pupae such as the Common Crow (*Euploae core*). The caterpillar lacks two key features of the adult – the ability to fly and to reproduce. It is impossible for wings to develop within the constraints of a caterpillar's body, especially the development of the flight muscles. The thorax, therefore, has to undergo considerable structural changes, since the muscles of the caterpillar are very different from the adult's, and cannot be attached to the larval cuticle.

Preparing to change

Once the caterpillar has entered its final instar, it moves away to find a suitable place to pupate, such as under or within a leaf, under leaf litter or in the ground. Caterpillars of the Nymphalidae suspend themselves from a silk pad under a leaf or branch, others grip with their claspers. Once in place, the caterpillar moults for the last time, and this can involve some manoeuvring to shed the old cuticle. For those attached by a silk pad, the pupa must resuspend itself without falling. Those that were suspended from claspers have a structure called a cremaster, which is an extension of the abdomen with a series of hooks that attach to the substrate.

The pupa is immobile, so it represents a vulnerable stage in the life cycle. Butterflies reduce this risk by camouflaging the pupa so that it blends with the background. Environmental factors have been found to determine

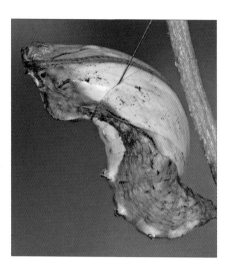

*Above: The distinctive pupa of the Spotted Swallowtail (*Papilio antenor*) is attached to a stem with silk.*

pupal colour in *Pieris* and *Papilio* species. These factors include day length, light, temperature, humidity and even the texture of the substrate. In *Papilio polytes*, short daylength in autumn leads to brown pupae that enter diapause. The pupae are brown, which gives better camouflage in the leaf litter. Caterpillars that experience a long daylength pupate and have green pupae, a colour that gives better camouflage among fresh leaves.

Transformation

The lepidopteran pupa is referred to as being obtect since all the appendages, such as legs and mouthparts are enclosed within a tight cuticle. During this stage, the pupa rarely moves, does not feed, and excretion is halted. Oxygen for respiration enters via the spiracles. The old tissues are broken down by histolysis and are replaced by adult tissues. The first changes involve the epidermis, which separates from the cuticle so that it can thicken and fold. Cell division takes place, followed by cell differentiation and the formation of new tissues; for example, cell

Butterfly life cycle

The life cycle of a butterfly varies from a few days to up to four years.

6. Mating adults

1. Egg (magnified)

5. Adult butterfly

2. Caterpillar

4. Adult butterfly emerging from pupa

3. Pupa

*Above: The pupa of the Ismenius Tiger (*Heliconius ismenius*) is dark brown, with several gold spots and abdominal spines.*

*Above: The pupa of the Variable Cracker (*Hamadryas feronia*) hangs beneath a branch, disguised as a withered leaf.*

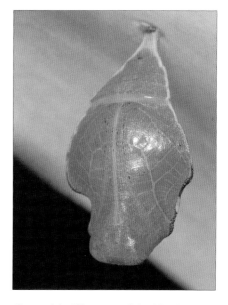

*Above: A leaf-like pupa of the Mamba (*Graphium colonna*) hangs beneath foliage, attached by a pad of silk.*

division creates a large fold which expands to form a leg. Epidermal thickenings called imaginal buds develop into adult tissues such as wings and reproductive organs. In *Pieris* sp., the imaginal disc that forms the wings is already present, albeit invaginated, in the second instar and it gets gradually larger. On the last moult, it everts and develops further.

Cocoons

Many moth pupae have an additional outer covering, called a cocoon. This conceals the pupa and reduces the risk of it being discovered. The cocoon is built by the caterpillar before it pupates.

*Below: The Oleander Hawkmoth (*Daphnis nerii*) pupates on the ground, spinning a loose cocoon among leaf litter.*

Cocoons are varied in nature; they can be hard or soft, white or coloured, be made from just silk or include other materials. Some moth caterpillars disguise their cocoon with leaves, twigs or even faecal pellets. Caterpillars with urticating hairs may incorporate these hairs into the cocoon for defence. The Emperor Gum Moth (*Opodiphthera eucalypti*) makes a brown cocoon, hidden under a gum leaf. The cocoon hardens and is waterproof and airtight within 24 hours, so the caterpillar makes a series of air holes along the side before pupating. It may spend up to five years in the cocoon before emerging. Some cocoons are made on the ground, others suspended from twigs. A few build their pupal cocoon underground, cementing particles of soil together with saliva, while those of

the genus *Cerura* (Puss moths) build a wooden chamber from wood fragments glued together, which forms a hard protective layer. Bagworms of the Psychidae family spin cocoons as caterpillars, and go through both larval and pupal stages within their cocoon.

Eclusion

Emergence, or eclusion, involves the splitting of the pupal cuticle, and of the cocoon if present. Within the pupa, the adult forces its body fluids into the head and thorax, causing them to swell and split the cuticle. Then the legs and abdomen can be freed. On emergence, the wings are soft and crumpled, so they have to be expanded by pumping haemolymph through the veins. The veins soon harden and the wings are then ready for flight. The final stage is the removal of uric acid from the body, which appears as a drop of red-pink liquid.

Moths with a cocoon have to break through the cocoon as well as the pupal cuticle. Some squeeze through a hole that is already present in the cocoon, or tear it open along pre-existing lines of weakness, but usually they have to make an opening using spines on the head or wings. A few, such as the Silkmoth (*Bombyx* sp.), use alkaline liquids to dissolve the silk threads.

DIAPAUSE AND MIGRATION

Lepidopterans have different ways of surviving periods of adverse weather such as cold during the winter and summer droughts. Some enter a state of dormancy known as diapause, in which development is halted, while others migrate to more favourable climes.

Diapause is a delay in the development process that allows the insect to survive periods of adversity such as cold or drought. Migration is a movement of transit that takes the animal beyond its normal habitat.

Diapause

This dormant state enables the species to survive in habitats that it would not otherwise be able to tolerate, for example during long cold winters and hot, dry months when there is a lack of food and water. Studies of the Pine caterpillar (*Dendrolimus tabulaeformis*) found that the caterpillars in diapause were more cold-tolerant than those that were active; this was due to an altered body composition in which levels of fats had been built up under the influence of hormones. One advantage of diapause is that it enables synchronization of development, so that there is a mass emergence of adults which increases the chances of successful mating.

There are several triggers for diapause, such as decreasing day length and change in the temperature. Diapause can occur during any of the four stages in the lifecycle, for example

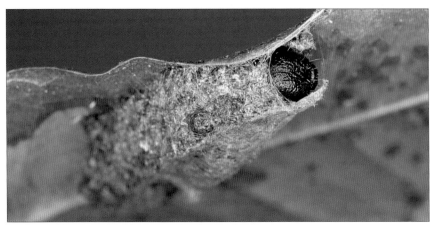

*Above: An overwintering caterpillar of the Sack Bearer (*Melsheimeri*) moth from Costa Rica is protected by a cocoon.*

in the egg of the White Letter Hairstreak (*Satyrium w-album*) in the Brown Argus caterpillar (*Aricia agestis*) and in the pupa of the Southern Festoon (*Zerynthia polyxena*) and in the adult Brimstone (*Gonepteryx rhamni*). In extreme cases the period of diapause may continue if conditions remain adverse; some caterpillars may remain in diapause for up to two years, while adult Yucca moths (*Prodoxus y-inversus*) have been reported to have emerged from pupae after 19 years of diapause.

Migration

Some species migrate during certain phases in the life cycle. Butterflies and moths frequently travel long distances to find food or mates, but sometimes the migration is a dispersal mechanism, and may involve only the females; female *Rhyacionia* sp., for example, migrate once they have mated.

The direction of the migration is influenced by both wind speed and direction, as this affects the insect's ability to move in a particular direction. Most migrations take place in one direction, and usually the butterflies or moths do not return. One

well-known exception is the Monarch (*Danaus plexippus*). During the summer months the butterfly is found across the USA and southern Canada. The butterflies cannot overwinter in the northern parts of their range, so in autumn they fly into the southern US states and Mexico. During the journey they roost in trees, clustering together on cold nights. They may remain in their roosts during cold periods, continuing their journey when temperatures rise above 13°C (55°F). Those butterflies that overwinter in the warmer southern regions of Mexico remain active through the winter months and may even breed, but

*Below: The camouflaged first-stage caterpillars of the Emerald moth (*Geometra dieckmanni*) overwinter on an oak bud.*

*Below: The adult Peacock butterfly (*Inachis io*) survives the winter by sheltering in outbuildings and sheds.*

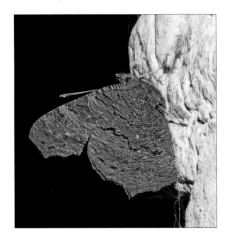

where temperatures are cooler, the butterflies roost in large numbers in trees, only becoming active on warm days to seek nectar. In February and March the temperatures increase and the butterflies start their journey north, taking up to two months to reach the northernmost points. Some butterflies that fly north are those that flew south earlier and survived the winter. Others are young adults that were bred in the south during the winter.

Another species with individuals that make the return journey is the Bogong moth (*Agostis infusa*), which is found in Australia. In late spring and early summer it migrates to the mountains to escape the heat, returning to the grasslands to breed in autumn. The Red Admiral (*Vanessa atalanta*) is known to make the return migration, but in this case it is the offspring of the generation that migrated that make the return journey.

*Above: A large group of Monarch butterflies (*Danaus plexippus*) drink water near the site in Mexico where they overwinter.*

In spring and summer, Red Admirals migrate to northerly parts of Europe where they breed. Then in autumn, the adults of this summer generation make the return journey south. In mild winters, Red Admirals may overwinter in southern England, emerging on warm days to feed and drink.

*Below: The Common Grass Yellow butterfly (*Eurema hecabe*), such as this one seen in Shiga, Japan, overwinters in snow.*

*Below: Unusually, it is the adult Herald moth (*Scoliopteryx libatrix*) that overwinters, usually in caves and outbuildings.*

*Below: A tree at an overwintering site in Michoacan, Mexico, is covered in Monarch butterflies (*Danaus plexippus*).*

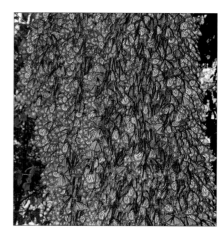

CLASSIFICATION

There are about 180,000 known lepidopteran species and probably as many as 300,000
awaiting classification. Until recently, classification was based on morphology but now much
of the classification makes use of studies of nuclear and mitochondrial DNA.

Often, DNA analyses reveal inconsistencies with traditional evolutionary development based on morphology, but there has been some consensus of opinion within the Lepidoptera.

Butterflies and moths are insects and are placed in the class Insecta within the phylum Arthropoda. They form the order Lepidoptera. Within the insects, the Lepidoptera are most closely related to the caddis flies (Trichoptera), and share key characteristics; for example, the females have heterogametic sex chromosomes, the caddis flies have dense hairs on their wings while lepidopterans have scales, and there are similarities in wing venation.

Together, Trichoptera and Lepidoptera form the superorder Amphiesmenoptera. Fossil records suggest that these two orders diverged just under 200 million years ago during the Jurassic period. The earliest lepidopteran fossils of primitive moth-like insects with scales on the wings, found in early Jurassic beds in Dorset, UK, were dated at 190-195 million years (Whalley, 1985).

The most primitive Lepidopterans are those that retain chewing mouthparts in the adult, the Micropterigidae and related moths. The other 98 per cent of species are placed in the suborder Glossata, as they have a coiled proboscis. Within this grouping, most belong to the Neolepidoptera, while there are a few unusual groups such as the archaic sun moths and bell moths. The Neolepidoptera are divided into the infraorders Heteroneura and Exoporia (ghost moths). Heteroneura is a clade, or ancestral grouping, that is characterized by different venation in the fore- and hindwings. It is divided into the Ditrysia (most moths and butterflies), the Incurvaroidea (leaf cutter moths, gall moths), Nepticuloidea (eye-cap moths) and several other small groups. The Ditrysia represent another natural clade or grouping of butterflies and moths that have two reproductive openings.

Further divisions produce a large natural group called the Macrolepidoptera, and within this is the Rhopalocera, containing the butterflies, skippers, and Heterocera with the moth superfamilies. This division is mostly based upon the shape of the antenna, which are club-shaped in the Rhopalocera.

Lepidopteran classification

This simplified representation of lepidopteran classification shows the suborder Glossata and the two divisions, Rhopalocera and Heterocera. All of the butterfly families are included along with some of the moth superfamilies.

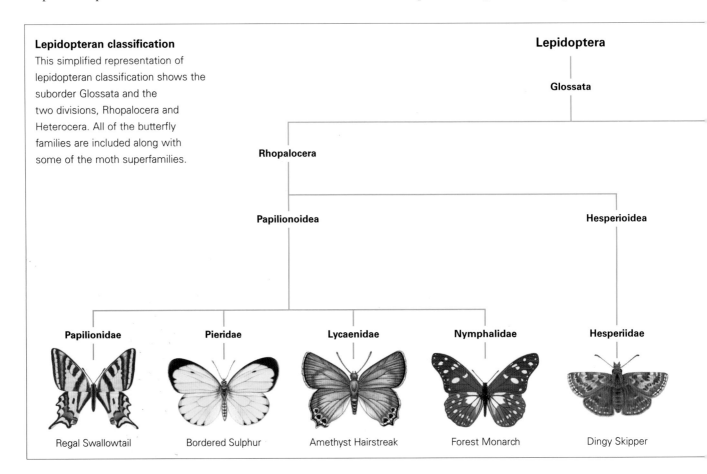

Lepidoptera

Glossata

Rhopalocera

Papilionoidea — Hesperioidea

Papilionidae — Pieridae — Lycaenidae — Nymphalidae — Hesperiidae

Regal Swallowtail — Bordered Sulphur — Amethyst Hairstreak — Forest Monarch — Dingy Skipper

Rhopalocera

This contains the two superfamilies: Papilionoidea (true butterflies); and Hesperioidea (skippers). Some classifications place the American moth-butterflies within the Rhopalocera, giving them a superfamily of their own, Hedyloidea. Alternatively, the 37 moth-butterflies of Central and South America are placed within the moth superfamily of Geometroidea. In this book they are found within the Geometroidea.

The Papilionoidea contains four families: Papilionidae, Pieridae, Nymphalidae, and Lycaenidae. Some classifications have a fifth family, Riodininae, the metalmarks, while others include the metalmarks as a subfamily within the Lycaenidae. In this book the metalmarks are included within the Lycaenidae.

Hesperioidea

The Hesperioidea comprises a single family, Hesperiidae. Within this family are more than 3,500 species of skipper, which are found around the world, with the greatest diversity being seen in

Above: In the field, identification of skippers, such as this Grizzled Skipper (Pyrgus malvae), is often difficult even for experienced lepidopterists.

Above: The Dingy Skipper (Erynnis lages) is often mistaken for the similar Grizzled Skipper (left) when flying in comparable habitats at the same time.

Central and South America. The members of the Hesperiidae are very similar in appearance, making an accurate identification in the field tricky and in some cases impossible, even for the experienced eye.

Heterocera

The superfamilies that form Heterocera are the large Geometroidea (inchworms) and Noctuoides (owlet

and tiger moths), which together represent about a quarter of all the lepidopterans, together with the smaller superfamilies of Bombycoides (silk worms), Lasiocampoidea (lappet moths), Mimallonoides (sack bearers), Callidulidea (Old World butterfly moths), Cimeliidae (gold moths), and Drepanoidea (hooktip moths related to the inchworms).

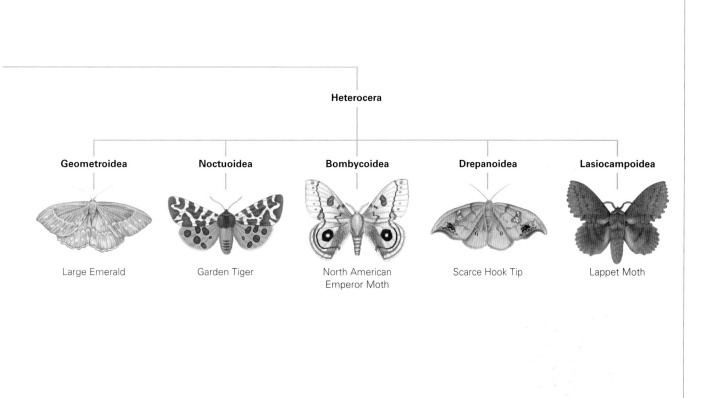

Heterocera

Geometroidea	Noctuoidea	Bombycoidea	Drepanoidea	Lasiocampoidea
Large Emerald	Garden Tiger	North American Emperor Moth	Scarce Hook Tip	Lappet Moth

BUTTERFLY FAMILIES

The butterfly superfamily Papilionoidea is divided into four families that vary greatly in appearance and habits: Papilionidae, Pieridae, Lycaenidae and Nymphalidae. Also classed as butterflies are the skippers of the superfamily Hesperioidea, which separate alone from the true butterflies.

Papilionidae

The Swallowtails are easily recognized by their large brightly coloured wings, which are usually tailed. Their caterpillars have a distinctive orange osmeterium behind the head, which is everted to release a foul-tasting liquid. The osmeterium is unique to the Swallowtails. Swallowtails are found across all the continents, with the exception of Antarctica, and are particularly common in tropical areas, especially rainforests.

There are more than 550 species of Swallowtail and they include the largest butterflies in the world, the birdwings. The Queen Alexandra birdwing (*Ornithoptera alexandrae*), with a wingspan of 30cm (12in) or more, is the world's largest butterfly.

The Papilionidae is made up of three subfamilies: the Baroniinae, Parnassiinae and Papilioninae. There is a single species, *Baronia brevicornis*, within Baroniinae and unlike other swallowtails, these caterpillars feed

Below: The Orange-Barred Sulphur butterfly (Phoebis philea) of the Pieridae is found from Brazil to Florida.

on host plants of the pea family. The Parnassiinae or Apollos are alpine butterflies found at high altitudes. The unique feature within this subfamily is the ability of the male Apollo to produce a sticky secretion that blocks the opening to the female reproductive tract after mating, to prevent other males from mating with her. The Parnassiinae is divided further into three tribes: Parnassiini, Luehdorfiini, and Zerynthiini.

The host plants of members of the Zerynthiini and Luehdorfiini belong to the Aristolochiaceae. The Papilioninae comprises about 225 species, divided into five tribes: Leptocircini, Teinopalpini, Troidini and Papilionini, and the Praepapilion, which consists of a single extinct species.

Pieridae

There are more than 1,100 species within the Pieridae, found mostly in Africa and Asia. The butterflies are typically white-, yellow- or orange-winged, and the sexes are frequently dimorphic. The forewing has a radial vein with three to four branches and the forelegs are well developed.

Above: The Emperor Swallowtail (Papilio ophidocephalus) has long tails on its hindwing, typical of the Papilionidae.

There are four subfamilies: Dismorphiinae, Pierinae, Coliadinae and Pseudopontiinae. The Dismorphiinae is a neotropical group that uses host plants from the pea family. The Pierinae comprise the Whites, Yellow and Orange-tips. Many of these species are migratory species which use a variety of host plants. The Coliadinae is made up of the Sulphurs, while the Pseudopontiinae consists of a single species, *Pseudopontia paradoxa:* found in West Africa.

Lycaenidae

This is the second largest family, with 6,000 species, representing 40 per cent of all butterflies. There are seven subfamilies: Polyomnatinae (blues), Lycaeninae (coppers), and Theclinae (hairstreaks), which are closely related and form a clade, their nearest relatives the Aphnaeinae, after that the Miletiae (harvesters) and Poritiinae, and the Curetinae. Members of the Lycaenidae are small and have brightly coloured

Above: The migratory Camberwell Beauty (Nymphalis antiopa) is one of the larger members of the Nymphalidae.

wings. They perch with their wings held open and flat. The male has reduced forelegs and no claws. The antennae are hairy with a ringed appearance.

The metalmarks or Riodininae are considered by some to be a family in their own right, while others include them within the Lycaenidae. There are about 1,000 species of metalmark, found mostly in the neotropics. Males have reduced forelegs, with the coxa (basal segment) of an unusual shape. The females have fully developed forelegs. Their wings have a unique venation, with a short humeral vein.

Below: Common Checkered Skipper (Pyrgus communis) of the Hesperioidea is common across the United States.

Nymphalidae
This large family consists of more than 5,000 species, which are found around the world. These medium to large butterflies usually have brightly coloured upperwings with underwings that are cryptically coloured for camouflage. The forelegs of these butterflies are very small or even absent, for which the family is named – the four-footed or brush-footed butterflies. The antennae have a clubbed tip and two grooves along

Below: A Small Copper Butterfly (Lycaena phlaeus) rests with its wings partly open, sunning itself in a patch of sunlight.

the underside. There are twelve subfamilies: Apaturinae, Biblidinae, Calinaginae, Charaxinae, Cyrestinae, Danainae, Heliconiinae, Libytheinae, Limenitidinae, Nymphalinae, Pseudergolini, and the Satyrinae.

Hesperioidea
The Hesperioidea comprises the skippers, a superfamily of lepidopterans with fast, darting flight. Classification of the Hesperioidea has changed in recent decades. They were, originally, classified as a butterfly. However, the skippers are not true butterflies, and have more features in common with moths; for example, they have a large, hairy body with relatively small wings, drab colours and antennae that are hooked rather than clubbed at the end. Many skippers do not hold their wings vertically in the same way as a butterfly, but fold them in a manner more reminiscent of moths. For these reasons the skippers are no longer included with the butterfly families, but stand alone as a link between butterfly and moth. In total, there are about 3,500 species, divided into seven families.

The close similarity among many of the species means that some species cannot be positively identified from external features, and instead close examination of internal features, especially their genitalia, is required.

MOTH SUPERFAMILIES

Moths are far more numerous than butterflies. Their classification is complex and still being debated. While the butterflies form a natural group, the same is not true of the moths. Some of the more significant moth superfamilies are described below.

Geometroidea

This large superfamily contains three families: Geometridae, Uraniidae, and Sematuridae. They are often called inchworms, after the manner in which the caterpillar moves. It has a looping movement in which the front of the caterpillar is extended and the back drawn up, giving the appearance of measuring the ground. The Geometridae contains about 26,000 species found around the world. The night-flying adults have broad wings which are held flat at rest. Often they are cryptically coloured to blend in with surrounding substrate such as bark. There are less than 1,000 species of Uraniids, a family that includes the butterfly-like Sunset moths. Moths of the little-known family Sematuridae are similar to the Uraniids, being large, colourful and often tailed.

Drepanoidea

These are the Hooktip moths that are related to the inchworms and with which they are often confused. They are named after the distinctive hook-tip to the forewing. The caterpillars of these moths communicate with each other by means of clicking sounds.

*Above: The large leaf-green Emerald Moth (*Geometra papilionaria*) is well camouflaged as it rests among foliage.*

Noctuoidea

The Owlet and Tiger moths form the largest of the superfamilies. Changes are still being made to the classification, so depending on this, there are between four and seven families. The largest family is the Noctuidae with about 35,000 known species. These night-flying moths are found around the world. Most have drab forewings, but more brightly coloured hindwings. The Arctiidae comprises 11,000 or so species which also have a world-wide distribution. The family includes the brightly coloured Tiger moths, Footmen, and Wasp moths. The caterpillars are very hairy and have been given the nickname 'woolly bears'.

Bombycoidea

This varied group of seven families contains about 3,400 species, which includes the Saturniidae (Emperor moths), the clade of Sphingidae (Hawk moths), Lemoniidae (Autumn Silkworms) and Brahmaeidae (Brahmin moths), the Bombycidae (Silkworm moths), Eupterotidae (Giant Lappet moths), and Mirina. These

*Left: The hindwings of the Owlet moth (*Caligo sp.*) have yellow-and-black eyespots designed to ward off predators.*

moths are mostly large and colourful, with pectinate antennae. The caterpillars spin cocoons in which to pupate. The Saturniids are medium to large sized moths with small heads and hairy, heavy bodies. This species includes the largest moths in the world. Their caterpillars are fleshy with raised bristles, some of which may be urticating.

There are about 1,000 species of Hawk or Sphinx moths worldwide. These moths have narrow wings and

*Below: The Oleander Hawk moth (*Daphnis nerii*) belongs to the Sphingidae. This nectar-feeding moth migrates over long distances.*

slender and streamlined bodies – adaptations for rapid flight. Many are day-flying moths seen hovering in front of flowers while they sip the nectar. The family gets its name from the horns found at the rear end of the caterpillar. The silkworms are economically important moths used in the production of silk.

Lasiocampoidea

The lappet moths are closely related to the Bombycoidea and in some classifications form a family within that superfamily. This group includes the tent caterpillar moths which are economically important forestry pests.

Pyraloidea

This superfamily comprises more than 16,000 species of small, drab-coloured moths, many of which are crop pests such as the European Corn Borer, Wax moths and Rice moths. Many are adapted to living in dry environments, with their larvae feeding on stored food such as flour, while others have parasitic larvae.

*Above: This Lappet moth (*Gastropacha quercifolia*) is well camouflaged as an autumn leaf while resting on a twig.*

*Below: The Bombycoidea contains the largest moths in the world, such as this Atlas Moth (*Attacus atlas*).*

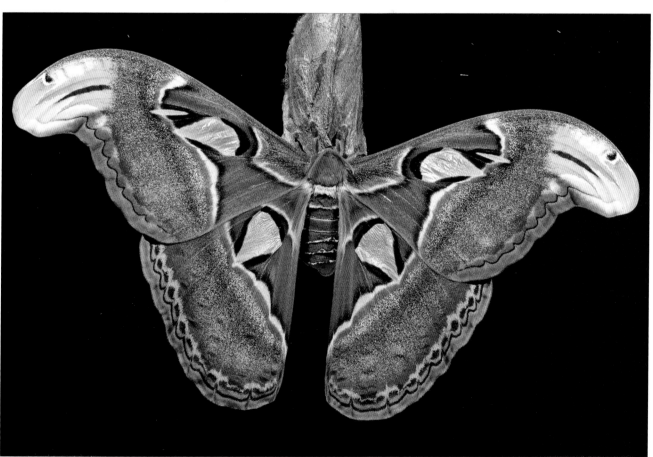

VARIATION AND SPECIATION

Study a collection of butterfly photographs of the same species and you will notice differences,
perhaps in the colour or the shape of the wing. These differences, or variations, are the key
to the process of speciation.

Variation

Within any population, there is always variation, for example a difference in size, colour, pattern or sex. This variation can be described as continuous or discontinuous. For example, wing size is an example of continuous variation, as there is a range of sizes, from the largest to the smallest, with the majority having an average wing size. Discontinuous variation is when there are two or more distinct forms within the population with no intermediates, for example sexual dimorphism, when the male and female have a different appearance, such as the Paradise Birdwing (*Ornithoptera paradise*) or the Orange-Tip butterfly (*Anthocharis cardamines*).

Polymorphism

The term polymorphism describes more than one appearance or form within a species; the Great Mormon (*Papilio memnon*), for example, is known to have four colour forms of males and 26 different forms of female. Polymorphism is genetic in origin and usually a result of mutation. The frequency of the different forms in the population, however, is often influenced by environmental factors such as predation.

There are many examples of polymorphism within the Lepidoptera, most of which involved the colours, patterns and shapes of the wing. A well-studied example is that of the Burnet Moth (*Zygaena ephialtes*) in which there are four different colour forms controlled by two genes.

Another example is that of the Peppered Moth (*Biston betularia*), studied by Kettlewell during the 1950s. The normal form is white with small

*Right: The Peppered moth (*Biston betularia*) in its normal mottled grey and white form (right) and the melanic form (left).*

black spots, but a melanic form became more common in industrial areas in response to the build up of soot on tree bark.

The black wing of the melanic form was better camouflaged in industrial areas; the frequency of the melanic form in the population rose to more than 90 per cent. The shift towards the melanic form happened quickly due to environmental pressures. In recent decades, the reduction in pollution has shifted the evolutionary advantage back to the natural spotted form, which has increased in frequency.

*Above: Burnet, or Forester, Moths (*Zygaena ephialtes*) are often differentiated by the number of spots on the wing.*

Mimicry

Yet another example of polymorphism is mimicry, whereby one species looks very similar to another species, known as the model, that has warning coloration due to its toxic nature.

Mimicry is one of the many strategies used to avoid predators. It is particularly common among tropical species, perhaps in response to the greater diversity of predators. Two

forms of mimicry exist, known as Batesian and Müllerian. Batesian mimicry, named after the naturalist Henry Bates, involves an edible species mimicking a poisonous or distasteful species. For example, *Papilio dardanus* has many polymorphic populations, in which the females mimic a number of a distasteful species. For this mimicry to work, the mimic must fly at the same time and in the same place, but be less numerous than the protected species, in case the predator learns that it is edible.

Müllerian mimicry involves two unrelated distasteful species having a similar appearance so both mimic and model benefit from the reinforcement of the warning colours, as with, for example, *Heliconius* butterflies. Both model and mimic have converged on the same warning coloration.

This form of mimicry is named after Fritz Müller, who came up with an explanation for convergence. The evolution of these forms of mimicry has been used to support the theory of natural selection, as the different mimics have probably evolved in response to predator pressure.

Isolation and speciation

In the examples of polymorphism described above, at no point have the differences between the two forms become so different as to prevent the individuals from mating.

*Above: The Viceroy (*Limenitis archippus*) is a Müllerian mimic of the Monarch butterfly, as both species are distasteful.*

Isolation is a key part of speciation. When a group of individuals become separated from the main population, perhaps by a geographic barrier, such as a river or from habitat fragmentation, there is no gene flow. The gene pool is restricted to those genes in the individuals of the population. Selection pressures may be different, and in time the population shows genetic drift away from that of

*Below: Habitat fragmentation may cause butterflies, such as this Speckled Wood (*Pararge aegeria*), to develop a larger thorax to fly over greater distances.*

the parent population. Isolated populations may display sufficient differences from the parent population for them to be classified as sub-species. In time, the differences may be sufficient to prevent individuals from mating, hence a new species is created.

Speciation can happen on small islands or isolated valleys, when a founding population of individuals becomes separated from the main species. For example, the Swallowtail *Battus devilliers* on Cuba has evolved separately from the widespread mainland species *Battus philenor*.

Speed of selection

Natural selection can work very quickly. Scientists have discovered one of the fastest known evolutionary changes in a butterfly, the Blue Moon butterfly (*Hypolimns bolina*) found in the South Pacific. The butterfly was under attack from a bacterium, *Wolbachia*, which was infecting eggs and killing male embryos before they hatched. In 2001 biologists observed that just 1 per cent of the butterflies on two Samoan islands were males, but by the time they carried out another survey in 2006, the males were back up to 40 per cent. The fightback was possible because of gene resistance to the bacterium. Scientists do not know whether this is due to a mutation or to the arrival of resistant males from other parts of South-east Asia.

TROPICAL RAINFOREST BIOME

The world's biosphere is divided up into biomes, each biome having its own climate, geographic location and community. Aspects of the physical environment, such as temperature and rainfall, have a major influence on the species that can survive in a particular biome.

Tropical rainforests cover about six per cent of the Earth's land surface. They form the most diverse biome on Earth, and are home to more than half the world's species. Not surprisingly, more species of Lepidoptera are found in this biome than in any other. Tropical rainforests are found in regions where there is strong sunlight, high rainfall and warm temperatures all year round. Huge expanses of rainforest occur across South America, Central and West Africa, South-east Asia and North Australia. The constant high temperatures ranging from 25–30ºC, plentiful rain (2,000mm/79in or so a year), and high humidity, create perfect conditions for plant growth.

A high canopy
Tall trees dominate this biome. The trees grow close together, creating a canopy that greatly reduces the light reaching the forest floor. Living on the trees are numerous epiphytes such as ferns, mosses, bromeliads and orchids, and vines including strangler figs and climbing palms, which all add to the

Above: Blue Morpho (Morpho sp.) spends much of its time near the forest floor.

Above: The Madagascan Sunset Moth (Chrysiridea riphearia).

Above: Blue Triangle (Graphium sarpendon) feeds on rotting fruit on the forest floor.

plant diversity. Much of the animal life is found in the canopy, where the leaves provide perfect concealment. Beneath the canopy there are few plants tolerant of the low light levels.

The forest floor

Because of the dense foliage above, little survives on the murky forest floor apart from a few shade-tolerant ferns, fungi and leaf litter. The warm, humid conditions mean that the rates of decomposition are high in the forest. Fallen leaves are broken down and disappear within weeks.

Colour in the forest

Colour is important in the forest and many animals make use of visual signals for communication. With the predominance of green, animals use complementary colours of red and orange to be seen. Many butterflies also make use of cryptic coloration to hide from predators. It is among tropical butterflies that mimicry is at its best.

Biodiversity

The lack of seasons in tropical rainforest means that butterflies are on the wing all year round, and comprise several generations. Many of the large tropical butterflies are long-lived, surviving up to nine months.

With the great diversity of plants existing in the rainforest, creating many different niches, it has been possible for the Lepidoptera to become diverse, demonstrating a great variety of shapes and colours. Each species occupies a particular niche in the rainforest, and many are important pollinators. As a consequence, the number of species found in a single area of rainforest can be many times the number found in a similar area of temperate forest.

*Above: Leaf Butterfly (*Kallima inachus*). When settled, the wings look like a dead leaf.*

*Above: The Owl Butterfly (*Caligo memnon*) has eyespots to scare away predators.*

*Above: Goliath Birdwing (*Ornithoptera goliath*) is from the forests of South-east Asia.*

GRASSLAND BIOME

Vast treeless plains stretch across the temperate zone, from the steppes of Asia and prairies of North America to the pampas of South America. Once home to herds of grazing animals, many have now been cleared to make space for crops.

Butterflies are common in grassland areas, where they are often the primary pollinating insect of herbaceous plants. In grasslands where there are abundant grasses, Skippers are common, while the butterfly diversity is greater in meadows and grasslands where there are more herbaceous plant species supplying food.

Moths are also present on grasslands. They include many Sphinx or Hawk moths. Day-flying moths seen over grassland include the Burnet and Hummingbird Hawk moths.

Temperate grassland

This type of grassland occurs in the interior of many continents such as

North and South America, Australia and Asia. Here the continental climate brings hot, dry summers and cold winters. Rainfall is usually in the range of 400–500mm (15–20in). The frequent summer fires and freezing winter conditions, together with the presence of grazing animals, prevents the growth of trees and shrubs, leaving

Above: The Common Brown (Heteronympha merope) *lays eggs singly on leaves of grass.*

Above: The moths of the Six-spot Burnet (Zygaena filipendulae) *pupate on long grass.*

Above: The Small Blue (Cupido minimus) *prefers grassland with shrubs for perching.*

the grasses to dominate. Within the grassland biome, there are areas of tall-grass vegetation, where the grasses reach 2m (79in) or more in height, and short-grass areas where the average height is just 60cm (24in). The grasses are good at outcompeting other species for light and water, due to their dense leaf growth and extensive networks of roots in the soil. However, some herbaceous plants can survive in the grass sward, especially those from the Papilionaceae, such as vetches and clovers, and Compositae, including daisies, cone flowers and corn marigolds. On the steppes, common examples include *Hipparchia*. *Melanargia*, *Colias*, and *Maniola* species, while in North America, common prairie species include the Regal Fritillary (*Speyeria idalia*), Satyrids, Skippers and Monarchs.

Tropical grassland

Situated in the tropical zone, the tropical grassland, or savannah, is characterized by warm temperatures all year round, with marked dry and wet seasons. These grasslands are found in parts of southern and eastern Africa, as well as in South America and Australia. The African savannah is home to many of the world's large ungulates (hoofed mammals) such as zebra and antelope.

Grazing animals

Grasslands are surprisingly productive inspite of a much smaller biomass than that of forests, so they can support large numbers of grazing animals. This is helped by the deep nutrient-rich soils, and rapid decomposition that recycles the nutrients back to the soil.

There is a wide range of grazing animals on grassland, together with invertebrate grazers such as locusts, grasshoppers and caterpillars.

*Above: Marbled Whites (*Melanargia galathea*) extract nectar from thistles and knapweeds.*

*Above: The night-flying Mother Shipton (*Callistege mi*) rests on meadow plants.*

*Above: The Grassland Copper (*Lucia limbaria*) is found on damp grassland in South Australia.*

WETLAND BIOME

The world's wetlands provide many different habitats for butterflies and moths. As well as the margins of lakes and rivers there are flood plains, marshes, bogs, fens, swamps, lagoons, mangroves and estuaries. All occur wherever there is abundant rainfall.

Swamp, marsh and bog

All wetlands have waterlogged soil, at least for part of the year. Swamps are habitats where there is standing water for much of the year. Dominant plants include water-loving species such as reeds and sedges. There is usually a rich diversity of birdlife, attracted by the wealth of invertebrates, fish and amphibians living in and near the water. Trees may colonize to form forested swamps. Marshes are similar, but are dominated by herbaceous plants. Bogs form where there is high rainfall and a rapid build-up of organic matter. In the tropics there are forested, elevated bogs while in the cooler temperate zones, bogs are dominated by mosses.

Mangrove swamps

Found along tropical shores, especially those of estuaries, mangrove swamps are coastal 'woodlands'. They are formed from very diverse plant communities, which vary according to salinity, substrate and the tides. Thick mud and organic debris covers the floor of the forest at low tide. This highly

*Above: The Swallowtail (*Papilio machaon*) female lays her eggs singly on the food plant.*

*Above: Orange-Tips (*Anthocharis cardamines*) are found in wet meadows in spring.*

*Above: The wings of the Large Copper (*Lycaena dispar*) are metallic orange in colour.*

productive habitat supports large populations of invertebrates, especially crabs, fish, reptiles and shorebirds.

Wetland lepidopterans

A diverse range of lepidopterans are found in wetland habitats. Some visit the wetlands for nectar, while others lay their eggs on the marginal plants. For example, the Bulrush Wainscot (*Nonagria typhae*) inhabits marshes, where its caterpillars feed on the stems of the reedmace (*Typha* sp.).

Some moths have aquatic larvae, for example the China-mark moths of the genus *Nymphula*. The larva feed on aquatic plants such as water lilies and pondweed of the genus *Potamogeton*. The larvae of *Paraponyx* sp. have gills and are cryptically coloured, so they are difficult to detect. In India they are considered a pest of the pondweed *Nymphoides cristatum*.

A range of different butterflies are found in the mangroves. For example, the Black and White Tiger (*Danaus affinis*) lays eggs on the mangrove milkweed (*Cynanchum carnosum*), while the Dull Jewel (*Hypochrysops epicurus*) lays eggs on the black mangrove (*Avicennia officinalis*).

Studies have found that seasonal flooding can affect the survival of diapausing caterpillars; for example, in the case of the Large Copper (*Lycaena dispar*), submergence in water for more than a month reduces survival rates.

Toledo Zoo in Ohio, USA, has a wetland butterfly project that aims to save three wetland butterfly species: Purplish Copper (*Lycaena helloides*), Mitchell's Satyr (*Neonympha mitchelli*) and Swamp Metalmark (*Calephelis muticum*). Host plants such as swamp thistles and tussock sedge are grown so that the butterflies can be raised and then released into protected sites.

*Above: The Black and White Tiger (*Danaus affinis*) is found in mangrove swamps.*

*Above: The Australian Fritillary (*Argyreus hyperbius*) is found in coastal swamps.*

*Above: Many Banded Daggerwing (*Marpesia chiron*) are found along rivers in rainforests.*

OTHER BIOMES

There are many other biomes, each with their own characteristic asemblage of plants and animals. Not only are there tropical forests, grasslands and wetlands, but temperature forests of cooler regions, deserts in low rainfall areas, distinctive montane biomes on each continent and a vast tundra in the Arctic.

The biomes below are among those most at threat from the consequences of global warming. Desert biomes are always vulnerable, dependent on unpredictable rainfall. The slightest shifts in rain patterns can lead to the local extinction of animals. Lepidopterans in particular are dependent on their host plants to complete their life cycle, and they can be wiped out by a lengthy drought. Montane vegetation is also very sensitive to changes in temperature, and already biologists are seeing butterflies moving to higher altitudes

Temperate Forests

These forests occur where there are distinct seasons and moderate rainfall over the year. Broad-leaved deciduous trees dominate the warmer forests. In cooler latitudes conifers dominate.

A few species of Lepidoptera are restricted to the forest, especially the canopy, for example the Purple Emperor (*Apatura iris*), but most are able to live in other habitats, especially along the forest margins, in hedgerows and on farmland.

Temperate forests, with clearings create more open conditions, and attract more butterflies. Clearings in a broadleaved forest, for example, create conditions favoured by Fritillaries, while other butterflies stay in the closed canopy.

Desert

Rainfall is the key factor in desert climates. Usually less than 25mm (1in) a year, it is concentrated in heavy rainfalls once a year. In the Atacama in South America rain may not fall for many years.

Desert lepidopterans are well adapted to the arid conditions, they are active at the cooler times of day and obtain water from all sources, including dew, dung and nectar.

Many species survive the dry months in diapause, either as eggs, caterpillars or pupae. The arrival of the rain is a trigger since it is followed by a burst of plant growth. Females lay their eggs while others come out of diapause. Larval growth is rapid and in some cases completed within a couple of weeks.

as temperatures become too warm lower down the mountain. However, the greatest changes are anticipated at the poles. The Arctic is already seeing significant changes in the pattern of ice melt. The snow and ice that cover the Arctic reflect much of the incoming solar radiation, keeping the environment cold. However, rising global temperatures cause more snow melt, so that the darker colours of the land and water absorb more heat, causing even more melt. Thaws take place earlier and more extensively. The changes have a significant impact on the many migrant animals that arrive each spring to feed and breed, although some adaptable species, including lepidopterans, may benefit.

Biodiversity

The world's biomes vary in their particular biodiversity or species richness. In general, biodiversity levels decline from the Equator to the poles. The tropical rainforests have the highest biodiversity, while the lowest levels are found in the Arctic and Antarctic. Biodiversity levels also decline with altitude. However, some of the least diverse biomes make up for their lack of diversity by having amazing levels of aggregations within a few species. This change in biodiversity is linked to climate and plant productivity.

Mountains

On a mountain, the climate changes with altitude, and there is a corresponding change in vegetation, from forested slopes at the bottom, up through alpine meadows to bare scree slopes. This is accompanied by a change in the butterfly and moth species. As a result, there is great lepidopteran diversity in alpine regions, especially in the larger mountain chains such as the Alps, Himalayas, Rockies and Andes. Butterflies and moths share many features in common with those of the tundra; they tend to be small and drab, and are adapted to survive the cold winters. Many enter diapause to survive the cold winter months, becoming active again as soon as the snow melts.

Tundra

Stretching from Scandinavia across Siberia to Alaska, northern Canada and Greenland is a vast treeless plain where the subsoil is permanently frozen. This is the Arctic desert, or tundra. Arctic butterflies and moths are adapted to survive the long, dark, cold winters. They tend to be small and drab, and are covered in scales and hairs to retain heat. Arctic moths are day-flying as it is too cold for them to be active at night. Caterpillars can survive in the frozen ground over winter, and may take several years to complete their larval stage. Lepidopteran diversity is low, although they may be present in large numbers. Better represented genera include *Colias*, *Boloria* and *Erebia*.

THE URBAN BIOME

As well as the natural biomes, there are anthropogenic biomes, where vegetation has been altered by people to create farmland, plantations, industrial sites and ever-expanding towns and cities. Today, the urban biome is home to a diverse array of animals and plants, not least butterflies and moths.

Some butterflies and moths are very specialist in their needs, and depend on certain food plants. If the food plant is absent, so is the butterfly or moth. However, there are generalist species that use a range of food plants, and this means that they are far more adaptable. It is mostly the generalists that have moved into the new urban habitats.

Concrete desert

The buildings and streets of a city can be likened to a desert, with the ground covered by buildings and tarmac. There are few plants with the exception of street trees and grass verges. The climate differs from that of the surrounding area, being several degrees warmer in winter and with lower

relative humidity. This enables species from subtropical zones to move north into the temperate zone. The walls of buildings with ledges and crevices resemble cliffs and are used by birds such as starlings and pigeons. Food waste dumped on the street and in landfills offers a source of food for scavengers such as foxes, rats and mice.

Above: Small Tortoiseshell (Aglias urticae) females lay their eggs on nettles.

Above: The Peacock butterfly (Inachis io) is often seen basking on sunny walls.

Above: The Red Admiral butterfly (Vanessa atalanta) is attracted to the Buddleia flower.

Garden oasis

In contrast to the concrete desert, gardens and parks are like oases. Here, plant life abounds, attracting many animals that are tolerant of the proximity of humans. In fact, a garden with lawns, herbaceous beds, ponds, and trees can attract a diversity of plant and animal life that competes with that of natural habitats.

Flower attraction

A garden can be further enhanced by the planting of nectar-rich flowers to attract butterflies and by allowing the development of wild areas with nettles and other useful food plants. Nettles, for example, are a food plant for many different butterflies and moths from around the world, including the Red Admiral (*Vanessa atalanta*), Small Tortoiseshell (*Aglais urticae*), Peacock (*Inachis io*), the Comma (*Polygonia c-album*), the Satyr (*Polygonia satyris*) and West Coast Lady (*Vanessa anabella*).

Many of those species that overwinter as adults, seek shelter in manmade structures such as sheds, garages and roof spaces. Our towns and cities are home to a surprising diversity of moths, many of which are attracted to the lights of houses and street lamps at night. A small urban garden can be visited by as many as 100 different species of moth. Moths benefit from plenty of plant debris, such as fallen leaves and twigs, in which they can hide or overwinter. However, not all moths are welcome visitors. Some are major defoliators of urban trees; for example, the Tent caterpillar, which is attracted to the bird cherry and other ornamental trees, and the Codling moth, which is a pest of apple and pear trees. In our homes, the caterpillars of clothes moths can eat holes in natural fabrics such as wool and cotton.

*Above: The Hummingbird Hawk moth (*Macroglossum stellatarum*).*

*Above: The Cabbage White (*Pieris brassicae*) lays its eggs on cabbages.*

*Above: Windfall apples attract butterflies such as the Painted Lady (*Vanessa cardui*).*

THREATS TO LEPIDOPTERANS

Biodiversity is usually considered to be a good environmental indicator of the health of a habitat. Lepidopterans are particularly good indicators of habitat health as they are sensitive to climatic and environmental changes caused by habitat fragmentation and loss, pollution and global warming.

It is due to lepidopteran's sensitivity to climatic and environmental changes that its relative abundance can reflect the diversity of the whole ecosystem.

As the human population increases, the pressure to clear natural habitats for development and agriculture increases too. Today there is massive deforestation of forests, both tropical and temperate, as well as the drainage of wetlands and the ploughing of grasslands. Pollution, too, has a role to play, with acid rain damaging trees and lakes, and the increased emissions of greenhouse gases such as carbon dioxide and methane causing global warming and climate change. In addition, there are the direct losses of insect populations associated with the increased use of pesticides.

Deforestation

The destruction of tropical forest continues despite many initiatives to reduce the logging. In 2007, a WWF report predicted that half the Amazon rainforest would be gone by 2030, and

Below: Huge tracts of the Amazon rainforest in Ecuador have been cleared for rubber plantations, oil explorations and roads.

*Above: The rainforest habitat of this Australian Birdwing (*Ornithoptera priamus euphorion*) is threatened by development.*

that this would release 100 billion tonnes of carbon dioxide in the atmosphere, the equivalent of double the world's annual emissions. The loss of tropical rainforests has had a severe effect on butterfly numbers. For example, Queen Alexandra's Birdwing (*Troides alexandrae*), the largest butterfly in the world, has in the past suffered greatly from illegal collection. Now the main threat comes from the oil palm industry in Papua New Guinea which clears huge tracts of rainforest to make way for new oil palm plantations, palm oil being much in demand as a biofuel in Europe.

Above: House building on green field sites in Europe has resulted in the loss of woodland and grassland butterfly habitats.

In addition, the forest is cleared for growing cocoa and rubber. In Mexico, the famous overwintering forest sites for the Monarch butterfly (*Danaus plexippus*) are threatened by deforestation. These pine forests are essential for the survival of hundreds of millions of Monarchs that arrive in autumn. The threats come mostly from illegal deforestation, caused largely by the spiralling costs of fuel wood. The illegal loggers arrive at night in convoys of trucks and can clear several hectares in a night. Despite annual crackdowns on illegal sawmills, the forest is still being lost. The Monarchs are very sensitive to small changes in their surroundings, so the felling of just a few trees can open up the canopy sufficiently to cause changes in humidity and temperature. The overwintering population has decreased since 2000, although this is in part due to other pressures such as loss of food plants, overuse of agrochemicals and even the planting of genetically modified crops.

Diminishing wetlands

More than half of the world's wetlands have been lost. The losses started thousands of years ago, when people started to drain wetlands, which were often considered to be disease infected,

Above: Intensive farming, with its increased use of pesticides and herbicides, has led to the decline of many species of butterfly.

and it is still continuing today. Most wetlands have been replaced by farmland. Along the coasts, mangroves have been cleared to make way for new coastal developments. Continued habitat loss is threatening the survival of many lepidopterans, such as the Large Copper (*Lycaena dispar*) in Europe and Kershaw's Brown (*Oreixenica kershawi*) and Sword Grass Brown (*Tisiphone abeona*) in Australia. In the USA, Mitchell's Satyr (*Neonympha mitchellii mitchellii*) has suffered from the loss of its habitats in Michigan and Indiana, where wetlands have been drained for agricultural use, together with the spread of alien species into the remaining fenland habitats. In addition, there has been contamination from pesticides and fertilizers, and overgrazing by livestock. As a consequence, in the USA this butterfly has been classed as endangered, and there are now fewer than 20 remnant populations.

Butterfly collectors

The collection of butterflies from the wild, in particular the attractive tropical Swallowtails, is controversial. The trade is worth millions of US dollars a year and there are hundreds of dealers. The collectors range from local people collecting a few specimens for adorning headdresses or amateurs collecting specimens for their personal collection or for research, to large-scale operations to supply the souvenir trade and other mass markets based in centres such as the Philippines. Prices range from a few cents for a common specimen to thousands of dollars for much-prized specimens of Queen Alexandra's Birdwing (*Ornithoptera alexandrae*) and the Paradise Birdwing (*Ornithoptera paradise*), which has commanded as much as US $7,000 (£4,480). Some subspecies also command high prices due to their rarity value for collectors. The trade in the low-value butterflies amounts to hundreds of millions of specimens a year, while there is a very much smaller trade in the high-value specimens.

There is also trade in live specimens that are sold to butterfly houses around the world.

Many conservationists argue that collection threatens species, but it is more likely that small-scale collection poses no real threat. In fact, many would argue that amateur butterfly collecting contributes greatly to our current knowledge of tropical butterflies. When a ban is put in place, it is the amateur collecting that stops, while the illegal collecting continues, and this does not benefit ongoing -- research.

For species that have several generations per year and lay plenty of eggs, collecting may not have an effect on their long-term survival, but for species such as the Birdwings, which lay only 30 or so eggs, the removal of too many females can have a big impact and needs careful control.

In contrast, studies in Brazil, where more than 50 million male Morphos are traded every year, have found the impact of collection to be minimal. Obviously, butterfly collection provides income for locals but it needs to be sustainable, and captive breeding schemes need to be in place to reduce the need to collect wild specimens. However, habitat destruction continues to pose much greater threats.

*Below: Tagging Monarch butterflies (*Danaus plexippus*) provides conservationists with information about their migration route.*

CLIMATE CHANGE

Butterflies and moths respond quickly to minute changes in temperature, so they are proving to be excellent indicators of the effects of climate change. Their success or failure to survive has knock-on effects on other species, as they are important consumers of plants, and all stages of the lepidoptean life cycle are preyed upon.

Any changes in butterfly and moth population size and diversity will have an impact on food webs and chains.

Generalist versus specialist

Climate change is unpredictable, and it can mean wet or cold winters, dry or wet summers, flood or drought. Those species that benefit most in a changing world are the generalists, the adaptable species that inhabit a variety of habitats and use a wide range of food plants. As a result they are able to exploit changes and take advantage of opportunities as they arise. In contrast, there are specialists, which, as the name suggests, have a restricted distribution, being found in just one or two habitats and using one food plant. These specializations make them vulnerable to climate change. If their habitat or food plant disappears, they are unable to make use of alternatives and die out.

Mapping the changes

Around the world biologists have been carrying out surveys of lepidopteran distribution in order to assess the impact of climate change. Britain has a long history of recording butterflies, with records dating back several

Below: The Brimstone butterfly (Gonepteryx rhamni) is appearing earlier in spring but it may be too early for many spring flowers.

hundred years. This wealth of information has proved to be valuable in monitoring the effect of climate change on butterfly distribution. One of the largest surveys, *Butterflies for the New Millennium: Mapping Butterfly Distributions in Britain*, was a five-year study between 1995 and 1999, which assessed broad-scale distribution changes over 20 and 200 years. A range of factors that affect butterfly distribution were noted, including habitat loss and fragmentation, but climate change was a key factor. The average spring and summer temperatures in central England had risen by about 1°C over 25 years, and this had an impact on butterfly distribution. Many of the species found in southern England were at the northernmost part of their range, so warmer summers and milder winters enabled them to survive; this was coupled with a northward shift of many species from mainland Europe. Warmer summers in southern Europe had also led to increased sightings of migrant species in northern regions of Europe.

Above: The Comma butterfly (Polygonia c-album) became extinct in Scotland in the 1870s, but is back due to climate change.

Overall, the survey showed that habitat specialists had declined in distribution over 20 years, in particular the High Brown Fritillary (*Argynnis adippe*). This once-widespread woodland species was found in just 50 sites, while the Wood White (*Leptidea sinapis*) and the Pearl Bordered Fritillary (*Boloria euphrosyne*) were lost from 62 and 60 per cent of their former sites respectively. In contrast, 14 generalist species expanded their distribution, for example the Comma (*Polygonia c-album*), which was found more than 200km (124 miles) further north, and the Brown Argus (*Aricia agestis*) which had reversed a previous decline and was found to be on the increase. The generalists made use of common habitats such as woodlands, roadside verges, hedgerows and even gardens to extend their range.

Tropical studies have also taken place. Studies of moths on Mount Kinabalu in Borneo that date back to

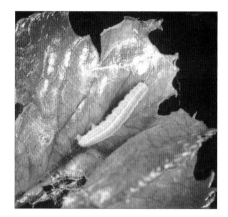

*Above: Winter Moth larvae (*Operophtera brumata*) may starve if they emerge too early in a warm spring.*

1965 were compared with a repeat study in 2007, and the results showed that on average, moth species had increased their range upwards by 67m (220ft) where it was cooler, to cope with changes in climate. However, the higher up the mountain, the less land there is available for colonization so biologists fear that there may not be enough habitat to accommodate them and some species will decline or even disappear.

An early spring

Another feature of climate change is the earlier arrival of seasons, such as that of spring in Europe. Historical records show that spring is definitely arriving earlier, and this can cause problems for some lepidopterans. For example, the caterpillars of the Winter Moth (*Operophtera brumata*) usually emerge as oak leaves open, but warmer temperatures have caused some of the caterpillars to hatch from overwintering eggs too early. They are emerging before the leaves, so they starve and die. However, biologists have now observed that the moths are adapting to change, and are hatching a few days later. Another species seen much earlier than before is the Red Admiral (*Vanessa atalanta*). This is a butterfly that is on the wing between May and September, so to see a Red Admiral on a snowdrop in February should not be possible. However, because of climate change, Red Admirals have, in recent years, been seen among snowdrops.

*Above: Warmer springs in the USA allow the Gulf Fritillary (*Agraulis vanilla*) to move north earlier than normal.*

*Below: Red Admiral butterflies (*Vanessa atalanta*) are seen much later in the year, flying in October or November.*

THREATENED SPECIES

With the threats from habitat loss, intensification of farming and climate change, it is not surprising that many species of Lepidoptera are under threat of extinction and more are classed as being critically endangered around the world.

Red List

For the last 40 years, the IUCN (International Union for Conservation of Nature) has assessed the conservation status of many species globally in order to highlight those at risk of extinction. The results are published in the IUCN Red List of Threatened Species. The lastest list, published in 2010, lists 425 species of butterfly and moth as being under threat. Of these, the most threatened family is the Swallowtails, of which 82 are listed. There are 27 species listed as being extinct, the majority of which are moths, including six species of the genus *Agrotis* within the *Noctuid* moths. *Agrotis* is a large genus of cutworms that can be serious pests, as

the caterpillar burrows in the ground and emerges at night to feed on grasses and crops. They are found through northern Europe and Asia, North America, and Australia. Although considered pests, this genus has some unusual biological features that make it of great interest to evolutionary biologists; for example, the adults have a pigment in their wings that is sensitive to temperature, and it changes colour from dark brown in cold weather to red-brown in warmer weather. They are the only moths that retain eggs within their body and give birth to larvae, rather than laying eggs. The extinct *Agrotis* species were found on Midway Island and the Hawaiian Islands.

National Red Lists

In addition to the main IUCN Red List, many countries publish their own lists based on national assessments for which there is an additional category of regionally extinct. In Britain the Red List for British butterflies, published every 10 years, listed four species as being considered extinct in 2007, eight

*Above: The Rothschild's Birdwing (*Ornithoptera rothschildi*), listed as Vulnerable, is found only in the Arfak Mountains of New Guinea.*

species are now listed as being Endangered, including the Large Blue (*Glaucopsyche arion*), which became extinct but has been reintroduced, and the High Brown Fritillary (*Argynnis adippe*). A further 16 species are classed as being vulnerable and 5 species as being Near Threatened. These 33 species represent 55 per cent of all butterfly species in Britain. This increases to 58 per cent if migrant species are excluded. In Europe, there are 435 species of resident butterflies, of which 37 are Threatened, mostly as

*Right: The reintroduction to Britain of the once-extinct Large Blue (*Glaucopsyche arion*) means it now has critically endangered status.*

The IUCN Red List of Threatened Species

The Red List is a list of all species that have been assessed as being under threat. There are different categories ranging from Least Concern to Critically Endangered and Extinct. The aim of the IUCN Red List is to identify and document those species most in need of conservation, in order to reduce rates of extinction and to provide a global index of the state of change of biodiversity. However, only a small proportion of the world species have been surveyed and assessed and some species were extinct before the programme started, so the Red List is only a snapshot of what is happening. The list is evaluated every four years, the most recent being in 2010. Over the years the list has grown, partly due to habitat changes but also due to improved methods of assessment. Individual countries use this data to develop their own programmes of conservation and to identify priorities in drawing up biodiversity action plans.

a result of change in land use. A further 44 species are classified as Near Threatened.

In North America there are 59 species of butterfly and moth in the national Red List. There are a number of species teetering on the brink of extinction, such as the Miami Blue (*Cyclargus thomasi bethunebakeri*). This species is endemic to Florida and has suffered as a result of increased urbanization and the loss of its coastal habitats. It was believed to have become extinct, but one isolated colony was discovered on Bahia Honda Key, so it is now listed as Critically Endangered. Part of the conservation programme involves a captive breeding programme, which is now underway. Another Critically Endangered species in Florida is the Schaus Swallowtail (*Heraclides aristodemus ponceanus*), which is restricted to the Upper Florida Keys. Its decline is due to the loss of its specialized habitat, hardwood hummock woodland, much of which was lost during Hurricane Andrew in 1992 and Hurricane Georges in 1998. In addition there is pressure from collection and from the increased use of pesticides against mosquitoes. Biologists estimate that its population may have fallen to fewer than 30. The Palos Verdes Blue butterfly (*Glaucopsyche lygdamus palosverdesensis*) was last seen in 1983 in tall grass near San Pedro, California, and was considered extinct; its last known habitat was bulldozed to make way for a sports field. However, ten years later, a small colony of 200 adults was found in San Pedro. The Lotis Blue (*Lycaeides idas lotis*) is now considered extinct. This small blue was found in coastal bog in Northern California, where droughts during the late 1970s led to a severe decline. It was last observed in 1994.

In Australia, there is just one species listed as being Critically Endangered, the Australian Fritillary (*Argynis*

*Right: Over-collection of the Apollo Butterfly (*Parnassius apollo*) has pushed this alpine butterfly into the Vulnerable category.*

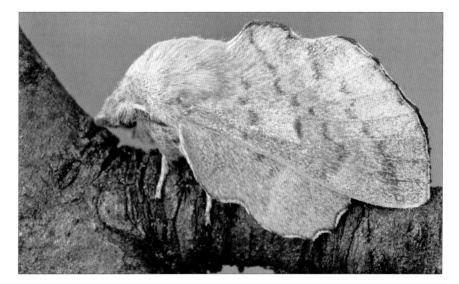

hyperbius inconstans); three species are listed as being Endangered; the Gove Crow butterfly (*Euploea alcathoe enastri*), the Graceful Sun Moth (*Synemon gratiosa*), and another moth *Phyllodes imperialis*. There is one species listed as being Vulnerable, the Bathurst Purple Copper (*Paralucia spinifera*).

Species that have a very limited distribution, such as those that occur on single islands, are under greater threat than those found over a wider geographical area. For example, the Island Marble butterfly (*Euchloe ausonides insulanus*) is found only on the islands of San Juan and Lopez in Washington State, USA. In 1908, it was believed to be extinct. This butterfly is dependent on field mustard and tumble mustard, which grows in coastal sites and, as coastal grasslands were cleared, the butterfly disappeared. However, it was rediscovered in 1998.

*Above: The Small Lappet Moth (*Phyllodesma ilicifolia*), now Endangered, once populated woodland areas of Europe.*

CITES

Further protection is gained through CITES (Convention on International Trade in Endangered Species of Wild Fauna and Flora), to which 175 countries are signatories. CITES controls the trade in about 5,000 species of animal and 29,000 species of plant. Appendix I species are at risk of extinction so all trade is prohibited, for example of the Queen Alexandra's Birdwing (*Ornithoptera alexandrae*) and the Homerus Swallowtail (*Papilio homerus*). Trade for species on Appendix II is tightly controlled through permits. This listing identifies 40 butterfly species including the Apollo butterfly (*Parnassius apollo*) and the remaining Birdwings.

CONSERVATION

There are many ways of conserving butterflies and moths which include giving protection to existing habitats, actively managing habitats to suit butterflies and moths, passing laws to give endangered species protection and captive breeding schemes.

For any conservation programme to be successful, the habitat of the butterfly or moth has to be protected, as the species is part of the community and it is the community that must be protected.

Habitat management

If they are to benefit the species in need of protection, habitats have to be managed. Woodland habitats, for example, can be managed to maximize the number of niches, and therefore the diversity of species. A broadleaved woodland may have a close canopy that suits some specialist species, but others would benefit by opening it up to create glades and rides, as many more species prefer edge habitats with a mix of sun and shade. Traditional management such as coppicing also favours insects. A coppiced woodland is divided into sectors, and each year the wood of one sector is harvested, leaving a few standards in place. The

Below: Monkton Nature Reserve in Kent, UK, is a former chalk pit. Butterflies thrive once vegetation cover is re-established.

Above: Popular with visitors, butterfly farms also help to raise awareness of the plight of the insect in the wild.

trees that are cut are those species that grow back quickly from stumps, such as hazel and willow. The bushy growth that is produced within a few years creates yet more niches. By rotating the harvest in this way, the woodland has a much greater biodiversity and therefore greater wildlife value.

Similarly, grasslands have to be managed. If they are neglected, succession takes place in which woody species move in and outcompete the grasses. In time, a climatic climax habitat such as a woodland is created.

Above: Hands-on experience of a Giant Atlas Moth (Attacus atlas) helps to educate the public about the conservation of moths.

To maintain the grassland, the grass has to be grazed to remove the shrub species, for example by grazing with sheep or cattle. Areas with a high rabbit population will be grazed, but often too heavily. Meadows are maintained with annual cuts for hay. Heathlands are maintained and pine seedlings removed by burning or using grazing animals.

Habitat re-creation

Often, valuable habitats have been lost by ploughing or felling, but in some cases it is possible to re-establish such habitats. For example, in North America just 23 per cent of the original prairie grassland remains, and sometimes the only way to conserve prairie species is to establish new prairie. There are now several examples of re-established prairie such as an old army site in Illinois where 60 square kilometres (23 square miles) of derelict land was restored to prairie grassland. Rainforest, too, can be replanted. The secondary forest that develops is more open than the primary forest, and the increased light levels lead to the establishment of more ground cover and vines. Biodiversity can be high for this reason, but it is generally different to that of the original closed forest that developed over thousands of years.

Above: These trays of pupae are being sorted at a captive breeding centre, and will be distributed around the world.

Captive breeding programmes

When habitat protection and management fails to protect a species, direct intervention in the form of captive breeding is needed. Some programmes have saved species from extinction, such as Lange's Metalmark butterfly (*Apodemia mormo langei*) in California. In 2006, just 45 adults were recorded in the wild, down from more than 200 just six years earlier. A captive breeding programme was quickly set up. Adults were captured and reared in captivity. In 2008, 30 females that had been mated were released back into an area of sand dunes, where its food plant, the naked-stemmed buckwheat (*Eriogonum nudum* ssp. *auriculatum*), had been established. Also under threat is the largest butterfly in the western hemisphere, the Giant Swallowtail (*Papilio homerus*), which is seen in just

two locations in Jamaica. Once found across the island, it has suffered from collection and habitat loss. One population is now protected in Jamaica's only national park, but the second population is threatened by bauxite mining. This species urgently needs a captive breeding programme to protect it from extinction.

Captive breeding programmes are relatively common in tropical regions, where large, attractive butterflies have, in the past, been collected from the wild. These captive breeding centres send live pupae around the world to supply several hundred walk-through butterfly houses. They also supply specimens to museums and the souvenir trade. Their value is in the way they raise awareness about the butterflies while providing an income for locals. By earning more money than is possible from subsistence farming, these 'butterfly farmers' have an incentive to protect the forest. In Papua New Guinea, money raised by the Insect Farming and Trading Agency

from butterflies sales goes to about 1,500 local farmers, who grow nectar and food plants on small garden plots near the forest, on which butterflies lay their eggs. The farmers sell some of the adults, and release the others, earning up to US $1,000 a year, ten times the average local income. Some of the large butterfly farms have become tourist attractions in their own right.

Reintroductions

When a species has become regionally extinct but the habitat still remains, it is possible to re-establish the species by releasing individuals from nearby populations. The reintroduction scheme of the Large Blue butterfly in southern Britain proved very successful. This butterfly had become extinct in the UK in 1979.

The key to the butterfly's survival is the red ant (*Myrica sabuleti*), on which the caterpillars depend. These ants need heavily grazed south-facing grassland. If the grasses grow longer than 4cm (1½in) high, the ant is replaced by another species that is not associated with the Large Blue. The recovery programme started in 1983 with the release of individuals from a Swedish population on a site in Dartmoor. Since then the species has been reintroduced to several other sites in the region. In 2010, more than 10,000 adults were flying at more than 20 sites. Not only has habitat management enabled the butterfly to survive, but it has boosted the populations of rare plants and other butterfly species.

*Below: Rows of Blue Morpho (*Morpho sp.*) pupae at a butterfly farm.*

BUTTERFLIES, MOTHS AND PEOPLE

Butterflies and moths have an essential role to play in nature through their role as pollinators, which undoubtedly benefits people too. Moths are kept for making silk, but there are many moths that are considered pests, including clothes moths, codling moths, cutworms, processionary and tent moths.

Above: The Chinese Tussah moth (Antheraea pernyi) is a major producer of Tussah silk, a type of wild silk. These moths can survive in the wild if they escape.

Pollination

The most vital role of lepidopterans for people is through the pollination of plants, both crop and ornamental.

Most people think of the honey bee as the most important pollinator of flowers, but butterflies and moths are just as important in many parts of the world. They visit flowers to sip nectar and in the process of extending their proboscis into the flower, they become covered in pollen which they transfer to other flowers. Butterflies generally prefer brightly coloured, scented flowers that have a sturdy landing platform. Moths, being mostly nocturnal, prefer large white tubular flowers with a strong scent.

Most native bees in North America are solitary, and the social honey bee was only introduced by Europeans about 300 years ago, so many North American flowers tend to be adapted for the butterfly or moth rather than the honey bee. Honey bees are efficient pollinators, but they tend to stay within a few kilometres of their hive, whereas some of the stronger-flying butterflies travel much greater distances, especially while they are on migration flights. This results in a much wider genetic mix of the plants that the butterflies pollinate, and more genetic diversity.

Among the moth pollinators are the Hawk moths. These active moths can hover in front of a flower, rather like a hummingbird, while they extend their proboscis into the flower. Some are day-flying, but most are nocturnal. Their fast wing beat means they need a good supply of energy-rich nectar in order to sustain their metabolism.

Few flowers rely solely on moths for pollination, but there is one notable exception, the yucca, which has a mutualistic relationship with the small white Yucca moths of the Prodoxidae. Both partners depend on each other for survival. The female moth gathers pollen from one flower and visits another flower, where she lays her eggs in the flower's ovaries and at the same time rubs pollen on to the stigmas of the flower. By laying her eggs in the ovaries, the caterpillars are assured of a ready supply of food in the form of seeds.

Silk production

The second most important beneficial role of moths is in the silk-making industry. Silk production goes back 4,000 years to China, where silk moths were bred specifically for their silk. The silk-making process was considered to be so important to the Chinese that the export of silk moths was banned, and anyone transgressing this rule was put to death. For thousands of years, there was a trade in silk goods, from the East to the West. Eventually some silk moth eggs were smuggled out to the west, where silk-making started in about 600AD.

The silk moth is a domesticated species, and the silk comes from its cocoon. The adults are short-lived and lack any mouthparts, living just long enough to lay eggs. The silkworm caterpillar takes about six weeks to complete its larval stage, and then it spins its silken cocoon from one continuous thread up to 1,000m (3,200ft) in length. This takes about six days. The pupal stage takes a few weeks, and in order to leave the cocoon the adult moth breaks the thread. Therefore the pupae have to be killed before they emerge. A few adults are allowed to pupate in order to

Below: The caterpillars of the Large White (Pieris brassicae) are major pests of brassica crops, causing extensive defoliation.

*Right: Migrant butterflies such as the Painted Lady (*Cynthia cardui*) help to boost the genetic diversity of the flowers they pollinate.*

maintain the breeding stocks. Today the silkworm industry is thriving in India and China and the annual production is about 60,000 tonnes. More than 50,000 cocoons are needed to make a kilogramme of raw silk.

Defoliators

A number of species have caterpillars that inflict serious damage to orchards and commercial wood plantations. The Gypsy moth (*Lymantria dispar*) is a common pest species. The caterpillar emerges just as deciduous trees are opening their buds. Over the next few weeks, the caterpillars damage most of the leaves. The caterpillars disperse over a large area, either when newly hatched, when they are carried on silken threads by the wind, or when eggs and caterpillars are picked up by animals or even on vehicles. The female moths cannot fly, and they remain on the trees on which they hatched. This pest species was introduced to North America in 1868, where it was able to spread due to a lack of natural predators. It is estimated that 4,000 km² or more of forest is defoliated most years by the Gypsy moth caterpillars. The Gypsy moth is not the only pest species of forests; others include the Forest Tent caterpillar (*Malacosoma disstria*), Winter moth (*Operophtera brumata*), Nun moth (*Lymantria monarcha*), Spruce Budworm (*Choristoneura fumiferana*), and the Large Aspen Tortrix (*Choristoneura conflictana*).

Fabric infestation

Clothes moths of the genus *Tineola* can be very destructive. The adults have a wingspan of just a centimetre or so, and they fly at night. The females crawl into dark places such as wardrobes, cupboards and in cracks under carpets where they lay their eggs

*Right: A Hummingbird Hawk moth adult (*Macroglossum stellatarum*) drinking nectar from, and pollinating, the lantana flower.*

on clothes, blankets and carpets made of natural fibres. The tiny caterpillars spin a protective silk tube in which they live and feed. An infestation can damage clothes, carpets and upholstered furniture.

Controlling pests

One way of controlling most pests is through the use of pheromones. The pheromone can act as an aphrodisiac, especially in Saturniidae moths, causing the male to want to mate with anything smelling of the pheromone. This feature has been exploited by fruit growers, who use pheromones to control pests in orchards, for example the Apple Clearwing and Codling Moth. Traps are baited with the smell of the pheromone to attract the male moths, which then enter the traps and become stuck on adhesive paper. With fewer male moths around, the females are less likely to lay fertilized eggs.

Biological control

Butterflies and moths are frequently parasitized by parasitic wasps. These parasitic wasps are useful in the biological control of pests such as Noctuid moths, whose larvae are called cutworms. The commercial process of raising the parasitic wasps for release in the field involves the use of eggs of the moth *Stilotroga cerealla*, which are used to raise the parasitic wasp. One moth species proving to be difficult to control is the Diamond-back moth (*Plutella xylostella*), a widespread pest of cruciferous crops around the world, now found to be infesting peas too. This moth has developed resistance to the main pesticides, and researchers are now seeking an alternative approach to its control, including biological control with parasitic moths. No one species has been found to be totally effective, so combinations of different species of wasps may be needed.

WATCHING BUTTERFLIES AND MOTHS

Collecting butterflies and moths has long been a popular hobby, but nowadays there is a growing trend for people to want to watch living butterflies rather than to catch and kill them. Armed with guidebooks, binoculars and cameras, they venture into the countryside to seek out suitable butterfly habitats.

Butterfly reserves

Many conservation organizations, including those specializing in butterflies and moths, have purchased habitats which are managed specifically to conserve lepidopterans; for example, Butterfly Conservation in Britain owns more than 37 nature reserves. They have open days where members of the public can visit and see the work that is being done. For those interested in seeing tropical butterflies there are companies specializing in butterfly-watching holidays in their natural habitats.

Moth watch

Projects such as National Moth Night in Britain help to raise people's awareness of moths. Launched in 1999, volunteers are asked to go out on a specific night and record the number and types of moth in a specific location, and all the results are gathered together to give a snapshot of moth populations. Each year National Moth Night takes place in a different

Below: Millions of preserved butterflies in collections, such as this one at Hogle Zoo in Salt Lake City, USA, provide biologists with references dating back hundreds of years.

Above: This is a lightweight portable moth trap, fitted with a mercury vapour lamp. It can be hung or placed on the ground.

Above: Moths are lured by the ultraviolet glow from the trap, and are funnelled down into a collecting box.

month so that a wide variety of moths are sampled. In 2008, the June count recorded 740 species at 458 sites. Many wildlife organizations set up Moth Watch nights where members of the public can go out with experts and take part in the survey.

Trapping moths

Since the majority of moths are night-flying, watching them is more difficult. Many are attracted to lights, so a good way of attracting moths is by the use

of lights. A mercury discharge bulb is the favoured type since it produces a light with a lot of the ultraviolet wavelengths which are favoured by moths. This light can be set up outside, supported on a tripod and powered by a battery. A white sheet is placed below the lamp to collect the moths. A more elaborate piece of equipment is the Skinner moth trap, which consists of a mercury discharge lamp placed above a box. The lid of the box is formed from two pieces of sloping perpex. The pieces do not meet; instead, there is a gap at the bottom through which the moths can fall into the collecting area. The trap is set up overnight and then examined. Careful release of the moths is important otherwise they may die or be predated. Ideally they should be released in small groups in sheltered spots, where they will not be found easily by predators.

Attracting butterflies and moths

One of the easiest ways to watch these insects is to attract them into the garden. Growing both nectar-producing flowers for the adults, and the food plants for the caterpillars, will

bring a wealth of these insects into the garden. Some plants have nectar-rich flowers, and act like magnets, such as the butterfly bush (*Buddleia davidii*), which gets its name from the fact that its long purple-blue flowers are much sought after by butterflies. Other attractors include the purple cone flower (*Echinacea purpurea*), ice plants (*Sedum spectabile*), French marigolds (*Tagetes patula*), thyme (*Thymus* sp.), lilac (*Syringa vulgaris*), yarrow (*Achillea millefolium*), sea holly (*Eryngium bourgatii*), lavender (*Lavendula angustifolia*), Michaelmas daisies (*Aster novae-belgii*) and verbena (*Verbena bonariensis*). With careful selection, it is possible to provide nectar from early spring through to late autumn.

Rainforest studies

The world's rainforests are home to a great diversity of butterflies and moths, but they are not the easiest habitats to study. In a temperate forest, butterflies can be surveyed by using a 'butterfly walk' in which the researcher walks slowly along a designated transect through the habitat for a set length of time, recording the numbers and species of butterfly seen within a fixed distance of the transect. However, in a rainforest, most of the species are found high up in the canopy, out of sight of the researchers on the ground. One way of surveying the canopy, is to climb up into the canopy, so research biologists use ropes to haul themselves up and then carry out a survey. In some forests there are aerial walkways through the forest which allows direct access, albeit to a small area of forest. The alternative is to use fogging. This involves directing a small jet of pyrethroid-based insecticide into the canopy to knock out the insects. The dead insects fall to the ground onto collecting trays. The disadvantage of the fogging method is that it kills the insects. However, the area fogged is small and often the specimens need to be killed in order that correct identification can take place.

*Above: Butterflies such as the Red Admiral (*Vanessa atalanta*) species are common visitors to gardens.*

Moths are attracted by scented flowers. Moth-attracting flowers are usually pale or dull-coloured flowers that are open from dusk, with a heavy fragrance and lots of nectar. Some moths hover in front of the flower, and extend their proboscis deep into the flower, such as the Hawk moths, while others need a flower with a landing platform. Moth flowers include night-scented stock (*Matthiola bicornis*), ornamental tobacco (*Nicotiana* sp.), yucca (*Yucca* sp.), honeysuckle (*Lonicera* sp.), morning glory (*Ipomoea* and *Convolvulus* sp.), and gardenia (*Gardenia* sp.)

A range of food plants can be grown, but one of the best is the stinging nettle (*Urtica dioica*). This common weed attracts many lepidopterans including the Small Tortoiseshell (*Aglais urticae*),

Red Admiral (*Vanessa atalanta*), Peacock (*Inachis io*), Painted Lady (*Cynthia cardui*), and Comma (*Polygonia c-album*).

As well as plants, there are design features that encourage butterflies and moths, including areas of paving for the butterflies to sun themselves, shady areas to cool down, fencing and climbing plants on walls to provide shelter from the wind and rain, and sheds and garages for overwintering.

Below: This colourful display of preserved butterflies is part of an educational exhibition. Many of the specimens come from butterfly farms.

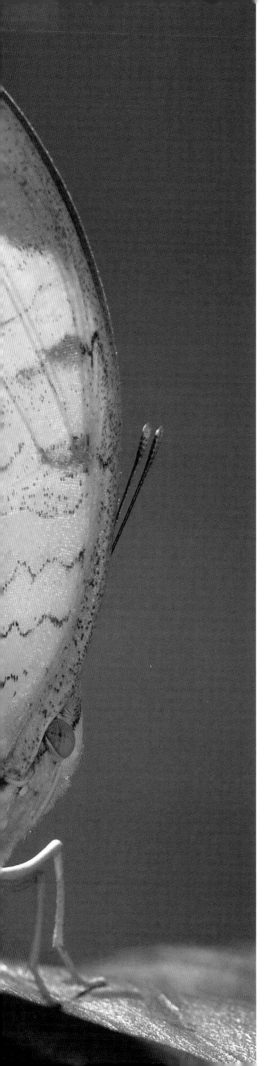

BUTTERFLIES AND MOTHS OF THE WORLD

Butterflies and moths are amazingly diverse in their size, shape and colour. You do not have to travel far to see them, as they can be found in most places on the planet, from the steaming jungles of the Equator to the barren plains of the tundra, from low-lying wetlands to mountain tops, and of course in the farmlands of our countryside, and the parks and gardens of our towns and cities. The following chapters will give you a glimpse of the diversity of butterflies and moths, with examples drawn from all parts of the world. Many of the entries are common species that occur in large numbers over a wide area, but others are so rare that they may soon become extinct.

More than 350 species of butterfly and moth are illustrated throughout these pages, each containing a stunning drawing that shows the shape, colours and intricate detail of the wings. In some cases there are additional illustrative details showing the underside of the wing or the caterpillar. Accompanying the illustration is information on each species' appearance, their distribution, food plants and biology. Information on a further 250 species of note has also been included. Following this page is an explanation of how the entries are grouped, and laid out, so that you can find the information you need as quickly as possible.

Left: This Mother of Pearl butterfly (Salamis parhassus) is well camouflaged as it rests with its wings open on a leaf.

HOW TO USE THE DIRECTORIES

The butterflies and moths featured in the following chapters are grouped according to the broad geographical region in which they occur. The three regions included here are: Europe, Asia and Africa; North and South America; and South Asia and Australasia.

Each of the regions covered are large land areas with a great variety of terrains, climates, habitats and, of course, biodiversity. Some of the lepidopteran species are found in very localized areas, but others are globally distributed species, found across all three regions.

Within each of the three regions, the featured butterflies are listed first, followed by the moths. The butterflies are grouped according to the family to which they belong: Papilionidae (Swallowtails), Pieridae (Whites), Lycaenidae (Blues) and Nymphalidae (Brush-footed). The butterflies are

Butterfly and moth families
Each species belongs to a family, the members of which have physical characteristics in common. The families and superfamilies belong to a larger group called an order.

followed by the Hesperioidea (Skippers). The moths are grouped according to their superfamily. In some chapters, you will find that more than one superfamily is featured.

The featured species represent a fraction of the 180,000 species of butterfly and moth known to science, but each is representative of the family to which they belong. They have been chosen for a variety of reasons. Many are well-known species, common throughout their region, while others are endangered species at risk of becoming extinct. Some have an interesting biology. A few are migratory species that have an unusual life cycle. Some are large and glamorous examples, but others are small and drab and are easily overlooked. Many are urban butterflies and moths that have moved

into our towns and cities, where they are important pollinators of garden flowers, but a few are major agricultural pests that damage trees and crops. Some are record breakers. Together, the featured species provide an overview of the huge diversity of butterflies and moths that are found in the world today.

Many species of butterfly and moth are at risk of becoming extinct. The IUCN has only assessed a few thousand, but already more than 700 species have been added to the Red List. The Red List status of each species is provided.

Learning to identify the different species of butterfly and moths, and studying their behaviour, can be a fascinating and rewarding pastime. The following directory will provide plenty of information to get you started.

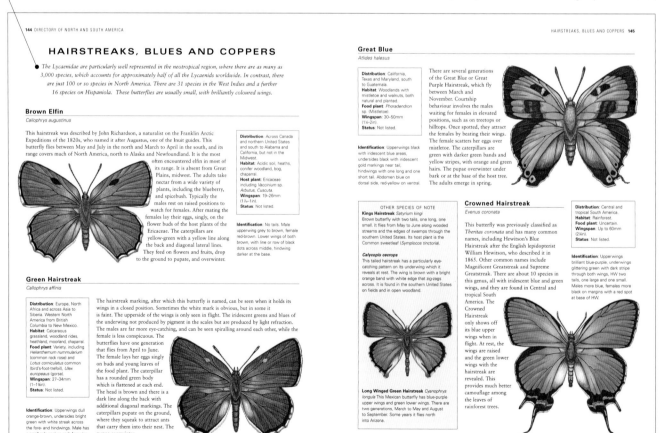

Common name
This is the most popular, non-scientific name for the butterfly or moth entry.

Latin name
This is the internationally accepted Latin name for the butterfly or moth entry.

Introduction
This provides a general introduction to the butterfly or moth and may include information on life cycle, habitat, behaviour and food sources.

Great Blue
Atlides halesus

Distribution: California, Texas and Maryland, south to Guatemala.
Habitat: Woodlands with mistletoe and walnuts, both natural and planted.
Food plant: *Phoradendron* sp. (Mistletoe).
Wingspan: 30–50mm (1¼–2in).
Status: Not listed.

Identification: Upperwings black with iridescent blue areas, undersides black with iridescent gold markings near tail, hindwings with one long and one short tail. Abdomen blue on dorsal side, red-yellow on ventral.

There are several generations of the Great Blue or Great Purple Hairstreak, which fly between March and November. Courtship behaviour involves the males waiting for females in elevated positions, such as on treetops or hilltops. Once spotted, they attract the females by beating their wings. The female scatters her eggs over mistletoe. The caterpillars are green with darker green bands and yellow stripes, with orange and green hairs. The pupae overwinter under bark or at the base of the host tree. The adults emerge in spring.

Identification
This description will enable the reader to identify the butterfly or moth. It gives an overall impression of the visual appearance of the species. Abbreviations for the wings, used where necessary, are as follows: FW; forewing, HW; hindwing, UFW; upper forewing, UHW; upper hindwing, LFW; lower forewing, LHW; lower hindwing.

Illustration
The portrait is an illustration of the butterfly or moth's upperwings, usually an adult male, unless otherwise stated.

Distribution
This describes the butterfly or moth's natural distribution throughout the world.

Habitat
The butterfly or moth's natural habitat. It may live, for example, in gardens, near streams, or among specific crops.

Distribution: California, Texas and Maryland, south to Guatemala.
Habitat: Woodlands with mistletoe and walnuts, both natural and planted.
Food plant: *Phoradendron* sp. (Mistletoe).
Wingspan: 30–50mm (1¼–2in).
Status: Not listed.

Food plant
Butterflies and moths have preferences for specific foods.

Wingspan
For many butterflies and moths, the wings are the main defining feature and method of movement.

Status
Describes whether or not the butterfly or moth is listed as endangered on the IUCN Red List.

Other Species of note
The butterflies or moths featured in this tinted box are usually lesser-known species of the order. They are included because they have some outstanding features worthy of note.

Species names
The name by which the butterfly or moth is most commonly known is presented first, followed by the Latin name and any other common name by which it is known.

Entries
The information given for each entry describes the butterfly or moth's main characteristics and the specific features it has that distinguishes it from similar species.

● OTHER SPECIES OF NOTE
Kings Hairstreak *Satyrium kingi*
Brown butterfly with two tails, one long, one small. It flies from May to June along wooded streams and the edges of swamps through the southern United States. Its host plant is the Common sweetleaf (*Symplocos tinctoria*).

●*Calycopis cecrops*
This tailed hairstreak has a particularly eye-catching pattern on its underwing which it reveals at rest. The wing is brown with a bright orange band with white edge that zig-zags across. It is found in the southern United States on fields and in open woodland.

Long Winged Green Hairstreak *Cyanophrys*
●*longula* This Mexican butterfly has blue-purple upper wings and green lower wings. There are two generations, March to May and August to September. Some years it flies north into Arizona.

DIRECTORY OF EUROPE, ASIA AND AFRICA

This section covers the geographical areas known as the Palaearctic and the Ethiopian Region (Tropical Africa). The Palaearctic extends from Europe to China and Japan, and includes North Africa, South-west Asia, the Middle East, and Asia north of the Himalayas. Climates range from subtropical in the south to the arctic in the north. There is a broad range of habitats including broad-leaved and coniferous forest, tundra, grassland and mountains. Within this region, the richest area in terms of species diversity is the central Asia zone and Tibet, due to the overlap with the Oriental zone to the south. The Ethiopian Region covers the rest of Africa. Africa, despite being mostly tropical, has far fewer species of Lepidoptera than other tropical regions. However, the Lycaenids (blues) are particularly well represented and make up almost half the butterflies.

Above from left: Antennae of a Giant Comet moth (Argema mittrei)*; Swallowtail (*Papilio ophidocephalus*) butterfly in flight; Emerald Swallowtail (*Papilio palinurus*) butterfly in flight.*
Right: A Giant Comet moth (Argema mittrei) *fills the palm of an adult hand.*

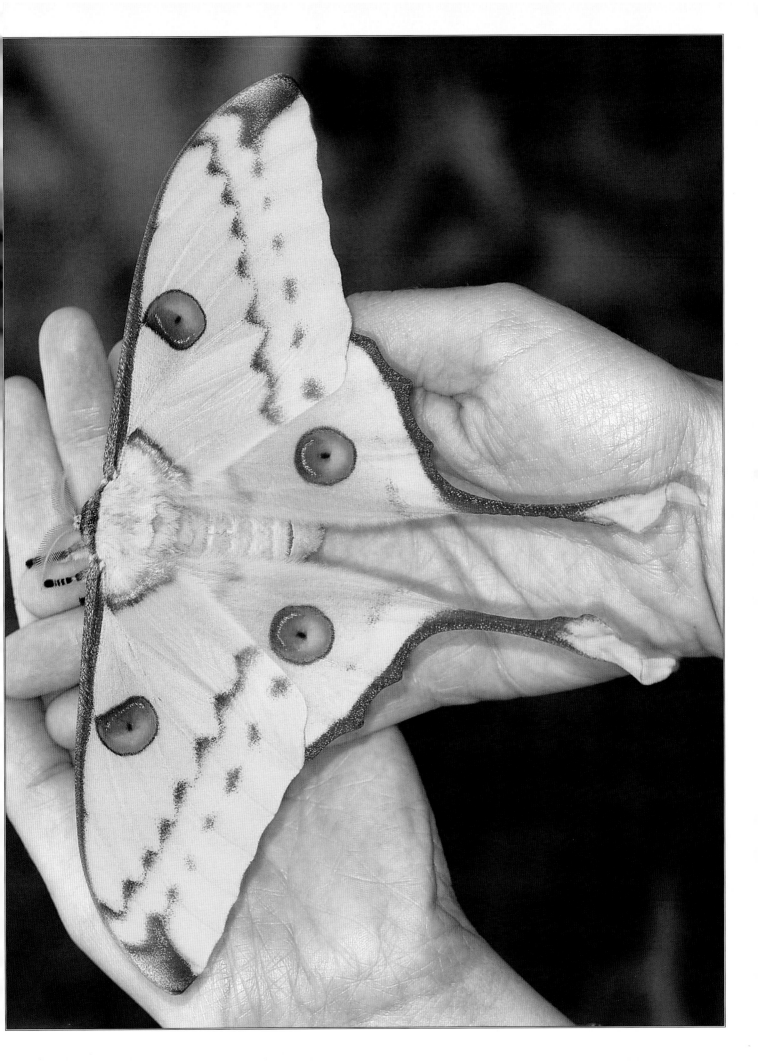

SWALLOWTAILS

There are about 170 species of swallowtail (Papilionidae) in this region. The Parnassius butterflies are mountain species and are found mostly in the Himalayas and Altai Mountains. These butterflies lack the distinctive tail. In Africa, one of the most impressive is the giant swallowtail (Papilio antimachus). The identification of many African swallowtails is difficult due to the existence of numerous mimics.

False Apollo

Archon apollinus

The False Apollo is a relatively common butterfly. This butterfly loses scales from its wings as it ages, especially the males. The loss of scales is most noticeable in older butterflies, some of which have completely transparent forewings. This gives the forewing a ghostly appearance in flight. There are four or five subspecies. There is one generation of butterflies per year; these fly between March and April. The caterpillar is brown and black, with many orange, thorny warts. It overwinters as a pupa.

Right: The underside has a similar pattern to the upper wing, with two black bars on the forewing, and a series of red spots on the hindwing.

Identification: FW mottled white, grey and black. Transparent in places. Two large black spots on leading edge. Chain of grey-black spots along the margin. HW white to yellow-white and partly transparent. Chain of black spots with blue centres and red surrounds. Females larger, with orange and red areas on the UHW, but very variable.

Distribution: Central and eastern Europe and west Asia.
Habitat: Woodland and scrub.
Larval plant: Birthwort *Aristolochia* sp..
Wingspan: 45–55mm (1¾–2⅛in).
Status: Not listed, but protected in Greece.

Glassy Graphium

Graphium agamedes

Identification: Black-brown wings with broad white band across fore- and hindwings. Black veins visible. Parts of wing may be transparent.

The Glassy Graphium or Westwood's White Lady is one of 39 species of *Graphium* found in Africa. These are a type of kite swallowtail known as swordtails. Unlike most of the other *Graphium* species, this butterfly lacks the characteristic tails on the hindwings. It is a fast flying butterfly. Caterpillars have three pairs of spines behind the head. This butterfly is becoming increasingly uncommon as its rainforest habitats disappear. If deforestation continues at its current rate, the species will be threatened and, due to its limited distribution, may even become extinct.

Distribution: West and Central Africa (Benin, Cameroon, Central African Republic, Congo, Democratic Republic of the Congo, Equatorial Guinea, Gabon, Ghana, Nigeria and Togo).
Habitat: Rainforests.
Larval plant: Uncertain.
Wingspan: 65mm (2½in).
Status: Not listed.

Large Striped Swordtail

Graphium antheus

Distribution: Africa, south of Sahara, not Madagascar.
Habitat: Woodland, savannah and forest edges.
Larval plant: Annonaceae species, including *Uvaria caffra*, *Cleistochlamys kirkii*.
Wingspan: 70–80mm (2¾–3⅛in).
Status: Not listed.

Identification: Large wings with long, curved tails. Upper sides black, with iridescent turquoise blue markings in bands across both wings. Underside similar but with pale green markings on grey-brown group. Sexes similar, although females are slightly larger than males.

This powerful flier is named after the long sword-like extensions to its hindwings. It flies high and fast. Both males and females visit flowers for nectar. Large numbers of males, often in their hundreds, are seen gathering around mud puddles with other species from the same genus. This is an attractive butterfly, and is one of several species of butterfly successfully farmed in Kenya. Parental stock and larval food plants are collected from forests, and are used to raise butterflies that are sold around the world. By farming them in this way, the butterfly populations are protected. The butterfly sales provide valuable revenue for the local people.

OTHER SPECIES OF NOTE

Eastern Festoon *Allancastria cerisyi*
This butterfly has white or yellow-white wings with black markings. There are small red spots on the hindwings, and each hindwing has a short tail. It is found across Eastern Europe and Turkey, flying from April to June, often in alpine meadows. The larval food plant is *Aristolochia* sp..

Luehdorfia puziloi
This butterfly has creamy white wings with black bars, red spots and a chain of blue spots on the hindwings. It flies from April to May in mixed mountain forests of northern China, the Kuril Islands, N Korea and Japan. The reported larval host plant is *Asarum sieboldii*.

Atrophaneura alcinous
This butterfly is found in mixed forests where its host plant, *Aristolochia manshuriensis* occurs. There are two generations of butterflies from May to August. Its distribution ranges from eastern China to Korea and Japan.

Mamba

Black Swordtail, *Graphium colonna*

The Mamba is a slow-flying butterfly, that keeps low, fluttering through the undergrowth of forests and coastal bush. The white tail tips are very conspicuous during flight. It drinks nectar from flowers of *Artabotrys monteiroae*, a woody climber found in forest habitats. The males are frequently seen gathering with other males on wet mud along roads and river banks. They do this to collect essential nutrients such as sodium and amino acids. Research suggests that the males transfer these nutrients to the female during mating, and this increases the hatch rate of eggs. There are continuous generations between October and April.

Identification: Large black butterfly with thin, pale blue-green blotches and stripes across both wings. Parts of the UHW lack stripes and spotting. Underside red-brown background with pale-green markings with pale markings. White tail tips. Sexes similar.

Distribution: West, Central and East Africa.
Habitat: Woodlands.
Larval food plant: Annonaceae e.g. *Artabotrys monteiroae* and *Uvaria caffra*.
Wingspan: 55–65mm (2⅛–2½in).
Status: Not listed.

Common Graphium

Graphium leonidas

Identification: Wings dark black-brown background with white to pale green blotches and a chain of white spots below the margin. The UHW has a large green area at its base and two chains of small white spots. The hindwings lack a tail.

The Common Graphium, or Veined Swallowtail, is a mimic of *Tirumala petiverana*, a poisonous butterfly. This is an example of Batesian mimicry, although some experts believe that the Common Graphium may have some protection of its own. Adult butterflies are seen in a range of habitats including gardens, where they visit flowers for nectar. A characteristic feature of the genus *Graphium* is the inrolled inner margin of the hindwing of the male, forming a hollow tube that surrounds a bundle of scales called the androconia. These scales are released during courtship, and carry pheromones to the female.

Distribution: South of the Sahara, including Madagascar.
Habitat: Woodlands, gardens.
Larval food plant: *Annonaceae*.
Wingspan: 90mm (3½ in).
Status: Not listed.

Below: The underwings have a similar appearance to the upperwings but are a paler brown.

Scarce Swallowtail

Iphiclides podalirius

Distribution: Europe and Asia Minor across to China.
Habitat: Hedgerows, scrub, waysides, grassland.
Larval food plant: *Prunus* sp. including blackthorn, hawthorn and rowan.
Wingspan: 70–90mm (2¾–3½ in).
Status: Not listed.

Identification: Large butterfly with tailed wings. Cream to pale yellow wings with vertical black stripes extending from fore- to hindwing. The upper hindwing has a chain of blue spots along the margin and a red and blue false eye on the inner margin.

There are just two species in the genus of *Iphiclides*. When flying, this butterfly gives the impression of flying backwards due the presence of an eyespot and the long 'antenna-like' tail on the hindwing. This is a form of back-to-front mimicry to distract any predator from the head region. There are three generations between March and October in the south parts of its range, and two in the north. The solitary caterpillar is found on trees and shrubs of *Prunus* species. The summer pupae are green while the autumn pupae are brown. These overwinter and the adult butterflies emerge in spring. This butterfly is experiencing a severe loss of habitat due to agricultural intensification and from collection.

Southern Swallowtail

Papilio alexanor

Distribution: France, Italy, Greece, and into central Asia.
Habitat: Alpine meadows to 1.2km (¾ mile) above sea level, and open woodland.
Larval food plant: Umbelliferae e.g. *Opopanax chironium* and *Seseli montanum*.
Wingspan: 75–90mm (3–3½in).
Status: Least concern.

Identification: Upperwings have black vertical stripes that extend across both fore- and hindwings, outermost stripe thick, becoming blue on the hindwing, black margin. Hindwings tailed, with single blue and red eye-spot on the inner margin. Underwings similar pattern with slightly iridescent appearance.

This large and increasingly rare butterfly flies from April through to July in open woodland where it feeds on nectar from brambles and red valerian (*Centranthus ruber*). Characteristically, it flutters its wings while feeding. There is a single generation. The female lays her eggs singly on a range of food plants of the Umbelliferae. The caterpillar has vertical bands of black and white with yellow spots. The adult butterfly is easily confused with *Papilio machaon*, which has more black on the wing, and with *Iphiclides podalirius*, which has paired black stripes and has a whiter background. There are a number of sub-species that are found in Asia Minor.

OTHER SPECIES OF NOTE

Graphium ridleyanus
This butterfly has brown wings with a pattern of red spots and blotches with no tails. It is a mimic of the poisonous *Acraea* species which has red wings. This is one of the smaller swallowtails, with a wingspan of 70–90mm (2¾–3½in).

Graphium illyris
This species is thought to be increasingly rare and occurs from Zaire into west Africa. It has brown wings with a yellow band that extends across the fore- and hindwings. The hindwings are slightly darker with a chain of creamy spots and a long tail. The females are slightly larger in size, duller with larger spots on the hindwings.

White Lady Swallowtail *Graphium morania*
This is a tail-less graphium that is found flying over grasslands and along forest edges. The sexes are similar with black and creamy-white spots, a broad area of cream-white on both the fore- and hindwings, and characteristic kidney-shaped white markings on the upper forewings. It is increasingly rare due to habitat destruction.

Mocker Swallowtail

Papilio dardanus

The Mocker Swallowtail is a common and widespread species of variable appearance. The yellow-and-black males are highly visible and are preyed upon by birds and monkeys. However, the females are highly successful Batesian mimics of poisonous swallowtails and therefore suffer from less predation. Within the eight races of *P. dardanus*, there are 39 different forms or morphs that mimic other butterflies. For example, the swallowtail *Amauris niavius* has ten different *P. dardanus* mimics across Africa. For the mimicry to be successful, the mimic and host butterfly have to live in the same habitat so the predators of the host butterfly are continually reminded that it tastes unpleasant. If the predator eats too many mimics it quickly learns that the butterfly is not poisonous.

Identification: Males yellow-cream background with black markings. UFW black tips, UHW scattered black markings and long tails. Females are extremely variable, usually smaller, darker and lacking tails. Variable combinations of black, white, yellow, cream and orange.

Distribution: Southern Africa including Madagascar.
Habitat: Forest, meadow.
Larval plant: Members of the Rutaceae and Monimaceae.
Wingspan: 10–12cm (4–4½in).
Status: Not listed.

Left: The underwings have brown-black spots and dark veins.

Citrus Swallowtail

Papilio demodocus

This common butterfly is also known as the African Lime, Christmas or Orange Dog butterfly. It is also known to be a pest of citrus fruit trees, because the female butterflies lay their eggs singly on the leaves. There are three generations per year. Young caterpillars look a bit like bird's droppings, being black, yellow and white with spikes. They moult and grow to about 15mm (⅝in) and change their appearance, becoming green with white or pink markings and an obvious eyespot. The older caterpillars deter would-be predators by everting their orange osmeeria from behind the head and releasing a pungent smell.

Identification: Wings yellow speckled with dark brown background, no tail. The upper hindwing has false eyespots. The female has larger blue spots on the upper hindwing, and is orange rather than yellow.

Distribution: Africa south of the Sahara, including Madagascar and Arabia.
Habitat: Open forests, orchards, gardens.
Larval plant: *Citrus* sp., *Clausena inaequalis*.
Wingspan: 11–12cm (4⅜–4¾in).
Status: Not listed.

Swallowtail

Papilio machaon

Distribution: Europe, North Africa, central Asia, and North America.
Habitat: Wetlands.
Larval food plant: *Umbelliferae*, such as carrot, fennel, milk parsley, *Artemisia* (North America).
Wingspan: 80–90mm (3⅛–3½in).
Status: Not listed.

There is one generation of butterflies that fly from May to July. The adults live for about one month. The females lay their eggs singly on host plants. The caterpillar changes appearance as it grows. At first it is green and orange with the appearance of a bird dropping, but as it grows it becomes creamy white with black and yellow spots. It has a pair of orange osmeteria behind the head, which extend when the caterpillar is threatened and release a pineapple-like smell to deter predators. Despite the warning colours and pungent smell, this species suffers a high mortality rate at all stages due to predation by birds, small mammals and spiders. There are a number of sub-species across the range, which vary in colour from almost black to black-and-orange.

Identification: Wings black with pale yellow or orange markings and black margin. Hindwings have short tails and a bright blue and red false eye on the inner margin. Undersides paler with more yellow.

Below: The later instars show much brighter warning colours.

OTHER SPECIES OF NOTE

Narrow-banded Swallowtail *Papilio nireus*
This butterfly is also called the Green-banded Swallowtail. There are four subspecies of this common African swallowtail, the difference being in the colour and width of the green or blue band that crosses the wings. Males have a striking white band on the lower hindwing. The females lay their eggs on citrus trees.

Emperor Swallowtail *Papilio ophidicephalus*
This is one of the larger African swallowtails. It is also called the Snake Wing due to the presence of snake-like eyespots on the hindwing. It lives in tropical rainforests through East and South Africa.

Papilio delalandei
This swallowtail is found only on Madagascar, where it can be seen in large numbers. Its forewings bear striking green spots along the front edge, and there is a yellow–white band running through the centre of the fore- and hindwings.

Giant African Swallowtail

Papilio antimachus

This is the largest African butterfly and is found in tropical rainforests. The females are secretive and are rarely seen as they stay high in the canopy where they lay their eggs. The males come down from the canopy to visit mud puddles and obtain essential nutrients. This species is one of the most poisonous of all butterflies, so has few predators. It has been classed as Rare since 1985, and its decline is due to the loss of its habitat of previously undisturbed rainforest.

Identification: Long curved forewings with orange and black-brown markings, dark brown tips. Hindwings orange with black spots and black border. Females much smaller.

Distribution: West Africa to Uganda and Zaire.
Habitat: Tropical rainforests.
Larval plant: Unknown.
Wingspan: 18–23cm (7–9in).
Status: Locally Rare.

Left: The underwings are similar to the upperwings but more creamy in colour.

Horniman's Swallowtail

Papilio hornimani

These spectacular butterflies have a limited distribution, as they are restricted to high-altitude rainforest. The males are seen more frequently, especially after rain, when they fly down from the canopy to gather around puddles. The females tend to stay in the canopy. The butterflies are seen all year and there are continuous generations. There are three subspecies in Tanzania: *P. h. hornimani* in the Usambara Mountains, *P. h. mwanihanae* in the Udzungwa Mountains and *P. h. mbulu* in the Oldeani-Mbulu Massif. This butterfly is named after the Victorian tea trader and avid collector Frederick Horniman.

Distribution: Central and eastern Africa.
Habitat: High-altitude tropical rainforest.
Larval plant: Unknown.
Wingspan: 10cm (4in).
Status: Not listed.

Identification: Large, black, tailed wings, with a bright metallic blue band across both wings. Hindwings have a chain of blue spots inside margin.

Regal Swallowtail

Papilio rex

The Regal or King Swallowtail is a common butterfly occurring widely in high-altitude rainforest. It is a mimic of the poisonous *Danaus formosa*, having similar markings but with larger wings. The female is particularly variable and there are several forms. In addition there are seven sub-species.

Distribution: West to East Africa (Nigeria, Cameroon, Sudan, Ethiopia, Congo, Zaire Uganda and Kenya).
Habitat: High-altitude rainforest.
Larval plant: *Rutaceae* e.g. *Calodendron* sp..
Wingspan: 12–14cm (4¾–5½in).
Status: Vulnerable.

Identification: Wings brown with cream spots, two bands of orange at base of the forewing. Similar pattern on the hindwing, with a band of yellow at the base. Females variable.

Apollo

Parnassius apollo

Distribution: Europe and central Asia.
Habitat: Alpine meadows and pastures, up to 2,000m (6,500ft) above sea level.
Larval plant: *Sedum* sp. and *Sempervivum* sp..
Wingspan: 80mm (3⅛in).
Status: Rare.

Identification: Wings shiny white with black spots of variable pattern, edges slightly transparent. The hindwing has large red to orange spots. The races and subspecies vary in the depth of their markings.

Apollo Butterflies are seen in midsummer and females lay their eggs on stonecrop (*Sedum*) and houseleek (*Sempervivum*). Once a male mates with a female, the female moves a special cap over the end of her abdomen to stop other males from mating with her. The caterpillars are velvety black with orange-red spots along the sides. They feed on the host plants and then pupate on the ground in a loose cocoon. The butterfly has a scattered distribution that is declining. It is believed that after the Ice Age, different populations of the butterfly became isolated in mountainous areas and evolved first into races, and then into sub-species.

The recent decline in numbers since the 1970s has been due to habitat loss, climate change, predation and increased competition from other species of butterfly. Its status is listed as Vulnerable, and it is listed on Appendix II of CITES.

OTHER SPECIES OF NOTE
Papilio zalmoxis
This striking butterfly is found in the tropical rainforests of Central Africa. The uppersides of both wings are vivid blue-green, while the undersides are pale grey. The wingspan is 15–17cm (6–6¾in). The body is bright yellow.

Small Apollo *Parnassius phoebus*
The Small Apollo is found in the mountainous regions of Europe, Central Asia and North America. It prefers alpine meadows at altitudes of 1,500m (4,900ft) or more. The females lay their eggs on *Sedum* sp. and *Saxifraga* sp.. There are about 45 subspecies across the range, which vary in the number and size of red spots.

Eversmann's Parnassian *Parnassius eversmanni*
This butterfly is found high in forested mountains of eastern Asia and Japan. It is also found in Alaska and western Canada. This Parnassian is a mostly creamy white butterfly, with two red spots and black markings on the hindwings. The females lays eggs on *Corydalis sp.*.

Southern Festoon

Zerynthia polyxena

Distribution: South and Central Europe.
Habitat: Herb-rich meadows, rocky slopes, mountains.
Food plant: *Aristolochia* e.g. *A. pistolochia* and *A. rotunda*.
Wingspan: 45mm (1¾in).
Status: Not listed, but Vulnerable in some parts of range.

Identification: Striking black and creamy white to yellow markings, the upper hindwings have a chain of small blue and red spots on inside of margin. Females are larger than males and are often more yellow.

Right: The underwings are paler with small areas of black and with an orange and black zigzag along the margin.

This shy butterfly is often seen fluttering close to the ground and resting on flowers and grass stalks. There is a single generation of butterflies that is seen from April to May. The females lay their eggs on *Aristolochia* (birthwort). The caterpillar is creamy white, with multi-coloured spots and spikes. It takes four to five weeks to mature and pupate. The stick-like pupa is brown and overwinters. This butterfly can be confused with the Spanish Festoon, but the only place the two species overlap is in southeast France. The Spanish Festoon has red on the forewings, no blue spots and a less pronounced zigzag.

Spanish Festoon

Zerynthia rumina

The Spanish Festoon is widespread and is relatively common in southeast France and across Spain and Portugal, although it is never found in abundance. There are two subspecies in North Africa: *Z. rumina africana*, which has more pronounced red spots on the forewings; and *Z. rumina tarrieri*, which is quite yellow. This butterfly occurs in a wide range of habitats, especially meadows and coastal mountains. There is one generation between April and May. The caterpillar has a white body with black dots and yellow and orange spikes. The similar Southern Festoon has virtually no red on the forewings and more prominent zigzags around the margins and blue spots on the hindwings.

Distribution: Spain, Portugal, and North Africa.
Habitat: Dry meadows and slopes, maritime mountains.
Food plant: *Aristolochia* sp..
Wingspan: 45mm (1¾in).
Status: Not listed.

Below: The underwings have a similar but paler pattern to the upperwings, and a row of red spots under the margin.

Identification: Striking black and creamy white marked wings, occasional red spot on forewing.

WHITES AND YELLOWS

There are about 300 species of the Pieridae within Europe, Asia and Africa. Some species range across the whole region, while others have a very localized distribution. Only 20 or so species of butterfly survive in the Sahara Desert, and they include a number of Pieridae, which tend to be medium in size, and are usually characterized by white or yellow wings with a black edge and no tails on the hindwings.

Black-veined White

Aporia crataegi

The Black-veined White has a powerful, soaring flight and is seen flying in May and June in meadows, scrub and along woodland margins and hedgerows. It is also seen in orchards. The females lay their eggs on a variety of food plants, both wild and cultivated, such as *Prunus* spp. (blackthorn, plum, peach, cherry), *Malus* spp. (apple) and *Pyrus* spp. (pear). Often, it is considered a pest of orchards. Large numbers of the caterpillars live together in the same cocoon all summer, they then pupate together, merging as adults the following May. This species is in decline across much of its range due to habitat loss and intensification of agriculture.

Distribution: Europe, Middle East, across Asia to Japan. North Africa.
Habitat: Meadows, gardens, orchard, woodlands.
Larval food plant: Fruit trees such as *Prunus, Malus, Pyrus, Crateagus*.
Wingspan: 60–70mm (2¼–2¾in).
Status: Not listed.

Identification: White wings crossed by black veins. Papery wings and scales lost easily giving parchment appearance.

Orange Tip

Anthocharis cardamines

A single generation of butterflies is seen from March to May. The males are first to emerge in spring and they often cluster together. Once the females emerge, the males patrol territories along ditches and streams, while the females search for food plants in wet meadows. The females lay their eggs singly on flower buds of the food plant. As they develop, the eggs change colour from green to orange. The caterpillars are blue-green, which is the perfect camouflage when among seed pods. They have forked hairs that secrete a sweet liquid which attracts ants. The pupa resembles a length of stem or fruit of the food plant, and overwinters.

Distribution: Europe and central Asia.
Habitat: Damp meadows, verges, hedgerows.
Larval plant: Cruciferae such as *Cardamine pratensis* (lady's smock), and *Allium petiolata* (garlic mustard).
Wingspan: 45mm (1¾in).
Status: Not listed.

Identification: Male forewing has an orange tip, which is absent in the female. Both sexes have green mottling on the underside of wing. When resting, the forewing moves backwards inside hindwings.

Right: The female lacks the orange spot, having white wings with grey-black tips and a single black spot on each forewing.

Diverse White

Appias epaphia

Distribution: Africa south of the Sahara, Madagascar.
Habitat: Open bush and open woodland.
Larval plant: Capparidaceae e.g. *Capparis, Boscia, Niebuhria*.
Wingspan: 50mm (2in).
Status: Not listed.

Identification: Male white with black tips on the forewing while the female is black with white base to the hindwing and white band and spots on the forewing.

The Diverse White or African Albatross is one of the few African representatives of this genus. Most of the other *Appias* species are found in Southeast Asia and Australia, while a few occur in the Americas. It is a relatively common species in the tropical regions of Africa, and is a migratory species that can suddenly appear in an area in large numbers and then disappear again.

OTHER SPECIES OF NOTE

Congo White *Appias phalola*
The male Congo White has white wings, while the females have pale grey wings. Both sexes have black tips to the forewings and a row of small black spots along the margin of the hindwing. The female lays eggs on members of the Capperidaceae family.

Moroccan Orange Tip *Anthocharis belia*
This Orange Tip is found across Morocco, Tunisia and Algeria. It also appears in Portugal, Spain and southern France during spring. The males have pale yellow wings with intense orange tips and a brown border on the forewings. The Moroccan Orange Tips occur in dry grassland and scrub where there are lots of meadow flowers. Their food plants include *Biscutella* sp., such as the Buckler Mustard.

Cleopatra Butterfly *Gonepteryx cleopatra*
This butterfly is found across Europe and North Africa. It looks similar to the brimstone; the female has pale yellow wings, the male is darker yellow with an orange patch on the forewing. Both sexes have brown dots in the centre of each wing, and the underside of wings is light greenish yellow. A number of subspecies exist, including some that are found on the Canary Islands.

Brimstone

Gonepteryx rhamni

The word butterfly, which means 'butter coloured' insect, was probably first used to describe this butterfly, later being called brimstone after the sulphur colour of its wings. The curved wings and colour of the underwings provide excellent camouflage when the butterfly rests in ivy leaves, its overwintering site. This is a long-lived butterfly, with adults surviving for up to a year. It emerges in spring and is an important pollinator of early flowers such as primrose. The females lay their yellow eggs singly near tips of the food plant. Caterpillars are green and they feed on leaves before pupation on the stems of the food plant.

Right: Females have pale yellow-green upperwings.

Distribution: North Africa, Europe, Asia to Japan.
Habitat: Woodland, scrub, verges and hedgerows.
Larval plant: *Rhamnus catharticus* (buckthorn) and *Frangula alnus* (alder buckthorn).
Wingspan: 65mm (2½in).
Status: Not listed.

Identification: Sexes different. Males have sulphur-yellow wings, females are pale yellow, looking almost white in flight. Both have a single orange spot in the middle of each curved wing.

Clouded Yellow

Colias croceus

Identification: Orange wings with black border on the outer edge of both fore- and hindwings, with conspicuous black dot in middle of FW. Female has pale yellow dots in the black border, and pink legs and antennae.

Distribution: Europe.
Habitat: Meadows, gardens.
Larval plant: Legumes, especially *Trifolium* spp and *Medicago sativa* (lucerne).
Wingspan: 50–55mm (2–2⅛ in).
Status: Not listed.

This common species of Pierid is usually seen flying from flower to flower in search of nectar, in meadows and other flowery places such as gardens. They rest with their wings in an upright position, so their upper wings are very rarely displayed. This migrant butterfly travels long distances across Europe in spring and early summer, reaching as far north as Scotland and Ireland. In more recent years, it has been shown that this species has successfully overwintered in the south of England. However, it is believed that the majority of individuals perish, since both larva and pupa of this continuously-brooded species are easily killed by damp and frost. In good years this species can produce up to three generations in the UK. The butterfly is on the wing from spring to late autumn, with as many as four generations. Each female can lay as many as 600 eggs, singly, on leguminous species. Initially the eggs are pale yellow, but they become orange just before hatching. They take up to 10 days to hatch. The caterpillar is green, with fine white hairs and a yellow stripe down each side of the body. There is evidence that this species is benefiting from global warming.

African Clouded Yellow

Colias electo

Identification: Upperwings orange with wide black border along margin, undersides yellow. Single conspicuous dot in the middle of FW. Female larger and brighter with eight pale yellow dots in the black border.

Distribution: Eastern and Southern Africa, Arabia.
Habitat: Grasslands of higher altitude.
Larval plant: *Trifolium africanum*, *Vicia sativa*, and *Medicago sativa* (lucerne).
Wingspan: 55mm (2⅛ in).
Status: Not listed.

The African Clouded Yellow is the only African representative of this genus of butterflies. Very similar in appearance to the Clouded Yellow (*Colias croceus*), above, it is a common species found on high-altitude grasslands from Arabia to Malawi and at lower altitude in southern Africa. It is a migrant species, always on the move in search of nectar and food plants on which to lay its eggs. It can turn up in large numbers, for example on lucerne and clover fields where it can damage the crops. The butterfly is also seen in gardens and on roadside verges. There are a number of subspecies occurring across its range. The African Clouded Yellow, along with many other species of butterfly in the region, is under stress from the effects of climate change. Research indicates that hot weather may make the butterfly more prone to bacterial and viral infections.

Purple Tip

Colotis ione

Distribution: Africa, south of the Sahara.
Habitat: Savannah, open woodland, scrub.
Larval plant: Various, including *Maerua racemulosa*, *Capparis* sp., *Boscia* sp..
Wingspan: 65–75mm (2½–3in).
Status: Not listed.

The Purple Tip is also known as the Violet Tip, both names referring to the purple tip on the wings of the male. The females can be difficult to identify as they are polymorphic, with several seasonal forms. The dry season form has predominantly yellow wings with red tips, but the wet season females have black wings and red tips. This butterfly is found on drier habitats, such as savannah grassland, and in open scrub and forest where it lays its eggs on plants of the Capparidaceae.

Left: The upper wings of the dry season female has red tips with a row of dark dots.

Identification: White wings with black veins. Male forewing has a purple tip bordered in brown. Females variable from yellow wings with red tip to black wings with white marks and red tips.

OTHER SPECIES OF NOTE

Pale Clouded Yellow *Colias hyale*
The male and female Pale Clouded Yellows look quite different. The males are pale yellow while the females are white, but both have forewings with a dark spot and black margins, and hindwings with an orange spot. This migrant species flies across Europe.

Eastern Pale Clouded Yellow *Colias erate*
This migrant yellow is widespread from eastern Europe, East Africa, through Russia to Afghanistan and India. It is seen on flower meadows. It has pale yellow wings with a dark outer margin. The females have yellow spots in the margin.

Double-banded Orange *Colotis aurigineus*
This upper wings of this butterfly are orange, crossed with dark bands and black veins. The margins are black with thin orange lines. It is found on grassland, alpine meadows and woodland through Central and eastern Africa.

Orange Patch White

Colotis halimede

This common and widespread butterfly goes under a variety of names, including Yellow Patch, White Orange Patch, Dappled White and Orange Halimede. It is found on dry grassland habitats across West, Central and East Africa and across into the Arabian Peninsula. Like other members of the genus *Colotis*, there are seasonal forms, although the differences are not as marked as in other species.

Distribution: S. Arabia, Senegal to Somalia and Tanzania.
Habitat: Savannah.
Larval plant: Various including *Capparis* sp., *Boscia* sp..
Wingspan: 45–55mm (1¾–2⅛in).
Status: Not listed.

Identification:
White wings with central orange patch across the forewing and hindwing, with grey towards the base. The forewings have grey tips and spots in males. The females' orange patch is smaller and paler, with more grey spots.

Wood White

Leptidea sinapis

This is a small, dainty butterfly with feeble flight. It flies slowly along the ground. For this reason it is particularly vulnerable to habitat loss, as it cannot fly long distances to populate new areas. Globally this butterfly is not threatened but it is considered to be rare or vulnerable in parts of its range, such as Britain. It does well in managed woodlands where there are open rides, disused railway tracks and similar open areas. The butterflies fly from May to June, with the males emerging first. They are frequently seen mud puddling. The females lay their eggs singly on the underside of the food plants. The caterpillars are green with a green-yellow stripe down one side. The pupa overwinters on the stems of shrubs and trees.

Distribution: Across Europe and Central Asia.
Habitat: Meadows, grassland, woodland rides.
Larval plant: *Lathyrus montanus* (bitter vetch), *Cardamine pratensis* (cuckoo flower).
Wingspan: 42 mm (1⅝ in).
Status: Not listed.

Identification: Small white wings with faint black veins. The forewings have grey tips in males. The undersides are mottled grey on white.

Bath White

Pontia daplidice

Distribution: Europe, North Africa, central Asia, India and Japan.
Habitat: Open, grassy or disturbed habitats.
Food plant: Brassicaceae including *Reseda* sp., *Sisymbrium* sp., Biscutella sp, *Sinapis* sp..
Wingspan: 45–55mm (1¾–2⅛ in).
Status: Not listed.

The Bath White gets it name from the English town of Bath. It is seen from March to October, and there are two or three generations. It is a strong, fast flier that migrates considerable distances. It is common on open habitats such as grassland and farmland. The females lay their eggs singly on the food plant. In the northern and eastern regions of Europe it is replaced by *Pontia edusa*. These two species are externally identical but they differ internally so they are unable to interbreed.

Identification: Upper forewing white with grey-black spots on tip, hindwing white with grey spots. Underwings creamy white with green blotches. The females have a chain of small grey-black spots along the upper hindwing margin.

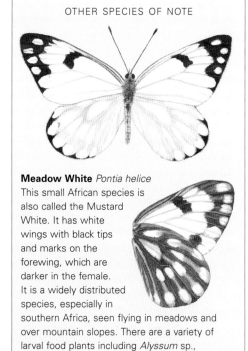

OTHER SPECIES OF NOTE

Meadow White *Pontia helice*
This small African species is also called the Mustard White. It has white wings with black tips and marks on the forewing, which are darker in the female. It is a widely distributed species, especially in southern Africa, seen flying in meadows and over mountain slopes. There are a variety of larval food plants including *Alyssum* sp., *Sisymbrium* sp., and *Reseda odorata*.

Dotted Border *Mylothris chloris*
The Dotted Border is a common butterfly of variable appearance. The males have white wings which may be tipped with black, and the females have white or orange forewings and hindwings, which are black on the lower half, and yellow on the upper half. It is found on grasslands, meadows and in gardens of West Africa across to Kenya.

Small White

Pieris rapae

Distribution: North Africa, Europe, Asia, Australia, and North America.
Habitat: Grasslands, meadows, gardens.
Larval plant: Cruciferae such as cabbage, rape seed, and nasturtium.
Wingspan: 48mm (2in).
Status: Not listed.

Identification: The forewings are white with black tips, males have one black spot and females two. Undersides are pale yellow.

This is a particularly common white butterfly that migrates over considerable distances. It is often seen flying in swarms. Part of its success is due to its ability to colonize a variety of habitats. Another reason is its reproductive capacity, having up to five generations each year between April and October. The green caterpillars grow quickly and can pupate within 14 days of hatching. The pupa is either green, brown or grey depending on the plant to which it is attached. The last generation overwinter as pupae on woody plants. It is considered a pest of brassica crops and can be difficult to control because it eats the innermost leaves first, so remaining undetected.

Tropical Dotted Border

Mylothris rhodope

The Tropical Dotted Border is a member of the genus *Mylothris*, which consists of 51 African species that are white or yellow. The genus, known as the Dotted Borders, is characterized by a single row of black dots along the margin of the underwings. Butterflies of this genus typically have rounded wings with a black apex on the forewing, and a row of marginal dots on the underwings. These butterflies, including the Tropical Dotted Border occur in the belt of tropical forest that extends from Cameroon, through Congo to Uganda. The Tropical Dotted Border is seen flying slowly in the canopy of tropical rainforests. It rarely flies to the ground, so often goes unnoticed. It is an unpalatable butterfly that is mimicked by other Pierid species such as *Appais*, *Belenois* and *Dixeia*. It is migratory, and during the rainy season it may be seen in more open habitats.

Identification: Forewing; male white with black margin, female variable from yellow to orange with black border, hindwing of both sexes white with black dots along margin, although dots on female larger. In both, row of marginal black dots on underwings.

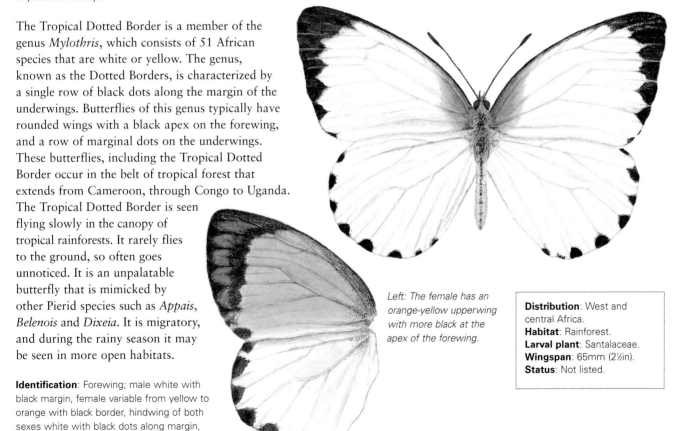

Left: The female has an orange-yellow upperwing with more black at the apex of the forewing.

Distribution: West and central Africa.
Habitat: Rainforest.
Larval plant: Santalaceae.
Wingspan: 65mm (2½in).
Status: Not listed.

BLUES, HAIRSTREAKS AND COPPERS

The Lycaenid butterflies are small, swift-flying butterflies, many of which have metallic colours.
The family is particularly well represented in Africa, where there are more than 1000 species, just under
half of all the butterfly species in the region, while there are just under 400 species in the Palaearctic.
The family is traditionally divided into the subfamilies of the blues, hairstreaks and coppers.

Brown Argus

Aricia agestis

Distribution: Europe, North Africa, Central Asia.
Habitat: Meadows, especially on chalky soils.
Larval plant: Members of the Geraniaceae such as *Erodium* sp..
Wingspan: 28mm (1⅛ in).
Status: Not listed.

The Brown Argus is a small butterfly that is found across most of Europe and North Africa. Unusually is lacks the characteristic blue scales on the upperside that are seen in other members of the family. Since the male and female are brown they closely resemble the females of several species, especially the Common Blue, *Polyommatus icarus*. On sunny days they are often seen clustered in small groups, feeding on the flowers of brambles, bird's foot trefoil and others. At night they roost together, head down, on grass stems. There are two generations a year, that fly May and June and July and August. The females lay their eggs singly on leaves of *Erodium* sp.. The caterpillars are found living with ants. The ants milk them to get sticky secretions that may deter predators. The caterpillars overwinter on leaves and the adults emerge in spring.

Above: The undersides of the wings are grey with black spots with orange spots near the margin.

Identification: Wings rich dark brown with orange half moons in a broken band along margin, with black spot in centre of the forewing. Unlike other blues, it never has any blue scaling on the upperside.

Northern Brown Argus

Aricia artaxerxes

The Northern Brown Argus was given a separate species status from the Brown Argus in 1967. There is one generation a year that flies from June to August. Unlike the Brown Argus, this butterfly is not found with others of the same species, but is more solitary. The males occupy territories which they defend against other males. The females lay their eggs singly on the upper side of leaves of Geraniaceae such as rock rose and storksbill. The caterpillar is green with white stripes down the side. The pupa, which is found at the base of the food plant is larger and paler than that of the Brown Argus.

Identification: Similar to Brown Argus, but with a white spot and fewer orange half-moon spots on the forewing.

Distribution: Scotland, Scandinavia, Balkans and scattered sites in Spain, Morocco, Turkey.
Habitat: Alpine meadows above 1.4km (1 mile) and 0.3km (0.2 miles) in Scotland.
Food Plant: Geraniaceae.
Wingspan: 28mm (1⅛ in).
Status: Not listed.

Left: The underwings are grey-brown with a row of orange-and-black spots along the margin.

White Letter Hairstreak

Satyrium w-album

Distribution: Europe, temperate parts of Asia to Kazakhstan, Korea and Japan.
Habitat: Woodland, hedgerow, with elm.
Larval plant: *Ulmus* sp..
Wingspan: 32mm (1⅜in).
Status: Not listed.

These butterflies are named after the white 'W' that is visible on the underside of the wings. They live for about three weeks between July and August. During this time, they are seen feeding on nectar of bramble and privet, as well as taking honeydew from aphids. They have a habit of walking over leaves opening and closing their wings. The females lay their eggs singly on twigs of the elm tree. The eggs overwinter and hatch in March. The caterpillars feed on the buds and then the young leaves. They are full-grown and ready to pupate in May and June.

Identification: Both sexes have dark brown upperwings with a small black tail tipped with white, undersides lighter brown with band of orange half moons near margin, white letter 'W' close to tail. Males have scent scales on forewing, and antennae with orange tips, females have longer tails.

Left: The white 'W' that gives the butterfly its name is visible on the underside of the wings.

OTHER SPECIES OF NOTE

Black-striped Hairtail *Anthene amarah*
The black stripes refer to the marks on the underside of the forewing. The upperwings are grey-brown and the undersides are grey. The females are larger and darker with more rounded wings. They are found on the open African grassland where their food plant, *Acacia*, is found.

Chapman's Green Hairstreak *Callophrys avis*
This butterfly has reddish upperwings, but these are rarely seen as the butterfly rests with its wings up, displaying its green underwings with a white hairstreak. The colour provides good camouflage among leaves. Its food plant is the strawberry tree, *Arbutus unedo*.

Protea Scarlet *Capys alphaeus*
The Protea Scarlet is a brightly coloured South African butterfly found near *Protea* plants. It has dark brown wing, with a wide orange band across both wings. Its underwings are light grey with a darker border. The hindwing has a slight tail.

Brown Hairstreak

Thecla betulae

This distinctive hairstreak is seen from July to September. It is a secretive butterfly that spends most of its time high in the canopy. The males tend to gather around 'master' trees such as *Fraxinus* sp. (ash) whereas the females fly to the ground to lay their eggs. They feed on nectar of hemp agrimony and bramble as well as honeydew from aphids. The females lay their eggs singly, between one and two metres above the ground, on blackthorn twigs. The eggs overwinter and hatch seven months later in spring, when the caterpillars can feed on young leaves.

Distribution: Europe from Spain and Ireland, Scandinavia to Greece.
Habitat: Woodland or open places with hedges or scrub with food plant.
Larval plant: *Prunus spinosa* (blackthorn).
Wingspan: 35mm (1⅜in).
Status: Not listed.

Identification: Upperwings dark brown with bright orange-brown patch on forewings, usually absent in the male. Underwings are brown with a wedge of darker brown bordered by white, creating the white hairstreaks. Tails orange-red.

Right: The rich orange-brown underwings bear two white hairstreaks.

Chapmans Blue

Agrodiaetus thersites

Chapman's Blue butterfly is found on open alpine meadows with *Onobrychis* (sainfoin) in France and North Africa. It is often mistaken for the Common Blue (*Polyommatus icarus*) butterfly. It flies from spring through summer and there are two to three generations. The butterflies feed on nectar and they are seen drinking water from between stones on river banks.

Distribution: North Africa, southern Europe, Asia.
Habitat: Warm, dry slopes.
Larval plant: *Onobrychis* sp. (sainfoin).
Wingspan: 30–35mm (1³⁄₁₆–1³⁄₈in).
Status: Missing.

Identification: Sexes different. Males are violet-blue with underwings of grey and brown with orange half-moon border, flushed blue at base. Females brown with orange half-moon border on upperwings.

They are able to survive long dry summers. The females lay their eggs on the sainfoin. The caterpillars are small and active through spring and summer. They are attended by ants of several genera, including *Lasius* and *Myrmica*. They pupate in leaf litter and overwinter as pupae. There are approximately 175 species in the genus *Agrodiaetus*, the greatest numbers being found in Iran and Turkey. This genus is of interest to biologists because it exhibits extreme diversity in the number of chromosomes, the haploid number of chromosomes varying between ten in *A. caeruleus* to 134 in *A. shahrami* and *A. achaemenes*.

Chalk-hill Blue

Lysandra coridon

Identification: Males silvery blue upperwings have dark edge with white margins, and row of black spots around margin of hindwings. Underwings brown with spots. Females brown, with white edge and row of orange spots on hindwings, underwings brown with chequered fringes.

There is a single generation of Chalk-hill Blue butterflies, flying from July to August. Like many blues the sexes are different. The males have brightly coloured wings to attract the females, while the females are drab and better camouflaged. The blue males are often seen basking in the sun with their wings open. These butterflies are found on open, chalky grassland where they feed on nectar from trefoils and vetches. They also take moisture from fresh dung. The females lay their eggs, singly, at the base of

Distribution: Europe.
Habitat: Chalk grasslands.
Larval plant: Horseshoe vetch.
Wingspan: 35mm (1³⁄₈in).
Status: Not listed.

Hippocrepis comosa (horseshoe vetch). Eggs overwinter and hatch in spring. The caterpillars are pale green and hairy, with yellow lines along their sides. They are protected by ants, and in return the ants milk them for honeydew. The species has experienced a decline due to loss of habitat throughout its range.

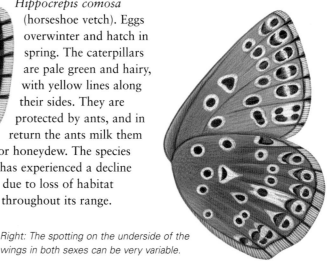

Right: The spotting on the underside of the wings in both sexes can be very variable.

Adonis Blue

Lysandra bellargus

Distribution: Europe and
Central Asia.
Habitat: Grassland.
Larval plant: *Hippocrepis
comosa* (horseshoe vetch).
Wingspan: 32mm (1³⁄₆in).
Status: Not listed.

Identification: Males vivid blue
upperwings, females brown. Both
have chequered white bands
around the wings. Undersides are
mottled brown with a white edge,
and black veins leading to the
edges of the wings.

*Far right: The butterfly rests with
its wings up, revealing the
mottled wings that are flushed
blue towards the base.*

This butterfly with its
striking blue wings is
named after the Greek god
Adonis. There are two
generations, May to June
and August to September.
They fly on flowery grasslands
and meadows, especially those
growing on chalk. The butterflies
feed on the nectar of clover, vetch
and trefoil. The males are often seen
clustered on damp ground and on fresh
dung taking up moisture and nutrients. The
females lay their eggs, singly on leaves of the
horseshoe vetch. The caterpillar is green with
yellow stripes along the sides. These
caterpillars are associated with ants. The
ants provide protection, and the caterpillars
provide the ants with honeydew. This
butterfly is in decline across much of its
range due to habitat loss caused by
agricultural intensification.

OTHER SPECIES OF NOTE

Congo-tailed Blue *Iolaus timon congoensis*
This eye-catching butterfly is about 45mm (1¾in)
across and has two pairs of tails on its hindwings,
one long and one short. The long white tail is
almost the length of the hindwing. The
upperwings are an iridescent green with black
tips, while the underwings are white with a few
black marks. They are found along forest edges.

Fig Tree Blue *Myrina silenus*
This is a stunning blue butterfly that is found in
wooded habitats with fig trees. The upperwings of
the males are violet-blue with patch of red-brown
surrounded by black. The females are larger with
more black, and a long brown tail on hindwings.

Common Blue *Polyommatus icarus*
The males have bright blue upperwings with a
white edge and metallic scales that catch the
light, while the females have brown upperwings
with a band of orange half-moons along the
margins and a white edge. The underwings of
both sexes are pale grey brown, with dark spots
with blue at the base.

Small Blue

Cupido minimus

The Small Blue may indeed be small, but it
is a strong flier. However, its speed causes its
scales to drop off, and it soon loses its vivid
colours and becomes frayed. Eventually it is
too weak to fly. It lives for about two weeks
in June. It is found in a variety of habitats,
where it visits flowers to obtain nectar. It
flies low over the vegetation and may be
found in thickets where it is well camouflaged
in the dappled shade. The female lays eggs
singly on the flowers of the food plant, the
kidney vetch. The caterpillars feed on
the flowers, then overwinter and pupate in
the spring.

Distribution: Europe.
Habitat: Grassland, coastal
cliffs and sand dunes,
disused railway cuttings.
Larval plant: *Anthyllis
vulneraria* (kidney vetch).
Wingspan: 22mm (⅞in).
Status: Not listed.

Identification: Both sexes are
brown, males have a hint of blue
on upperwing. Both sexes have
pale brown underwings with
tiny dark spots flushed to blue
at base.

Short-tailed Blue

Everes argiades

Butterflies of the genus *Everes* are found in Europe and Asia, and a few are found in Australia. A subspecies, *E. argiades comyntas*, is found in North America. This is a migrant species and occasionally it flies north into northern Europe. It frequents meadows rich in leguminous species such as trefoils and medicks. There are two to three generations each year, made possible by the fast growth rate of the caterpillars. The last generation of caterpillars overwinter in the leaf litter and the adults emerge in spring.

Identification: Males have violet-blue upperwings, females brown with some purple scales at wing bases. Both sexes have very small tail on hindwings.

Right: The underwings of both sexes are blue-grey with a row of orange spots and smaller black spots under the margin.

Distribution: Central Europe, central Asia, Australia and North America.
Habitat: Grassland, marshes and heaths.
Larval plant: *Medicago* sp. (medick), *Lotus* sp. (trefoil).
Wingspan: 10–25mm (⅜–1in).
Status: Not listed.

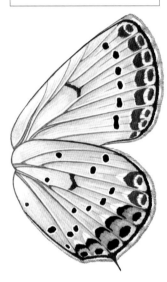

Silver-studded Blue

Plebejus argus

This attractive blue butterfly flies from June to August. The males are often seen gathered together on plants such as brambles, basking in the sun with their wings open. The females lay their eggs singly on new shoots of bramble and gorse in July and the eggs overwinter until spring. The caterpillars hatch and feed on the leaves. The caterpillars are green, with black and white strips along the body. They have a close relationship with ants that feed on the sugary honeydew produced by the caterpillars. The ants protect the caterpillars and will even carry them to new food plant to make sure there is an ample supply of honeydew. The caterpillars pupate at the base of the food plants.

Distribution: Europe and Central Asia.
Habitat: Grassland and heathland.
Larval plant: *Ulex* sp., (gorse), *Cytisus* sp. (broom), *Calluna* sp. (heather).
Wingspan: 35mm (1⅜in).
Status: Not listed.

Identification: Male upperwings are silvery blue with white margin and black line. Females are brown with orange half-moon markings.

Left: The underwings of both sexes are pale brown with spots of black, orange and blue which give the impression of silver studs.

Large Copper

Lycaena dispar

Distribution: Europe into central Asia and China.
Habitat: Wetlands.
Larval plant: *Rumex hydrolapathum, Rumex crispus, Rumex aquaticus*.
Wingspan: 38mm (1⅜in).
Status: Near threatened and extinct in UK and Ireland.

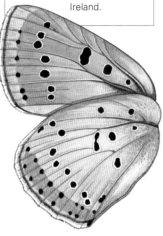

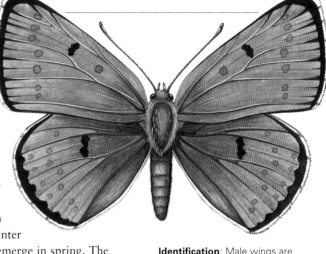

The metallic orange of the Large Copper's wings catch the light as it flies over its wetland habitat. It is on the wing from July to August, and the females lay their eggs on *Rumex hydrolapathum* (water dock). The caterpillars are green and they feed in a very distinctive pattern, feeding only on the underside of leaves, leaving a thin 'window'. The caterpillars overwinter amongst dying docks leaves and emerge in spring. The species is under threat from loss of its wetland and damp meadow habitats, as well as from collection. It became extinct in the United Kingdom in the 1850s and is classed as endangered in Europe. There have been unsuccessful attempts to re-introduce the butterfly to the United Kingdom and Ireland, using individuals from Sweden.

Left: The band of coppery orange below the margin of the hindwing is very distinctive.

Identification: Male wings are bright metallic coppery-orange, fringed with black, underwings are silvery-blue with black spots. Some have several black spots on the upper wing. Females have orange forewings with black spots and margin, hindwings are brown-orange with a pale margin.

OTHER SPECIES OF NOTE

Hutchinson's High Flier
Paraphnaeus hutchinsoni
Hutchinson's High Flier has two small tails on its hindwings, a characteristic of the genus of two-tailed blue hairstreaks. The upperwings are bright blue, with black tips and white spots. The underwings are particularly distinctive, being orange-brown with numerous large silver eye-spots ringed in black. It is found in southern Africa, where its food plant is the *Acacia*.

Purple Shot Copper *Lycaena alciphron*
The Purple Shot Copper is found on dry grassland of North Africa, Europe and Asia. Its food plant is *Rumex* sp. (sorrel). It gets its name after the bright purple, often iridescent forewings of the males. The hindwings are orange. The females are brown with an orange band along the margin of the hindwing.

Molomo Copper

Aloeides molomo

The Molomo Copper is one of 53 species of the African genus *Aloeides*, all of which are small orange-brown butterflies. It has one of the wider distributions, being found across South and East Africa. The genus is facing a number of threats. Many are found on the unique fynbos vegetation of Cape Province in South Africa, which is under threat from development. Another threat comes from the introduced Argentine ant. The caterpillars, like many other caterpillars of blue butterflies, have a close association with ants. The Argentine ant is replacing the indigenous ants, and so is an indirect threat to the caterpillars.

Distribution: Southern and eastern Africa.
Habitat: Grassland.
Larval plant: *Aspalathus* sp..
Wingspan: 30mm (1⅜in).
Status: Not listed.

Identification: Upperwings are orange-brown with a broad brown band and brown mark along the leading edge, underwings are similar but paler, no tail.

BRUSH-FOOTED BUTTERFLIES

The brush-footed butterflies of the Nymphalidae family represent more than half of all the species of butterflies found in the Palaearctic and a third of those species found in the Ethiopian region. The family is made up of around 5,000 species. Brush-footed butterflies may vary in appearance but they all have four, rather than six, functional legs, and many are brightly coloured.

Garden Inspector

Precis archesia

The Garden Inspector belongs to the genus of Pansy butterflies that have two seasonal forms. In some texts it is referred to as *Junonia archesia*. The differences in appearance enable the butterfly to be better camouflaged. The dry season form looks more like a dead leaf, so it blends well with dead grasses during the long hot months. The wet season form blends well with the lush vegetation that appears after the rains. This is a common butterfly and is often seen in gardens as well as on grassland. It has a strong, rapid flight, staying close to the ground.

Distribution: Southern Africa
Habitat: Grassy and rocky hillsides, gardens.
Larval plant: *Coleus* sp. and *Plectranthus* sp..
Wingspan: 65mm (2½ in).
Status: Not listed.

Identification: Both sexes are similar, but there are distinct seasonal forms. The wings are brown with a broad band curving across both wings. In the dry season the band is red-brown with white spots with lilac-blue patches on forewing. In the wet season the band is light yellow-brown with small brown spots. Underwings have a mottled pattern, giving the appearance of a dead leaf.

White Admiral

Limenitis camilla

This eye-catching butterfly was given its name in the 18th century. It inhabits shady, overgrown woods where honeysuckle, its food plant, grows well. It often goes unnoticed as it lives high in the canopy. The males defend territories, flying around their patch to keep other butterflies away. The adults visit bramble flowers to feed on nectar. During their month-long life span, their wings become shredded by bramble thorns. Females lay eggs singly on the edges of honeysuckle leaves. The caterpillars have a dark green body with a double row of branched red-brown spines. They attach their droppings to their body to provide better camouflage. In autumn the caterpillars hide inside a folded leaf where they overwinter. They emerge in spring to feed on young leaves and then they pupate. The chrysalis is green and purple with silver points, two horns on the head and a knob halfway down.

Distribution: Europe from northern Spain and UK to Turkey, Latvia, across Asia to China and Japan.
Habitat: Shady, overgrown woodlands.
Food plant: *Lonicera* sp. (honeysuckle).
Wingspan: 60mm (2⅜ in).
Status: Not listed.

Identification: Upperwings are dark brown with a distinctive white band across both wings. Underwings paler, but have a similar pattern, with black-and-white spots and white close to the body.

Red Admiral

Vanessa atalanta

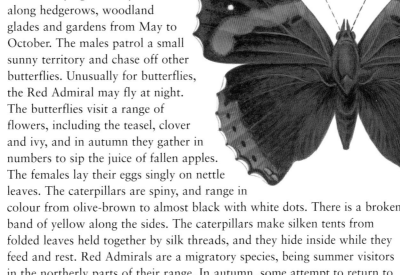

Distribution: North and Central America, across Europe and Asia to Iran, Australia, and Africa north of the Sahara.
Habitat: Wide-ranging, including grassland, mountain and garden.
Food plant: *Urtica* sp. (nettle).
Wingspan: 62–64mm (2–2½ in).
Status: Not listed.

Identification: Forewings have a distinctive diagonal red band on a black background with white markings near the tip. Hindwings are edged with red with tiny black spots and a blue patch at the bottom.

This fast-flying butterfly is found along hedgerows, woodland glades and gardens from May to October. The males patrol a small sunny territory and chase off other butterflies. Unusually for butterflies, the Red Admiral may fly at night. The butterflies visit a range of flowers, including the teasel, clover and ivy, and in autumn they gather in numbers to sip the juice of fallen apples. The females lay their eggs singly on nettle leaves. The caterpillars are spiny, and range in colour from olive-brown to almost black with white dots. There is a broken band of yellow along the sides. The caterpillars make silken tents from folded leaves held together by silk threads, and they hide inside while they feed and rest. Red Admirals are a migratory species, being summer visitors in the northerly parts of their range. In autumn, some attempt to return to warmer areas but most overwinter, although few survive.

OTHER SPECIES OF NOTE

Gaudy Commodore
Junonia octavia
The two seasonal forms of the Gaudy Commodore are very different, so much so that they were once considered to be different species. The wet-season form is a rich brown with an orange band along the wing margins, while the dry-season form is orange with black borders and small dots. It is possible that the production of the different pigments in the scales is linked to temperature, rather than rainfall.

Mycalesis rhacotis
This drab brown butterfly belongs to the brush-footed genus. It has curved forewings with brown eyespots. Like many African butterflies, it has wet- and dry-season forms.

Comma

Polygonia c-album

The Comma's distinctive ragged wings are perfect camouflage. The broken edges blend with the ground or bark as the butterfly rests. It feeds on the nectar from brambles, thistles, buddleia and the late-flowering Michaelmas daisy, and sips juice from rotting fruit. There are two generations in July and October. The female lays her eggs on the upper sides of leaves of the hop, nettle and currant. The caterpillars of the first generation are light coloured compared with the darker caterpillars of the second generation. This species is extending its range north into regions that were formerly too cold in winter.

Distribution: Europe, North Africa and Asia to Japan.
Habitat: Gardens, meadows.
Larval plant: *Humulus* sp. (hop), *Urtica* sp. (nettle), *Ribes* (currants).
Wingspan: 47mm (1¾in).
Status: Not listed.

Identification: Easily identified ragged wings, underwings of both sexes have distinct white comma mark. Upper side of wings orange-brown with blackspots, underwings much darker mottled brown.

Below: The butterfly gets its name from the white comma mark on the underwing.

White-barred Acraea

Acraea encedon

The White Barred or Common Acraea is often seen flying along banks of streams and rivers, especially where there are reeds. This is a poisonous species as indicated by its bright wing colours. Unlike many other butterflies that gain poison from the food plant, this species creates the hydrocyanic acid itself. When caught by a predator it exudes a yellow foam containing the poison. This species is a mimic of *Danaus chrysippus*, but in this case both species are poisonous, reinforcing the message to predators. This is an example of Müllerian mimicry. Scientists have studied this species extensively because some females produce only female offspring, while others produce both males and females. It seems this is caused by the death of the male embryos.

Distribution: Africa south of Sahara, Madagascar, Arabia.
Habitat: Grassland, banks of rivers and streams.
Food plant: *Commelina* sp..
Wingspan: 55mm (2⅛ in).
Status: Not listed.

Identification: Red-brown wings with darker spots and black border. The forewings are slightly pointed with pale orange-yellow band. Both sexes are variable.

Desert Acraea

Acraea miranda

The Desert Acraea is a large, brown-orange, poisonous butterfly. Despite its bright warning colours, it flies low over its desert habitat, staying close to shrubs rather than flying in the open to avoid being seen by predators such as birds. The genus *Acraea* is a large and very diverse group of just over 200 species. Most are found in Africa, although a few species are found in South and Southeast Asia.

Distribution: Somalia, southeast Ethiopia, north Kenya.
Habitat: Deserts and semi arid grassland.
Food plant: *Loewia tanaensis*.
Wingspan: 55mm (2⅛ in).
Status: Not listed.

Identification: Wings are long, orange-red, with two thin black lines across the forewing. Underwings similar, shown here. The hindwing is crossed with black lines. Dark band around the margins. Sexes similar, although females are more yellow-orange.

Forest Monarch

Tirumala formosa

The Forest or Beautiful Monarch is a relatively common butterfly, found in a wide range of habitats, in fact in any habitat in which its food plant grows. It is a poisonous butterfly that gains its poison, a type of pyrrolizidine alkaloid, from the food plants eaten by the caterpillars. It is mimicked by the swallowtail *Papilio rex*. It is larger than its imitator, but the pattern of brown and cream are very similar. The genus *Tirumala*, the Blue Tigers, consists of 13 species, and is closely related to the genus *Danaus*; in some older classifications, the Forest Monarch may be given the name *Danaus formosa*. There are four subspecies.

Distribution: Cameroon to Ethiopia, Kenya and Tanzania.
Habitat: Gardens, tropical forests and woodlands.
Food plant: *Secamone* sp., *Cryptolepsis* sp..
Wing span: 90mm (3½in).
Staus: Not listed.

Identification: Dark-brown wings with large cream patches, the base of the forewings are orange-brown. Both sexes are similar in appearance.

OTHER SPECIES OF NOTE

Acraea horta
A common butterfly in southern Africa, where it is found on the poisonous wild peach *Kiggelaria africana*. The caterpillars take up the poisonous compounds and become poisonous themselves. The males have red wings with black forewings, while the females are pale brown. Both sexes have almost transparent wing tips.

Acraea zetes
This species is found throughout Africa, south of the Sahara, especially on grassland and forest margins. It has distinctive black margins to its hindwings and black bands over the forewings.

False Monarch *Pseudacraea poggei*
This butterfly has orange wings with black margins. The black apex to the forewings is crossed by a row of white marks. It is a mimic of the African Monarch (*Danaus chrysippus*), and ranges from Namibia and Angola to Zaire and Tanzania. The genus *Pseudacraea*, the False Acraeas, comprises 15 species, many of which are mimics.

Blood Red Glider

Cymothoe sangaris

The Blood Red Glider is a member of the all-African genus *Cymothoe*. It is named after the unique blood-red colour of the male's wings. These are highly variable butterflies. Not only are the sexes different, but the females are also variable. They have more orange-coloured wings and show regional differences. Blood Red Gliders are found in forests, where the females tend to stay high in the canopy.

Distribution: West Africa, Zaire.
Habitat: Forests.
Food plant: Uncertain.
Wingspan: 70mm (2¾in).
Status: Not listed.

Identification:
Large, curved forewings. Male has blood-red wings. The female is red-orange with dark margins with white dots on the forewing and a zig-zag pattern on the hindwing.

Two-tailed Pasha

Charaxes jasius

This butterfly is seen flying around strawberry trees (*Arbutus unedo*) on coastal hills of the Mediterranean, from Spain to the Balkans and in North Africa. They are often found gathered on tracks and paths. There are two generations, from May to June and from August to October. The males often defend territories and drive away other insects. The females lay their eggs on the upper surface of the leaves of the strawberry tree. The caterpillars are green, with large heads that bear four backward-pointing spikes. After feeding they return to a silken pad on a leaf, where they rest.

Distribution: Mediterranean.
Habitat: Wooded hillsides, also gardens.
Larval plant: *Arbutus unedo* (strawberry tree).
Wingspan: 80–100mm (3⅛–4in).
Status: Not listed.

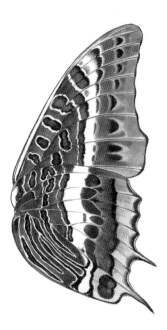

Identification: Upperwing dark brown with paler band towards the tips. Upper hindwings are edged with black, each with two unequal length tails.

Right: Underwings maroon, with patches of dark brown; lighter brown band along margin, white stripe across middle of both wings.

African Map Butterfly

Cyrestis camillus

The genus *Cyrestis*, the map butterflies, is named after the fine lines that cross the forewing giving the impression of a map. The African Map Butterfly is the only African representative of the genus. The pattern on its wings is seen when it settles on the underside of leaves and opens its wings. The butterflies fly for much of the year as there are several generations. They are found in forests, where they often gather on damp mud.

Distribution: West Africa to East Africa, Mozambique and Madagascar.
Habitat: Forests.
Larval plant: *Morus* sp., *Ficus* sp., *Zizyphus* sp..
Wingspan: 55mm (2³⁄₁₆in).
Status: Not listed.

Identification: Cream wings with bands of orange and brown, often edged in black. Hindwings have a tail and two blue spots on the inside margin of each hindwing.

Blue Temora

Salamis temora

Distribution: Nigeria across Africa to Tanzania, Kenya and Ethiopia.
Habitat: Forests up to 1,500m (4,900ft).
Larval plant: *Aystasia* sp., *Mellera* sp., *Justicia* sp., *Mimulopsis* sp., *Paulowilhelmia* sp..
Wingspan: 80–90mm (3⅛in–3½in).
Status: Not listed.

Identification: Brilliant blue-purple hooked wings with black dots inside the margin. The hindwing has a yellow-brown band around the margin with black spots and eye-spot, underwings are mottled brown with eye-spots.

This is a common African butterfly, often found in the central and eastern countries of the continent, with a wide distribution from West to East Africa. The Blue Temora is mostly found in forested areas, where it is seen throughout much of the year as there are several generations. The butterfly rests with its wings up, revealing a mottled brown pattern, which provides excellent camouflage in the forest when resting on bark and dead leaves.

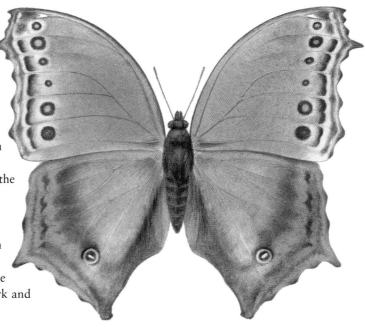

OTHER SPECIES OF NOTE

Charaxes ameliae
The males have dark wings with bands of pale blue spots, while the females have white spots. It is found across western Africa across to Malawi and Uganda. This forest butterfly drinks fermenting sap that oozes from the bark of damaged trees.

Pearl Charaxes *Charaxes varanes*
The forewings of the Pearl Charaxes are brown with orange spots, while the inner wing is white. The underwing is marbled brown and yellow with a chain of dark spots. This butterfly is found across South Africa where it flies all year.

Charaxes smaragdalis
This butterfly is a powerful flier found in the forests of West Africa. It feeds on the juice released by rotting fruits. The males have dark upperwings with patches of blue, while the female has paler wings.

Mother of Pearl

Salamis parhassus

This widely distributed butterfly is common in forests and dense shrub throughout tropical Africa. For much of the time it rests on leaves and makes short flights through the canopy. There are two generations, one in the wet season and one in the dry season. The wet-season butterflies are darker and smaller compared with the dry-season ones.

Distribution: Africa south of the Sahara.
Habitat: Forests and dense scrub.
Larval plant: Acanthaceae e.g. *Asystasia* sp. and *Isoglossa* sp..
Wingspan: 90mm (3½in).
Status: Not listed.

Identification: Pale greenish yellow wings with black hooked tip on forewing, dark spots on both wings, series of smaller black spots near margin, eyespot on inside margin of hindwing, small tail. Underwings pearly, with eight small red dots. Seasonal differences, wet-season form shown here.

Below: The paler underwings with their ragged edge provide good camouflage when the butterfly is at rest.

Dark Green Fritillary

Argynnis aglaja

This fast-flying butterfly is seen from July to August. It moves quickly from flower to flower in search of nectar, then rests on trees. In late summer, the females lay their eggs on the stems and leaves of violets. On hatching, the caterpillar eats its shell then overwinters until March. Then it feeds on the newly open leaves. The fully grown caterpillar is black with a red stripe down the side. It pupates at the base of a violet plant, and an adult emerges about four weeks later. This species is declining due to the loss of its habitat, and from agricultural intensification.

Identification: Upperwings have orange-brown background with dark spots and blotches. Underwings olive green and pale brown with silver spots. Similar in appearance to *Argynnis paphia* and *A. adippe*.

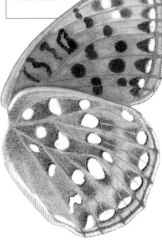

Right: The Dark Green Fritillary is most easily identified by the presence of the green colour and silver spots on the underwings, seen here on the female wing.

Distribution: Europe, Morocco, Iran, Siberia, China, Korea and Japan.
Habitat: Meadow, woodland edges, sea cliff, moorland.
Food plant: *Viola* sp. (violet).
Wing span: 55–60mm (2³⁄₁₆in–2¼in).
Status: Not listed.

Silver-washed Fritillary

Argynnis paphia

The Silver-washed Fritillary is found flying in open glades and rides of woodlands, and along woodland edges. In early mornings, groups of the butterflies can be seen basking in the sun to warm up. At night they roost in trees. There is a single generation that flies in July and August. The dark bars across the forewings of the males have pheromone-producing scales to attract females with. Unusually, the females lay their eggs singly on the bark of trees. The caterpillars overwinter and then in spring they crawl to the grounds to feed on violet leaves. They pupate and the adults emerge in summer.

Identification: Upperwings are orange-brown with dark markings. Males, dark bars on top of the forewing, females have spots. Underwings of both sexes have a greenish hue with silver wash markings across the hindwing.

Below: The darker female is similar to the male, but the forewing is less curved and lacks the black scent marks across the forewing.

Distribution: Europe, North Africa and across Asia to Japan.
Habitat: Woodland.
Food plant: *Viola* sp. (violet).
Wing span: 70mm (2¾in).
Status: Not listed.

Below: The lighter female form, known as the Valezina, is much paler with a green hue.

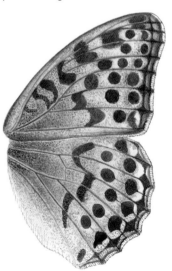

Weaver's Fritillary

Clossiana dia

Distribution: Europe, Asia to West China.
Habitat: Meadow, grassy woodland.
Food plant: *Viola* sp. (violet), *Rubus* sp. (blackberry).
Wing span: 30mm (1³⁄₁₆in).
Status: Not listed.

Identification: Upperwings orange with black spots. The leading edge of the hindwing is strongly angled and straight. Underwings have violet tinge over outermost parts, base of wings are dark. The females often have dark markings and some are virtually melanic.

The Weaver's Fritillary is also known as the Violet Fritillary, due to the purple hue of the underside. It is a fairly widespread and common species, occurring across Europe and Asia. It is one of the smallest fritillaries, and from the top the males resemble the Pearl-bordered Fritillary. It is also one of the first butterflies to emerge in spring and flies throughout the summer until September. It is a restless butterfly, easily disturbed, and it flutters from flower to flower in search of nectar. There are several generations. The females lay their eggs, singly, on the leaves of the violet. The late caterpillars overwinter and pupate in spring.

OTHER SPECIES OF NOTE

Cranberry Fritillary *Boloria aquilonaris*
The Cranberry Fritillary is a specialist butterfly that is found on peat bogs. Its distribution has become very fragmented and is classed as Endangered in parts of its range. It is found in Northern Europe and Central Asia at lower altitudes, and at higher altitudes in southern Europe. Its food plant is *Vaccinium* sp. (cranberry).

Marbled Fritillary *Brenthis daphne*
This rare butterfly is widely distributed from southern Europe across Asia to Japan. It occurs on warm, grassy banks and slopes where there are plenty of flowers. The caterpillars feed on violet and bramble, then overwinter and pupate in spring. The upperwings are orange with distinctive black markings, and the underwings are pale yellow to orange.

Spotted Fritillary *Melitaea didyma*
The Spotted Fritillary is found on grassland and in woodland across North Africa, southern Europe and Central Asia. Its appearance, especially that of the female can be variable. The males have orange-red wings with dark markings, and the females are darker, almost black.

Cardinal

Pandoriana pandora

This is the largest of the European fritillaries. There is a single generation in Europe that flies from May to October; however, there are two generations in North Africa, from May to June and from August to September. Large groups of butterflies tend to gather in open meadows, on slopes and banks where there is an abundance of flowers, especially thistles. The caterpillar feeds on the leaves of violets, such as *Viola tricolor*. This species is declining due to habitat loss.

Identification:
Sexes different. Male upperwings are orange with black pattern of markings and a row of spots towards margin, the underside of the hindwing is grey-green. The females are larger and darker.

Distribution: Southern Europe, Morocco, western Asia to India.
Habitat: Meadow, woodland edges, moorland, and sea cliff.
Food plant: *Viola* sp. (violet, pansies).
Wing span: 65mm (2½in).
Status: Not listed.

Left: The undersides of the female forewings are red-orange with a green apex. The hindwing is pale green.

Duke of Burgundy Fritillary

Hamearis lucina

The Duke of Burgundy Fritillary flies from May to June. It is an active butterfly that can be seen flying from flower to flower in woodlands, and basking in the sun in woodland clearings. The female lays her eggs on the leaves of primrose and cowslip. The caterpillar is small, brown and hairy. It feeds on the underside of leaves, where it is out of sight of predators. It pupates in early autumn and overwinters. Although this butterfly looks very similar to the fritillaries featured on the previous pages, and is given the name fritillary, it is a member of the sub-family *Riodininae*, or Metal Marks. Members of the genus Hamearis are found mostly in South America.

Distribution: Southern and central Europe, Turkey.
Habitat: Woodland.
Food plant: *Primula veris*, *Primula vulgaris*.
Wingspan: 30–34mm (1³⁄₆in–1³⁄₆in).
Status: Not listed.

Identification: Dark brown wings with orange spots and a white margin, males have degenerate front legs, females retain all six.

OTHER SPECIES OF NOTE
Lilac Tree Nymph *Sallya amulia*
African species with rich violet blue upperwings. The underside of the forewings are orange and the hindwings blue with orange bands, similar to a fritillary pattern. These butterflies are found in forests but migrate over large areas.

The Hermit *Chazara briseis*
This butterfly is found in North Africa, southern and central Europe and Asia. It favours rocky slopes and grassland such as the steppes in Asia. There is one generation which flies from June to September. The caterpillars feed on grasses belonging to the genus *Sesleria*.

Queen of Spain Fritillary *Issoria lathonia*
This fritillary is found in North Africa, Europe and Asia. The underwings have large silver-grey patches that catch the sun and give the appearance of liquid silver. The females lay their eggs on violets in woodland clearings and along paths. There are two to three generations a year.

Gatekeeper

Pyronia tithonus

The Gatekeeper is seen in June, often flying along hedgerows and woodland edges. It looks similar to other brown butterflies found in the same habitats, such as the Meadow Brown and the Wall. The butterflies visit flowers for nectar, including bramble, marjoram and valerian. The male Gatekeepers guard a territory and chase all other insects. The females lay their eggs singly at the base of grass stalks, especially those of the meadow grass *Poa annua*. The caterpillar is brown with white stripes along the sides and is active at night. It overwinters and emerges again in spring, when it continues to feed. It pupates in early summer.

Distribution: Europe, north Africa, into central Asia.
Habitat: Hedgerows, woodland edges.
Food plant: Grasses.
Wingspan: 35–40mm (1³⁄₈–1½in).
Status: Not listed.

Identification: Upperwings are orange, with brown borders and a false eye on the forewing. The lower hindwings are brown with three or four tiny white dots. Males have dark richer colours and are smaller than the females.

Right: The lower wings of the female bear the same eyespots as the male, but the lower hindwings are generally paler.

Meadow Brown

Maniola jurtina

Distribution: Canary Islands, North Africa, Europe to the Urals, Asia Minor and Iran.
Habitat: Grasslands, meadows and gardens.
Food plant: Grass species, e.g. *Poa annua*.
Wingspan: 50mm (2in).
Status: Not listed.

Right: The female has paler lower wings than the male, with a light band across the lower hindwing.

Identification: The male is smaller and darker than the female, with a false eye on each forewing. The brown female wings have an orange band along the margin. The hindwing has a duller band.

This is a common butterfly that is on the wing from May to July. There is a single generation. The butterflies are active near meadows and they feed on nectar from thistles. Unusually they fly most days, even in wet weather. At night they rest on grass stems in their characteristic pose with head up and wings down. The prominent eyespots are used to deter predators, such as birds. The females lay their eggs, singly, on grass. The caterpillars are two-tone green and they feed at night and rest during the day. They overwinter, then emerge and continue to feed until they pupate in early summer.

Wall

Lassiommata megera

The Wall gets its name from its behaviour of basking in the sun on walls, with its wings open. They visit flowers near hedgerows and walls to feed on nectar. Unlike many other butterflies, the Wall is active at dawn and dusk. The males have territories which they guard. They patrol walls and paths and chase off any other insects. There are usually two generations a year, from May to June and from July to August, and occasionally there is a third generation in early autumn. The females lay their eggs singly on the underside of grass leaves. The late caterpillars overwinter, and pupate the following spring.

Distribution: N. Africa, Europe, Asia Minor, Syria, Lebanon and Iran.
Habitat: Grasslands, meadows and gardens.
Food plant: Grass species.
Wingspan: 50mm (2in).
Status: Not listed.

Right: Upperwings of the female show less black than the male.

Identification: Orange-brown wings with black markings and white-centred false eyes on the upper forewing and upper hindwing. The lower hindwing has a silver-grey and brown pattern with two rows of false eyes. Males have more black, with a scent mark across wing.

Left: The lower hindwings of both sexes have a silver-grey and brown pattern with two rows of false eyes. There is a single large eyespot on the lower forewing.

Marbled White

Melanargia galathea

Identification: Black with white patterns across both wings. Females are larger, and the underside of the wings has a similar pattern but is paler.

Left: Although the underwings can be seen when the butterfly feeds, when it rests it holds its wings open.

Distribution: Europe, southern Russia, central Asia, Iran and Japan.
Habitat: Chalk grassland, meadows, moors, wasteland.
Food plant: Grass.
Wingspan: 55mm (2⅛in).
Status: Not listed.

This distinctive black-and-white butterfly was once called the half-mourner, because its wings reminded people of the black and white clothing worn by 19th-century women who were halfway through their period of mourning. The butterflies are seen from July to August. They feed on the nectar of thistles, knapweed and scabious. They rest with their wings open. Unusually, the females lay the eggs while they are flying over grass. The eggs fall to the ground, where they stick to blades of grass. The caterpillar is green and feeds on the grass at night. It overwinters and in spring it pupates in the soil.

Speckled Wood

Pararge aegeria

This is a common butterfly that is found in woodlands, gardens, parks and commons. The brown patterned wings provide excellent camouflage when the butterfly rests in dappled shade under trees. They visit bramble flowers for nectar. This is a territorial species, and the males defend a small sunny patch in woodland clearings. One male will chase off another male and they may even be seen fighting, where two males spiral around each other until one gives up and flies away. There are two generations per year, in early and late summer. There are differences in appearance between the generations, with the early males being paler than the late ones. The females lay their eggs on blades of grass. The caterpillars of the late generation overwinter and pupate the following spring.

Distribution: Europe, north Africa, across Middle East and Asia.
Habitat: Woodlands, gardens and parks.
Food plant: Grass.
Wingspan: 45mm (1¾in).
Status: Not listed.

Identification: Dark brown with pale brown patches, a false eye on each forewing, and three false eyes on each hindwing. Females have larger patches than the males.

Right: The forewing of the female has more rounded tips than the male, but the pattern is very similar.

Ringlet

Aphantopus hyperantus

Distribution: Europe, temperate Asia.
Habitat: Shady places such as woodlands and hedgerows.
Food plant: Grass.
Wingspan: 48mm (2in).
Status: Not listed.

Below: The male Ringlet (right) has more prominent eyespots on the lower wings than the female (left).

The name 'ringlet' comes from the string of eyespots on the underwings. These are designed to deter predators. The Ringlet is seen from June to August in grassy corners of fields and in woodland clearings, where it feeds on the nectar of bramble and thistles. Unusually, it is active on both sunny and rainy days. The females lay their eggs while flying low over grass, just like the Marbled White *Melanargia galathea*. The caterpillar is brown-yellow with a brown stripe down the back and yellow-brown stripes down the side. It emerges on warm nights to feed. It evades predators by dropping to the ground if it is disturbed. The caterpillar is unusually long-lived, some live for 90 months before pupating.

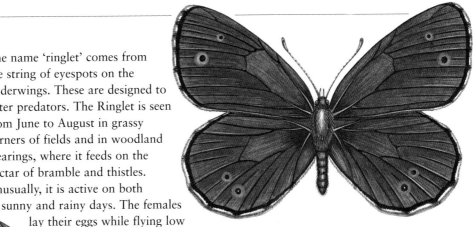

Identification: Dark brown wings. Small spots on upper forewing. Underwings have eyespots, three on each forewing and five on the hindwing, Females are darker than males, males are larger with more obvious eyespots on upper forewing.

OTHER SPECIES OF NOTE
Russian Heath *Coenonympha leander*
This butterfly is found in the Balkans and across to Siberia and Asia Minor on dry grasslands and lower alpine meadows between June and July. Its food plant is grass of various species.

Small Heath *Coenonympha pamphilus*
This small butterfly is found across Europe and Asia, as far as Mongolia, and in North Africa. It inhabits a number of habitats including grassland and coastal dunes. It is active on sunny days from April to September. It stays low, rarely rising more than a metre above the ground.

Spanish Gatekeeper *Pyronia bathseba*
This butterfly has orange upperwings with brown borders and a distinctive white stripe on the underside of the hindwing. It flies from April to July over grassy meadows and scrub. The larval food plant is *Brachypodium* species.

Grayling

Hipparchia semele

This butterfly is incredibly hard to spot when it lands on stony or sandy ground. It tucks its forewings behind the hindwing and tilts slightly to the side to cast a shadow. This, together with its mottled colouring, provides excellent camouflage. When threatened, the butterfly lifts its forewings to reveal the eyespots to startle any predator. The butterflies are seen from June to July. They do not usually visit flowers, but drink sap from oak and pine trees. The females lay their eggs singly on blades of grass. The caterpillar feeds on grass and remains active through winter, emerging on warm days to feed. It pupates in a small underground chamber in spring. There are a number of subspecies across the range, which vary in colour and size.

Distribution: Europe, southern Russia.
Habitat: Coastal grassland, heath, grasslands.
Food plant: Grass.
Wingspan: 50–55mm (2–2³⁄₁₆in).
Status: Not listed.

Identification: Upperwings light brown with straw-coloured wavy lines and eyespots. Lower forewings grey border, orange centre with two obvious eyespots with white centres. Underwings marbled silver-grey and brown divided by zigzag boundary separating dark from light half.

SKIPPERS

The Skipper butterflies belong to the family Hesperiidae and to the superfamily Hesperioidea. There are about 3,500 species of Skipper throughout the world, approximately two-thirds of which inhabit Europe, Asia and Africa. Their strong, well-developed wing muscles enable them to travel quickly. These butterflies live mostly in grassy habitats, where the males defend a patch of grasses.

Red Underwing Skipper

Spialia sertorius

Distribution: Western Europe to Italy, north Africa, central Asia to China.
Habitat: Meadows and scrub to 2,000m (1.2 miles).
Food plant: *Sanguisorba minor* (salad burnet) *Rubus* sp. (bramble), *Phlomis* sp..
Wingspan: 24mm (1in).
Status: Not listed.

This is a fast-flying grassland butterfly that stays close to the ground, stopping only to feed on nectar flowers such as dandelion and dog rose. It frequently basks on bare ground in the sun where its brown-patterned wings provide perfect camouflage against the soil. It settles on damp ground to take up water and salts. Groups of up to 100 individuals may be seen in summer. There are two generations a year, in May to June and July to August. Caterpillars of the second generation overwinter and complete their life cycle the following spring.

Identification: Upperwings are chequered dark brown and white, with distinctive square patches of white along margins. Underwings are a pale reddish brown and white with a flush of red.

Left: When resting, the paler brown-coloured underwing is clearly visible.

Mallow Skipper

Carcharodus alceae

This butterfly is frequently seen sunbathing in a sunny spot on the ground with its wings open, its brown wings being well camouflaged against stony ground. The mallow skipper is a strong flier and it may fly long distances to colonize new habitats. It is on the wing for much of the year, with as many as three generations between April and September. The female lays eggs on mallow and they hatch in fast-growing caterpillars. The caterpillar produces a cocoon in which to pupate.

The Mallow Skipper is frequently confused with the False Mallow Skipper (*C. tripolinus*) which is virtually impossible to distinguish without examining the male genitalia.

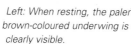

Distribution: North Africa, southern and central Europe to Central Asia.
Habitat: Dry grassy banks.
Food plant: *Malva sylvestris* (mallow) and *Hibiscus* sp..
Wingspan: 25–30mm (1–1³⁄₆in).
Status: Not listed.

Identification: Wings are dark brown with paler orange-brown bands. Two white bands on the upper forewing.

Paradise Skipper

Abantis paradisea

Distribution: Southern Africa
Habitat: Grassland and open woodland.
Food plant: Euphorbiaceae such as *Bridelia cathartica* and *B. micrantha*.
Wingspan: 25–30mm (1–1³⁄₁₆in).
Status: Not listed.

This is one of the more brightly coloured skippers. It is on the wing for much of the year, but it is particularly common from August to October. It occurs on shrubby grassland and rocky hills. For much of the time it flies slowly from flower to flower, but if disturbed can fly speedily away with a great burst of speed. It is frequently seen mud puddling to obtain essential salts. There are several generations per year.

Identification: Black wings with white spots. The upper hindwing is white or has a yellow band towards the base of hindwing. Orange-red spots on thorax, and orange bands on the abdomen. Females are similar but duller in colour and larger in size.

OTHER SPECIES OF NOTE

Large Chequered Skipper *Heteropterus morpheus* A wide-ranging butterfly that occurs from Spain across Europe and Asia to Korea. It occurs on grassland, damp meadow and woodland clearings where its food plant *Calamagrostis canescens* and *Brachypodium syvaticum* occur.

Large Skipper *Ochlodes venatus*
This is an adaptable butterfly found on a range of habitats from grassland to alpine meadow from Scadinavia to Japan. Its food plant is grass, on which the caterpillar overwinters.

Grizzled Skipper *Pyrgus malvae*
The Grizzled Skipper is found across much of Europe and Asia to China, but not northern Europe. It prefers grassy habitats such as meadows, marshes and peat bogs. There are two generations and the late caterpillars overwinter and pupate the following spring. The butterfly occurs in small colonies of fewer than 100 adults, emerges in late April and flies until the end of August.

Dingy Skipper

Erynnis tages

The sun-loving Dingy Skipper is found in habitats where there are bare patches for basking in the sun, for example woodland clearings, grassland, disturbed or derelict ground. Unlike most other skippers, they do not raise their forewings while at rest. During the late afternoon they can be seen landing on dead flowerheads and grass stalks to catch the last of the sunlight. Then they wrap their wings tightly around the stem and roost overnight. The females lay their bright orange eggs at the base of their food plant, such as bird's-foot trefoil and horseshoe vetch. The caterpillar produces silk to form a tent of leaves in which it hides during the day, emerging at night to feed. The caterpillar pupates in spring.

Distribution: Western and central Europe to China.
Larval food plant: Bird's-foot trefoil (*Lotus corniculatus*), Horseshoe vetch (*Hippocrepis comosa*).
Habitat: Dry grassland and steppes.
Wingspan: 25mm (1in).
Status: Not listed.

Identification: Pattern of browns and greys on UW, more uniform brown on the HW. Male wings are a duller and more uniform colour with a pronounced fold on the leading edge of the FW.

Right: A freshly emerged Dingy Skipper reveals a subtle pattern of browns and greys that is lost over time, resulting in a drab appearance.

TIGER MOTHS

The large and varied Arctiidae family is made up of around 11,000 species and includes the brightly coloured Tiger Moths, as well as the less conspicuous Ermines, Footmen and Buffs. Many species have hairy caterpillars that are affectionately known as woolly bears or woolly worms, which will roll into a tight coil if disrupted. Many of the Tiger Moth adults and caterpillars are active during the daytime.

Cinnabar Moth

Tyria jacobaeae

This night-flying moth is named after the Red Mineral Cinnabar because of its crimson-scarlet hindwings. This moth flies particularly late in the evening, and is attracted to bright lights. During the day the adults rest in low vegetation. There is a single generation which flies between May and July. Females lay large batches of eggs on the underside of ragwort leaves. The poisonous caterpillar has striking warning colours of a bright orange body with black stripes and shiny black head. The poison comes from the ragwort, a pernicious weed that can be fatal to animals such as horses. The caterpillars can be used as a form of biological control because of the quantity of ragwort they eat. In fact, the caterpillars eat so much that they can exhaust their food supply before they are ready to pupate. During food shortages they are known to become cannibalistic.

Distribution: Europe, East and central Asia, Australasia, North America.
Habitat: Grassland, rough pasture and wasteland.
Food plant: *Senecio jabobaea* (common ragwort).
Wingspan: 35–45 mm (1⅜-1¾in).
Status: Not listed.

Below: The distinctive caterpillar with its black and orange bands feeds on ragwort.

Identification: Brightly coloured. FW, dark grey with red streak towards the front edge and two red spots on the outer edge. HW is crimson, edged with black.

Clouded Buff

Diacrisia sannio

The Clouded Buff moth is also known as the Clouded Ermine. As well as differences in appearances between the male and female, there are also behavioural differences between the sexes. The males, who are more brightly coloured, are active during the day, whereas the paler-coloured females tend to be active at dusk and through the night. The female moths rest in vegetation during the day, but they are easily disturbed. There is one generation that flies during June and July. The females lay their eggs on *Calluna* sp. (heather) and other low-growing plants on heathland. The caterpillar is slow-growing and overwinters, pupating the following May.

Distribution: Europe, Russia, eastern Asia, Japan.
Habitat: Heathland and rough grassland.
Food plant: *Calluna* sp. (heather).
Wingspan: 35–50mm (1⅜–2in).
Status: Not listed.

Identification: Sexes different. Males forewing yellow with reddish discal mark. Hindwing is pale yellow-white with darker band towards outer margin. Females forewing dark orange with dark veining. The hindwing has a darker basal patch. Males are larger.

White Ermine

Spilosoma lubricipeda

Distribution: Europe, across Asia to Korea and Japan.
Habitat: Woodland, heathland, grassland, rough scrub.
Food plant: Various, including *Rumex* sp. and *Urtica*.
Wingspan: 35–50mm (⅜–1in).
Status: Not listed.

Identification: Hairy, white to cream-coloured moth. Both wings speckled with variable number of black dots. Thorax hairy and white, abdomen yellow and black.

The White Ermine is a night-flying moth. It has few predators due to its foul taste. It rests during the day and is relatively difficult to disturb. It will also drop to the ground and pretend to be dead. Also it releases a poisonous yellow secretion from its thorax. Most years there is a single generation that flies from May to July, but some years there may be a second generation in August. The adults do not feed during their short life. The female lays her eggs in large clusters on common plants such as *Rumex* and *Urtica* sp. The caterpillar is black-brown with a dark red line along the back and many hairs. It is fast-growing and eats a variety of foods including weeds such as docks and bracken. It will cover considerable distances in its search for food. In autumn the caterpillar spins a silken cocoon in which to pupate.

OTHER SPECIES OF NOTE

Basker Moth *Euchromia lethe*
This moth arrived in Europe hidden in bananas imported from Africa. Its long tapering black wings have yellow-orange blotches. The thorax is black and orange and the abdomen is striped black, blue and orange. The genus *Euchromia* comprises approximately 100 species, most of which occur in Southeast Asia.

Common Footman *Eilema lurideola*
This moth has green-grey forewings with a leading yellow stripe, tapering to a point. The hindwings are yellow. At rest, the forewings are folded back over the body. It normally flies at night, but it can be seen during the day visiting flowers to obtain nectar. This species is often considered to be an air pollution indicator as the caterpillar feeds on lichens that are restricted to areas of clean air.

Muslin Moth *Diaphora mendica*
The males are creamy brown while the females are white, and both are speckled with black. It is seen from May to June, when it flies in damp woodland, bogs and marshy areas. The caterpillars feed on dock, plantain and dandelion.

Buff Ermine

Spilosoma luteum

This common night-flying moth is easily attracted to lights. It is found in a range of habitats including grasslands, waste ground and gardens. The moth is preyed upon by birds, and it is believed that the moth may benefit from mimicking the White Ermine, which is poisonous. It flies slightly later than the White Ermine, so predators will have learned to avoid the White Ermine by the time the Buff Ermine emerges. There is a single generation from May to July. The female moth lays her eggs in clusters at the base of food plants such as dandelion and dock. The pupa overwinters in a cocoon amongst the leaf litter.

Distribution: Europe, Asia and North America.
Habitat: Woodland, grassland, parks, gardens and waste land.
Food plant: *Rumex* sp. (dock), *Taraxacum* sp. (dandelion).
Wingspan: 34–42mm (1⅜–1⅝in).
Status: Not listed.

Identification: Variable wing markings and colouring. FW buff yellow with variable number of small black marks. HW pale buff with fewer black marks. Females paler but similar in appearance. Head and thorax buff and hairy. Abdomen yellow with black stripes.

Jersey Tiger

Euplagia quadripunctaria

The Jersey Tiger flies both in the daytime, when it can be found feeding on various flowers, as well as at night, when it is attracted to light. It is seen from July to September. The adults are well-camouflaged when they rest, as their wings are completely folded and this hides the bright-orange colour. The colour is only revealed during flight. The female lays her eggs on a variety of food plants such as dandelion. The caterpillar is dark brown with a yellow stripe along the back and down the sides of the body. The caterpillar overwinters and pupates the following spring. In southern Europe many Jersey Tiger moths migrate to the Greek island of Rhodes to overwinter in one particular valley, known as Valley of the Butterflies.

Distribution: Central and southern Europe, Asia Minor, Russia, Urals.
Habitat: Grasslands, woodlands, mountain slopes.
Food plant: *Taraxacum* (dandelion) *Plantago* sp. (plantain), *Urtica* (nettle), *Lonicera* (honeysuckle).
Wingspan: 42–52mm (1⅝–2in).
Status: Not listed.

Identification: This striking moth. has cream forewings with black stripes, the hindwings are bright orange with black patches. The thorax is brown with yellow sides, and the abdomen is bright orange.

Ruby Tiger

Phragmatobia fuliginosa

This is a widely distributed moth that is commonly seen on coastal habitats and heathland. Although it flies mostly at night, it is occasionally seen during the day, especially on warm, sunny days. There are two generations a year in the southerly regions of its range, April to June and August to September, but in the northern parts there is a single generation in June. It shows a gradual variation in colour, with the brightest individuals in the south, and much duller specimens in the north of its range. The female lays her eggs on a variety of food plants including heather, purple moor grass and dock. The dark, and very hairy, caterpillar feeds on a wide range of plants during the summer months. The full grown caterpillar overwinters and becomes active again in spring. The caterpillar pupates in a silk cocoon among leaf litter on the ground.

Distribution: Europe, northern Asia and North America.
Habitat: Coastal grassland and heathland.
Food plant: *Calluna vulgaris* (common heather), *Molinia caerulea* (purple moor grass), *Rumex* sp..
Wingspan: 30–35mm (1³⁄₁₆–1⅜in).
Status: Not listed.

Identification: Forewings are red-brown with prominent veins and single black mark. Hindwings are pink-red with grey towards outer margin. The thorax is hairy and red-brown. The abdomen is red with a dark dorsal stripe.

Yellow Tiger

Arctia flavia

Distribution: Central Europe, Siberia, central Asia, China.
Habitat: Alpine meadow to 3,000m (9,800ft).
Food plant: *Cotoneaster, Leontodon, Taraxacum, Urtica.*
Wingspan: 50–70mm (2–2¾in).
Status: Not listed.

Identification: Conspicuous moth. The upper forewing is white with large prominent black blotches. The upper hindwing is cream with black spots. Thorax black and hairy.

The Yellow Tiger is also called the Alpine Yellow Tiger moth, as it is found high up in mountain regions. It tends to be seen in July, close to glaciers where the air is more humid. It is a night-flying moth that hides under rocks during the day. The caterpillar is brown-black with long black and yellow hairs. It feeds at night on plants such as alpine cotoneaster and other low-growing plants. This moth species has an exceptionally long life cycle, because the caterpillars grow slowly and have to overwinter twice before they mature.

OTHER SPECIES OF NOTE

Swamp Tiger Moth *Diacrisia metalkana*
This moth is found across central and southern Europe and Asia as far as Japan. The forewings are pale yellow with a few black spots and the hindwings are orange-to-red with larger black spots. The females have redder wings than the males.

Garden Tiger *Arctia caja*
The Garden Tiger is a common moth found across Europe, Asia and North America, where it occurs in a wide range of habitats from alpine meadows to farmland. These night-flying moths have an unusual behaviour pattern, in that they are not attracted to lights during the first part of the night, but at about midnight they can be seen gathering around lights in large numbers.

Four-spotted Footman *Lithosia quadra*
Only the females have spots and sometimes there are only three. It flies in woodlands where there are plenty of lichens, the food plant of the caterpillars. Occurring across Europe and in Siberia, China and Japan, the moth is also a migrant species that is extending its range.

Cream-spotted Tiger

Arctia villica

The Cream-spotted Tiger is also known as the Black Bear, after the appearance of the caterpillar. This moth varies greatly in appearance and there are a number of geographical races in which the spots merge to form bands or where the spots on the forewings have disappeared completely.

There is a single generation that flies in May and June. This night-flying moth is easily attracted to light. It inhabits a number of habitats including coastal sand dunes, grassland, gardens and even industrial wasteland. The females lay their eggs in large clusters on the leaves of various plants, including dandelions and nettles. The caterpillars are dark brown and covered in long hairs. They overwinter and pupate the following spring.

Distribution: North Africa, southern Europe, Russia and central Asia.
Habitat: Woodland, grassland, gardens, wasteland.
Food plant: *Achillea, Centaurea, Taraxacum, Plantago, Urtica* sp..
Wingspan: 45–60mm (1¾–2¼in).
Status: Not listed.

Identification: Forewing black, tapering, with eight white blotches. Hindwing yellow with black spots and margin. Thorax black. Abdomen orange with black dots and red tip.

LAPPETS AND TUSSOCKS

The Tussock moths of the Lymantriidae family occur across Europe and Asia, but they are particularly well-represented in sub-Saharan Africa and on Madagascar where there are more than 250 species, while there are just 11 species in Great Britain. The Eggars, Snout moths, Lackey and Lappet moths belong to the smaller family, Lasiocampidae.

Lappet Moth

Gastropacha quercifolia

The species name of this moth, *quercifolia*, does not refer to the food plant, but to the appearance of the resting adult moth that resembles a dead oak leaf. This provides excellent camouflage in its woodland habitat. The caterpillar has flaps, or folds, on its body and this gives it its English name, lappet, a term once used to describe the flaps on a lady's hat. There are two generations between May and August in the more southerly parts of its range, and one generation in the north. The female moth lays her eggs in large clusters on the underside of leaves of the food plant. When resting, the colour of the caterpillar, together with its folds, helps it to look like a twig. When threatened, it displays two blue bands behind its head.

Identification: Red-brown to purple-brown wings with faint lines in dark brown and a wavy margin, females larger than males.

Distribution: Europe, Russia, China and Japan.
Habitat: Woodland, orchards, gardens.
Food plant: *Corylus*, *Crateagus* (hawthorn), *Prunus spinosa* (blackthorn), *Malus*, *Quercus*, *Salix*.
Wingspan: 90mm (3½in).
Status: Not listed.

Below: At rest, the brown moth looks just like a dead oak leaf.

Oak Eggar

Lasiocampa quercus

The Oak Eggar does not feed on oak. Its name is derived from the acorn-like appearance of the cocoon. This is a widespread species, but it is not particularly common and is suffering from a loss of its heathland and moorland habitat, especially in the eastern regions of its range. The males fly during the day and night, while the females are active at night. The females drop their eggs while in flight. The caterpillars are black, brown and red with orange hairs. They pupate in autumn and overwinter. Historically this species has been divided into two subspecies: *Lasiocampa quercus quercus*, which has a one-year life cycle and flies in July and August; and *Lasiocampa quercus callunae*, which has a two-year life cycle and flies in May and June. However, this division has been called into question in recent years.

Distribution: Europe, Canary Islands, central Asia to China.
Habitat: Moorland, heathland and bogs.
Food plant: *Calluna*, *Corylus*, *Crateagus* (hawthorn), *Prunus spinosa* (blackthorn), *Salix*.
Wingspan: 50–75mm (2–3in).
Status: Not listed.

Identification: Males have dark red-brown wings with a small white spot on upper forewing and a diffuse yellow band across both wings. The females are yellow-brown and larger with similar markings.

Left: The white spot on the forewing is clearly visible when the moth rests.

Pale Tussock

Calliteara pudibunda

Distribution: Europe, central Asia, China, Japan.
Habitat: Woodlands, hedgerow.
Food plant: *Betula* sp. *Corylus*, *Quercus* sp. *Ulmus* sp..
Wingspan: 40–60mm (1½–2¼in).
Status: Not listed.

Identification: Forewings light grey to grey-brown, with dark spots along outer margin and two wavy transverse bands. Hindwings pale grey to white. Front pair of legs white and very hairy. Females paler, with three wavy bands on the forewing.

The Pale Tussock is a woodland species of moth. It is a night flier that is attracted to light, especially the males. The moths fly from May to June. The females lay their eggs in clusters of up to 300 on the bark and leaves of trees, such as oak and birch. The caterpillars have a yellow body with black bands and there are thick tufts of hairs sticking out the tops and sides. They rest during the day and emerge at night to feed on leaves *en masse*, creating holes and even eating whole leaves. The moths can be considered pests as large numbers of caterpillars cause severe defoliation and this results in mortality in young trees. In the past it was a serious pest of hop (*Humulus lupulus*) before pesticides were in common use.

Below: The hairy caterpillar used to be called a 'hop dog' when found in the crop by hop pickers.

OTHER SPECIES OF NOTE

Dark Tussock *Dicallomera fascelina*
The Dark Tussock moth is found on a variety of habitats from moorland and heathland to sand dunes and even on shingle beaches. They fly in July and August. The dark-coloured caterpillars have five distinctive tufts of pale hairs on the back.

Lackey *Malacosoma neustria*
This common moth is seen in lowland and coastal areas in summer. They are identified from the two yellow lines running across the forewings and dotted fringes to the wings. The caterpillars feed in groups under the protective cover of a silken tent. They disperse when they are ready to pupate.

Brown-tail Tussock *Euproctis chrysorrhoea*
These moths are considered pests. The caterpillars group together and spin a protective silken tent under which they feed, often defoliating shrubs and trees. The hairs of the caterpillar can detach and cause skin rashes which are particularly irritating.

Yellow Tail Tussock

Euproctis similis

This moths are seen from July to August, especially in coastal areas. During the day the adults rest on shrubs and in trees, and their white wings give them the appearance of fluffy feathers. They are night-fliers and are attracted to lights and are seen at windows. The distinctive caterpillars are black with a red stripe down the back and a white stripe along each side. They are covered in hairs that cause skin irritation. The caterpillars stay together and feed on the leaves of trees such as birch, oak, and elm. In autumn the caterpillars spin a silken shelter in which to overwinter. They emerge in spring to continue to feed before pupating in early summer.

Distribution: Europe, central Asia, China, Japan and North America.
Habitat: Woodlands and coastal habitats.
Food plant: *Betula* sp., *Alnus glutinosa*, *Malus domestica*, *Sorbus aucuparia*.
Wingspan: 28–35mm (1³⁄₁₆–1³⁄₈in).
Status: Not listed.

Identification: White body with yellow anal tuft. Wings are silky white. Males have a single small dark spot on lower part of the FW.

THE LOOPERS

Moths of the Geometridae are characterized by caterpillars that move around by pulling their bodies up into loops, hence they are often referred to as Loopers. The caterpillars are characteristically thin and hairless. There are approximately 26,000 species of geometrids, of which about 3,500 are found in the Palaearctic and a similar number are found in Africa.

Magpie Moth

Abraxas grossulariata

The Magpie Moth is a common species of carpet moth that is seen on lowland woodlands, gardens and northern moorlands. It is a day-flying moth and is often mistaken for a butterfly. The females lay their eggs on the underside of the leaves of currants, gooseberries and hawthorn. The caterpillars have similar markings, with a black and white patterned body with an orange stripe. This is quite variable, with some caterpillars almost completely black or white. The caterpillars move with a looping movement. The young caterpillars overwinter and emerge in May to feed on young leaves. This species can be a problem as the caterpillars soon defoliate entire fruit bushes.

Above: The caterpillar has black spots with a red-orange line down the sides.

Distribution: Europe to Siberia.
Habitat: Gardens, hedgerows and woodlands.
Food plant: *Crateagus, Ribes* sp..
Wingspan: 35–48mm (1⅜–2in).
Status: Not listed.

Identification: Wing pattern of black and white, with orange stripe across the forewing, and orange flush near the body.

Peppered Moth

Biston betularia

The original name for this species was the pepper-and-salt moth because of its speckled wings. This pattern provides excellent camouflage on bark. There is a second form that has dark wings, and this is associated with the darkened tree trunks caused by industrial pollution. The dark forms appeared during the Industrial Revolution as a means of being camouflaged on darkened bark, so reducing predation. This is an example of natural selection and evolution, and this moth has been extensively studied since the 1950s. However, both forms are the same species so they can interbreed. Nowadays the melanic form is less common as there is less sooty air pollution from coal fires. The moths fly from May to June. The females lay their eggs in chains on leaves of deciduous trees. The looping caterpillars are green or brown and are active at night. They pupate in autumn and the pupae overwinter.

Identification: Pale upperwings. Body speckled with dark markings, males smaller than females.

Distribution: Central and southern Europe, North Africa.
Habitat: Woodland, hedgerows, parks, gardens and moorland.
Food plant: *Crateagus, Ribes, Salix.*
Wingspan: 45–55mm (1¾–2³⁄₁₆in).
Status: Not listed.

Left: The dark form, known as carbonaria, was prevalent during the mid-19th century.

Large Emerald

Geometra papilionaria

Distribution: Europe across northern Asia to Japan.
Habitat: Woodland.
Food plant: *Betula, Corylus, Fagus.*
Wingspan: 50–65mm (2–2½in).
Status: Not listed.

Identification: Blue-green wings crossed with faint pale wavy lines. Small white dots along the outer margin of both wings.

The Large Emerald is a night-flying moth seen between June and August. It prefers open woodland with rides and clearings, and sandy birch woodland as well as wet heathland and bogs. They rest with their wings spread out flat on the surface. The females lay their eggs on leaves of trees such as birch and alder. Young caterpillars are reddish brown, but after they have overwintered they become green in order to be camouflaged against leaves. The caterpillars are often called Loopers after the way in which they move; pulling the end of the abdomen up to the front to form a loop and then moving the front end forwards. This moth is often confused for a butterfly because of its uniform green colouring and shape.

OTHER SPECIES OF NOTE

Mottled Umber *Erannis defoliaria*
Unusually this moth flies through the winter months when it is seen in gardens, woodlands and parks. The males are attracted to light. The females are wingless. The caterpillars are found on trees such as oak and birch during the summer. They pupate in autumn and the adults emerge. The eggs overwinter and hatch in spring.

Brindled Beauty *Lycia hirtaria*
This common moth gets its name from the bands on its wings, which provide good camouflage when the moth rests on bark during the day. It is active at night. It is a woodland species and is on the wing during April and May. The females lay their eggs on the bark of a number of tree species such as apple, willow and birch. The caterpillars are black with yellow bands, becoming grey or brown with age. They pupate in late summer and the pupae overwinter.

Swallow-tailed Moth

Ourapteryx sambucaria

This large butterfly-like moth is named after the small tails on the hind wings. However these are often hidden when the moth is at rest. Their wings are easily damaged and they fade quickly. It flies at dusk from June to August and it is attracted to lights. It is found in a range of habitats, including gardens and woodlands. The moths rest during the day; however, they are easily disturbed. The females lay their eggs on plants such as ivy and honeysuckle, and the caterpillars are seen from August through to May.

Distribution: Central and southern Europe to Siberia.
Habitat: Woodlands, gardens and parks.
Food plant: *Hedera, Lonicera, Sambucus.*
Wingspan: 40–60mm (1½–2¼in).
Status: Not listed.

Identification: Wings pale yellow to white, with narrow orange margin and two orange stripes. The hindwing has tail-like projections on the apex. Pale yellow body.

OWLET MOTHS

The sturdy Owlet moths belong to the Noctuidae family. This is the largest of the moth families, with more than 35,000 species worldwide, of which about 1,450 are found throughout Europe. There is little difference between the sexes. Most species have dull forewings, although some have brighter hindwings. Most owlets are active at night and feed on sweet liquids such as sap, fruit or the nectar of flowers.

Blue Underwing

Catocala fraxini

Identification: Forewings are mottled light and dark grey. Hindwings are dark brown with a dull blue band and a white fringe.

The name Catocala comes from two Greek words, 'kato' meaning behind and 'kalos' which means beautiful. This refers to its brightly coloured hindwings that are usually hidden by the mottled forewings. The moth reveals its bright hindwings if they are disturbed by predators such as birds. The adults are night-flying and during the day they rest on walls, fence posts and tree trunks, especially oak. There is a single generation on the wing from August to October. The females lay their eggs in crevices in the bark of the aspen, where they overwinter, and hatch the following spring. The large, grey caterpillars spin their cocoons in the leaf litter. This migrant species appears in northern Europe in the late summer and autumn.

Distribution: North America, Western Europe.
Habitat: Woodlands.
Food plant: *Populus tremula* (aspen).
Wingspan: 75–95mm (3–3¾in).
Status: Not listed.

Red Underwing

Catocala nupta

The Red Underwing is a difficult moth to spot at rest as its forewings provide perfect camouflage against tree bark. However, when disturbed it takes off and flashes its brightly coloured hindwings to confuse its predators. The moth flies in August and September, occurring in habitats where willow and poplar grow. The female lays her eggs in crevices on the bark of the food plants. The caterpillar is grey-brown with wart-like bumps on the back, which blend well with the bark. It rests during the day and feeds on leaves at night. The caterpillars descend to the leaf litter to spin a cocoon in which they pupate and overwinter.

Distribution: Europe, northern Asia to China and Japan.
Habitat: Open woodland, parks and gardens.
Food plant: *Salix sp.* and *Populus*.
Wingspan: 80–85mm (3⅛–3⅜in).
Status: Not listed.

Identification: Forewings mottled grey brown. Hindwings red and black.

Right: When the moth rests, the mottled forewings hide the red hindwings.

Mother Shipton

Callistege mi

Distribution: Europe, northern Asia and China.
Habitat: Meadows, railway embankments, woodland rides.
Food plant: *Elymus arenarius, Lathyrus pratensis, Vicia* sp., *Calluna vulgaris*.
Wingspan: 30–34mm (1³⁄₁₆–1³⁄₈in).
Status: Not listed.

Identification: The forewings are mottled brown with a wavy white lines. Hindwings are dark brown with paler spots and a pale chequered margin.

Mother Shipton is a small, day-flying moth that is particularly active on sunny days in May and June. It gets its unusual name from the shape outlined in white on its forewing that is said to resemble to profile of a well-known Yorkshire witch. The moths fly at night, and during the day they rest on the leaves and flowers of meadow plants. However, they are easily disturbed and fly off at the slightest movement. The females lay their eggs on grass and other meadow plants such as vetch and heather.

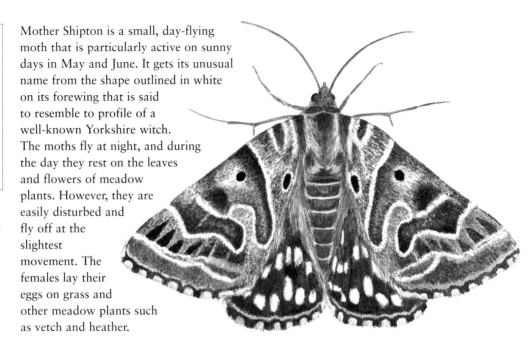

OTHER SPECIES OF NOTE

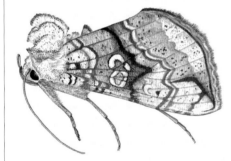

Golden Plusia *Polychrysia moneta*
This moth has a golden sheen to its forewings and a wingspan of about 40mm (1⅛in). This is a migrant species that is found across Europe and central Asia on meadows and in gardens, where the caterpillars feed on *Delphinium*.

Cabbage Moth *Mamestra brassicae*
The Cabbage moth or Cabbage Army moth has reddish-brown marbled coloured wings, and it is very similar to other species, such as the White Colon (*N. albicolon*). A distinguishing feature is a curved spur on the tibia of the foreleg. The caterpillars feed on cabbage and other brassicas.

Shark Moth *Cucullia umbratica*
The large forewings of the Shark moth are grey and brown with black streaks. The males have grey hindwings and the females have brown. The females lay their eggs on species of sow thistle (*Sonchus* sp.).

Angle Shades

Phlogophora meticulosa

The name Angle Shades comes from the angled markings on the forewing and from the characteristic way in which the moth rests. The forewings are held creased, with the leading edge folded over so it resembles a dead leaf and casts an irregular shade. A newly emerged moth has bright green and brown wings, but the colours soon fade. The moths are seen all year, especially in summer when migrants add to the numbers. There are two generations. The caterpillars are seen through the year, feeding on a range of plants including bramble, broom and oak. They are green or brown with reddish spots along the sides and faint dark chevrons along the back, and have the ability to take on the colour of the plant on which they are resting so they are well camouflaged. When they are ready to pupate, the caterpillars move to the ground where they spin a loose cocoon just below the surface of the soil.

Distribution: Europe.
Habitat: Meadows, woodlands, parks and gardens.
Food plant: Variety including *Cytisus, Quercus, Rubus* sp..
Wingspan: 40–50mm (1½–2in).
Status: Not listed.

Identification: The forewing has a scalloped outer margin, with colours ranging from olive-green to orange-red, dark central band edged in paler colours, dark patch near apex. The hindwing is pale yellow-white, dark margin and veins.

THE PROMINENTS

The Prominent moths, so called because of the tuft of hair that protrudes from the leading edge of the forewing in adults, and the dorsal humps in the larva, belong to the Notodontidae family. There are just over 500 species known in the Palaearctic region. These moths are nocturnal, have stubby, hairy bodies, and colouring that makes them difficult to see on bark or twigs.

Puss Moth

Cerura vinula

Distribution: Europe, central Asia, China.
Habitat: Woodlands and hedgerows.
Food plant: *Populus, Salix*
Wingspan: 45–70mm (1¾–2¾ in).
Status: Not listed.

Identification: Wings white or grey with yellow-brown zig-zag lines over the FW, small dots along the margin. HW white with yellow veining. Hairy grey abdomen with black bands.

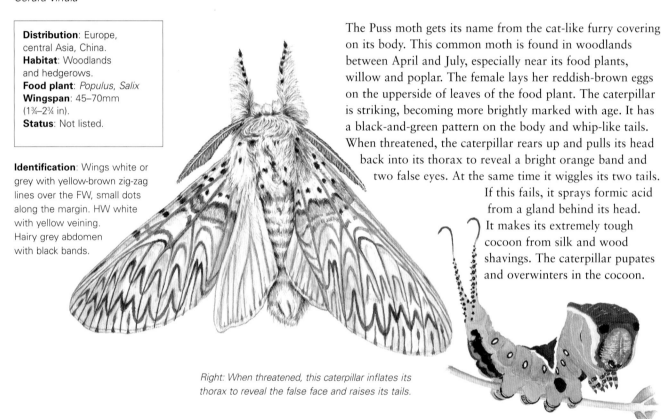

The Puss moth gets its name from the cat-like furry covering on its body. This common moth is found in woodlands between April and July, especially near its food plants, willow and poplar. The female lays her reddish-brown eggs on the upperside of leaves of the food plant. The caterpillar is striking, becoming more brightly marked with age. It has a black-and-green pattern on the body and whip-like tails. When threatened, the caterpillar rears up and pulls its head back into its thorax to reveal a bright orange band and two false eyes. At the same time it wiggles its two tails. If this fails, it sprays formic acid from a gland behind its head. It makes its extremely tough cocoon from silk and wood shavings. The caterpillar pupates and overwinters in the cocoon.

Right: When threatened, this caterpillar inflates its thorax to reveal the false face and raises its tails.

Lobster Moth

Stauropus fagi

Distribution: Europe, northern Asia to China.
Habitat: Woodlands, heathland, scrub.
Food plant: *Betula, Fagus, Quercus* sp..
Wingspan: 40–70mm (1½–2¾in).
Status: Not listed.

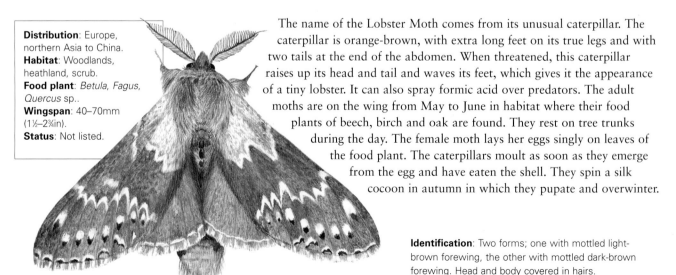

The name of the Lobster Moth comes from its unusual caterpillar. The caterpillar is orange-brown, with extra long feet on its true legs and with two tails at the end of the abdomen. When threatened, this caterpillar raises up its head and tail and waves its feet, which gives it the appearance of a tiny lobster. It can also spray formic acid over predators. The adult moths are on the wing from May to June in habitat where their food plants of beech, birch and oak are found. They rest on tree trunks during the day. The female moth lays her eggs singly on leaves of the food plant. The caterpillars moult as soon as they emerge from the egg and have eaten the shell. They spin a silk cocoon in autumn in which they pupate and overwinter.

Identification: Two forms; one with mottled light-brown forewing, the other with mottled dark-brown forewing. Head and body covered in hairs.

Sallow Kitten

Harpyia furcula

The Sallow Kitten is on the wing in spring, when it can be found in places where its food plant, the willow, grows, such as damp woodland and scrub willow. Their grey wings blend well with willow bark on which they rest during the day. They fly by night. In the southern regions of the range, there are two generations per year, the first in May to June and the second in August. However, in more northerly locations, there is one generation in June to July. Females lay their eggs in small groups on the underside of leaves. The caterpillars are black and green and are similar in appearance to the Puss moth. The caterpillars feed on leaves through summer and make a tough cocoon from silk and wood shavings in autumn. They pupate and overwinter in the cocoon. May also be classified as *Furcula furcata*.

Identification: Wings grey-white with dark band across each forewing. Margins have a row of small black dots. Hindwings are pale grey with brown veins and black dots along margin. Abdomen has black and white bands.

Distribution: Europe, central Asia, China.
Habitat: Damp woodland.
Food plant: *Betula, Fagus, Populus, Salix* sp..
Wingspan: 27–35mm (1–1⅜in).
Status: Not listed.

OTHER SPECIES OF NOTE

Coxcomb Prominent *Ptilodon capucina*
This moth has red-brown wings with scalloped margins and cross lines, so that it resembles a dead leaf when at rest. The Coxcomb Prominent is found in a variety of habitats such as woodland, gardens and heathland, where it can find its food plant, including alder, birch, hazel and oak.

Figure-of-eight *Diloba caeruleocephala*
The name Figure-of-eight comes from the white mark on the forewing which is shaped like a number eight. It is seen in woodland and along hedgerows in autumn, from October to November. The caterpillars feed on hawthorn, blackthorn and apple.

Chinese Wild Silk Moth *Bombyx mandarina*
This is the closest relative to the domesticated silk moth, and it is found in China, Japan and India. It is still able to hybridize with the silk moth, with the male Chinese Wild Silk moth mating with female domesticated silk moths.

Silk Moth

Bombyx mori

This species has been domesticated for thousands of years and no longer exists in the wild. Its appearance has been changed by selective breeding, so it can no longer survive without the help of humans. The adults cannot eat because they have undeveloped mouthparts, and they are also flightless. The female lays tiny eggs and then dies. The caterpillars grow rapidly for about six weeks, feeding on white mulberry leaves, and then they spin silk to make their cocoon. A cocoon is made from a single fine silk thread up to 900m (0.6 miles) long, and about 3,000 are needed to make 500g (1lb) of silk. The pupa would normally secrete enzymes to dissolve the silk threads so it can emerge, but since this would damage the silk, the producers boil the cocoons to kill the pupae and make the cocoon easier to unravel.

Distribution: Originally China, Japan and Korea, but now domesticated worldwide.
Habitat: Woodland.
Food plant: *Morus alba*.
Wingspan: 40–60mm (1½–2¼in).
Status: Not listed.

Identification: Wings buff with pale-brown lines. Forewing has a hooked tip. Heavy, rounded and hairy white body. Females are larger than males.

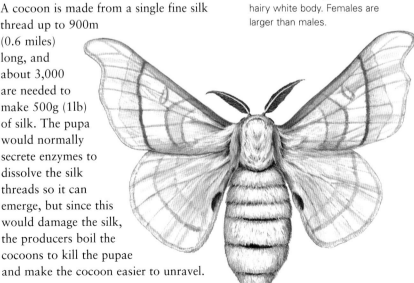

SATURNIIDS

The Saturniids are large, heavy moths which are covered in hair-like scales and have smaller mouthparts than usual. Some of the largest moths in the world, such as the Giant Silkmoth and the Royal Moth, belong to this family. There are about 1,500 species of Saturniids worldwide, of which just over 20 occur in the western Palaearctic.

Emperor Moth

Saturnia pavonia

This attractive moth is seen during April and May. The males are active during the day, when they fly quickly over their habitat in search of the resting females. Females are active at night. The eyespots are used to startle predators such as birds. The adults do not feed but rely on food stores built up when they were caterpillars. The females lay their eggs in a cluster around the stems of a great variety of food plants. The caterpillars stay together at first while they feed on leaves. Young caterpillars are black and hairy, and as they grow, they change to green and yellow with orange warts and black hairs. The caterpillars spin a tough cocoon among the leaves of their food plant and overwinter within it.

Distribution: Europe, northern Asia, North America.
Habitat: Moorland, heathland, alpine slopes, woodland.
Food plant: Various including *Alnus, Betula, Calluna vulgaris, Quercus, Salix.*
Wingspan: Male 70–80mm (2¾–3⅛in).
Status: Not listed.

Identification: Male forewing is grey to brown, hindwing is orange. One large black and yellow eyespot on each wing. Females have eyespots on grey-brown to white background.

Great Peacock Moth

Saturnia pyri

The Great Peacock or Viennese Emperor is the largest moth in Europe. It is seen flying at night from April to June, and there is a single generation. The females lay batches of 10 or so eggs on leaves and twigs of the food plant. The caterpillars are black initially, but become increasingly green with each moult. The fully grown caterpillars are yellow-green with blue warts and black hairs. There is a yellow line along the side. Just before the caterpillar pupates it becomes golden brown. They feed on leaves, often completely eating one leaf before moving on to the next. They either spin a cocoon at the base of the food plant, or find a suitable spot between rocks or in walls. They overwinter as a pupa.

Distribution: Southern Europe, Africa, and Middle East.
Habitat: Grassland, parks, orchards and vineyards.
Food plant: *Juglans regia, Malus, Prunus.*
Wingspan: 9–17cm (3½–7in).
Status: Not listed.

Below: From the third instar stage, the caterpillars focus on eating leaves in one spot before moving some distance away and resuming feeding.

Identification: Grey-to-brown wings, edged with white-yellow, prominent eyespot in the middle of each wing.

Tau Emperor

Aglia tau

Distribution: Europe across to Russia, Iran, China and Korea.
Habitat: Deciduous woodland.
Food plant: *Alnus, Betula, Corylus, Quercus, Salix.*
Wingspan: 60–80mm (2¼–3⅛in).
Status: Not listed.

Identification: Sexes different. Males orange-brown wings, with submarginal black line and speckled black dots. Prominent white-and-black eye spot on each wing. Females are larger and paler.

This distinctive moth appears in March and flies until June, with a single generation. The females are nocturnal, but the males are active during the day. They are seen zigzaging through woods in their search for females. The females lay their eggs in neat rows on trunks and branches of the food plants. The young caterpillar is yellow-green, with a yellow stripe along the side of the body and two pairs of long yellow and red spines that stick out of the thorax and another pair at the end of the abdomen. These disappear as it goes through the moults. The fully grown caterpillar has a scalloped outline as the segments become increasing hump-like in shape. The caterpillar pupates in leaf litter, but unlike other Emperor moths, it does not spin a cocoon.

OTHER SPECIES OF NOTE

Jackson's Emperor *Bunaeopsis jacksoni*
Striking African emperor moth with reddish wings, dark brown towards the margins and pale brown margin. Four large red, black and brown eyespots, one on each wing. Underside has a similar, but paler pattern.

Sloe Emperor Moth *Saturnia spini*
This nocturnal species resembles the Emperor Moth (*Saturnia pavonia*). There is a single generation that flies from April to June. It occurs from Eastern Europe to Kazakhstan where it is found on dry grassland and steppe, although in some parts of its range it occurs up to 1,500m (1 mile).

African Moon Moth *Argema mimosa*
This huge tailed silkmoth with a wingspan of up to 12cm (4½in) is found along the east coast of South Africa. Its forewings have a distinctive grey-coloured 'furry' edge, giving a very rough surface. When it rests, its long tails often cross over. The caterpillars feed on the mango and related species.

Steindachner's Emperor

Athletes steindachneri

This species is also known as *Athletes gigas*, a name which refers to the moth's large wing span of almost 16cm (6¼in). It is one of six large species of the African genus *Athletes*. The underwings are cryptically coloured to provide camouflage when the moth is at rest. There is a small eyespot on each of the underwings. Steindachner's Emperor is found in forested habitats of up to 1,700m (5,570ft). The caterpillar is green and blue with metallic yellow spines. The food plant, *Julbernardia*, is a genus of leguminous trees found in tropical Africa.

Distribution: Central Africa.
Habitat: Woodland.
Food plant: *Julbernardia.*
Wingspan: 13–15.5cm (5–6in).
Status: Not listed.

Identification: FW mottled grey towards body, dark and light-brown margins, tapered and slightly hooked. HW is red-brown with dark-brown margins and large eyespot on each wing.

HAWK, SUNSET AND BURNET MOTHS

*Hawk moths are fast-flying day moths that occur around the world. There are approximately
1,300 species which are divided into three subfamilies: Smerinthinae, Sphingidae and Macroglossinae.
The Sunset moths belong to the family Uraniidae while the Burnet moths, often identified and named by
the number of spots they have, belong to the Zygaenidae.*

Death's Head Moth

Acherontia atropos

Distribution: Europe, Africa, Madagascar, Middle East.
Habitat: Farmland, gardens and parks.
Food plant: Mostly Solanaceae but also others including Bignoniaceae and Oleaceae.
Wingspan: 11–13cm (4½–5in).
Status: Not listed.

Identification:
Forewings black with brown, some lighter scales, with white spot. Hindwings bright yellow, two thick black cross lines. Abdomen wide dark dorsal stripe with yellow patches along sides.

The unusual name of this moth comes from the skull-and-cross-bones marking on the dorsal side of the thorax. The moths are seen in late summer and early autumn. When handled, the moth makes a loud squeaking noise that is produced through its proboscis. The adult moths love honey, and raid beehives in search of this energy-rich food; surprisingly the bees allow the moths into the hive. Usually the female lays her eggs singly on the leaves of plants of the Solanaceae (potato family), but other plants can be used. The caterpillar is yellow-green with dark green oblique stripes down the side. Like the adult, it makes alarm sounds when disturbed, rubbing its mandibles together to produce a clicking sound. The fully grown caterpillar digs itself into the ground to a depth of about 15cm (6in) and then presses hard on the soil to form an underground chamber in which it pupates.

Elephant Hawk Moth

Deilephila elpenor

The attractive Elephant Hawk Moth is seen from May to August. There may be one or two generations. The adults are nocturnal and visit flowers for nectar, especially honeysuckle (*Lonicera* sp.). The female lays her eggs singly on the leaves of the food plant. The moth's name comes from the behaviour of the caterpillar. When threatened, it pulls its head into its thorax which becomes larger and causes two eyespots to become more prominent, giving the appearance of an elephant's head. This defensive behaviour startles any would-be predator. The nocturnal caterpillars feed on willowherb, *Fuchsia* and bedstraw. During the day they may be seen resting on the plants. The caterpillars pupate in the soil, where they form a cocoon in which they overwinter.

Distribution: Europe, Asia to China and Japan, introduced to British Columbia.
Habitat: Damp woodland, flood plains, wasteland and alpine meadows.
Food plant: Variety including *Epilobium, Fuschsia, Galium*.
Wingspan: 45–60mm (1¾–2⅜in).
Status: Not listed.

Identification: Forewings olive-brown, flushed with pink, with a pink margin. Hindwings pink with a dark basal patch. Thorax and abdomen flushed with pink.

Left: The caterpillar is a freckled grey-brown to green, with a strongly tapering head and an abdominal horn.

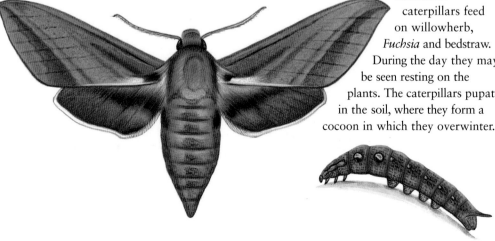

Spurge Hawk Moth

Hyles euphorbiae

Distribution: Southern Europe, North America.
Habitat: Woodlands, meadows with spurge.
Food plant: *Euphorbia* sp..
Wingspan: 55–75mm (2³⁄₁₆–3in).
Status: Not listed.

Identification: Forewings pale yellow-grey to lilac-grey, brown spot at centre, base and brown band from wing tip to inner margin, flushed with pink. Hindwings black with green-brown outer margin, bright pink-brown median band.

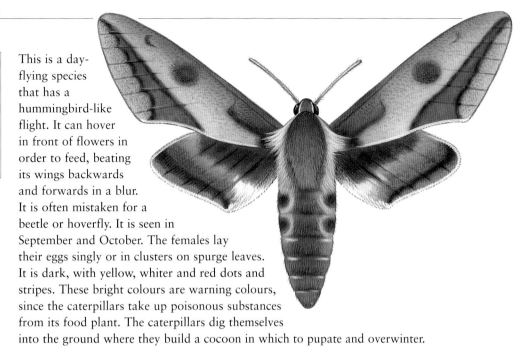

This is a day-flying species that has a hummingbird-like flight. It can hover in front of flowers in order to feed, beating its wings backwards and forwards in a blur. It is often mistaken for a beetle or hoverfly. It is seen in September and October. The females lay their eggs singly or in clusters on spurge leaves. It is dark, with yellow, whiter and red dots and stripes. These bright colours are warning colours, since the caterpillars take up poisonous substances from its food plant. The caterpillars dig themselves into the ground where they build a cocoon in which to pupate and overwinter.

OTHER SPECIES OF NOTE

Beautiful Antinephele *Antinephele maculifera*
This hawk moth is found in west and central Africa. Its forewings are patterned dark brown to pale brown while the hindwings are dark brown. Its abdomen is orange-red. It is thought that the bright abdomen is an example of flash coloration, in which it is suddenly revealed by the forewings which normally cover it up.

Verdant Sphinx Hawk Moth *Euchloron megaera*
This African Hawk moth has unusual green forewings and body, with bright orange and brown hindwings. The caterpillar feeds on *Vitis* (vine) and *Parthenocissus* (Virginia creeper).

Morgan's Sphinx *Xanthopan morgani*
This very large Hawk moth has an exceptionally long proboscis that enables it to reach to the bottom of the extra-long flowers of African orchids of the genus *Angraecum*. It was Charles Darwin who first theorized that this moth's proboscis was a pollinator. The moth's wings are patterned brown and grey, giving good camouflage when resting. The caterpillars feed on *Annona senegalensis*, *Hexalobus crispiflorus*, *Uvaria*, *Ibaria* and *Zylopia* species.

Poplar Hawk Moth

Laothoe populi

This common night-flying moth is often spied resting on walls and fence posts during the day. It rests with its hindwings held above the forewing, so its outline looks like dead leaves. It lives in a range of habitats including wasteland, parks, damp woodland and alpine meadows. It flies from May to July and there is usually one generation. However, to the south of its range there may be two generations. The female lay her eggs in small clusters on the underside of leaves of the food plant. The caterpillar burrows into the soil to pupate and overwinter.

Distribution: Western Europe to Asia.
Habitat: Woodlands, meadows, gardens, coasts.
Food plant: *Poplar* sp. and *Salix* sp..
Wingspan: 7–10cm (2½–4in).
Status: Not listed.

Identification: Forewing is pink-grey to brown with dark central band and small white spot, scalloped edge. Hindwing also pink-grey with large red basal patch.

Right: The caterpillar is green, with oblique yellow stripes and small red spots.

Hummingbird Hawk Moth

Macroglossum stellatarum

This day-flying moth is seen hovering in front of flowers from which it sips nectar. It is this hovering flight and the way that it flits between flowers that gives the Hummingbird Hawk moth its name. It can be confused with the Bee Hawk Moth, which has a similar flight. This is a migrant species that flies north in summer, especially during warm summers. It is most common during June and July, but can be seen on the wing from April to October. It prefers to fly in bright sunshine, but it may be seen at dawn, dusk and even at night. On the hottest days it becomes inactive, only flying during the cooler parts of the day. The females lay their eggs on bedstraw. The caterpillars are green with yellow stripes, and a horn at the end of the abdomen which identifies it as a Hawk moth caterpillar.

Identification: Forewings various from brown to grey, with darker cross lines. Hindwings orange. Thorax is hairy and abdomen brown-black with white patches on sides; it has a dark anal tuft.

Distribution: Europe, North Africa, central, south and Southeast Asia.
Habitat: Grassland, coastal habitats, gardens.
Food plant: *Galium* sp. (bedstraw).
Wingspan: 40–50mm (1⁹⁄₁₆–2in).
Status: Not listed.

Above: When feeding, Hummingbird Hawk moths beat their wings at such speed they emit an audible hum.

Eyed Hawk Moth

Smerinthus ocellata

The Eyed Hawk moth gets its name from the eyespots on its hindwings. When resting, it holds its forewings over its hindwings and curls its body upwards. If threatened, it quickly reveals its eyespots to startle any would-be predator. The moths are seen from May to July, mostly over marshy or boggy ground and damp woodland where its food plant, willow, can be found. The females lay their eggs on the leaves of willow and apple. There are two colour forms of the caterpillar. One is yellow-green with whitish stripes and red rings on the side, while the other is blue-green with white lateral stripes. However, all caterpillars become yellow-brown prior to pupation, which takes place just under the surface of the soil. The pupa overwinters and the moth emerges the following summer.

Identification: Forewings pink-brown, slight scallop to the margin with series of dark-brown spots. Hindwings brown, with pink tinge, large blue and black eyespots. Body brown.

Left: At rest, the eyespots are covered by the forewings, but when disturbed the moth moves the forewings forward to reveal the bright eyespots.

Distribution: Europe, across Asia to Siberia.
Habitat: Marsh, bog, woodland, gardens.
Food plant: *Malus* sp., *Salix* sp..
Wingspan: 70–90mm (2¾–3½in).
Status: Not listed.

Madagascan Sunset Moth

Chrysiridia madagascarensis

Distribution: Madagascar.
Habitat: Forest.
Food plant: Euphorbiaceae.
Wingspan: 75–90mm
(3–3½in).
Status: Not listed.

Identification: Forewings are black with iridescent green blotches, pale margin. Hindwings are brown giving way to blue and orange with black marks, invaginated margin.

This butterfly-like moth is a member of the Uraniidae family, and the name comes from its colourful wings. Like the Morpho butterflies of South America, the iridescent colours come from the refraction of light off the surface of the scales rather than from pigments. In its native Madagascar, it is called 'noble butterfly' or 'noble spirit'. It has long attracted the attention of collectors, and during Victorian times its wings were used to make jewellery. The Sunset moth is day-flying and the wing colours warn predators that it is toxic. The toxin, a type of alkaloid, is found in plants of the Euphorbiaceae, the food plants of the caterpillar. The toxin remains active in the caterpillar, pupa and adult. The caterpillar is yellow-white with black spots and hairs, and red feet.

OTHER SPECIES OF NOTE

Five-spot Burnet Moth *Zygaena trifolii*
This moth has five red spots on the forewing. It is abundant across parts of its range. In some places it can be seen flying with the Six-spot Burnet moth. Some individuals are known as aberration as their spots are merged together. There are two subspecies that are similar in appearance but differ in flight time and habitat.

Forester *Adscita statices*
The day-flying Forester has iridescent yellow and green wings and is seen in June and July. It occurs on chalk grassland, meadows and on heathland. The females lay their eggs on the leaves of common sorrel (*Rumex acetosa*).

African Sunset Moth *Chrysiridia croesus*
The day-flying African Sunset Moth is found in east Africa. It belongs to the African genus *Chrysiridia*, of which the only other member is the Madagascan Sunset Moth. The bright wing colours in red, orange and green, are a warning of its toxicity. The caterpillars are specialists, feeding solely on species of the Euphorbiaceae. The caterpillar spins a cocoon, either among the leaves or near the ground.

Six-spot Burnet

Zygaena filipendulae

Distribution: Europe.
Habitat: Grassland, meadow, waste land, woodland.
Food plant: *Lotus* sp..
Wingspan: 30–38mm
(1⅛–1½in).
Status: Not listed.

Identification: FW Metallic black with three pairs of red spots. HW Red with black margin. Body black.

The Six-spot Burnet moth is a brightly coloured day-flying moth. When it flies it reveals it bright-red hindwings, which, together with the red spots, warn predators that it is poisonous. There are a number of species of Burnet moth, and they are identified by the number of spots on the forewings. The origin of the name 'burnet' is uncertain and may be linked to the salad burnet, a plant of chalk grassland, or to its fire-like burnt colours. It is one of the most common of day-flying moths in Europe, where it is seen living in colonies close to patches of vetches and clovers. It flies from June to July, and the females lay their eggs in groups on leaves of the bird's-foot trefoil. The caterpillar is yellow with black markings. It spins a boat-shaped cocoon around a grass stem in which it pupates and overwinters. The species is not threatened but it is suffering from a loss of habitat, especially grasslands. It is also considered to be vulnerable to drought.

MICRO MOTHS

The moths featured on this and the following pages are the small moths, or Microlepidoptera. They do not belong to any one family, rather to a range of families that are simply grouped together because of their size, in an artificial (unranked and not monophyletic) grouping. Smaller moths generally have wingspans of under 20mm (³⁄₄in) although some species are large enough to be grouped with the Macrolepidoptera.

Green Longhorn

Adela reaumurella

Longhorn moths or Fairy moths, such as the Green Longhorn, are characterized by long antennae. They do not belong to one family, but to several closely related families. However, those of the family Adelidae have the longest antennae. They are also noted for their metallic scales. The day-flying Green Longhorns fly in May and June, and are often seen in groups dancing around oak trees and shrubs in a mosquito-like manner. The caterpillars spend the autumn and winter feeding on leaf litter. They create cases from pieces of leaves, in which they pupate. Climate change is causing the population size of this species to decline in parts of its range.

Distribution: Europe.
Habitat: Woodlands.
Food plant: *Quercus* and *Betula*.
Wingspan: 14–18mm (⁹⁄₁₆–1¹⁄₁₆in).
Status: Not listed.

Identification: Upperwings metallic green, underwings metallic bronze. Males have very long white antennae, rough black hairs under head. Females short antennae and short, light hairs on the head.

Acorn Moth

Blastobasis glandulella

This species may also be classified as *Valentinia glandulella*. The Acorn moths belong to a family of micro moths that are very small. They are characterized by a fringe along the hind margin of the forewing and on both sides of the thin hindwing. The Acorn moth flies from April to September, and there are several generations. The females lay their eggs on oak and sweet chestnut trees. The female lays her egg beside the tiny hole in an acorn left by an exiting acorn weevil larva. The caterpillar hatches and crawls through the hole. The hole is sealed and the caterpillar feeds on the contents of the acorn. In this way, they can cause economic damage to forests, as they eat so many acorns that the trees fail to reproduce.

Distribution: Europe and North America.
Habitat: Woodlands.
Food plant: *Quercus* and *Castanea sativa*.
Wingspan: 15–25mm (⁹⁄₁₆–1in).
Status: Not listed.

Identification: Forewings grey-brown, banded dark and light, black dots, fringe to hind margin. Hindwings shiny grey, dark veins. Fringe of long hair-like scales on both margins in the small wing.

Above: The fat, maggot-like caterpillars feed and often pupate inside acorns.

Twenty Plume

Alucita hexadactyl

Distribution: Eurasia, North America.
Habitat: Gardens, woodlands, hedgerows.
Food plant: *Lonicera* sp, *Symphoricarpos* sp..
Wingspan: 14–16mm (⁹⁄₁₆–⁵⁄₈ in).
Status: Not listed

The Twenty Plume moth belongs to the family of Many Plumed moths, characterised by fore- and hindwings that are divided into six segments with fringes around the edges. This creates a feather-like appearance. The Twenty Plume moth has wings with six segments, like the rest of the family, despite its name. The word 'Alucita' means 'gnat' and relates to the moth's fly-like appearance. It is on the wing for much of the year, although few are seen in the height of summer. There are several generations. The females lay their eggs on the leaves of honeysuckle. The caterpillars tunnel through the leaves and buds.

Identification: Wings spread out like a fan at rest. Each wing is divided into six segments or plumes. Zig-zag pattern in brown and black across the wings.

OTHER SPECIES OF NOTE

Nematopogon swammerdamella
This Longhorn moth is found in European woodlands, and has also been known to live in hedgerows, moorland, heathland and other open habitats. Its antennae are incredibly long for its size. It flies from May to June. The caterpillars are unusual in that they feed on the dead leaves of oak and beech trees. They hibernate twice and pupate inside the case.

Alucita dohertyi
This many-plumed moth is found only in Kenya where it is locally abundant. Its divided, feathery wings are patterned in shades of brown and white. The wingspan reaches up to 40mm (1½in).

Beet Moth *Scrobipalpa ocellatella*
This moth is seen through April and May. As its name suggests, it lays its eggs on the leaves of the beet family such as sea beet (*Beta maritima*), also orache (*Atriplex* sp.) and *Amarathus* sp.. There are two generations, with adult moths on the wing from May to July and again between August and October.

White Plume

Pterophorus pentadactyla

The White Plume moth is the largest of the plume moths, reaching up to 34mm (1⅜in). It is an eyecatching moth with long white feathery wings and long spiked legs. It is common and widespread across its range. It is seen flying at night from August to April and it is easily attracted to light. It roosts on vegetation during the day. The females lay their eggs on the leaves of bindweed. The caterpillars emerge and feed on the leaves. They overwinter and pupate the following spring.

Distribution: Europe, Middle Asia and Iran.
Habitat: Woodlands, hedgerows and gardens.
Food plant: *Convolvulus* and *Calystegia*.
Wingspan: 26–34mm (1–1⅜in).
Status: Not listed.

Identification: White narrow wings deeply divided into six segments, each finely feathered.

Lilac Leaf Miner

Caloptilia syringella

Distribution: Northern Europe and Canada.
Habitat: Woodlands, gardens.
Food plant: *Ligustrum, Fraxinus, Syringa*.
Wingspan: 10–13mm (⅜–½ in).
Status: Not listed.

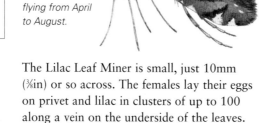

Right: The adult moths are seen flying from April to August.

Identification: Forewings grey-brown with irregular silvery yellow patches and bands.

The Lilac Leaf Miner is small, just 10mm (⅜in) or so across. The females lay their eggs on privet and lilac in clusters of up to 100 along a vein on the underside of the leaves. The caterpillars hatch and tunnel through the leaves. They are green-white while within the leaf, but as they mine through the leaf they change colour, becoming darker. Then they move out of the leaf. They curl up the tip of the leaf using strands of silk and continue to feed within the roll. At the end of summer the caterpillars drop from the leaves and pupate in the ground, where they overwinter.

Goat Moth

Cossus cossus

Distribution: Europe.
Habitat: Woodland.
Food plant: *Betula, Salix, Ulmus*.
Wingspan: 6.5–10cm (2½–4in).
Status: Not listed.

Identification: Forewings grey-brown, with fine but dark lines crossing the wing, feathery lower margin. Hindwings mottled shades of brown, small and feathery.

Below: The fully grown caterpillar is about 10cm (4in) long and bright red in colour.

Goat moths get their name from the goat-like smell of the caterpillars. Goat moths are relatively large moths, with forewings that are long and narrow. The adults lack a proboscis and are unable to feed. Unusually, the long-lived caterpillars can bore into wood of trees such as willow and elm. They take up to four years to reach maturity. The distinctive smell lingers in the wood long after the caterpillars have crawled out of the wood to pupate.

Ghost Moth

Hepialus humuli

> **Distribution**: Central and southern Europe.
> **Habitat**: Grassland and meadows.
> **Food plant**: *Urtica dioica, Arctium tomentos*.
> **Wingspan**: 50mm (2in).
> **Status**: Not listed.

Identification: Males have white wings. Females have larger, yellow-white wings with orange markings.

Below: Unlike many other species of moth, it is the female moth that is attracted to the males.

This moth is one of the largest micro moths. It gets its name from the ghostly appearance of the white wings of the male when it hovers over tall grasses at dusk. In a suitable location, several moths may display together. The term 'ghost moth' is sometimes used as a general term for all Hepialids. The moths are seen in June and July, when they fly over grasslands and hillsides. The males gather in small groups at dusk; however, they are not attracted as easily to light as the females. The females scatter their eggs while in flight over grassland. The maggot-like caterpillars feed on the roots of grasses and other grassland plants and so spend much of their larval development underground. They grow slowly and may take as long as two years to mature. The caterpillar can become a pest in commercial nurseries.

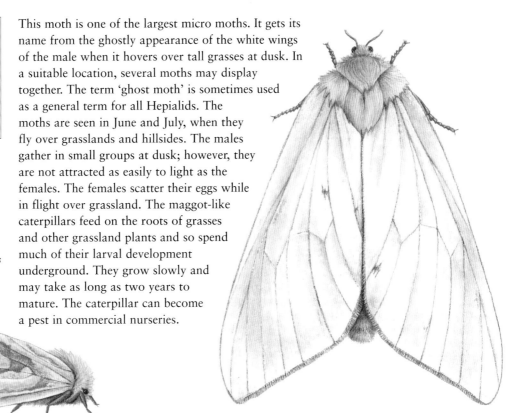

Festoon

Apoda limacodes

> **Distribution**: Europe, Middle East, South Asia.
> **Habitat**: Woodland.
> **Food plant**: *Quercus, Fagus*.
> **Wingspan**: 24–28mm (1–1³⁄₆in).
> **Status**: Not listed.

Identification: Forewings are orange-brown with dark-brown line in 'V' across wings. Hindwings dark brown to black.

Apoda is a genus of moths that is widespread in Europe, parts of Africa and temperate and Southern Asia. There are some species in North America as well. The Festoon Moth flies from June to July. During the day it rests on bark, with its wings angled and abdomen raised to give the appearance of a piece of bark. The females lay their eggs on oak leaves. The caterpillar looks remarkably like a slug, and for this reason, this genus of moths is often called the Slug moths. The caterpillar is green, with three rows of warts and yellow lines along the back, edged with red, together with a yellow line along each side. They appear to be almost legless and they use mucus to glide over surfaces like a slug.

Apple Pygmy

Stigmella malella

This is a pest of apple trees. The first generation of these tiny moths appears in March and April, and then further generations occur throughout the summer. There can be as many as four generations in the southern parts of the Mediterranean. The females lay their eggs on the underside of apple leaves. The tiny caterpillar burrows inside the leaf, creating a mine that damages the leaf. Once it is fully grown, it drops to the ground and overwinters as a pupa. Small numbers of caterpillars cause limited damage, but in some years severe infestations can lead to extensive leaf death, a reduced crop and economic losses.

Identification: Small wings, black with silver band on the forewings.

Distribution: Europe.
Habitat: Orchards, gardens.
Food plant: *Malus* sp. (apple).
Wingspan: 4mm (⅜in).
Status: Not listed.

Right: The conspicuous mines created by the caterpillars on the leaves of apple trees start as linear winding mines and end in a large blotch.

Left: The caterpillar of the Apple Pygmy is tiny, just a few millimetres long, with a brown head and pale yellow body.

Long-horned Moth

Nemophora degeerella

Distribution: Europe.
Habitat: Woodlands, hedgerows, gardens.
Food plant: Leaf litter.
Wingspan: 18–23mm (¾–1 1/16 in).
Status: Not listed.

Identification: Forewings are brown with yellow and dark-brown band. Antennae are five times the length of the body. Females are smaller.

Species belonging to the genus *Nemophora* occur around the world, with the exception of New Zealand. They are most abundant in Europe, Asia and Africa. The attractive Long-horned Moth is common throughout its range. Its extra-long antennae are the longest of all the European moths, extending to five times its body length. It holds them out in front of its head as it flutters over hedgerows. The female lays her eggs on the ground. The caterpillars feed on leaf litter from the safety of a case, which they form from pieces of leaf glued together with silk. They also pupate in this case. The moths fly from May to July, when small groups may be spotted 'dancing' around in the sunlight. They rest on leaves in shady places.

Right: The male Long-horned Moth is larger than the female (above) and has longer antennae.

Red-belted Clearwing

Synanthedon myopaeformis

Distribution: Europe, north Africa, Middle East, and North America.
Habitat: Gardens, orchards, woodland.
Food plant: *Crataegus* sp., *Malus* sp., *Prunus* sp., *Syringa* sp..
Wingspan: 18–26mm (¾–1in).
Status: Not listed.

Identification: Wings clear. Forewings narrow. Hindwings shorter and triangular with veins. Dark blue-black thorax, abdomen black with red band giving the appearance of a wasp.

This moth is also called the Apple Clearwing Moth, and over the last 50 years it has become a significant pest of apple trees. The moths are active from June to August, and although they are day-flying they are not commonly seen. The female moth lays her eggs on the bark of fruit trees, especially apple, and the grey-white caterpillars bore deep tunnels into the trunk. Here they cut into the phloem, the main food transporting vessels of the tree, in order to obtain an easy source of food. They pupate and the adults emerge from holes in the bark. Nowadays the caterpillars can seriously retard the growth of young apple trees, especially those on dwarfing rootstocks, common in modern orchards. They are controlled by the use of pheromone traps.

OTHER SPECIES OF NOTE

Summer Fruit Tortrix *Adoxophyes orana*
The Summer Fruit Tortrix is a devastating pest of apple and pear trees. The moth flies in two generations from May to November. The female moths lay large numbers of eggs on the leaves of the fruit trees, and the caterpillars eat the leaves and fruits. The moth has developed resistance to pesticides, so the best method of control is a form of biological control using a virus.

Clematis Window Freckle *Thyris fenestrella*
The caterpillars of this European moth are found on *Clematis*, chewing the leaf in such a way as to create a tent. It is found in woodlands and woodland edges which are favoured by *Clematis* plants.

Apple Leaf Miner *Lyonetia clerkella*
This tiny night-flying moth is common in Europe, North Africa and across northern Asia to Japan. It is silvery white in appearance with a wingspan of 7–9mm (¼–⁵⁄₁₆in). It is a pest of orchards as its larvae eat their way through leaves, creating the characteristic leaf mines. This reduces the productivity of the trees and their yield. It is a highly successful species of moth, having as many as four generations each year between April and October.

Spindle Ermine

Yponomeuta cagnagella

The Spindle Ermine gets its name from its white wings. It is just one of 70 species in the genus *Yponomeuta*, which are found around the world. Most are specialists found on one particular species of food plant. Spindle Ermines are seen from June to July in deciduous woodland, as well as on waste land, verges and grassy hillsides. The female lays her eggs on the bark of the spindle tree. The newly hatched caterpillars overwinter and do not start to grow until the following spring. The caterpillars live together in a colony, under a silken web. As the caterpillars grow, they extend the webbing, and eventually the plant is encased in silken threads and most of its leaves are eaten. They spin a white cocoon that hangs vertically from the webbing.

Distribution: Europe, Middle East, North America.
Habitat: Deciduous woodland, chalk grassland.
Food plant: *Euonymus europaeus* (spindle).
Wingspan: 20–26mm (¾–1in).
Status: Not listed.

Identification: White wings. FW three rows of small black spots. HW grey-brown with fringe.

Below: The caterpillar is yellow-white with two rows of black spots along its back.

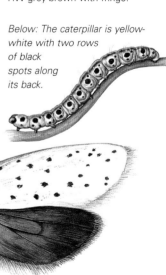

DIRECTORY OF NORTH AND SOUTH AMERICA

North and South America represent the geographical regions of the Nearctic and Neotropics. The Nearctic region includes North America as far south as the northern part of Mexico. The Neotropical region covers Central and South America. The neotropical region is home to more species of lepidopterans than any other region, where approximately 45,000 have already been identified. This figure includes about 10,000 species of butterfly, which is half the butterfly species of the world. In contrast, far fewer species inhabit North America, with its great belt of coniferous forests and tundra that stretches across northern Canada and Alaska. The region is home to about 10,500 species of moth and just 700 species of butterfly, with the skippers representing about a third of all the species. The greatest diversity of species exists in the warmer southern zone from California and Mexico to Florida.

*Above from left: Zebra Longwing (*Hiliconius chartihonia*) caterpillars; a chrysalis of* Colubura dirce *camouflaged on a plant stem; Ismenius Tiger (*Heliconius ismenius*); Right: Red Postman (*Heliconius erato*) emerging from pupa.*

SWALLOWTAILS

Most members of the Papilionidae family are found in Central and South America. Here there are about 170 known species, of which all but a few are endemic. There are just 25 resident species in North America, together with a handful of migrants. Swallowtails are mostly brightly coloured, large butterflies, that usually have long tails on the hindwings.

Short-horned Baronia

Baronia brevicornis

The Short-horned Baronia is of interest to biologists, as it is considered to be the most primitive of the swallowtails and is described as a living fossil. Its wing venation has more in common with the Pieridae and Nymphalidae than other members of the Papilionidae, so it is assumed that it diverged from the Papilionidae before the changes in venation occurred. The butterflies are seen in thickets where *Acacia* trees are found. The males are territorial, and perch on high branches from where they dive down to chase off intruders. The females lay their eggs singly, a few on each tree. The caterpillars protect themselves when threatened by releasing a noxious secretion from their osmeteria which they attempt to wipe over their attacker. This species is endemic to Mexico, and although it is not under threat in Mexico, its restricted distribution puts it at risk on a worldwide basis, and its habitat is under increasing pressure from the growing human population.

Distribution: Mexico
Habitat: Deciduous scrub forest with Acacia.
Food plant: Acacia *Acacia cochliacantha*.
Wingspan: 55–65mm (2⅛–2⁹⁄₁₆ in)
Status: Near threatened.

Right: The female is larger, and more brightly coloured.

Identification: Dark brown wings, lacking tails, with variable pattern of yellow markings. Upper forewings have three rows of yellow spots. Upper hindwings are yellow patches and yellow spots.

Pipevine Swallowtail

Battus philenor

Identification: UFW blue-black, LFW grey, UHW iridescent blue to blue-green with submarginal row of cream-orange spots. Males brighter blue than females with smaller spots on upper wing.

The flight time of this butterfly varies, depending on the location. In Mexico they are present all year round, but in the United States they fly in late spring and summer. Females lay batches of eggs on the underside of host plants growing in sunny spots. Caterpillars are black, with yellow-orange spines and spots along their back. Initially, they feed in small groups, but they spread out as they get older and are eventually solitary. The pipevine is a poisonous plant, but these caterpillars are unaffected. However, the toxic chemical is retained in their body making them distasteful to predators, such as birds. The caterpillars pupate and overwinter as a chrysalis. There are two colours of chrysalis, depending on where the caterpillar pupates.

Distribution: Southern United States and Mexico
Habitat: Open grassland, scrub and open woodland, woodland edges, gardens
Larval plant: *Aristolochia* sp. (pipevine).
Wingspan: 7–13cm (2½–5in).
Status: Not listed.

Polydamas

Battus polydamas

Distribution: Southern US, Bahamas, through Central and South America to Argentina.
Habitat: Open woodlands and disturbed areas, gardens
Larval plant: *Aristolochia* sp. (pipevine).
Wingspan: 90–120mm (3½–4¾ in)
Status: Not listed.

This is a common butterfly, although the adults only live about a week. They fly all year round in the tropics. The eggs are laid on stems or tips of pipevine leaves. Caterpillars are dark brown with black-tipped orange tubercles with an orange collar.

Below: The underwings of the male and female butterfly have the same pattern of colours.

Identification: Only *Battus* species that lacks tails on wings. Upperwings black with yellow bands near margins. Underwings black with row of yellow spots on FW and wavy red lines on HW. Black body with red spots.

OTHER SPECIES OF NOTE

Bee Butterfly *Chorinea faunus*
These tropical butterflies are easily identified by their clear wings and black veins, and a distinctive red patch on the hindwing. The males have reduced front legs that they do not use for walking, but the females have six normal legs.

Eurytides marchandi
This yellow-brown butterfly has wings with long tails. It is found in tropical rainforests of Mexico, Central America, Columbia and Ecuador.

Eurytides bellerophon
This is one of 50 Kite butterflies in the New World, and is found in southeastern Brazil, Bolivia and northern Argentina. Its wings have black stripes on a white background. The hindwings have long tails and the uppersides have a small red patch. This species is listed as Threatened, a decline which is due mostly to loss of habitat.

Zebra Swallowtail

Eurytides marcellus

The Zebra Swallowtail is named after its zebra-like black and white banding. It is also called the Jamaican Kite Swallowtail. The adults drink moisture from sand and mud. There are two generations a year, in spring and summer. The spring butterflies are smaller and lighter in colour than the summer generation and their tails are half the length. The females lay single pale green eggs on young leaves of the pawpaw. Young caterpillars are dark with black, yellow and white transverse bands, while older caterpillars are green with blue, black and yellow bands. The caterpillars only feed on young leaves, so this limits reproduction in late summer and autumn. The caterpillars pupate and overwinter. These butterflies have an ecological relationship with the moth *Omphalacera munroei*. The moth defoliates the pawpaw, stimulating the plant into producing new growth. Those caterpillars emerging late in the season depend on this new growth in order to obtain sufficient nutrients.

Distribution: Eastern states of the USA.
Habitat Water courses, swamps, marshes and sometimes in abandoned fields.
Food plant: *Asimina* sp. (pawpaw).
Wingspan: 64–100mm (2½–4in).
Status: Not listed.

Identification: Long, triangular wings with sword-like tails. Black stripes on a white background on four wings. UHW bright red stripe and blue spots on the margin, LHW red stripe.

Dark Kite Swallowtail

Eurytides philolaus philolaus

There are two generations between March and November. The numbers of Dark Kite butterflies are at their greatest at the start of the rainy season, when the butterflies are seen gathering in large numbers around muddy pools of water in woodlands to drink and obtain essential nutrients. This butterfly is often confused with the related species *Eurytides philolaus* in the southern regions of the United States, where their ranges overlap.

Identification: Males' upper wings broad black bars on cream, Upper hindwings two red marks on inside margin, long tails. Lower hindwings paler brown with red streak and red spots. Females different, see below.

Distribution: South Texas to Costa Rica.
Habitat: Low-altitude tropical deciduous forest.
Larval plant: Annonaceae (custard apple) family, including pawpaw.
Wingspan: 90mm (3½ in).
Status: Not listed.

Above: The underwing of the female is a paler brown than the upperwing, and the red marks are less noticeable than those of the male.

Ruby-spotted Swallowtail

Papilio anchisiades

The Ruby-spotted Swallowtail flies from May to October. The females lay eggs in clusters on the leaves of citrus trees. The caterpillars are green and brown with white markings. The caterpillars are social, sheltering together during the day and feeding at night. When threatened, the orange scent glands (osmeteria) behind the head spray an odour to deter any predators. The caterpillars also moult at the same time. The pupae are light brown, with pale green spots.

Distribution: Texas to Argentina.
Habitat: Lowland tropical forests, citrus groves, gardens.
Food plant: Rutaceae family including Citrus, *Casimiroa*, and *Zanthoxylum* sp..
Wingspan: 70–100mm (2¾–4in).
Status: Not listed.

Identification: Mostly black wings with no tails. Hindwings have pink to purple spots. Females' upper forewings have a diffused white to pink patch.

Broad-banded Swallowtail

Papilio astyalus

Distribution: Mexico south to Argentina.
Habitat: Subtropical forests.
Food plant: Citrus trees.
Wing span: 11–12cm (4½in).
Status: Not listed.

Left: The female has dark brown wings. The hindwings have additional blue and orange submarginal bands and very short tails.

Identification: Males' upper FW broad diagonal yellow band and rows of submarginal yellow spots. HW large yellow spots along margin. Black, narrow tail. Females different, see below.

This tropical butterfly flies from April to October. The adults feed on nectar, particularly the Lantana flower. The males are found flying in open habitats whereas the females prefer wooded habitats where there are citrus trees (Rutaceae) on which to lay their eggs.

OTHER SPECIES OF NOTE

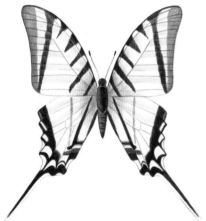

Short-lined Kite Swallowtail *Eurytides agesilaus*
This swallowtail has white wings with black bands and long tails. It feeds on plants of the custard apple (Annonaceae) family including *Rollinia emarginata*. It is found in seasonal monsoon, in swampy areas and along rivers in rainforests from Mexico to Brazil and Bolivia.

Palamedes Swallowtail *Papilio palamedes*
This butterfly has dark wings with a yellow band across the upperwings. It is common around swampy woodlands, and is the signature swallowtail of the great swamps in Florida, USA.

Papilio lycophron
The smallest member of the family Papilionaeae, this butterfly has dark brown wings with broad yellow bands and spots. The hindwing margin is ridged and there is a brown tail. The female butterfly looks similar but lacks the yellow bands.

Dusky Swallowtail

Papilio aristodemus ponceanus

The Dusky or Schaus Swallowtail is a slow-flying butterfly that is seen flying between the dense trees of hammock vegetation. There is one generation from April to July, which corresponds to the rainy season. The females lay their eggs singly on new growth of food plants so the caterpillars can feed on the leaves. The young caterpillars are brown with creamy patches. The bark-like pupae attach to twigs, where they overwinter. The butterfly is listed as Endangered across its range in Florida due to drought, habitat loss through fire and hurricane damage, and pesticide use. The population is estimated at fewer than 1,000.

Distribution: Florida with subspecies in the Caribbean.
Habitat: Tropical hardwood hammocks.
Food plant: *Zanthoxylum fagara* (Rutaceae) and *Amyris elemifera* (sea torchwood).
Wing span: 85–130mm (3⅜–5¼in)
Status: Listed as endangered in Florida.

Identification: Sexes similar but males have yellow-tipped antennae and females are larger. Upperwings brown with row of yellow submarginal spots and broad yellow band through middle. HW with yellow outline. Undersides yellow with brown markings, blue and orange-red band.

Eastern Tiger Swallowtail

Papilio glaucus

This butterfly is considered to be the 'American butterfly', symbolic in a similar way to the bald eagle. It is common and occurs in a variety of habitats. There are three generations per year in the south, and two in the north, between May and September. The adults feed on nectar. The males are territorial and they patrol their territory in search of females. Both sexes are seen flying high over the tops of trees. The two forms of the female have benefits. The tiger-like stripes of the yellow form distracts predators, while the dark form mimics the unpalatable blue swallowtail. Females lay their eggs singly on a wide range of woody plants including apple, ash, magnolia and poplar. The caterpillars feed on leaves at night and rest within in-rolled leaves during the day. The pupae overwinter.

Distribution: North America.
Habitat: Deciduous woods, forest edges, river valleys, parks, and gardens.
Food plant: Many including *Prunus* (wild cherry), *Populus* (cottonwood), *Salix* sp. (willow) *Magnolia* sp..
Wingspan: 90–160mm (3½–6¼in).
Status: Not listed.

Identification: Males yellow with black stripes, black border around edge of wings. Females occur in two forms, one like the male, the other black with dark stripes; both forms have iridescent blue scales and an orange marginal spot on upper wing and band along margin on underside of forewing.

Above: In the dark morph form of the female underwing, the normally yellow areas become dark grey and black.

Above: The underwings of the male and female light form have submarginal rows of blue and orange on the hindwing.

Spicebush Swallowtail

Papilio troilus

This common butterfly is seen in a wide range of habitats from woodlands through to gardens. There are two generations per year, between April and October. The male butterflies are frequently seen mud-puddling on damp areas on the ground, where they drink and obtain nutrients. The female lay their eggs on the underside of leaves. The young caterpillars look like bird droppings. As they get larger, they gain the appearance of a snake with eyespots. The caterpillars are social and make a leaf shelter in which they hide during the day, emerging at night to feed. When disturbed, the orange scent gland behind their head releases an odour to deter their would-be predator.

Distribution: North America.
Habitat: Woodlands and swamp forest, parks, gardens.
Larval food: Lauraceae such as spice bush (*Lindera benzoin*).
Wingspan: 80–110mm (3⅛–4¾in).
Status: Not listed.

Identification: Upper forewing brown-black with cream spots along bottom margin, orange spot on costal margin. Hindwing bottom margin cream spots, broad tail. Underwings in both sexes have pale green spots under the margin.

Western Tiger Swallowtail

Papilio rutulus

Distribution: Western North America.
Habitat: Woodlands near rivers and streams, wooded suburbs, canyons, parks, gardens and roadsides.
Food plant: *Populus* (Cottonwood, aspen), *Salix* (willows) *Prunus* (wild cherry) and *Fraxinus* (ash).
Wingspan: 70–100cm (2¾–4in).
Status: Not listed.

Identification: Upper forewing has separate yellow spots forming marginal band. Upper hindwing has marginal spot yellow or lacking, underside narrow marginal spots and no orange tint except for two spots near end of inner margin.

An attractive butterfly that tends to fly slowly unless threatened, when it can fly at speed. It takes nectar from a range of flowers including *Abelia*, thistles, and Zinnia. The males gather with other swallowtail species for mud-puddling in Western Canyons. There is one generation that flies from June to July. The females lay their eggs singly on the surface of leaves of trees such as cottonwood, aspen and willow. The caterpillars feed on leaves and rest on silken mats within in-rolled leaves. The pupae overwinter.

OTHER SPECIES OF NOTE

Giant Swallowtail *Papilio cresphontes*
This yellow and black swallowtail occurs through much of eastern North America, where it is found along streams, citrus groves and even gardens. The larval food plant are members of the Rutaceae (citrus) family. The caterpillars are nicknamed 'orange dogs' by fruit farmers because they defoliate citrus trees.

Papilio zagreus
This is a large and common butterfly in South America, and is found in Venezuela, Colombia, Ecuador, Peru, Bolivia and western Brazil. With a wingspan of 10–30cm (4¾–12in), the forewings are dark brown to black with yellow and orange spots. The hind wings are orange with black spots, and they lack a tail.

Mylotes Cattleheart *Parides eurimedes*
A member of the Cattlehearts, belonging to the genus *Parides*, this species is common in the rainforests of Mexico and Central America. Both male and female are black, with a red patch on the hindwing. The hindwings lack tails.

Giant Homerus Swallowtail

Papilio homerus

The Giant Swallowtail is probably the largest true Swallowtail in the world, with some specimens having a wingspan of 25cm (10in). This attractive butterfly is found in rainforest, both wet forest on limestone and lower montane forest, as well as disturbed land around the edge of forests. It flies from February to April and September to October. It is found only in two populations on Jamaica, where its rainforest habitat is under threat from deforestation. Another threat comes from collectors. Being a relatively slow-flying butterfly, it is easy to catch so has been over-collected. The rainforest in which it occurs is now protected under the Blue Mountain and John Crow Mountains National Park Project. Trade in the butterflies has been stopped as the species is protected by CITES. Captive breeding schemes have been established to safeguard the future of the butterfly, and it is being re-established in protected sites.

Distribution: Jamaica.
Habitat: Tropical rainforest.
Food plant: *Hernandia catalpaefolia* (water mahoe).
Wingspan: 15–25cm (6–10in).
Status: Endangered.

Identification: Sexes similar. Upper forewing black with yellow band, central bar and spots. Hindwing black with broader transverse yellow band with row of blue spots and red dashes at base of tails.

WHITES AND YELLOWS

There are approximately 50 species of the Pieridae in North America. There are many more in Central and South America, where most of the genera present are endemic to the region. Some species are particularly common with a widespread distribution, for example the Green-veined White and the Large White.

Green Veined White

Pieris napi

This widespread butterfly can be found in a range of habitats, but it prefers damp, sheltered areas. When resting among leaves the greenish veins on the underwings provide good camouflage. Its host plants are wild crucifers, unlike other Pierids, such as the Cabbage White, that favour brassicas grown as crops. There are two generations per year, the first in April and a second one in July/August. The females lay their eggs singly on the underside of leaves. The pupae overwinter and emerge in spring. In warm years, a third generation may be produced.

Distribution: Europe, parts of North Africa, across Asia and North America.
Habitat: Hedgerows, ditches, meadows, woodland clearings, moorland.
Food plant: Wild crucifers including *Alliaria petiolata* (garlic mustard), *Cardamine pratensis* (cuckoo flower), and *Sisymbrium officinale* (hedge mustard).
Wingspan: 40–50mm (1½–2in).
Status: Not listed.

Identification: Upper wings yellow white. FW black tips. Males have centre dark spot on FW, females two spots. Underside yellow-green veins.

Cabbage or Large White

Pieris brassicae

The Cabbage White is a common butterfly that can reach pest proportions in some years. The caterpillars destroy brassica crops in fields, gardens, and allotments. It is a strong-flying butterfly that can cover long distances in its search for new food plants. There are two generations a year in the northern parts of its range, but as many as eight in the south. The female Cabbage White lays her eggs in groups of up to 40 on the upper and lower leaf surfaces. The larvae are pale green with black spots and a yellow line along the back and on each side, the conspicuous colours being a warning to predators that they contain poisonous mustard oils. The caterpillars feed together, eating the outer leaves of the food plant first and working inwards. In contrast, the Small White prefers the inner leaves. The older caterpillars are solitary and move away from the food plant to pupate on fences, tree trunks or under an overhanging roof, where they overwinter.

Distribution: North America, Europe, North Africa, across Asia to the Himalayas.
Habitat: Almost any, especially meadows, hedgerows, parks and gardens, farmland.
Food plant: Crucifers including *Tropaeolum majus* (nasturtium), cultivated brassicas including *Brassica oleracea*, *B. napus*
Wingspan: 50–65mm (2–2½in).
Status: Not listed.

Identification: Upperside of wings white. Forewing has a black tip. Two black spots in female, one in male. Underside of the hindwing and tip of forewing is yellow-green.

Right: The lower forewing of the male is white with a yellow tip and black spot, while the lower hindwing is a creamy yellow.

Large Marble

Euchloe ausonides

Distribution: Western North America.
Habitat: Sunny areas such as meadows, grassy slopes and fields.
Food plant: Brassicaceae including *Arabis drummondi* (rock cress), *Isatis tinctoria* (dyers wood), *Brassica* sp. (mustards).
Wingspan: 35–55mm (1⅜–2⅛in).
Status: Not listed.

The Large Marble is also known as the Creamy Marblewing. There are one or two generations per year, May to July in the north, and February to April and May to August in the south. They feed on nectar from flowers of the Brassicaceae family. The males are seen patrolling sunny valleys and hillsides in their search for females. The females lay eggs singly on unopened flower buds of rock cress and other members of the Brassicaceae family. The caterpillars eat the flowers and fruits. The pupa overwinters.

Identification: FW white with black bar, black pattern on tip of FW. HW dense green marbling.

OTHER SPECIES OF NOTE

Olympic White *Euchloe olympia*
This small white butterfly is found in the Midwest of the United States and Canada, flying on open dry areas such as prairies, dunes and meadows. There is a single generation on the wing from April through to July. The females lay their eggs singly on the unopened flowers of the host plant. The caterpillars are green with grey and yellow stripes. They feed on the flowers and buds. The butterfly overwinters as a pupa. This species is uncommon but has been extending its range eastwards since the 1970s, perhaps benefiting from global warming and from the restoration of prairie habitats.

Sonoran Marble *Euchloe guaymasensis*
Creamy white butterfly with black tips and single black spot on the upper forewings and marbling on the hindwings. Underwings have yellow-green marbling.

Charcoal Mimic *Pereute charops*
The charcoal mimic belongs to a genus of Central and South American butterflies that are characterized by dark wings with a bright band. It occurs from the western United States south to Columbia and Ecuador. Its food plants belongs to the Loranthaceae.

Pine White

Neophasia menapia

The Pine White is a widespread species, which flies from June to September. The males are seen patrolling host trees, such as pine and fir, waiting for females. The females lay their eggs in a row along a conifer needle. These overwinter and hatch in spring. The green caterpillar has white specks and creamy yellow stripes down the sides. The caterpillars stay together while young, becoming solitary when older. They drop down from the tree and pupate at its base. This species is considered a pest, as its main food plant is the Ponderosa pine, Douglas Fir and Lodgepole Pine. Large numbers of caterpillars on a tree can defoliate its needles. Older trees are less able to withstand the defoliation than young, faster-growing trees.

Distribution: South from British Columbia to California and New Mexico.
Habitat: Coniferous forests.
Food plant: Conifers including pines, *Pseudotsuga menziesii* (Douglas Fir), and *Abies* species (true firs).
Wingspan: 45–58mm (1¾–2¼in).
Status: Not listed.

Identification: Forewing white with black band along edge. Underside of the hindwing has black veins. Female is duller, hindwing has red edges and is tinged with yellow.

Northern Clouded Yellow

Colias hecla

This Arctic butterfly is also known as the Hecla Sulphur and Greenland Sulphur. It is seen from June to August, flying across grassy slopes and tundra of the Arctic. It is one of several *Colias* species in the Arctic. The female lays eggs on the alpine milk vetch. The caterpillars are green and laterally striped. The caterpillars or the pupae may overwinter. Growth is slow and the caterpillar may take two years to mature.

Distribution: Circumpolar region, Arctic Eurasia, North America (Alaska, northern Canada, Greenland).
Habitat: Tundra.
Food plant: *Astragalus alpinus* (Alpine milk vetch)
Wingspan: 35–48mm (1⅜–2in).
Status: Not listed.

Identification: Upperwings of males dull orange with dark borders to wings, female dull orange to yellow. Both have pink fringe and red-orange spot. Underwings green-yellow, lower forewing black spot, lower hindwing elongated spot and silver and pink edged.

Clouded Sulphur

Colias philodice

Distribution: Alaska, south to Guatemala.
Habitat: Open areas such as fields, lawns, meadows.
Food plant: Pea family such as *Medicago sativa* (alfalfa), *Trifolium repens* (white clover), and *Pisum sativum* (pea).
Wingspan: 22–31mm (⅞in–1¼in).
Status: Not listed.

Identification: Both greenish-yellow in spring and yellow in summer. Hindwing single silver spot surrounded by two red rings. Males light yellow with black border. Females yellow or white with yellow-spotted black border.

The Clouded Sulphur is a common and widespread species that has benefited from the expansion of agriculture as it favours open ground such as meadows and clover fields. It flies quickly but tends to stay within a metre of the ground, hence its preference for open ground. The mating is unusual. The female lands and the male beats his wings against her to release pheromones. If the female detects the pheromones, she allows the male to mate with her. There are several generations per year, from April to October. The female has a wide choice of food plants of the pea family on which to lay her eggs, including milk vetch, clover, pea, trefoil and vetch. The caterpillar is green with pale yellow sides. Clouded Sulphurs may hybridize with the Orange Sulphur where their range overlaps.

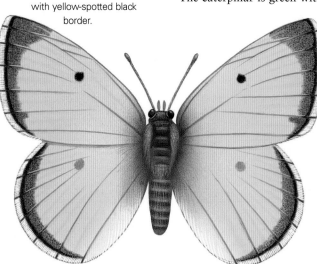

OTHER SPECIES OF NOTE
Catasticta uricoecheae
The forewings of this butterfly are mottled brown and white with a row of white spots just inside the margin. The hindwing is red with brown markings. The males are known to land on water to drink, and then be able to take off again.

Red Splashed Sulphur *Phoebis avellaneda*
This butterfly is endemic to the island of Cuba. The males have orange-red wings with yellow bases and black tips and black spots, while the females have red wings. The body of both sexes is red and yellow.

California Dogface *Colias eurydice*
This is the state butterfly of California, and it is named after the appearance of the markings on the males upperwings. The forewings are yellow-orange with black tips and small black 'eyes', while the hindwings are yellow with tiny black dots. The females have yellow wings, with a black dot on each forewing. These fast-flying butterflies are seen on a variety of habitats such as open woodland, woodland clearings and mountain slopes.

Apricot Sulphur

Phoebis argante

Distribution: Texas to Paraguay.
Habitat: Cleared areas in rainforests, clearings, gardens and fields.
Food plant: Pea family including *Cassia biflora* and *Inga vera*.
Wingspan: 54–70mm (2³⁄₁₆–2¾in).
Status: Not listed.

Identification: Male upperwings bright orange with black border on forewing. Females white-to-yellow, pale black borders.

Right: The underwings of the Apricot Sulphur are revealed when the butterfly rests. In both sexes, the underwings are a deep yellow.

This butterfly is seen all year round in Central and South America and it migrates north to Texas in June to October. The females lay their eggs singly on new leaves of the food plant, often laying many on each plant. The food plants include members of the pea family such as *Cassia* and *Inga* species. Unlike many species that are found in tropical rainforest, this species has gained from forest clearance as it favours clearings. It is also seen in open deciduous woodland, scrubby grassland, beach headlands, farmland and gardens.

Cloudless Sulphur

Phoebis sennae

Distribution: Southern United States to Argentina.
Habitat: Disturbed open areas in woodland, scrub, fields and gardens.
Food plant: *Cassia* species.
Wingspan: 57–80mm (2⅛–3⅛in).
Status: Not listed.

Identification: Male upperwings lemon yellow, no markings. Female yellow or white, wings edged in brown black line, upper forewing has a dark spot.

Right: Both sexes have lower HW with 2 pink-edged eye spots.

Left: There are two forms of caterpillar; one is yellow with black stripes, the other is pale green with a yellow stripe down each side and black spots.

The range of this butterfly is wide, from South America to southern Canada. It is most common from Argentina to southern Texas and Florida. There are many generations each year over most of the range, although in California they only fly from April to May. The males have a rapid flight and they patrol in search of females. The butterfly rarely lands and opens its wings. The adults visit a variety of tubular flowers to obtain nectar, including *Bougainvillea*, *Hibiscus* and *Lantana*. The females lay their eggs singly on young leaves and flower buds. The caterpillars feed on the leaves. The pupae overwinter and the adults emerge in spring. The genus name *Phoebis* means 'pure' or 'radiant' in Greek, while the species name *sennae* refers to the host plant.

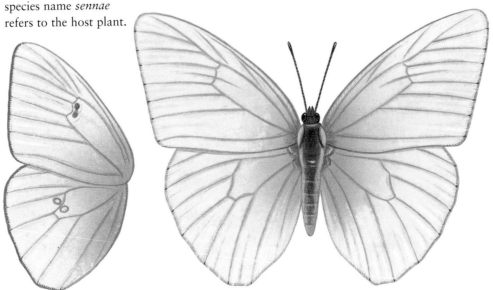

Checkered White

Pontia protodice

Identification: Males' upperwings white with black chequered pattern, underside white with faint pattern; females upperwings more heavily patterned, undersides white with yellow markings.

The Checkered White, also known as the Southern Cabbage, is a common butterfly in North America and has three generations between March and November. The male flies over low-lying ground seeking females. After mating, the females lay their eggs singly on leaves and flowers of the host plants. The caterpillars eat the buds and flowers first, moving on to leaves later. The pupae overwinter. The Checkered White is a permanent resident in the southern regions of its range, but is a summer visitor in the northern parts and may occasionally appear in Canada.

Distribution: Western United States, Mexico.
Habitat: Fields and meadows, roadside verges, scrubland, abandoned ground.
Food plant: Mustard family (Brassicaceae), capers (Capparidaceae).
Wingspan: 38–63mm (1½–2½in).
Status: Not listed.

Tiger Pierid *Dismorphia amphione*
This brightly coloured butterfly is found from Southern United States through South America. It has the appearance of a heliconid butterfly and the warning colours deter predators. It is a relatively rare butterfly seen flying along forest edges.

Creamy White *Melete lycimnia isandra*
This butterfly has creamy white upper forewings with faint grey veins, the underside of the forewing is tipped with pale yellow while that of the hindwing is pale yellow with dark yellow veins.

Western White *Pontia occidentalis*
This white is found in the western region of North America, from Alaska to central California and Arizona. It occurs in a variety of habitats, including grassland and verges, gardens, and mountain slopes, in which its food plant, the mustard, is found. There are one or two generations.

Yellow Brimstone

Anteos maerula

This butterfly, also known as the Yellow Angled-sulphur, flies rapidly at height. The adults sip nectar from the flowers of *Hibiscus* and *Bougainvillea*. This is a migrant species, and early generations fly north into the southern states of the United States. The migrants appear in a range of habitats, not just the more usual subtropical forests. There are two generations per year in the northern part of its range, April, and August to December, while in the south it flies all year round. The female lays a number of eggs singly on just one plant. The caterpillars feed on the leaves.

Distribution: Southern USA south to Peru, also Cuba.
Habitat: Subtropical forest, clearings.
Food plant: *Cassia* sp. (senna).
Wingspan: 80–120mm (3⅛–4¾in).
Status: Not listed.

Identification: Forewings are tip hooked. Male upperwing is bright yellow, female paler. Both sexes have a black spot on the forewing.

Barred Yellow

Eurema daira

Distribution: Southern United States to Argentina.
Habitats: Meadows, fields, open woodland, dunes.
Food plants: Pea family.
Wingspan: 30–41mm (1¼–1½in).
Status: Not listed.

Below: The male has far more black on its wings than the female.

The Barred Yellow is also known as the Barred Sulphur, and it is a migrant butterfly. It is a strong flier that is found on a variety of habitats that are open and full of flowers, such as meadows. Its food plants belong to the pea family and are widely available, for example, joint vetches (*Aeschynomene* sp.) and pencil flowers (*Stylosanthes biflora*). The males patrol open areas searching for females. The females lay their eggs singly on the new growth of the food plants, and the caterpillars feed on the leaves. The green caterpillars are difficult to spot at rest on the host plant, as they lie along stems and leaf midribs. In the southern parts of its range the butterfly is seen all year round, but in more northerly regions it appears as a migrant in summer and autumn. Some of these adults are known to overwinter.

Identification: Male forewings yellow with brown tip and brown bar, hindwings white with brown margin. Female forewings yellow or white with brown tip. Wet season form smaller with black areas, undersides hindwings white. Dry-season hindwings brick red with two black spots.

Little Jaune

Eurema proterpia

Distribution: Peru north to Mexico and southern United States.
Habitat: Desert, subtropical open scrub, fields, forest edges.
Food plant: Pea family including *Prosopis* (mesquite), *Cassia* (senna); *Desmodium.*
Wingspan: 45–57mm (1¾–2⅛in).
Status: Not listed.

Right: The dry-season female has a black margin on the forewing and hindwing, together with a tail that is absent in the wet-season form.

The Little Jaune, or Tailed Orange, flies throughout the year in the tropical parts of its range, but in Texas it is only seen between August and November. The males patrol over flat ground and in gullies looking for the females. The dry-season form will not mate until the start of the rainy season, after which it dies. This ensures that the caterpillar benefits from the arrival of the rains and the new growth of leaves. The adult is similar in appearance to the Sleepy Orange (*Eurema nicippe*), but its hindwing is pointed.

Identification: Orange butterfly with differences between the male and female, wet-season and dry-season forms. Upperwings orange with FW tip squared off. Angled hindwing. Males' FW leading black edge with black scales along veins, females dull orange HW black margin. Dry-season has small tails on HW, wet-season lacks tails.

HAIRSTREAKS, BLUES AND COPPERS

The Lycaenidae are particularly well represented in the neotropical region, where there are as many as 3,000 species, which accounts for approximately half of all the Lycaenids worldwide. In contrast, there are just 100 or so species in North America. There are 31 species in the West Indies and a further 16 species on Hispaniola. These butterflies are usually small, with brilliantly coloured wings.

Brown Elfin

Callophrys augustinus

This hairstreak was described by John Richardson, a naturalist on the Franklin Arctic Expeditions of the 1820s, who named it after Augustus, one of the Inuit guides. This butterfly flies between May and July in the north and March to April in the south, and its range covers much of North America, north to Alaska and Newfoundland. It is the most often encountered elfin in most of its range. It is absent from Great Plains, midwest. The adults take nectar from a wide variety of plants, including the blueberry, and spicebush. Typically the males rest on raised positions to watch for females. After mating the females lay their eggs, singly, on the flower buds of the host plants of the Ericaceae. The caterpillars are yellow-green with a yellow line along the back and diagonal lateral lines. They feed on flowers and fruits, drop to the ground to pupate, and overwinter.

Distribution: Across Canada and northern United States and south to Alabama and California, but not in the Midwest.
Habitat: Acidic soil, heaths, conifer woodland, bog, chaparral.
Host plant: Ericaceae including *Vaccinium* sp. *Arbutus*, *Cuscuta*.
Wingspan: 19–26mm (1⅙–1in).
Status: Not listed.

Identification: No tails. Male upperwing grey to brown, female red-brown. Lower wings of both brown, with line or row of black dots across middle, hindwing darker at the base.

Green Hairstreak

Callophrys affinis

Distribution: Europe, North Africa and across Asia to Siberia. Western North America from British Columbia to New Mexico.
Habitat: Calcareous grassland, woodland rides, heathland, moorland, chaparral.
Food plant: Variety, including *Helianthemum nummularium* (common rock rose) and *Lotus corniculatus* common (bird's-foot-trefoil), *Ulex europeaus* (gorse).
Wingspan: 27–34mm (1–1⅜in).
Status: Not listed.

Identification: Upperwings dull orange-brown, undersides bright green with white streak across the fore- and hindwings. Male has a small pale spot on each forewing.

The hairstreak marking, after which this butterfly is named, can be seen when it holds its wings in a closed position. Sometimes the white mark is obvious, but in some it is faint. The upperside of the wings is only seen in flight. The iridescent greens and blues of the underwing not produced by pigment in the scales but are produced by light refraction. The males are far more eye-catching, and can be seen spiralling around each other, while the female is less conspicuous. The butterflies have one generation that flies from April to June. The female lays her eggs singly on buds and young leaves of the food plant. The caterpillar has a rounded green body which is flattened at each end. The head is brown and there is a dark line along the back with additional diagonal markings. The caterpillars pupate on the ground, where they squeak to attract ants that carry them into their nest. The pupae overwinter.

Great Blue

Atlides halesus

Distribution: California, Texas and Maryland, south to Guatemala.
Habitat: Woodlands with mistletoe and walnuts, both natural and planted.
Food plant: *Phoradendron* sp. (Mistletoe).
Wingspan: 30–50mm (1¼–2in).
Status: Not listed.

Identification: Upperwings black with iridescent blue areas, undersides black with iridescent gold markings near tail, hindwings with one long and one short tail. Abdomen blue on dorsal side, red-yellow on ventral.

There are several generations of the Great Blue or Great Purple Hairstreak, which fly between March and November. Courtship behaviour involves the males waiting for females in elevated positions, such as on treetops or hilltops. Once spotted, they attract the females by beating their wings. The female scatters her eggs over mistletoe. The caterpillars are green with darker green bands and yellow stripes, with orange and green hairs. The pupae overwinter under bark or at the base of the host tree. The adults emerge in spring.

OTHER SPECIES OF NOTE
Kings Hairstreak *Satyrium kingi*
Brown butterfly with two tails, one long, one small. It flies from May to June along wooded streams and the edges of swamps through the southern United States. Its host plant is the Common sweetleaf (*Symplocos tinctoria*).

Calycopis cecrops
This tailed hairstreak has a particularly eye-catching pattern on its underwing which it reveals at rest. The wing is brown with a bright orange band with white edge that zig-zags across. It is found in the southern United States on fields and in open woodland.

Long Winged Green Hairstreak *Cyanophrys longula* This Mexican butterfly has blue-purple upper wings and green lower wings. There are two generations, March to May and August to September. Some years it flies north into Arizona.

Crowned Hairstreak

Evenus coronata

This butterfly was previously classified as *Theritas coronata* and has many common names, including Hewitson's Blue Hairstreak after the English lepidopterist William Hewitson, who described it in 1865. Other common names include Magnificent Greatstreak and Supreme Greatstreak. There are about 10 species in this genus, all with iridescent blue and green wings, and they are found in Central and tropical South America. The Crowned Hairstreak only shows off its blue upper wings when in flight. At rest, the wings are raised and the green lower wings with the hairstreak are revealed. This provides much better camouflage among the leaves of rainforest trees.

Distribution: Central and tropical South America.
Habitat: Rainforest.
Food plant: Uncertain.
Wingspan: Up to 60mm (2¼in).
Status: Not listed.

Identification: Upperwings brilliant blue-purple, underwings glittering green with dark stripe through both wings, HW two tails, one large and one small. Males more blue, females more black on margins with a red spot at base of HW.

Tailed Copper

Lycaena arota

The Tailed Copper is seen from May to August when there is a single generation of butterflies. Like many other members of the Lycaenidae, the males perch in open places to watch for females. The females lay their eggs singly on the leaves of gooseberry and currant bushes. The eggs remain on the plant until the following spring, when the caterpillars hatch and eat the young leaves. There are several subspecies including the Clouded Copper, *L. arota nubila*, which is critically endangered and has likely become extinct. This is because it is found only in the Los Angeles region where much of its habitat has been lost.

Distribution: Western United States.
Habitat: Chaparral, sagebrush, open woodland.
Host plant: Grossulariaceae family including gooseberry.
Wingspan: 30–35mm (1¼–1⅜).
Status: Not listed, although a subspecies is critically endangered.

Identification: Underwings of both, shown here, are brown-grey with black spots. Male upperwings are copper-brown with iridescent purple sheen, females are brown with orange markings. Hindwings have white crescents under the margin.

American Copper

Lycaena phlaeas

The American or Small Copper may be small, but it makes up for this by being one of the most territorial and aggressive members of the Copper family. There are one or two generations in northern parts of its range, May to June and August to October, and three generations from April to September in the south. The males patrol their territory and chase away any other butterfly that intrudes. They are frequently seen basking in the sun while they wait for females to fly by. The females lay their eggs on the underside of leaves of the sorrel family. The caterpillars hatch and feed on the surface of the leaves leaving tell-tale surface damage. The pupae overwinter and emerge the following spring. The species is still relatively abundant, and this is due in part to it being a generalist. Its food plant is common, enabling it to colonize a range of habitats.

Identification: Variable shades of orange. Upper forewing orange with darker orange bands at tips, with dark spots. Upper hindwing dark bronze with tiny patches of blue scales. Underwings grey, lower hindwings submarginal row of orange zigzags.

Distribution: Europe, North Africa, Asia to Japan, North America.
Habitat: Heaths, moorland, grassland, parks, coastal cliffs.
Food plant: *Rumex acetosa* (common sorrel) and *R. acetosella* (sheep's sorrel).
Wingspan: 24–30mm (1–1¼in).
Status: Not listed.

Above: The caterpillar is variable in colour. It is usually green but some have red lines down the back and sides. The short white hairs covering the body aid camouflage.

Mormon Metalmark

Apodemia mormo

Distribution: United States.
Habitat: Arid grassland and desert.
Food plant: *Eriogonum* (Wild buckwheat).
Wingspan: 21–33mm (¾–1¼in).
Status: Not listed, although one subspecies Critically Endangered.

Identification: Upperwings orange-brown to black, with chequered squares of pearly white with black borders. Red patch on forewing. Lower forewing pale brown with white squares with white spots, Lower hindwing grey to white with white squares and other shapes.

The characteristic pose of the Metalmark is a butterfly perched vertically, with either head up or down, in bright sunshine. This is a swift-flying butterfly found on dry grassland and desert habitats. Its metallic colours reflect light as its flies, making it difficult to follow against the sand and desert rocks. It flies between July and September in the north, and March to October in the south. The males perch and wait for the females, which lay their eggs in small clusters of up to four eggs on the leaves of the host plant. The caterpillars shelter during the day, and feed by night. There are a number of subspecies, of which one, *Apodemia mormo langei*, is Critically Endangered. It occurs only in California, where it is suffering from loss of habitat.

OTHER SPECIES OF NOTE

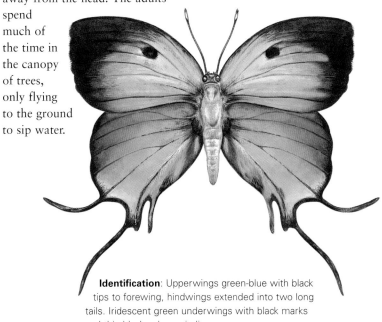

Bitias Hairstreak *Thecla bitias*
The stunning metallic blue wings of the male are conspicuous in the tropical rainforests of South America. However, at rest the butterfly raises its wings to reveal a dull brown underside with a hairstreak, which provides camouflage. The females have blue wings too, but their wings are much duller with black borders.

Thecla draudti
This Central American hairstreak has hindwings with four tails of differing lengths. The upperwings are metallic green while the lower wings are a mix of iridescent green, black, and red.

Jamaican Hairstreak *Callophrys crethona*
An attractive tailed butterfly has blue upper wings. The hind wings have a distinctive red eyespot at the base of the longer tail. The under wings are green and brown with a pale hair streak.

Imperial Sunstreak

Arcas imperialis

This genus of butterflies occurs mostly in South America, from Mexico to Bolivia and in Columbia. The butterflies have a unique wing profile. The forewings are rounded and elongated, while the hindwings are pulled out into two unequal tails. Some have hairy tails that they move constantly to confuse predators and to direct any attack away from the head. The adults spend much of the time in the canopy of trees, only flying to the ground to sip water.

Distribution: Southern Mexico to Brazil and Ecuador.
Habitat: Varied from sea level to 1,500m, rainforests.
Food plant: Uncertain.
Wingspan: 20–22mm (¾–⅞in).
Status: Not listed.

Identification: Upperwings green-blue with black tips to forewing, hindwings extended into two long tails. Iridescent green underwings with black marks and thin black submargin line.

Cranberry Blue

Vacciniina optilete

This violet-blue butterfly has a widespread distribution from North America across Northern Asia to Europe. It is found in a variety of habitats including montane forests, scrub, open moorland, bog and tundra. There is a single generation which is on the wing from June through to August. The butterfly has a weak flight, staying close to the ground. The females lay their eggs on plants belonging to the Ericaeae family, such as the cranberry and blueberry (*Vaccinium* sp.). Approximately halfway through their development, the caterpillars overwinter and complete their growth the following year.

Distribution: North America from Alaska to Western Canada, North Eurasia, Mongolia, Korea and Japan. **Habitat**: Bogs, heathland, wet tundra. **Food plant**: *Vaccinium* sp. such as cranberries and blueberries. **Wingspan**: 22–25mm (⅞–1in). **Status**: Not listed.

Identification: Upperwings violet blue, undersides blue with row of black spots and a single large orange spot and pair of blue spots, hindwings single black edged spot. Females dark scales on upperwings.

Pygmy Blue

Brephidium exilis

Distribution: California to Texas and south of Mexico, Hawaii. **Habitat**: Coastal, disturbed ground such as wasteland, gardens. **Food plant**: *Chenopodium* sp, *Atriplex* sp. **Wingspan**: 12–15mm (½–⅝in). **Status**: Not listed.

Identification: Upperwings brown, blue towards the base, white margin, underwings light brown to grey, blue towards the base, with four black submarginal spots and four black dots near margin.

This small blue butterfly is the smallest butterfly in North America, with a wingspan of just over a centimetre. It has a weak flight and it flutters slowly from one food plant to another. It is on the wing for much of the year, but is particularly common in autumn when large groups can be seen. There are several generations each year. This species has benefited from using weed species, such as goosefoot and tumbleweed, as its food plants, which occur widely and are increasing. There are two subspecies, the Western Pygmy Blue and the Eastern Pygmy Blue.

OTHER SPECIES OF NOTE

Eumaeus minyas
A black-winged butterfly with rows of blue-green iridescent spots along the hindwing. The lower side of the hindwing has a red-orange spot and three rows of pale blue spots below the margin. It occurs through Bolivia and Peru.

Estemopsis inaria thyatira
This is a genus of South American butterflies that occur in the Amazonian rainforest. The upper wings of the male are bright orange with thick dark borders. The females are paler with orange-yellow colours.

Spring Azure *Celastrina ladon*
The Spring Azure is found from Alaska to Canada, occurring as far south as Columbia. It is found along the edges of woodlands, wooded swamps and wetlands. Food plants include meadowsweet (*Spiraea salicifolia*) and dogwood (*Cornus florida*). Adults are seen from April to June. The species is easily confused with the Summer Azure (*C. neglecta*) and the Appalachian Azure (*C. neglectamajor*).

Miami Blue

Cyclargus thomasi bethunebakeri

Distribution: Florida.
Habitat: Tropical coastal hummocks.
Food plant: Balloon vine (*Cardiospermum corrindum*), yellow nickerbean (*Caesalpinia bonduc*).
Wingspan: 22–30mm (⅞–1¼in).
Status: Subspecies listed as Endangered in Florida.

This small butterfly is only found in Florida in the United States, with a couple of other subspecies of *Cyclargus thomasi* in the Caribbean. There are several generations each year, with a short dormant period in winter. The females lay their eggs on the balloon vine and yellow nickerbean. The caterpillars are variable in colour, ranging from green to almost red-brown, and they feed on the flower buds. Like many species of blues, they are tended by ants. This butterfly was once abundant and widespread, but has suffered a severe decline in recent decades due to the urbanization and loss of habitat. Now a single, small colony remains within Bahia Honda State Park in the Florida Keys. The University of Florida is managing a captive breeding programme.

Left: The female has a different appearance from the male, with a row of orange and black eyespots on the upper hindwings.

Identification: Male upperwings bright blue. Female upperwings grey with blue towards the wing bases and orange-capped black submarginal eyespots on each hindwing. Underwings of both grey, with white band and four basal black spots.

Eastern Tailed Blue

Everes comyntas

Distribution: Eastern North America, south to Costa Rica.
Habitat: Weedy habitats such as waste ground.
Food plant: Papilionaceae e.g. *Melilotus* sp., *Medicago* sp., *Vicia* sp. *Trifolium* sp..
Wingspan: 15–20mm (⅝–¾in).
Status: Not listed.

These blues are found in sunny, open habitats where there are weeds, so they are widely distributed. In the northern parts of their distribution there are three generations between April and November, while in the south there are multiple generations throughout the year. The males patrol the food plants, watching for females. The females lay their eggs on the flower buds of the plants of the pea family. The caterpillars feed on the flower buds, flowers and even the seeds. Caterpillars of the last generation of the year overwinter and pupate the following spring.

Identification: Sexes different. Male upperwings iridescent blue, hindwings have a narrow tail. Undersides of male and female pale grey with black bar and black spots, three orange spots near base of tail.

Right: There are two forms of female. The spring female (top right) has blue-grey upperwings with a flush of blue at the base, while the summer form (bottom right) has brown wings.

BRUSH-FOOTED BUTTERFLIES

This varied family of butterflies is well-represented across the region, with more than 200 species in North America and more than 1,000 in Central and South America. Among the tropical representatives are the well-known Heliconids, Morphos and Owl butterflies. Most adult species have a reduced pair of forelegs, which gives the family its name of brush-footed or four-footed butterflies.

Red Admiral

Vanessa atalanta

The name of Red Admiral comes from the 18th-century word 'admirable', as the red bands reminded people of uniforms. This fast-flying butterfly is found along hedgerows, woodland glades and gardens. It is territorial and the males patrol a small sunny territory and chase off other butterflies. Unusually for butterflies, the Red Admiral may fly at night. The adult butterflies visit a range of flowers, including the teasel, clover and ivy. In autumn they gather in numbers to sip the juice of fallen apples. In late spring the females lay single eggs on the upper surface of nettle leaves. The caterpillar is spiny, ranging in colour from olive-brown to almost black with white dots, and a broken band of yellow along each side. The caterpillar makes a silken tent from folded leaves held together by silk threads in which it hides while it feeds and rests. The chrysalis forms inside the caterpillar's last tent. Red Admirals are a migratory species, being summer visitors in the northerly parts of their range.

Distribution: North and Central America, across Europe and Asia to Iran, Australia, Africa north of the Sahara.
Habitat: Wide ranging, including grassland, mountain and garden.
Food plant: *Urtica* sp. (nettles).
Wingspan: 62–64mm (2¼–2½in).
Status: Not listed.

Identification: FW distinctive diagonal red band on a black background with white markings near the tip. HW edged with red with tiny black spots and a blue patch at the bottom. Underwing of FW a paler version of the upperside, HW mottled brown.

Camberwell Beauty or Mourning Cloak

Nymphalis antiopa

This attractive and distinctive butterfly was named after the village of Camberwell, now part of London, in 1748. It had other names, such as White Petticoat, which referred to the white margins of the wings. It is a migrant species that extends its range northwards in summer. However, the migrants rarely survive the cold northern winters. Being a strong flier it can fly across stretches of water, such as the North Sea from Scandinavia to Britain. It is seen from March to August, flying in areas that are populated by willow trees. The female lays her eggs on willow leaves. The adults hibernate from late summer to early spring and during this time their colours become quite faded, especially the borders, which become white and the wings ragged.

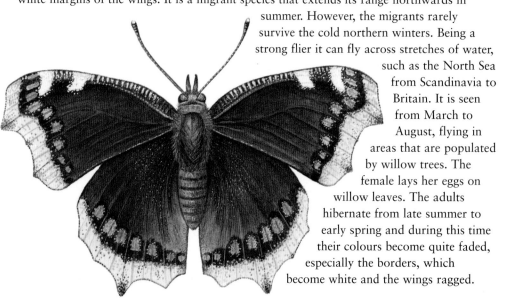

Distribution: North America, Europe.
Habitat: Damp woodland with willow.
Food plant: *Salix* sp. (willow).
Wingspan: 60–65mm (2¼–2½in).
Status: Not listed.

Identification: Dark maroon wings with cream margins, with sub marginal row of blue spots on both wings. Underwings similar but lack the blue spots.

American Painted Lady

Vanessa virginiensis

Distribution: Southern US to Columbia, Canary Islands, Madeira, Hawaii, Galapagos.
Habitat: Meadows, parks and gardens, wasteland.
Food plant: Various including Asteraceae, Malvaceae, Fabaceae, Urticaceae, Scrophulariaceae, Boraginaceae.
Wingspan: 45–67mm (1¾–2⅝in).
Status: Not listed.

The American Painted Lady, or simply the American Lady, flies all year through much of its range, and there are as many as four generations. It is a strong flier, and this has enabled it to colonize islands such as the Galapagos, Hawaii and the Canary Islands. It is a migratory species that flies north and westward each year, appearing across the the northern United States and to the Caribbean, where it is seen from May to November. The adults feed on nectar from a wide range of flowers such as aster, goldenrod and marigold. The females lay their eggs on the leaves of the food plant. The caterpillars are solitary, and they live inside a tent of leaves held together with silken threads. The adult overwinters. Although the migrant butterfly can breed during the summer, the adults are unable to survive the cold winters.

Identification: Wings patterned brown, yellow and orange. FW black apical patch, with small white spot below, white bar at leading edge. LHW two eyespots. Winter form smaller and paler.

OTHER SPECIES OF NOTE

Lorquin's Admiral *Limenitis lorquini*
The upperwings of this North American butterfly are black with white bands on both wings, with an orange tip to the forewing. The larval plant of this species include cherries, willows, cottonwoods and orchard trees.

Red-spotted Admiral *Limenitis arthemis*
There are three forms of *Limenitis arthemis* which occur in North America; the northern black and white form, which is often called the White Admiral, the western form with red spots on the hindwing, and is called the Western White Admiral, and the southern form which is black and purple, and called the Red Spotted purple.

Band-celled Sister *Adelpha fessonia*
This butterfly has brown wings with an orange apex to the forewings and a white diagonal band across the fore and hindwing, forming a distinctive 'V' shape. This butterfly is found in the southern United States and south to Central America where it is seen from March to December, and in the tropical part of its range where it is seen all year round. Its food plant includes the hackberry (*Celtis lindheimeri*).

Painted Lady

Cynthia cardui

The Painted Lady is the world's most widespread butterfly. This powerful flier can reach speeds of 15km/h (9m/hr) and fly distances of 1,000km (620 miles). It is a migrant species, and swarms of many thousands fly across the Mediterranean from North Africa and spread out over Europe. It is a highly adaptable butterfly, and able to feed on a wide range of plants. Its northerly distribution is limited by its inability to survive cold winters. It is likely to benefit from global warming, as more northerly regions become warmer in winter. The female lays single eggs on the underside of leaves of thistles, mallow, burdock and nettles. The caterpillar is black with yellow or black spines and yellow stripe along each side. It spins a silken web over the underside of a leaf, under which it hides, while eating the leaf. Eventually it forms a tent over several leaves and pupates inside the tent. The pupa is grey-pink with gold highlights.

Distribution: North and Central America, Europe and Asia, Australasia and North Africa.
Habitat: Meadows, hedgerow, waste land, garden.
Food plant: Many, including the thistle and mallow.
Wingspan: 57mm (2⅛).
Status: Not listed.

Identification: Forewing chequered black, brown and orange, almost black tips with small white spots. Small patch of blue on bottom corner of hindwings. Undersides of forewings similar pattern, undersides of hindwings mottled brown, grey, white and blue with small blue and black eyespots.

Variable Cracker

Hamadryas feronia

The Variable Cracker gets its name from the cracking noise made by the males when they fly. The sound is believed to be produced when swollen veins in the forewing rub each other during the upstroke of the wing. It is on the wing all year round in the southern parts of its range but only seen from July to December in Texas. The adults perch head down on tree trunks with their wings open, the patterned brown colours providing good camouflage. They descend to the ground to feed on dung and the juices of rotting fruits. The females lay their eggs on vines of the Euphorbia family.

Distribution: Texas, south to Argentina.
Habitat: Edges of tropical forests, second growth tropical forests.
Food plant: *Dalechampia* (Euphorbiaceae).
Wingspan: 70–85mm (2¾–3¼in).
Status: Not listed.

Identification: Upper forewings brown and white, red bar near leading edge. Hindwings patterned brown with eyespots that are black and white surrounded by blue line. Underwings white-brown or white, with submarginal black spots on lower hindwing.

OTHER SPECIES OF NOTE

Tropical Leafwing *Anaea aidea*
The under wings of this tropical butterfly resemble a dead leaf, providing excellent camouflage when it rests on the ground. The adults feed on dung and decaying fruits on the ground. They fly along the edge of tropical forests and the banks of streams. from the Southern United States to Costa Rica. It is becoming increasingly rare at the extremes of its range.

Queen Cracker *Hamadryas arethusa*
The male Queen Cracker has beautiful velvet black wings with iridescent blue spots while the female's black wing has more blue spots and a white band in the centre of the forewing. Like all crackers, the males make a crackling sound when they fly. This species occurs in Central America and the Caribbean.

Stinky Leafwing *Historis odius*
The Stinky Leafwing occurs in Central and South America as well as the West Indies. It is a large black and orange butterfly that inhabits tropical forest. It is a strong-flying butterfly, which perches on tree trunks with its head pointing downwards. Its food plant is the Cecropia tree.

Common Buckeye

Junonia coenia

A common butterfly, often spotted resting in a sunny spot on bare ground, surrounded by low vegetation. The distinctive eyespots on the uppersides of the wings are believed to startle and deter predators. The butterfly flies all year in the southern parts of its range and from March to October elsewhere, and there are several generations each year. The summer generations are migratory and fly north. There are two seasonal forms, an example of seasonal polymorphism. Although the males are not territorial they patrol and perch on shrubs to watch for females. The caterpillar is green-black with orange and yellow markings.

Distribution: Southern United States, Mexico, Caribbean.
Habitat: Grassland, waste ground, gardens, parks.
Food plant: Varied, especially Scrophulariaceae e.g. *Plantago* sp., *Antirrhinum* sp..
Wingspan: 50–65 mm (2–2½in).
Status: Not listed.

Identification: Brown scalloped wings. Upper forewing has two orange bars and a creamy-white band, two eyespots. Upper hindwing has submarginal orange band and two eyespots. Underwings; summer form brown, autumn form red-pink.

California Ringlet

Coenonympha california

Distribution: North America, from Alaska to New Mexico and east to New England.
Habitat: Grassland, meadows, tundra.
Food plant: Grass species.
Wingspan: 34–38mm (1⅜-1½in)
Status: Not listed.

Identification: Wings pale cream to yellow-brown. Lower forewing has small eyespot near tip. Lower hindwing is grey-green with wavy white line across the middle.

This species is often mistaken for a white Pierid butterfly due to its plain white wings. However, Pierids have a much longer length of forewing. It is a weak flier, staying close to the ground. For this reason it tends to prefer low-growing grassland habitats. It flies from March to August, and there are as many as three generations. The females lay their eggs on the leaves of grasses. The summer butterflies have wings with a yellowish-brown hue, unlike those of the spring generation which are white. The summer butterflies undergo a short dormant period before becoming active again in September. The caterpillars overwinter among leaves of dead grass.

Question Mark

Polygonia interrogationis

The unusual name of the Question Mark butterfly comes from the silver-white marking on the underside of the hindwing that resembles a question mark. The adult butterflies emerge in spring, and the females lay their eggs on the plants that unusually are not the food plant. The caterpillars hatch and then crawl over the ground in search of their food plant, including elm, nettle, and hackberry. These caterpillars pupate and emerge as the summer form butterfly. The summer form has a black hindwing with a short tail. It flies from May to September. Its eggs develop into winter-form adults which have orange and black hindwings with violet-tipped tails. This butterfly emerges in August and overwinters.

Identification: FW hooked, red-orange, black spots, UHW black with tail. Underwing light brown. LHW white question mark in centre. Summer and winter forms.

Left: The winter-form butterfly has orange and black hindwings. In summer, the upperwings are predominantly orange with a longer tail.

Distribution: Southern Canada, Eastern United States.
Habitat: Woodlands, parks and gardens.
Food plant: *Celtis* sp., *Ulmus* sp., *Urtica* sp..
Wingspan: 57–76mm (2⅛–3in).
Status: Not listed.

Great Spangled Fritillary

Speyeria cybele

Distribution: Eastern
North America.
Habitat: Temperate forest,
meadows, prairie.
Food plant: *Viola* sp..
Wingspan: 70–100mm
(2¾–4in).
Status: Not listed.

Identification: Wings scalloped.
Male upperwings orange-brown
with black scales, female tawny
brown. Undersides of both brown
with pale submarginal band, and
silver spots.

These large and common fritillaries get their
name from the black spots along the edges
of the wings. They are seen in the eastern
temperate forests and meadows of North
America from June to September. There is a
single generation and the adults feed on the
nectar of a range of forest flowers such as
milkweeds, verbena and purple coneflower.
The females lay their eggs on or near to the
food plant, violets. However, the caterpillars
do not feed when they hatch but overwinter.
They become active in spring, feeding on the
young leaves of the violet.
The caterpillars have a
black body with large
orange spines.

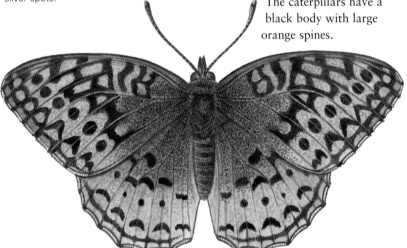

OTHER SPECIES OF NOTE

Mexican Fritillary *Dione moneta*
The Mexican Fritillary, or Mexican Silverspot, is
found from the southern United States, south
through Central and South America. Its food
plant is the passion vine, *Passiflora* sp..

Gulf Fritillary *Agraulis vanillae*
This bright orange butterfly is found from the
southern United States to northern parts
of South America. It prefers secondary
subtropical forests where its food plants, the
common buckeyeplant and the passion vine
(*Passiflora* sp.) can become established. It is a
migratory species that appears in the midwest
United States.

Great Basin Fritillary *Speyeria eglais*
This fritillary occurs in the western half of
North America from British Columbia south to
California, where it inhabits mountain meadows
and forests. There is a single generation on the
wing from June to August. The food plant is the
violet (*Viola* sp.) The caterpillars hatch but do
not feed. Instead, they overwinter and emerge
the following spring when there are plenty of
violet leaves to feed upon.

Nokomis Fritillary

Speyeria nokomis

This butterfly is seen in damp meadows and along streams from July to September.
The adults feed on nectar from flowers such as thistles. The males are seen patrolling for the
females. There is a single generation. The females lay their eggs on the ground close to
the food plant, violets. The caterpillars
hatch and do not feed. They overwinter
and then become
active in spring,
when they feed
on violet leaves.
This species is in
a decline due to the
loss of its habitat
through drainage
schemes and increasing
urbanization.

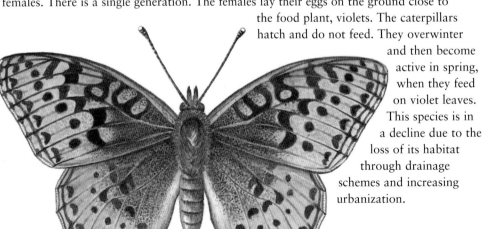

Distribution: Western
United States, Mexico.
Habitat: Damp meadows,
marshland, banks of streams
and ditches.
Food plant: *Viola* sp..
Wingspan: 60–80mm
(2¼–3⅛in).
Status: Not listed but
requiring conservation.

Identification: Male upperwings
brown-orange with dark markings,
female outer half of the forewing
brown with cream spots, basal
half brown with dark markings.
Underwings of both brown with
dark markings, Lower hindwing
black bordered with silver spots.

The Diana

Speyeria diana

Distribution: North America
Habitat: Montane forest
and meadow.
Food plant: *Viola* sp..
Wingspan: 85–115mm
(3¼–6in).
Status: Not listed, but
considered Vulnerable
in parts of its range.

*Below: The female has blue-black
wings with lighter blue patches
and white spots towards the
wing margin.*

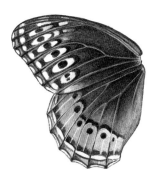

This large, attractive butterfly is found
along the edge of montane forest where
its food plant, the violet,
can be found.
There is one
generation
that flies
from June to
September. The
males are the first to
emerge in spring, and they
patrol the forests looking
for females. In August, the
females lay their eggs singly on
twigs and leaves on the ground.
The caterpillars hatch but do not
feed. Instead, they hibernate until spring when they become
active and start feeding on the leaves and flowers of violets.
The species is under threat from both collecting and from
habitat loss. Its main distribution is in the Southern
Appalachians, where forests are being lost due to logging,
pests and from the activities of the strip mining industry.

Identification: Sexes different.
Male upperwings, basal half
black, outer half orange with black
spots and veins. Female outer
half of wings are black with white
spots, with blue spots on outer
hindwing. Undersides are dark
green-brown.

Regal Fritillary

Speyeria idalia

Distribution: Eastern
United States.
Habitat: Prairies.
Food plant: *Viola* sp..
Wingspan: 70–100mm
(2¾–4in).
Status: Not listed.

Identification: Sexes different.
Male upper forewings orange
with black markings, upper
hindwings brown-orange with
row of orange spots and white
spots. Female upper forewings
orange with black markings and
submarginal row of white spots,
upper hindwings brown to black
with yellow spots.

*Right: The female has a dark
patch at the apex to the forewing
and a row of white spots.*

This striking
orange and
black
butterfly is
seen only on
tall grass prairie.
From a distance it is
easy to confuse with the
more common Monarch.
The butterfly is on the wing
during the summer months,
and there is a single generation.
Unlike other species of fritillary, the
Regal Fritillary females do not lay their eggs close to the
food plants but instead almost anywhere on the prairie.
The caterpillars have to find suitable food plants, such as
the birdsfoot violet and the prairie violet. For this reason,
the females lay several thousand eggs, far more than
other species. The newly hatched caterpillars overwinter,
and start feeding the following spring. The caterpillars
are black and yellow with spines. The range of this
butterfly has declined over the last 50 years due to its
dependence on the prairie species of violets. Prairie
grassland has been ploughed up for farmland, and the
populations of the Regal Fritillary have become fragmented.

Arctic Fritillary

Clossiana chariclea or *Boloria chariclea*

Distribution: North America, Northern Asia.
Habitat: Tundra, alpine meadows, taiga.
Food plant: *Viola* sp., *Salix* sp., *Vaccinium* sp..
Wingspan: 30–39mm (1¼–1½in).
Status: Not listed.

Identification: Orange-brown wings with dark markings. Lower hindwings brown, orange to purple with silver-white spots.

The Arctic Fritillary is one of the few butterflies to be able to survive the freezing temperatures of the high Arctic. It is active from June to August and there is a single generation. The males are seen patrolling along the edge of bogs and in valleys, searching for females. They feed on nectar from flowers of the goldenrod. The females lay their eggs singly on the leaves of a variety of bog plants such as violets and blueberries. The newly hatched caterpillars overwinter and become active in spring, when they feed on leaves. However, they are slow-growing, and in some places the caterpillar overwinters again. It pupates and emerges as an adult in early summer.

Polar Fritillary

Clossiana polaris, Boloria polaris

This Arctic butterfly is on the wing from June to July, although in parts of Labrador in Canada it can be seen to the end of August. It is found on ridges within the tundra and on the flat, rocky areas that occur below mountain summits where they can find their food plants. On hatching, the caterpillars overwinter and then become active the following summer. The caterpillar is pale brown with black spines.

Distribution: Alaska, Northern Canada, Greenland, Northern Europe.
Habitat: Tundra.
Food plant: *Dryas octopetala* (mountain avens), *Vaccinium uliginosum* (blueberry).
Wingspan: 30–39mm (1¼–1½in).
Status: Not listed.

Identification: Upperwings orange-brown with black markings. LHW frosted white and brown with submarginal black triangles, black spots.

OTHER SPECIES OF NOTE

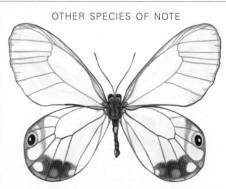

Cithaerias esmeralda
This South American butterfly is one of a genus of ten rainforest butterflies that have mostly transparent wings and very thin bodies. There is an eyespot on each hindwing. While most rainforest butterflies seek out sunlit clearings, these butterflies are seen flying in the darkest parts of the rainforest.

Caligo idomeneus
This is a particularly large owl butterfly, reaching up to 140mm (5½in) across. It is seen at dawn and dusk. The females lay their eggs on leaves of bananas (*Musa* sp.) and in some places are considered to be a pest of banana plantations.

Cocoa Mort Blue *Caligo teucer*
From the underside this huge butterfly looks like the other Owl butterflies with its prominent eyespot. However, its upperwings are black and iridescent blue. It is found in the Caribbean, and its striking colours make it a target for collectors.

Julia

Dryas julia

The distinctive bright orange colours of the Julia make it an easy butterfly to identify. It flies throughout the year in much of its range. It is a strong flier, and in summer flies north to central parts of the United States. The adults feed on nectar from flowers such as the creeping Lantana. They are seen to have regular routes along which they fly in search of food. The males patrol the edge of woodlands looking for females. The Julia's bright colours act as a warning to predators that it is unpalatable. The females lay their eggs singly on the young leaves of the passion vine. The caterpillars are brown with white spots and have spiky outgrowths on each segment.

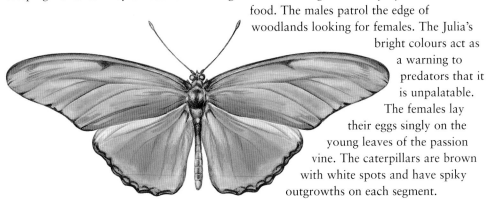

Distribution: Southern United States south to Brazil. **Habitat**: Edges of Subtropical hammock woodland and surrounding fields. **Food plant**: *Passiflora* sp.. **Wingspan**: 80–95mm (3⅛–3¾in). **Status**: Not listed.

Identification: Forewing elongated. Sexes different; males bright orange, lower hindwing narrow black border along outer margin. Females dull orange with more black markings.

Owl Butterfly

Caligo memnon

This is a member of the genus of Owl butterflies, large butterflies with distinctive patterned wings which bear prominent owl-like eyespots on the underwings. The eyespots are conspicuous when the butterflies rest with their wings raised, and are designed to startle and scare away would-be predators. The butterflies are active all year, and occur in particularly large numbers during the rainy season. They are seen at dawn and dusk, when they seek out rotting fruit on the forest floor. The females lay their eggs on leaves of the banana and *Heliconia*. The large caterpillars are shades of brown with black spikes and have an armoured head piece. Additional protection is gained from an unpleasant secretion that is released when threatened.

Identification: Upper forewings basal pale cream-brown, outerwing brown, upper hindwings brown to black with lighter marks. Underwings patterned brown and grey with eyespots, one large with black centre surrounded by cream and dark brown.

Distribution: Central and South America. **Habitat**: Tropical forests. **Food plant**: *Musa* sp., *Heliconia* sp.. **Wingspan**: 120–130mm (4¾–5⅛in). **Status**: Not listed.

Below: The distinctive owl-like eyespots on the lower underwings, which give the butterfly its name, are only revealed when the butterfly lifts its wings.

California Patch

Chlosyne californica

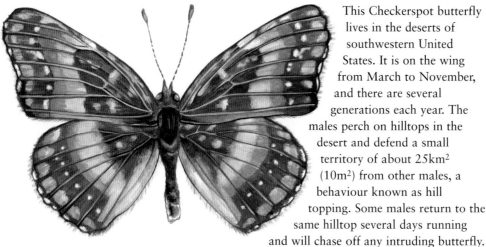

This Checkerspot butterfly lives in the deserts of southwestern United States. It is on the wing from March to November, and there are several generations each year. The males perch on hilltops in the desert and defend a small territory of about 25km² (10m²) from other males, a behaviour known as hill topping. Some males return to the same hilltop several days running and will chase off any intruding butterfly. A female flying into a territory is pursued and mated by the resident male. The females lay their eggs in small groups on the underside of leaves of the food plant. The caterpillars feed on the leaves, then overwinter before completing their growth and pupating in spring.

Distribution: Southwest United States and Mexico.
Habitat: Desert canyons.
Food plant: Asteraceae such as *Viguira deltoides* and *Helianthus annuus*.
Wingspan: 32–35mm (1¼–1⅜in).
Status: Not listed.

Identification: Variable. Upperwings brown-black with orange band across the middle, large orange submarginal spots and row of smaller white spots. Lower hindwing light orange with red spot near the base and white spots.

Silvery Checkerspot

Chlosyne nycteis

Distribution: Eastern United States.
Habitat: Meadows, clearings in forests, banks of streams and rivers.
Food plant: Compositae including *Rudbeckia* sp. (black-eyed Susan), and *Helianthus* (sunflower).
Wingspan: 35–50mm (1⅜–2in).
Status: Not listed.

The Silvery Checkerspot is seen from May to September over much of its range, although in the more northerly areas it flies in June and July. There are as many as four generations in the south. The males perch in prominent positions and patrol in their search for females. The females lay clusters of up to 100 eggs on the underside of leaves of the food plant. The caterpillars are black with black spines. They stay together, steadily eating the leaves of the plant. Caterpillars of the last generation overwinter and complete their growth in spring. The white-centred black spots near the margin of the upper hindwing are features that distinguish it from similar species such as the Pearl Crescent (*Phyciodes tharos*) butterfly.

Identification: Upperwings orange to yellow with black borders and markings. Hindwings white-centred submarginal spots. Underwings creamy-yellow with brown markings, submarginal orange line and large white crescent-shaped spots.

OTHER SPECIES OF NOTE

Orange-banded Shoemaker *Catonephele orites*
This Central and South American butterfly gets is name from the distinctive orange band across the black wings of the male. The species shows sexual dimorphism as the female has black wings with blue spots.

Queen Butterfly *Danaus gilippus*
The Queen Butterfly is similar to the Monarch and the Viceroy with its orange and black markings. This poisonous species is distinguished by the lack of black veins on the forewings and white spots, which are particularly noticeable. The caterpillar gains its toxin from the leaves of its food plant, the milkweed. The butterflies are on the wing all year round in Florida and Texas, Central and South America, but are seen only in July and August in the central states of the USA, where it is a migrant species.

Little Soldier *Chlosyne saundersii*
This orange-brown butterfly is found from Mexico to Paraguay and in the Caribbean. The wings have a black border and black base, although there is considerable variation over the range. It is considered by some to be a subspecies of the Bordered Patch (*Chlosyne lacinia*). The caterpillar is a pest of the sunflower (*Helianthus annuus*) in Venezuela and Brazil.

Monarch

Danaus plexippus

Distribution: North and South America, Australia, New Zealand, parts of Asia, Canary Islands, southern Europe.
Habitat: Meadows, grassland, waste land, gardens.
Food plant: *Asclepsis* (milkweed).
Wingspan: 86–120mm (3¼in–4¾in).
Status: Not listed, although the migration is classed as a Threatened Phenomena by IUCN and overwintering sites are protected.

The Monarch is probably the best known butterfly in North America. It overwinters in huge numbers in specific forests in California and Mexico. A powerful flier, in spring it flies north and may occasionally cross the Atlantic to reach Europe and North Africa. Monarchs in South America and Australia exhibit similar migratory patterns. There are several generations a year, and adults of the last generation return to the overwintering sites. The distinctive orange and black colours are a warning to predators that it is poisonous. The poison comes from the food plant, the milkweed, which is eaten by the caterpillars.

Identification: Bright orange wings with black borders, black veins and white spots on borders and toward tip. Hindwings have patch of scent scales. Female has wider black borders and thicker veins.

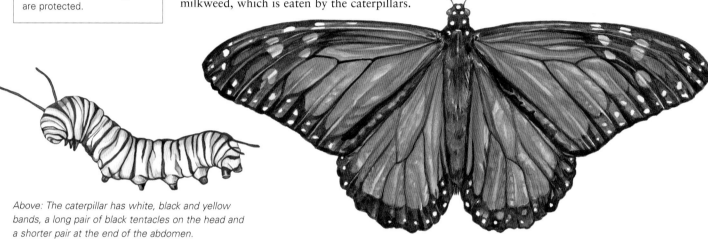

Above: The caterpillar has white, black and yellow bands, a long pair of black tentacles on the head and a shorter pair at the end of the abdomen.

Viceroy

Basilarchia archippus

The Viceroy, found throughout North America, looks very similar to several species of Danidae, including the Monarch and Queen Butterfly, although it is the only one to have a black band across the hindwing. For a while, scientists believed that the Viceroy used mimicry to gain protection, but in fact the Viceroy is also poisonous. This is an example of Müllerian mimicry, in which one poisonous species mimics another to reinforce the message that it is poisonous and should be avoided. The adults fly from May to August and there are two generations. In Florida it is on the wing all year round. It can be found in or near wet meadows with willow trees. The caterpillars are active at night, feeding on the leaves and catkins of the willow. The young caterpillars build a leaf ball from bits of leaves stuck together with silk. These are dangled from the leaves on which they are feeding to distract predators.

Identification: Orange wings with black borders and veins, white spots with a black band across the hindwings.

Distribution: North America.
Habitat: Wet meadows with willow, gardens.
Food plant: *Salix* sp. (willow).
Wingspan: 60–70mm (2¼–2¾in).
Status: Not listed.

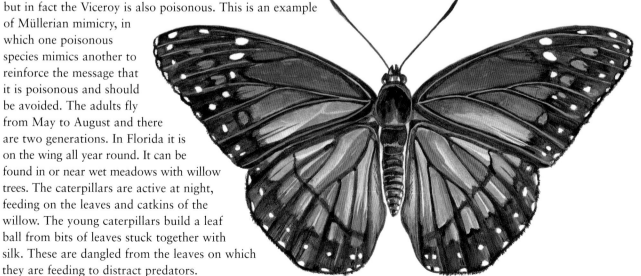

Hackberry Emperor

Asterocampa celtis

Distribution: Eastern United States, Mexico.
Habitat: Deciduous woodland with hackberries.
Food plant: *Celtis* sp. (hackberry).
Wingspan: 40–60mm 1½–2¼in).
Status: Not listed.

Identification: Variable. Upperwings yellow, red and brown, forewings have submarginal eyespot and scattered white-yellow spots, black bar and black spots. Hindwings pale yellow-brown with submarginal black jagged line and row of black spots.

The Hackberry Emperor is a fast-flying butterfly that is seen from May to October. There are two generations. The adults are seen resting head-down on tree trunks, and they feed on plant sap, fluid from dung and carrion, and even human sweat. The males perch while they wait for females to fly by. The females lay their eggs in clusters on the food plant. The caterpillars are bright green with yellow, buff and blue-green stripes, and spikes at the head and tail ends. They stay together and at the end of autumn they overwinter together, protected inside rolled up dead leaves on the ground.

OTHER SPECIES OF NOTE

Blue Night *Cepheuptychia cephus*
The male Blue Night has iridescent blue fore- and hindwings edged in black. The females are brown with a thin blue line around the outer margins. It is a day-flying species, occurring in Columbia and Brazil.

Sparkling Cherub *Doxocopa cherubina*
This striking blue and brown butterfly is found in the forests of Central and South America. It is often seen on the forest floor feeding on rotting fruit and carrion.

Appalachian Brown *Satyrodes Appalachia*
This brown butterfly has a series of eyespots on the underwing. Found from Quebec and New England south to Florida, it occurs in wooded swamp and along woodland edges. Its food plant is the sedge (*Carex lacustris*).

Tawny Emperor

Asterocampa clyton

A common butterfly that is seen in a variety of habitats including gardens, gravel driveways, near water, muddy places, and woodlands. It is on the wing from June to August in the north where there is one generation, and from March to November in the south where there are two generations. The males perch in sunny spots watching for females. The females lay their eggs in large clusters on the bark of the hackberry, its only host plant, or on the undersides of the leaves. Adults feed on carrion, dung and plant sap. The caterpillar is green with yellow and pale green stripes, and small spikes on the head and tail. The older caterpillars overwinter together inside rolled up dead leaves.

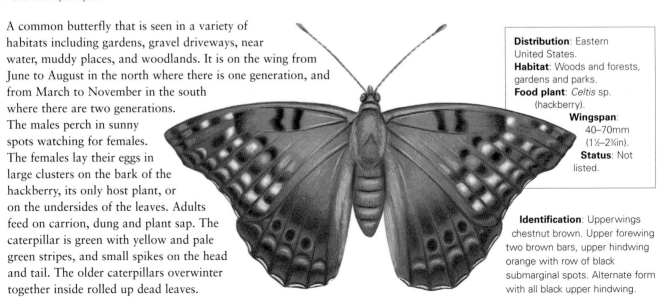

Distribution: Eastern United States.
Habitat: Woods and forests, gardens and parks.
Food plant: *Celtis* sp. (hackberry).
Wingspan: 40–70mm (1½–2¾in).
Status: Not listed.

Identification: Upperwings chestnut brown. Upper forewing two brown bars, upper hindwing orange with row of black submarginal spots. Alternate form with all black upper hindwing.

Silver Emperor

Doxocopa laure

Distribution: Northern Mexico and southern United States to Brazil.
Habitat: Subtropical woodlands.
Food plant: *Celtis* sp. (Ulmaceae).
Wingspan: 70–82mm (2¾–3⅛in).
Status: Not listed.

Identification: Male upperside dark brown, hint of iridescent blue, band across both wings that is orange on forewing and white on hindwing Female upperwings dark brown, white band across both wings ending with yellow spot on leading edge of forewing. Undersides grey with silver.

The Silver Emperor is a woodland butterfly that is seen flying from July to December in the southern United States and all year round in lowland tropics from northern Brazil to northern Mexico. The adults fly down from the canopy to feed on rotting fruit, dung and even carrion on the woodland floor. Here, the wing colours blend well and provide good camouflage. The female lays her eggs singly on the new leaves of the food plant. The caterpillars emerge and feed on the leaves. They find resting perches on the top of the leaves.

Southern Pearly Eye

Enodia portlandia

The Southern Pearly Eye is found in eastern Oklahoma and eastern Texas through the southeastern United States. The males perch on tree trunks, sometimes head downwards, to wait for females. Eggs are laid singly on or near the host plant, bamboo switch cane (*A. tecta*), on which the caterpillars feed when they hatch. Older caterpillars hibernate. There are three generations from March to October. The adults feed on rotting fruit, carrion and dung. The Southern Pearly Eye's preferred habitat is shady, damp woods near stream-fed swamps, but these areas of swamp forest are gradually disappearing in the southeastern United States, and although apparently secure globally, there is some concern that it might be quite rare in parts of its range, especially at the periphery.

Distribution: South east United States.
Habitat: Shady, damp woods.
Food plant: Sap, rotting fruit, carrion.
Wingspan: 55–70mm (2–2¾in).
Status: Not listed.

Identification: Antennal clubs are orange. Upperside is brown with dark eyespots at the margins. Underside is light brown; submarginal row of four or five spots on the forewing is slightly curved and brown line inside this spot row is straight or zigzagged.

Left: A distinctive caterpillar, with horns on the head and tail. The body is brown with dark wavy lines and white dots. There is also a green form.

Zebra

Heliconius charithonia

Distribution: Central and South America, Caribbean, southern states of United States.
Habitat: Tropical hummock, moist forest, meadows.
Food plant: *Passiflora* sp..
Wingspan: 70–100mm (2¾–4in).
Status: Not listed.

Identification: Wings long and narrow. Black, with narrow yellow stripes across both wings.

Right: The early instars are brown, but the later ones are white with black spines.

This striking butterfly is found in tropical forests, where it flies all year round. It is a strong flier and migrates northwards through the USA during the summer months. The adults feed on nectar from the flowers of a wide range of plants, including *Lantana*. At dusk the adults come together to roost, often in groups of up to 30. They will use the same tree each night, dispersing in the morning. The males patrol for females. A male will also sit by a female pupa, waiting for the female butterfly to emerge, at which point it mates with her. He leaves a secretion on her abdomen that repels other males, ensuring that only his sperm fertilize the eggs. The females lay their eggs in clusters of up to 10 or so on the leaves of the food plant. The caterpillars are white with six rows of black spines. Despite its wide distribution, there are few regional differences and only one known subspecies that occurs in dry forest of Ecuador and Peru.

Postman

Heliconius melpomene

This poisonous butterfly is found in tropical rainforest, from Mexico to northern South America, and has a long life span of up to nine months. It has a very variable appearance, and there are about 30 subspecies, each found in a specific area and with a distinctive colour of wing. It is a mimic of *Heliconius erato*. Interestingly, the females in Central America will only lay their eggs on specific species of *Passiflora*, but in South America they lay their eggs on any *Passiflora* species The caterpillars have black thorns and spots on a white body, an orange head with two sharp black horns and a yellow anal plate. They eat the leaves of the passion vine, choosing the young leaves first because they contain less poison. As they grow, they become more tolerant of the poison and start accumulating it in their body.

Distribution: Central America south to Brazil.
Habitat: Rainforest.
Food plant: *Passiflora* sp..
Wingspan: 60–80mm (2¼–3⅛in).
Status: Not listed.

Identification: Many variants of the basic pattern of black-brown wings with orange and yellow or white bands. Most typical; upper forewings black-brown with orange band across middle, upper hindwings black-brown with a band across the basal half.

Sara Heliconian

Heliconius sara

Distribution: Mexico
south to Brazil.
Habitat: Rainforest.
Food plant: *Passiflora* sp..
Wingspan: 55–60mm
(2⅛–2¼in).
Status: Not listed.

Identification: Wings long and
rounded. Upper forewings black
flushed with metallic blue near
the base and crossed by two
broad creamy white bands.
Underwings are dark brown
with red spots at the base.

This rainforest butterfly is seen in
clearings and along the edge of the
forest, where it visits flowers such as
Lantana and *Hamelia* for nectar. Large
numbers gather at dusk to roost together on a
single branch. There are several
generations each
year. Like the
Zebra butterfly,
the males are
attracted to the
female pupae by
pheromones, and they sit
by the pupae waiting for the female
butterfly to emerge. The females lay their yellow eggs on young leaves of the *Passiflora* vine.
The leaves contain a poison that is accumulated by the caterpillars, making them poisonous.
The caterpillars pupate on the vine. The chrysalis is camouflaged to look like a leaf. The
poison is retained within the adult body.

OTHER SPECIES OF NOTE

Tiger Longwing *Heliconius hecale*
This heliconid butterfly, with black, orange and
yellow wings, occurs from Mexico to South
America. It is found in a variety of habitats,
including rainforest, and lays its eggs on a
number of *Passiflora* species.

Banded Orange Heliconian *Dryadula phaetusa*
This butterfly has bright orange-and-black striped
wings, warning of its unpalatability. They are
easily recognized by the distinctive patterns,
elongated forewings and characteristic delicate,
fluttering flight. Large numbers of males are
seen clustered on patches of moist ground,
obtaining essential minerals. It occurs from the
southern United States to Brazil. The female lays
her eggs on leaves of *Passiflora* species.

Little Callicore *Callicore hydaspes*
The Little Callicore has black wings with large
patches of red and iridescent blue on the
uppersides and black with a circular pattern of
yellow lines on the underside. It occurs from
Mexico to Argentina, and is mainly present in
humid forests.

Isabella's Heliconian

Eueides isabella

This brightly coloured butterfly is seen all
year round in the tropical regions of its
range, but only from April to July in
northern Mexico and Texas. It is a
poisonous butterfly and a Müllerian mimic
of poisonous *Danaids*. It prefers hilltops,
where the males are seen patrolling for
females. The adults feed on nectar of white
and yellow flowers, and at night roost alone
on the underside of leaves. The females lay
their eggs singly on the underside of leaves
or tendrils of the food plant. This genus was
once part of the genus *Heliconius*, but has
now been placed in a separate genus.

Distribution: Texas, south
to Brazil, Caribbean.
Habitat: Forest and
woodland edge, scrub.
Food plant: *Passiflora* sp..
Wingspan: 75–90mm
(2¾–3½in).
Status: Not listed.

Identification: Forewing elongated,
rounded tip. UFW black with yellow
and orange stripes, UHW orange
with two black stripes and white
dots along margin. Underwings of
similar pattern. Males have black
antennae, females are yellow.

Blue Morpho

Morpho menelaus

This butterfly is well known for its beautiful iridescent blue wings that catch the light. The colour comes not from a pigment, but from the way light is reflected from the surface of the scales. The butterfly's colours increase its visibility in the gloom of the rainforest, and alerts rival males of its presence. In contrast the dull underside provides camouflage as the butterfly rests with its wings folded up to reveal the brown leaf-like markings.

The butterfly has a slow flight and, as the wings are raised and lowered, the blue appears to flash, appearing and then disappearing and this helps to distract predators. They are seen throughout the forest, especially along streams and above the canopy where groups of males are seen to gather. The females lay their eggs on plants of the pea family. The caterpillar is red-brown with lime green patches and irritating hairs. The butterfly is not considered to be under threat, but is suffering due to deforestation and over-collecting.

Distribution: Central America to Colombia.
Habitat: Tropical rainforest.
Food plant: Papilionaceae.
Wingspan: 180mm (7in).
Status: Not listed.

Identification: Upperwings bright blue with black borders. Underwings mottled brown, black and red with eyespots. Males wings are broader and brighter than females.

Morpho

Morpho cypris

Like all the other butterflies of the genus *Morpho*, this is a brilliantly blue butterfly that is seen flying in the sunshine. It prefers high-altitude rainforest. The females are rarely seen as they stay in the forest canopy. The males are seen flying along the edge of streams and rivers as well as in the canopy, and fly to the ground to feed on the rotting fruit. The females lay their eggs on the *Inga marginata*, a member of the pea family. The older caterpillars are yellow, with thin lines of red and grey. This species is also suffering from loss of habitat and over-collection.

Identification: Male upperwings bright blue with white band and spots, females are larger, upperwings orange brown with brown margin. Underwings of both sexes mottled brown and white, with large eyespots.

Distribution: Panama, Nicaragua to Colombia.
Habitat: Tropical rainforest.
Food plant: *Inga marginata*.
Wingspan: 120–140mm (4¾–5½in).
Status: Not listed.

Below: The eyespots are revealed when the butterfly lifts its wings.

American Snout

Libytheana carinenta

Distribution: Argentina to Mexico, Caribbean, southern United States.
Habitat: Forest, scrub, roadside verge, meadows.
Food plant: *Celtis* sp..
Wingspan: 35–50mm (1⅜–2in).
Status: Not listed.

Identification: Forewing squared end, upper forewing brown with orange at base and along margin, four white spots on outer half. Upper hindwing brown with small areas of orange. Lower forewing orange and black with white tips near tip. Lower hindwing mottled grey-brown. Labial palps large and long, extend forwards.

The name American Snout comes from the shape of the labial palps. The colour and wing shapes are perfect for camouflage. When the butterfly perches, it holds its wings up to reveal the patterned undersides that resemble leaves, and it extends its palps out to look like leaf petioles. There are two generations, May to June and in August. The butterfly is a strong flier and migrates north into California, Nevada, Colorado and across the eastern United States in large numbers. The adults feed on nectar from flowers such as the dogbane, dogwood, and goldenrod. The males patrol in search of females, which lay their eggs in small clusters on leaves of the food plant. The dark green caterpillars feed on the leaves and pupate. The adults overwinter, although not in the more northerly parts of its range.

OTHER SPECIES OF NOTE

Common Blue Morpho *Morpho peleides*
This Morpho is one of the most common species, seen in tropical rainforest from Mexico to Colombia and in Trinidad. The females lay their eggs singly on a variety of plants including *Pterocarpus*, *Dahlbergia*, *Paragonia* and *Swatria*.

Morpho aega
The sexes are different, with the males having iridescent blue upperwings and the females being yellow-brown with a brown margin. The *Morpho aega* is found in Brazil, where the female lays her eggs on species of bamboo. This butterfly is collected extensively and used in jewellery.

Mechanitis isthmi
The bright forest butterfly is variable in appearance, with differing amounts of orange and yellow on the wings. It inhabits the rainforests of Mexico and Brazil.

Dynastor Napoleon

Dynastor napoleon

Butterflies of the genus *Dynastor* are found in Central and South America. *Dynastor napoleon* is a rare forest butterfly found only in Brazil, where it is seen flying at dawn and dusk. The adults are well camouflaged when they come to rest with their wings raised. The green caterpillars have spines on the thorax and a forked tail. The pupa is coloured to look like the head of a snake, complete with eyes and scale-like markings, which is thought to be a deterrent to predators.

Distribution: Brazil.
Habitat: Tropical rainforest.
Food plant: Bromeliaceae such as pineapple.
Wingspan: 125mm (5in).
Status: Not listed.

Identification: Upperwings are orange brown, with the upper forewings having a broken yellow bar. The underwings are leaf-like with a mottled brown appearance. The females are larger than the males.

Mosaic Butterfly

Colobura dirce

The mosaic butterfly is found around the edge of rainforests and in secondary forests which are less dense. They fly for much of the year and there are continuous generations. The adults fed on a range of foods including rotting fruits, banana skins, and fresh dung in order to obtain water and nutrients. They rarely visit flowers. The female lays her eggs in clusters at the top of the leaves of the *Cecropia* tree. The caterpillar is black with two yellow horns. The caterpillars stay together, eating the leaves. During the day they make a leaf shelter.

Distribution: Mexico through Central and South America, Caribbean.
Habitat: Rainforest from low to high altitude with *Cecropia* trees.
Larval food: *Cecropia* sp..
Wingspan: 60–70mm (2¼–2¾ in).
Status: Not listed.

Identification: Brown wings with a yellow strip across the forewing. Undersides pale brown background with a mosaic pattern of dark brown stripes and patches, with blue eyespots on the hindwing.

Brown Page

Siproeta epaphus

This is one of three members of the genus *Siproeta*, common in North and South America. All are large butterflies with a rapid, fluttering flight. The Brown Page ranges from south Texas and, rarely, southern New Mexico, south through both eastern and western Mexico to the Guyanas, Brazil, Bolivia and Peru. It lives all year round in tropical areas of its distribution, and is found along the edge of highland forests and roadsides, where they visit flowers as well as rotting fruit and fresh dung. The males fly to the ground to drink from

puddles and muddy patches. They are often seen basking in the sun. The female lays her eggs in clusters on the food plant. The caterpillars are red-orange with orange spikes along the back and sides, and black horns.

Distribution: Central and South America, Caribbean.
Habitat: Edge of subtropical forest, fields and roadsides in highland areas.
Larval food: Acanthus e.g. *Blechnum* sp. and *Ruellia* sp.
Wingspan: 10cm (4in).
Status: Not listed.

Identification: Outer part of upperwings red, dark brown on the inner half and separated by a white band across both wings. Hindwings have small tails.

Right: The caterpillars are dark-bodied, with yellow-orange spines along the back and sides and orange horns.

Glasswing Butterfly

Greta oto

Distribution: Southern
Mexico to Panama.
Habitat: Rainforest.
Food plant: *Cestrum
lanatum, Cestrum standlevi.*
Wingspan: 55–60mm
(2⅛–2¼in).
Status: Not listed.

Identification: Forewing shape is
broad at tip with almost straight
leading edge, wing almost
transparent; black or orange-
brown apex with white bar,
margins brown, dark veins.

There are 24 species in the genus *Greta* known as Clearwings, and they are found in
rainforests of Central and South America. *Greta oto* is one of the more common
Clearwings. Its common name 'glasswing' refers to its transparent wings. Its local Spanish
name is 'espejitos', which means 'little mirrors'. This butterfly is on the wing all year round,
although its numbers vary from season to season. The adult feeds on nectar from a variety
of flowers. It is a strong flier, covering long distances in a short time. The females lay their
eggs singly on nightshade species. The
caterpillars are pale green with a yellow
line down the side. They take up toxic
alkaloids from the food plant, which
makes them
distasteful to
predators.
The adults
are also
poisonous.

OTHER SPECIES OF NOTE

Siderone nemesis
This butterfly is found in Colombia, Venezuela,
and Brazil. Its wings have an unusual angular
shape, with pointed tips on the forewing and a
small stubby tail on the hindwing. Two red bars
cross the forewing. The under wings have leaf-
like markings, camouflaging the butterfly when it
rests. Their front pair of legs are generally much
reduced in size and give them the appearance of
having only four legs.

Mylitta Green Wing *Dynamine mylitta*
This small and attractive butterfly, is found in
Central and South America, where it is seen
visiting flowers for nectar. The male has blue-
green wings with dark borders and markings.

Small-eyed Soldier *Dynamine artemisia glauce*
This butterfly occurs through Central America to
Bolivia, and is one of 50 members of the genus
Dynamine. The upperwings are patterned in
brown and white with small blue patches.

Malachite

Siproeta stelenes

This forest butterfly has two to three broods
during the summer months (wet season),
while the brood of the winter form (dry
season) hibernates. The females lay their
eggs, singly, on leaves of the host plant.
During the day, the males perch on high
branches at the forest edge and may patrol
for females. The adults roost in groups on
small shrubs. The adults feed on rotting
fruits on the forest and orchard floor. They
are also seen taking nectar from flowers.

Distribution: Central and
South America and as far
north as Florida.
Habitat: Tropical forest and
mango and citrus orchards.
Food plant: Acanthaceae.
Wingspan: 85–100mm
(3¼–4in).
Status: Not listed.

Identification: Upperwings dark
brown to black with yellow-green
markings. Underwings orange-
brown with green markings.

Harmonious Tiger Clearwing

Tithorea harmonia

Identification: The *T. harmonia hermias*, shown here, has forewing with a rounded tip, upper forewing brown-black with creamy white spots, orange towards base, upper hindwing orange with black-brown margin and spots. Similar pattern on underwings, with small yellow dots along margin of the lower hindwing. Antennae cream, tapered, and drooping.

The bright orange and black colours of this clearwing are warning colours of its poisonous nature. The poisons are alkaloids taken up by the caterpillars from the food plant, a vine with a clear sap. Adult males gain the poison from bird droppings. It is a mimic of a number of Danaids and Heliconids, and each of the 26 named subspecies have a slightly different appearance. It is also mimicked by non-poisonous species, *Protogonius pardalis* and *Dismorphia egaena*, these latter being an example of Batesian mimicry. The best way to distinguish this species from its many mimics is to study the antennae and legs. The subfamily Ithomiinae, to which the glasswings and tigers belong, have two pairs of very long functioning legs that give the appearance of stilts. It is a relatively common species that is seen in low-altitude dry forest, where its food plant occurs, as well as cocoa plantations. However, its life cycle has not been studied.

Distribution: Mexico to northern parts of South America.
Habitat: Dry tropical forest.
Food plant: *Prestonia portobellensis*.
Wingspan: 60–70mm (2¼–2¾in).
Status: Not listed.

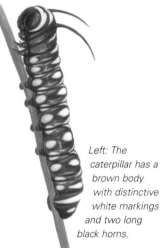

Left: The caterpillar has a brown body with distinctive white markings and two long black horns.

Common Wood Nymph

Cercyonis pegala

The distinctive eyespots on the upper forewings of this butterfly earn it the nickname 'goggle eyes', but apart from this it can vary greatly in appearance; some may have many other eyespots on the hindwing, and in the southeastern part of its range it has a large yellow patch on both surfaces of the forewing. Despite its common name, these butterflies are not seen in woodlands, preferring open habitats such as meadows. The adults are seen from May to October and there is a single generation. The males are active first. They have a characteristic up-and-down flight when patrolling for females. The females lay their eggs singly on the leaves of the food plants. The caterpillars are yellow-green with two red tails, a dark green strip along the top of the body and two paler ones along the side. The caterpillars do not feed after hatching, but overwinter before resuming their development in spring. There are 13 subspecies, which vary in depth of colour and in the amount of yellow on the wing.

Distribution: North America.
Habitat: Grassland and meadow.
Food plant: Grasses such as *Tridens flavus* (purple top).
Wingspan: 38–58mm (1⅜–2³⁄₁₆in).
Status: Not listed.

Identification: Wings rounded, brown to brown-red. Upper forewing has two large, yellow-ringed eyespots with white centre. Underwings mottled brown to orange, under forewings have two unequal eyespots, under hindwings have a row of small eyespots.

Many banded Daggerwing

Marpesia chiron

Distribution: Southern United States, south to Argentina.
Habitat: Swamps. marshes, tropical rainforest.
Food plant: *Ficus* sp., *Anacardium* sp..
Wingspan: 65–80mm (2½–3⅛in).
Status: Not listed.

Identification: Upperwings orange-brown with three vertical dark lines that cross both wings. Forewing has an irregular margin. Three white spots near tip. Hindwing has a dark margin and two tails of unequal length. Underwings pale brown to orange with a hint of purple, with white stripes.

The daggerwing butterflies are characterized by long tails on their hindwings. The adults fly all year round in Central and South America, but only from July to October in the northern parts of their range. They are seen feeding on the nectar of plants such as *Cordia* and *Lantana* sp., as well as mud-puddling. This butterfly is a strong flier, and mass migrations are seen in years that they are abundant. Large numbers of daggerwings roost together in the forest. The females lay their eggs singly on the buds of the food plants. Caterpillars feed on the leaves and rest on a platform that they build from their droppings, held together with silken threads.

OTHER SPECIES OF NOTE

Painted Crescent *Phyciodes picta*
The Painted Crescent has dark mottled upper wings with a yellow spot, while the undersides of the hindwings are creamy yellow. The females lay their eggs in clusters on the underside of leaves of the food plant, such as the field bindweed (*Convolvulus arvensis*). There are three generations between April and October. Caterpillars of the last generation overwinter, and the adults emerge in April.

Taygetis albinotata
Like other members of the genus *Taygetis*, this butterfly has a row of distinctive eyespots on its underside. The upper wing is brown with a row of white spots along the margin of the scalloped hindwing. The undersides are brown with white stripes and eyespots.

Taygetis chrysogone

Taygetis chrysogone

The genus *Taygetis* is found in South America, and numbers about 27 species. These large, brown butterflies are found in tropical rainforest, where they prefer the shade of the understorey, rather than sunny clearings. They fly in late afternoon, coming down to the forest floor to feed on rotting fruits and dung and for the females to lay their eggs on grasses.

Distribution: Central and South America.
Habitat: Tropical forests.
Food plant: Grass species.
Wingspan: 10cm (4in).
Status: Not listed.

Identification: Wings rich brown. Upper forewing is pointed, brown. Upper hindwing has a scalloped margin with short tail, brown with gold-orange thick margin. Underwings brown-grey with rows of false eyes.

SKIPPERS

The skippers are particularly well-represented in the Americas, with more than 2,300 species out of a worldwide total of about 3,700. Approximately 250 species occur in North America, most of which belong to the family of Common Skippers (Hesperiidae). Skippers have small wings but large bodies with, a fast flight. The colours of the wings are mostly shades of brown, which makes identification tricky.

Southern Cloudy Wing

Thorybes bathyllus

Distribution: Southern United States and Mexico.
Habitat: Meadows, scrub, prairies.
Food plant: Pea family, including *Astragalus* sp. (milk vetch) and *Trifolium* sp. (clover).
Wingspan: 33–35mm (1¼–1⅜in).
Status: Not listed.

The butterfly is seen from June to July. The adults visit a wide range of nectar plants including dogbane and thistle. There is a single generation in the northern parts of its range, and two to three generations elsewhere. The males are seen perching on high vegetation on hilltops, from where they watch for females. Some males use the same perch through their lifespan, which lasts about two weeks. The females lay their eggs singly on the underside of leaves of the food plants. The caterpillars hatch and feed on the leaves. They roll up the leaves to form shelters. The caterpillars overwinter and pupate the following spring.

Identification: Upperwings dark brown. Upper forewing has a wide band of transparent spots, upper hindwing is elongated in shape.

OTHER SPECIES OF NOTE
Yucca-borer Skipper *Megathymus yuccae*
The yucca-borer, or yucca giant skipper, is a fast-flying butterfly found across the southern United States, south to northern Mexico. There is a single generation on the wing from February to May, occurring in habitats with yucca, such as coastal dunes, scrub, grassland, old fields and desert. The caterpillars feed on the yucca leaves, where they build silk tents. As they get older they bore deep into the plant and feed on the root. They overwinter in their burrows, pupating in early spring.

Dusted Skipper *Atrytonopsis hianna*
The Dusted Skipper gets its name from the white dusting over its otherwise grey under hindwings. Its dark eyes are bordered by a white eye stripe above and white palps below. In the northern parts of its range, there is a single generation, but in Florida there are two. The adults visit a wide variety of nectar flowers. The females lay their eggs on grass. The caterpillars are pink-purple on the back, with grey sides and long yellow hairs.

Long-tailed Skipper

Urbanus proteus

There are three generations of this butterfly during the summer months. The adults feed on nectar from a variety of flowers such as *Bougainvillea* and *Lantana*. They roost upside down under leaves. The females lay their eggs in clusters on the underside of leaves. The caterpillars are green, with black speckles and a yellow to orange strip, brown head and black face. They cut flaps in the leaves and fold them over to form a small tent, under which they shelter. They pupate within the tent for about three weeks. The caterpillars are common pests of crops in the southern United States, where they damage bean crops as well as garden plants such as wisteria. For this reason it is often called the bean-leaf roller butterfly.

Distribution: Southern United States, south to Argentina.
Habitat: Edges of woodlands, scrub, gardens, waste land.
Food plant: Plants of the pea family, especially beans.
Wingspan: 45–60mm (1¾–2¼in).
Status: Not listed.

Identification: Upperwings dark brown to black, base of wings iridescent blue-green as is the body, hindwings have two long tails. Lower hindwings have a dark band. Males leading edge of the forewing has a costal fold with scent scales.

Leonard's skipper

Hesperia leonardus

Distribution: North America
Habitat: Grassland, prairie.
Food plant: Grasses such as
Agrostis sp., *Eragrostis* sp.,
Panicum sp..
Wingspan: 30–45mm
(1¼–1¾in).
Status: Critically Endangered
subspecies.

Identification: Upperwings red-
orange with wide black borders.
Lower hindwing is brick red with
a band of white and yellow spots.

This skipper is seen during late summer and autumn, from August to October, when there is one generation. The adults visit a range of nectar flowers, especially *Liatris punctata* (blazing star). The males perch close to the nectar flowers and watch for females. The females scatter their eggs on the food plant. The caterpillars hatch and feed on the leaves, sheltering in the tent of leaves. The caterpillars overwinter and complete their growth in spring. There are three sub-species which look quite different, varying in colour and range. The Pawnee Montane Skipper (*Hesperia leonardus montana*) that is found on open grassland has a very small range and low numbers, and is classed as being Critically Endangered.

Silver-spotted Skipper

Hesperia comma

The Silver-spotted Skipper is also called the Common Banded Skipper. This widespread skipper is seen from June to September, and there is a single generation. They are active on sunny days, when they can be seen basking in the sun on grass stalks. Bare patches in the grassland, such as those created by rabbits, are critical to this species' survival. The females land in a bare patch and walk to the edge to look for the food plant, sheep's fescue. They lay their eggs singly on the leaves. The eggs overwinter and hatch the following spring. The caterpillars emerge in spring and start to feed on grass leaves. They are olive green with a black band behind the black head. They pupate in a cocoon on the ground. In parts of its range, especially Europe, the Silver-spotted Skipper is in decline due to loss of grassland habitat, and lack of management of the remaining grassland. When grassland is left ungrazed, it becomes overgrown with shrubs. It is also reliant on one food plant: sheep's fescue.

Distribution: North America,
North Africa, Europe and
temperate Asia.
Habitat: Grassland.
Food plant: Grasses such
as *Festuca ovina*
(sheep's fescue).
Wingspan: 25–30mm
(1–1¼in).
Status: Not listed.

Right: This skipper gets its name from the silver spots that are seen on the underside of the wings.

Identification: Upperwings orange brown with pale spots. Underwings pale brown with silvery spots. Males black band on upper forewing.

Essex Skipper

Thymelicus lineola

The Essex, or European Skipper, is very similar in appearance to the Small Skipper; the distinguishing feature is the black tip to the antennae, while that of the Small Skipper is orange-brown. These two butterflies are often found together, adding to the confusion. The butterfly is on the wing from May to July and there is one generation. The adults visit a range of flowers for nectar. They roost on grass stalks at night and bask in the morning sun. The female lays her eggs in strings on blades of grass, where they stay throughout the winter and hatch in spring. The caterpillars feed on the leaves. The Essex Skipper was introduced to North America in 1910, and since then it has spread south to South Carolina and west to British Columbia, possibly as a result of eggs being moved in hay. The global range has also increased, helped by the fact that it overwinters as an egg, which is more able to survive winter flooding and cold than other species which overwinter as caterpillars or adults.

Distribution: North America, North Africa, Europe, across Asia.
Habitat: Grassland, meadows, verges and woodlands.
Food plant: Grasses, especially *Dactylis glomerata* (cock's foot).
Wingspan: 25–30mm (1–1¼in).
Status: Not listed.

Right: The underwings are plain orange-brown and lack any mottling.

Identification: Wings burnt orange. Upperwings black borders with thickened black veins towards the margins. Male upper forewing has a thin black scent mark. Tips of antennae black.

Chequered Skipper

Carterocephalus palaemon

Distribution: North America, Europe, across Asia to Japan.
Habitat: Woodlands, damp meadows, banks of streams.
Food plant: *Molinia caerulea* (purple moor grass), *Brachypodium sylvaticum* (false brome).
Wingspan: 20–30mm (¾–1¼in).
Status: Threatened in Japan and United Kingdom, Vulnerable in Europe.

This small, chocolate-brown butterfly is also known as the Arctic skipper. It is seen from May to June, and there is a single generation. The female lays her eggs singly on blades of grass. The summer caterpillar is green with dark green and white lines. It creates a leaf tube by spinning the edges of the blade of grass together. Then it shelters within the tube, only emerging to feed. At the end of autumn it spins several leaves together to create a larger shelter in which it overwinters. When it emerges in spring it is brown-white with brown and white lines. It is generally considered a woodland butterfly, and breeds in and around damp woodland, favouring clearings and woodland paths, and seems to have a particular attraction to blue woodland flowers. Although widely distributed in northern and central Europe, North America, southern Canada, Asia and Japan, this species is declining across its range. It is thought that this is due to loss of woodland habitats and changes in the management of the remaining woodlands, for example the switch from deciduous to coniferous plantings, decline in coppicing and other management practices that create woodland glades.

Identification: Wings chequered pattern of browns and creamy yellow. Upperwings dark brown with orange-yellow square-shaped markings, lower forewings orange with brown spots, lower hindwings red-orange with cream spots with black outline. Females larger than males.

Right: Initially, the caterpillars have a white body but as they mature their body turns pale green with dark green and white lines.

Sickle-winged Skipper

Achlyodes thraso

Distribution: Central and South America, as far north as Texas.
Habitat: Open forest, gardens and parks.
Food plant: Leaves of *Citrus* sp..
Wingspan: 3.5–4.5cm (1⅜–1¾in).
Status: Not listed.

Identification: The forewing has a characteristic hooked apex. The male is dark brown with brown spots, and a purple sheen over the surface, while the female is brown with pale brown-grey spots scattered across both wings.

This butterfly gets its name from the hooked shape of the forewing. It is seen all year, although numbers peak in late summer and autumn. The female lays her eggs, singly, on the top of Citrus sp. The caterpillars stay in groups, protected inside a nest of leaves, stuck together with silk. The adults feed on the nectar of a wide range of flowers. Some entomologists divide the Sickle-wing Skippers into two species, the Northern Sickle-wing (*Eantis tamenund*) and Southern Sickle-wing Skipper (*A. thraso*).

OTHER SPECIES OF NOTE

Mimoniades versicolor
The pattern of yellow spots and iridescent blue bands on the wings of this South American skipper are variable. The underwings are blue and red with a yellow band. It is a widespread species occurring above 2,000m (6,561 feet). Unlike most Skippers, it quite a slow flight.

Gold Skipper *Argopteron aureipennis*
This Skipper is found in Chile and Argentina. The upperwings are brown with three golden spots on the forewing. However, the underwings are very different, a stunning metallic gold colour.

Tawny-edged Skipper *Polites Themistocles*
This widespread species of grass skipper is found across much of North America from British Columbia and Nova Scotia in the north to Florida and Mexico. The upperwings are dark brown with an orange band and orange spots on the forewing. The underwings are orange-brown. There is a single generation in the north in June to July but two in the south. The female lays her eggs singly on grasses.

Common Chequered Skipper

Pyrgus communis

This species is very difficult to distinguish from *P. albescens* (White Chequered Skipper). Its fringe is partially chequered, while *P. albescens* is completely so. It is seen from February to October in the southernmost parts of its range, and March to September in the rest. There is a single generation. The males patrol in the afternoon, watching for females. During the late afternoon, the adults settle on tall plants where they roost. The females lay their eggs singly on the upper surface of leaves and on leaf buds of the food plants. Like other skippers, the caterpillars fold over leaves to make tents in which they shelter. The caterpillars overwinter and complete their growth the following spring. The Common and the White Chequered Skipper overlap in the southeastern United States, where the White Chequered Skipper is replacing the Common Chequered Skipper.

Distribution: North America, south from Ontario to Mexico.
Habitat: Meadows, prairies, gardens.
Food plant: Malvaceae including *Althea*, *Abutilon* and *Malva* sp..
Wingspan: 25–38mm (1–1½in).
Status: Not listed.

Identification: Male upperwings blue-grey, fringe partially chequered, costal fold on upper forewing. Female black. Both have band of large white spots across both wings. Underwings white with green to olive band.

TIGER MOTHS

The tiger moths are most diverse in the tropical regions of the world, with the Neotropics being home to more than 6,000 species. In contrast, there are about 250 species in the Nearctic region. Tiger moths are small- to medium-sized moths, many of which have bright colours of red, orange and yellow. The hairy caterpillars are commonly known as 'woolly bears'. They feed on lichens and the leaves of trees and shrubs.

Garden Tiger

Arctia caja

This attractive moth only reveals its bright orange hindwings when in flight. This moth was collected by the early lepidopterists, who bred the moths to create unusual colour forms. The bright colours are a warning to predators that it is distasteful. If the flash of bright colours fail to deter a predator, it releases a yellow liquid from behind its head. The moth is on the wing during July and August, and is attracted to light. It also flies during the day and can be mistaken for a butterfly. The caterpillar is covered in long hairs, which can cause irritation if touched by bare skin. The caterpillar overwinters and pupates in spring, it feeds on the leaves of nettles, docks and garden plants.

Distribution: North America, Europe, Asia.
Habitat: Gardens, scrub land, wasteland and hedgerows.
Food plant: Many common plants including *Allium* sp., *Ribes* sp., *Rubus* sp, *Rumex* sp. and *Urtica dioica* (stinging nettle).
Wingspan: 45–65mm (1¾–2½in).
Status: Not listed.

Right: The caterpillar is black-brown and densely covered in long hairs, giving it the nickname 'woolly bear'.

Identification: Forewing has pattern of brown and white markings. Hindwing is orange with blue-black spots, revealed in flight. Pattern of markings highly variable. Some have yellow or brown abdomen and hindwings.

Painted Tiger Moth

Arachnis picta

The Painted Tiger moth is one of 15 species of North and Central American tiger moths belonging to the genus *Arachnis*. Like many of the tiger moths, it is brightly coloured to warn that it is distasteful to predators such as birds. During the summer months, it can be seen flying over grassland areas. The females lay up to 200 eggs on or near the food plant. The caterpillar has a black-brown body covered in dark hairs. It is active at night. The caterpillar enters a diapause that can be several months or more in duration. In the arid grasslands, diapause is broken by the arrival of the rains. There are a number of subspecies that occur in localized regions, such as *A. picta meadowsi* in California.

Distribution: Colorado, California, Mexico.
Habitat: Grassland.
Food plant: *Acanthus* sp. and *Lupinus sp.*.
Wingspan: 48mm (2in).
Status: Not listed.

Identification: Forewing white with wavy grey to brown bars, hindwing red-orange with spots of grey. Abdomen red, with blue spots outlined in black.

Milkweed Tiger Moth

Euchaetes egle

Distribution: Canada
to Florida.
Habitat: Grassland.
Food plant: *Asclepias* sp.
(milkweed).
Wingspan: 30–42mm
(1¼–1½in).
Status: Not listed.

Identification: Wings creamy
grey-brown. Forewings may have
brown bands edged in black.
Yellow, hairy body with row of
black dots along dorsal surface.

This common tiger
moth is seen in the
latter part of summer.
It is a poisonous moth
containing cardiac
glycosides that are taken
up from the food plant
by the caterpillars and
retained in the adults.
Unlike many species of
butterflies and moth, it does not
rely on warning colours, as it is a
night-flying moth and the main predator is bats.
Instead, they produce clicks from their tymbal
organs which are detected by the bats. Sounds are
also used to attract females. There are one or two
generations a year. The females lay their eggs in large clusters on the underside of leaves.
The caterpillar has tufts of black, white and orange hairs. At first the caterpillars stay together
but the later instars move away. They pupate in a hairy grey cocoon and overwinter.

OTHER SPECIES OF NOTE

Zuni Tiger Moth *Arachnis zuni*
This tiger moth is not as brightly coloured as the
Painted Tiger Moth. The forewings are brown
with white spots, and the hindwings have small
areas of yellow. The abdomen is brown and
yellow. This moth is found in New Mexico,
Arizona and Mexico.

Amaxia chaon
This Ecuadorean moth has long yellow forewings
with blood-red markings. The hindwings are
much smaller and pale yellow with red hue.

Black-and-Yellow Lichen Moth
Lycomorpha pholous
This moth has a blue-black body and wings, with
the basal part of both wings being bright red
or orange. The wingspan is about 25mm (1in).
It is found east of the Rockies, from southern
Canada to Mexico. The caterpillar looks like
a lichen and feeds on lichens. Lichens are
excellent monitors of air pollution because of
their sensitivity to sulphur dioxide in the air. The
moths, in turn, are also indicators, because of
their dependence on the lichens. The moth is a
day-flier, often seen on flowers.

Fall Webworm

Hyphantria cunea

The Fall Webworm gets its name from the
way the caterpillars spin a web to enclose
leaves and even small branches of the food
plant. The caterpillars stay together, and
their web gets larger as they eat more leaves.
They can completely defoliate a tree, so the
Webworm is considered a pest species. The
females lay their eggs in clusters of several
hundred which hatch in a few days. There
are two races of Fall Webworm, a northern
and southern race. They can be
distinguished by their caterpillars. Northern-
race caterpillars have a black head and
yellow to green body with a dark stripe
along the back, black and orange warts with
long white hairs. Southern-race caterpillars
have an orange to red head, and a yellow
body with orange-red warts and brown
hairs. The pupae
overwinter in
bark or leaf litter.
This moth has
been introduced to
other regions of the
world, from where it
has spread, so its range
now includes much of
Europe, Japan and
eastern Asia.

Distribution: Canada to
Mexico, introduced to Europe,
Japan, Korea and China.
Habitat: Woodlands.
Food plant: Deciduous trees.
Wingspan: 30–45mm
(1¼–1¾in).
Status: Not listed.

Identification: Varies across
range. Usually white but may
have black spots on FW. Yellow-
orange patches on the front legs.

*Below: This caterpillar belongs to
the northern race of Fall Webworms.*

CUTWORMS, OWLETS AND UNDERWINGS

Cutworm, Owlet and Underwing moths belong to the Noctuidae, the largest family within the Lepidoptera. There are about 26,000 described species and probably more than 30,000 actual species, of which 8,600 are found in the Neotropics and 3,000 in the Nearctic. The Noctuids are a variable group, from the very small to the large, and are mostly nocturnal. The caterpillars are leaf-feeders and borers, and many are classed as pests.

Spotted Cutworm

Amathes c-nigrum, Xestia c-nigrum

Cutworms are a pest species of moth as the caterpillars damage a variety of crops. The Spotted Cutworm is a pest of apple trees and mint plants. Damage to the plants can occur from spring to autumn. The caterpillars have a red-brown head with two black bands, and a brown-red body with black triangle-shaped spots on last three abdominal segments. Paler triangles are seen on the forward segments and a pale yellow-orange stripe along the side. During the day, the caterpillars stay in the shelter of leaf litter on the ground, and emerge to feed on the food plant during the night. They lay a chemical trail so they can retrace their path to the ground. Most damage is done to young shoots. The caterpillars overwinter and resume feeding in spring, when they target fruiting buds.

Distribution: North America, especially west of the Cascade Mountains.
Habitat: Orchards.
Food plant: *Malus* sp..
Wingspan: 30mm (1¼in).
Status: Not listed.

Identification: Dark grey-black wings, with white pyramid-shaped spot, bordered with black, brown spot.

Large Yellow Underwing

Noctua pronuba

The Large Yellow Underwing is a relatively common and abundant moth found in a variety of habitats. It is a migrant species that flies north through the summer months. During the day it rests on plants such as as grasses with which its mottled colours blend well and provide good camouflage. When disturbed it will fly away, flashing its yellow hindwings in an attempt to deter any predator. The females lay mats of up to 1,000 eggs on blades of grass. The green or brown caterpillars are commonly known as cutworms because of their habit of chewing through low-growing plants at ground level. They rest among grass during the day and emerge at night to feed. They overwinter in the soil and pupate in spring. It is considered a pest because of the damage it does to garden plants and crops.

Distribution: Europe, central Asia, North Africa, North America.
Habitat: Many including grasslands, woodlands, gardens.
Food plant: Variety of low growing plants.
Wingspan: 60mm (2¼in).
Status: Not listed.

Identification: Forewing light to dark brown, even grey or orange-brown, ranging from unmarked to heavily patterned, black spot near tip, small dark patch in middle. Hindwing yellow with black band under margin.

Sweetheart Underwing

Catocala amatrix

Distribution: North America
Habitat: Woodlands, orchards, gardens.
Food plant: *Populus* sp., *Salix* sp..
Wingspan: 75–95mm (3–3¾in).
Status: Not listed.

Identification: Forewing dark brown-grey with zigzag, and mottled pattern, hindwing red with black sub-marginal band, and band across the middle of the wing, narrow white margin.

The Sweetheart Underwing is seen from August to October in the northern parts of the range, and from June and July further south. The adults are night-flying, and rest during the day on tree trunks, in caves and under bridges. They lay their wings flat against the surface with their head pointing downward. The females lay their eggs on tree bark during the autumn months, and the eggs hatch the following spring. Melanic forms of the moth have been seen. It is similar in appearance to *Catocala cara*, and in places where they occur together, they hybridize.

OTHER SPECIES OF NOTE

Brou's Underwing *Catocala atocala*
The genus name is a combination of two Greek words, *kato* (behind), and *kalos* (beautiful).This Underwing is seen in July and August in the southeast United States. The forewings are a mottled grey-brown while the hindwings are dark brown. The female lays her eggs on the bark of the walnut tree (*Juglans* sp.) in the autumn. The eggs overwinter and hatch the following spring.

Bay Underwing *Catocala badia*
The Bay Underwing is seen from Maine to New Jersey in the United States, mostly in coastal habitats in which its food plant, bayberry (*Myrica* sp.) and sweetfern (*Comptonia* sp.) are found.

Splendid Dagger Moth *Acronicta superans*
This dagger moth occurs from Newfoundland south to Kentucky. Its upper forewings are a mottled pale grey and black, while the upper hindwings are grey-brown. The moths are seen between May and August. The females lay their eggs on a variety of trees including *Betula* sp., *Prunus* sp. and *Malus* sp..

White Witch

Thysania agrippina

This moth has several common names, including Birdwing Moth and Great Owlet Moth. It has the largest wingspan of any moth, including the Atlas Moth (*Attacus atlas*), although the Atlas has a greater wing area. This moth flies at night, and its wings are so large that it is commonly mistaken for a bat. The female lays clusters of eggs on the bark of trees. The caterpillar has a black body, with blue-green bands and hairs, and feeds on leaves. The closely related Black Witch, *Thysania zenobia*, is one of North America's largest moths. It has a similar appearance but the lines are less regular.

Distribution: Central America, tropical South America.
Habitat: Tropical forests.
Food plant: Various trees.
Wingspan: 230–305mm (9–12in).
Status: Not listed.

Identification: Creamy white to yellow wings with black and grey zigzag pattern across both wings. Hindwing scalloped margin. Underwings blue-purple sheen with white spots, brown towards the body.

LOOPERS AND PROMINENTS

The Loopers of the Geometriidae form the second largest group of moths in North America. They are small to medium moths with slender bodies. The Prominents of the Notodontidae are medium-sized moths with a stout body. Their wings are often drab, and when they rest they either hold their wings over their body or they roll them to disrupt the wing shape and provide camouflage.

Gypsy Moth

Lymantria dispar

Distribution: Europe, Asia, North America.
Habitat: Forests.
Food plant: Varied, especially *Quercus* (oak).
Wingspan: 30–60mm (1¼–2¼in).
Status: Not listed.

This moth is one of the most devastating pests of North American forests. During the late 1860s, French scientist Leopold Trouvelot brought some Gypsy moths across from Europe into order to create a hybrid with the native Silk moth. However, some Gypsy moths escaped and since then they have spread steadily across North America. Today the largest numbers occur in the forests of the Appalachian Mountains, the Ozark Mountains and the northern lake states. The females lay an egg mass containing up to 800 eggs on the bark of trees, the eggs being protected by hairs from their abdomens. The eggs overwinter and the caterpillars emerge the following spring to feed on newly opened leaves. They tend to feed at night and rest during the day in crevices in the bark. The young caterpillars disperse by hanging from leaves on silken threads in order to catch the wind. In cases of severe infestation, a tree may be completely defoliated. If this happens regularly over a number of years, the tree may die. The moths are controlled by pesticides. A number of natural predators have been introduced as biological controls, the latest being a fungus.

Identification: Male mottled brown-grey wings. Females twice the size of the male, with creamy-white to buff wings with scattered small brown spots and thin zigzag lines.

Yellow-necked Apple Moth

Datana ministra

The Yellow-necked Apple Moth, or Egg Maiden Moth, is a member of the Notodontidae. A characteristic of this family is the way the moth rolls its wings around its body when at rest, to produce an irregular outline that is well-camouflaged on a surface such as bark. The outline of this particular moth resembles a short length of bark or twig. As the name suggests, this species can be a pest on apple trees, although it is found on a wide range of trees such as birch, hawthorn, oak and willow. There are as many as three generations per year. The female moth lays her eggs in a cluster on the underside of leaves. The caterpillar is black with yellow stripes and a distinctive yellow-orange band behind the head. The caterpillars stay together as they move through the plant, eating leaves. The pupae overwinter and the adult moths emerge in early summer.

Right: When the caterpillar is threatened it raises its head and end of the abdomen to look larger.

Distribution: North America.
Habitat: Forests, orchards.
Food plant: Varied, especially *Malus* (apple).
Wingspan: 30–50mm (1¼–2in).
Status: Not listed.

Identification: Forewing red-brown with thin dark lines and scalloped margin, Hindwing pale creamy-white to buff lacking any pattern. Thorax dark orange-brown.

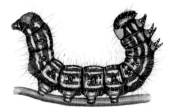

White-spotted Prominent

Nadata gibbosa

Distribution: North America.
Habitat: Forests, orchards.
Food plant: *Acer* (maple),
Quercus (oak).
Wingspan: 38–60mm
(1½–2¼in).
Status: Not listed.

Identification: Forewing pointed,
yellow to buff brown with two
prominent brown lines and two
small white spots in the centre,
thin white margin. Hindwing pale
yellow-buff, with maroon head
and thorax and brown abdomen.

The White-spotted
Prominent, named
after the two white
spots on the forewing,
is a relatively common
species that is found
across North America. At
rest, the moth has a tent
shape as the wings are held
close to the body, although
it may be seen lying with its
wings held flat. It is a night-
flying moth. One generation flies in the northern
parts of the range, from May to July, although two
may occur in the south. The caterpillar is green with a thin pale white line running along its
body. It feeds on leaves from a range of deciduous trees, including birch, oak and maple.
It overwinters as a pupa and the adult moth emerges in spring.

OTHER SPECIES OF NOTE

Red-washed Prominent *Oligocentria
semirufescens* This member of the
Notodontidae lays its eggs on a variety of forest
trees and shrubs, including apple, birch, and
willow. There are two generations a year. It is
found in Arkansas, USA.

Morning Glory Prominent *Schizura ipomoeae*
This moth has mottled grey-brown forewings and
pale creamy white hindwings, with the occasional
brown spot. It has a scattered distribution across
North America. Its food plant is *Ipomoea*
(morning glory). Its alternate name is the False
Unicorn, after the appearance of the caterpillar.

Spiny Looper *Phigalia titea*
This moth occurs in the midwest states of the
USA, where the caterpillar is found on a range of
trees such as hickory, maple and oak. The adult
male has powdery grey wings, with three black
lines running across the forewings. This colouring
provides excellent camouflage when the moth
rests on bark. There is a melanic form which is
much darker. The females are wingless and lay
their eggs on the tree on which they were
hatched. The males are on the wing from March
to April.

Teak Moth

Hyblaea puera

The Teak moth is a common and
widespread species that is classed as a pest
because of the damage it does to tropical
trees, especially high-value ones such as the
teak. Although teak is the primary food
plant, the caterpillars feed on other species
too. The caterpillars eat leaves and damage
buds, which reduces shoot growth. In some
plantations the level of defoliation can result
in as much as a 40 per cent reduction on
growth, and trees can be completely
defoliated. The females lay their eggs singly
on the underside of young leaves. The
caterpillars hatch and feed on the buds.
They make a shelter by folding over a piece
of leaf which they secure with silk. They
hide during the day and emerge at night to
feed on leaf tissue, leaving behind
a skeleton.

Distribution: Pantropical,
where teak occurs.
Habitat: Rainforest and
tropical plantations.
Food plant: *Tectora* sp.
(Teak).
Wingspan: 40mm (1½in).
Status: Not listed.

Identification: Upper forewing
mottled brown-grey, upper
hindwing brown with orange-red
markings, either in a band or
series of blotches. Under
forewing brown with two yellow
marks, under hindwing orange
with dark mark.

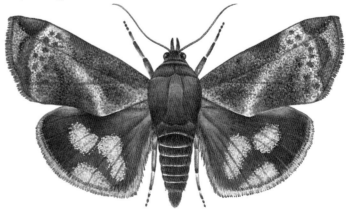

SATURNIIDS

The greatest diversity of the Saturniid moths occurs in the Neotropics, where there are several hundreds of species. There are 68 species in the Nearctic. Saturniids are heavy moths with small heads and a large wingspan to 15cm (6in). They include one of North America's largest native moths, the Cecropia moth (Hyalaphora cecropia). The caterpillars are equally large and feed mostly on leaves.

Luna Moth

Actias luna

The Luna or Moon moth is a common night-flying North American moth. This large, distinctive moth has no mouth and so cannot feed. It is a short-lived moth, surviving just long enough to mate and lay eggs. There is one generation a year in the northern parts of the range, from June to July, but in the southern parts there may be as many as three generations. The females lay clusters of up to seven eggs on the underside of leaves such as birch. The caterpillars move away from their hatching place, feeding on leaves of various trees. The mature caterpillar is about 9cm (3½in) long, bright green with a yellow stripe along the side of the body, narrow yellow bands between each segment and orange spots. It spins a cocoon in which it pupates.

Distribution: Eastern North America, Northern Mexico.
Habitat: Woodland.
Food plant: Various, including *Betula* sp., *Carya* sp., *Diospyros* sp., *Rhus* sp..
Wingspan: 70–100mm (2¾–4in).
Status: Not listed.

Identification: Lime green wings. Forewing pink-brown leading edge and brown eyespot, pink-brown veins. Hindwing long tail and one central eyespot. Sexes similar other than antennae.

Polyphemus Moth

Antherea polyphemus

This large night-flying silkmoth is common across North America. The large eyespots are believed to be defensive, as the moth opens its wings to reveal the eyespots and deter any would-be predator. The eyespots are where it gets its name – from the Greek myth of the Cyclops, Polyphemus. There is a single generation in the northern parts of its range, May to July, but two in the south. The female lays her eggs in groups of up to five on the underside of leaves. The caterpillar can eat 86,000 times its weight at emergence in a little less than two months. The mature caterpillar has a brown head and bright green body, with orange-brown spots and forward-pointing spines. It spins a cocoon on the ground or hangs from a tree and pupates. Pupae of the second generation overwinter and complete their life cycle the following spring.

Distribution: North America.
Habitat: Woodland.
Food plant: Various including *Prunus* sp., *Quercus* sp..
Wingspan: 10cm (4in).
Status: Not listed.

Identification: Forewing pink-brown with eyespot, two submarginal stripes, one dark brown-black and the other pink, similar stripes near the body. Hindwing large brown and black eyespot and two submarginal stripes, one black, one pink. Male hindwing darker than female. Underside shades of dark brown with one small eyespot on each wing.

Giant Silk Moth

Automeris moloneyi

Distribution: Central America.
Habitat: Tropical forests, mangroves.
Food plant: Various including *Robinia* sp..
Wingspan: 70–80mm (2¾–3⅛in).
Status: Not listed.

Identification: Forewing mottled shades of red-brown with pale line across the wings. Hindwing red-brown with prominent black eyespot with white centre and ringed in yellow; curved lines in black and yellow beyond the eyespot. Female similar, but paler.

Most of the members of the large genus *Automeris*, with the exception of a few such as *Automeris io*, are found in Central and South America. The Giant Silk moth is found throughout Central America, where it is locally common. The caterpillars are covered in irritating spines, a feature which deters predators. The caterpillars are gregarious at first, but become increasingly solitary with age. This species, along with other large moths, are under threat from collectors and from the deforestation of their habitat.

OTHER SPECIES OF NOTE

Promethea *Callosamia promethea*
This eye-catching moth is found in North America, especially the eastern states. The sexes are different. The males have mostly purple-black wings with a patterned border, while the females are larger, and have patterned wings with more red-brown. The caterpillar has a pale green body, with small black spots, with two pairs of red spines behind the head and a single yellow spine near the end of the abdomen.

Sweetbay Moth *Callosamia securifera*
The Sweetbay moth occurs in the southeastern United States. The wings are shades of yellow-brown, with the male being darker than the female. There are two generations per year, from April to May and August, with the occasional third generation in autumn. Both sexes are active during the day, and mating takes place between 1pm and 3pm. Females lay eggs at dusk, in rows on the leaves of the host plant, sweetbay (*Magnolia* sp.). Eggs hatch in about a week, and the caterpillars are gregarious feeders.

North American Emperor Moth

Automeris io

The Emperor or Io Moth is a spectacular moth with a large eyespot on each hindwing. This remains hidden when the moth is at rest, and is revealed to deter any would-be predator. There is a single generation in the northern parts of its range, and as many as three or four generations in the south. The female lays a cluster of about 20 eggs on the underside of leaves. The young caterpillars stay together, moving from plant to plant in search of food, but become solitary with age. They feed on a variety of deciduous leaves. The mature caterpillar is bright green with red and white stripes and is covered in barbed irritating hairs. The caterpillars climb down to the ground to spin a cocoon in the leaf litter. The pupa overwinters and emerges the following spring.

Distribution: North America.
Habitat: Woodland.
Food plant: Various including *Acer* sp., *Betula* sp., *Populus* sp., *Prunus* sp..
Wingspan: 50–80mm (2–3⅛in).
Status: Not listed.

Identification: Sexes different. Male FW pale yellow to red-brown with small patches of brown, HW yellow with red inner margin, large black eyespot with white centre, curved thin black line outside of the eyespot, and submarginal thin red-pink band. Female FW shades of brown, red and grey.

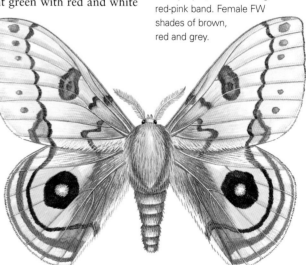

Ailanthus Silk Moth

Samia cynthia

The Ailanthus Silk moth was introduced to North America from China along with its food plant, the Chinese Tree of Heaven (*Ailanthus altissima*), during the late 19th century. It was hoped to establish a silk-making industry. This failed, but the moths colonized local parks and gardens. The moths have since spread along the east coast of America. It is a day-flying species that is seen from June to July. The adults do not feed. In the evening, females lay eggs on the host plant in rows of 10–20. The eggs hatch in 2–3 weeks, and the young caterpillars feed in tight groups, but separate as they get older. The caterpillar spins a cocoon of red-brown silk which is attached to the petiole of a leaf and falls to the ground with the leaf in autumn.

Distribution: Eastern United States, southern Asia, Japan, Philippines, parts of Europe.
Habitat: Cities, parks, gardens.
Food plant: *Ailanthus altissima*.
Wingspan: 10–14cm (4–5½in).
Status: Not listed.

Identification: Large olive-brown wings with pink-brown bands across the middle, crescent shaped transparent spot on each wing.

Orizaba Silk Moth

Rothschildia orizaba

Distribution: Arizona, through Central America to Venezuela.
Habitat: Woodland.
Food plant: Various including *Prunus* sp., *Rhus.*, *Salix* sp..
Wingspan: 10–12cm (4–4¾in).
Status: Not listed.

Identification: Forewing patterned red-brown wings, with triangular translucent patch, white and black thin stripe across middle of wing, pinky-brown to margin. Hindwing rounded, similar pattern and patch, submarginal row of small black spots. Female similar pattern, but paler.

This moth has a variety of common names including the Orizaba, Window-winged, and Mexican Emperor Silk moth. It is an attractive night-flying moth. Like the other members of this genus, this Silk moth has distinctive 'windows' in each wing. The moths are nocturnal and rest on tree trunks or on piles of dead leaves during the day, where the patterns of browns and orange provide good camouflage. The caterpillar has a green body, the dorsal half being bright green and the ventral half being a darker green with a white strip along the side and small white-yellow spots. The caterpillars have various appetites, feeding on large quantities of leaves, and often defoliate whole branches. The genus *Rothschildia* is named after Walter Rothschild (1868–1937) who built up a huge collection of Lepidoptera, much of which now forms part of the collection at the Natural History Museum in London, England.

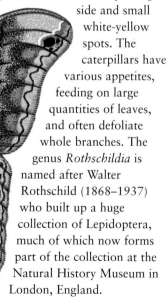

Royal Walnut Moth

Citheronia regalis

Distribution: North America.
Habitat: Woodland.
Food plant: Varied including *Carya* sp., *Juglans* sp..
Wingspan: 95–155mm (3¾–6in).
Status: Not listed.

Identification: Forewing brown with red-orange veins and creamy yellow spots, Hindwing orange with yellow at base.

Right: The fifth instar caterpillar is bright green, with silver and orange spots on the side and long spines.

The Royal Walnut Moth, or Regal Moth, is one of the largest North American moths. Its spectacular caterpillars are nick-named the Hickory Horned Devils. There is a single generation from June to August. The female moths lay their eggs on the upper surface of leaves of the food plants, including walnut and hickory. The young caterpillars are solitary and emerge at night to feed. During the day they curl up, giving the appearance of a bird dropping. The older caterpillars are bright green with black-tipped red horns, reaching lengths of 15cm (6in), and are frequently described as being the 'size of a large hotdog'. When threatened, they rear up and wave their horns to put off a would-be predator. To pupate, the caterpillar crawls to the ground where it digs a chamber. In adverse conditions it can remain as a pupa for several seasons.

OTHER SPECIES OF NOTE

Glover's Silkmoth *Hyalophora gloveri*
Glover's Silkmoth is very similar in appearance to the Cecropia Moth, although it has more grey and white along the margins. It is a little smaller, with a wingspan of 10–11cm (4–4⅜in). It is found in the Rocky Mountains of North America. Its food plants are varied, such as willow and *Prunus* sp.

Columbian Moth *Hyalophora columbia*
The Columbian moth is found in the woodlands of Canada and USA, where it flies from May to June. It has red-brown wings with white crescents, and grey beyond the white post-median band. The females lay their eggs singly at the bases of larch needles. The solitary caterpillars usually spin their cocoon on a branch or the trunk. Other food plants include cherry, birch and willow.

Cecropia Moth

Hyalaphora cecropia

Distribution: Southern Canada, USA, Mexico.
Habitat: Woodlands, gardens.
Food plant: Various including *Acer* sp., *Malus* sp., *Populus* sp., *Prunus* sp., *Salix* sp..
Wingspan: 15cm (6in).
Status: Not listed.

Identification: Wings dark brown with red flush at base, crescent-shaped spot, red post-median band, pale margin. Body red with white bands.

The Cecropia or Robin Moth is the largest native butterfly or moth in North America. It is a relatively common night-flying moth. There is usually a single generation that flies from March to June. However, a second generation may be seen a few weeks later. The adults lack a mouth so cannot feed. They live for less than two weeks. The females lay their eggs in rows on the underside of leaves. The impressive caterpillar is pale yellow-green, with blue and yellow tubercles ending in short black spines, with are four red-orange tubercles on the thorax. It reaches lengths of 15cm (6in) or more. It pupates inside a tough cocoon, overwinters and emerges the following spring.

SPHINGIDAE

There are about 125 species belonging to the Sphingidae in North America, and more than 300 known species in Central and South America. They are commonly called Sphinx or Hawk moths, and are medium to large moths with a rapid wing beat. Most species of Sphingidae feed by hovering in the air in front of flowers, like hummingbirds.

Pink-spotted Hawkmoth

Agrius cingulata

This day-flying moth is frequently seen sipping nectar from tubular flowers such as the moonflower and petunia. It is a strong-flying, migrant moth that can cover considerable distances. For this reason it can appear almost anywhere throughout its range, and has even been found in Hawaii, the Galapagos, Europe and West Africa. There is a single generation in the northern parts of its range, which flies from June to October, and as many as three in the far south, where adult moths can be seen throughout the year. The female lays her eggs on leaves of the food plant. The caterpillar is usually green, with black 'V' shaped markings along the sides and a black horn at the end of the abdomen; however, brown and yellow variants can be seen. In some places it is considered a pest, as it damages garden plants.

Distribution: Canada, USA, Central and South America, occasionally Western Europe.
Habitat: Woodlands, gardens.
Food plant: *Calonyction aculeatum, Convolvulus* sp. *Lonicera* sp., *Petunia* sp..
Wingspan: 90–120mm (3½–4¾in).
Status: Not listed.

Identification: Forewing tapered, mottled pattern of shades of black, brown and pink. Hindwing smaller with pink base and bands. Pink bands on abdomen.

Carolina Sphinx

Manduca sexta

The Carolina Sphinx or the Tobacco Hornworm, as it is also known, is a common Hawk moth found across the southern states of North America. It is a day-flying moth that is seen taking nectar from flowers. Generally, there are two generations each year, but in the southern states there are as many as four. The female moths lay their eggs singly on the underside of leaves of the tobacco and other food plants. The caterpillar is lime green, with seven pale diagonal marks on its sides and a red horn on the last abdominal segment. When mature, the caterpillars drop to the ground where they burrow into the ground and pupate. The pupae of the last generation overwinter, and emerge the following spring. The caterpillars are considered pests as they can defoliate plants and cause damage in gardens and crops such as the tomato, tobacco, and potato. The caterpillars are frequently parasitized by wasps and the caterpillars carry the cocoons of the parasitic moths on their backs.

Distribution: Southern United States, Central America.
Habitat: Farmland, gardens.
Food plant: *Solanum* sp..
Wingspan: 10cm (4in).
Status: Not listed.

Identification: Forewings mottled black, grey and white with spotted white fringe. Hindwings black and white bands, two zig-zag median lines. Abdomen black and orange.

Snowberry Clearwing

Hemaris diffinis

> **Distribution**: North America and Mexico.
> **Habitat**: Fields, gardens.
> **Food plant**: *Lonicera* sp. *Symphoricarpos* sp., *Viburnum* sp..
> **Wingspan**: 30–50mm (1¼–2in).
> **Status**: Not listed.

Identification: Variable. Wings clear with brown veins, margins and base. Thorax golden-brown with black sides, abdomen black with a couple of yellow segments, ending with tufts of black hairs.

The Snowberry or Bumblebee Moth is seen across North America from Canada to Mexico. The adult moth is a mimic of the bumble bee with its transparent wings and yellow and black abdomen. It is active during the day, when it is spotted hovering around flowers such as honeysuckle, snowberry and *Lantana*. Its wings beat at a high frequency producing a buzzing sound, which contributes to the mimicry. There are two generations a year between March and September. The female moth lays her eggs singly on leaves of the food plant. The caterpillar is lime green with a brown stripe along the underside, blue spots and a terminal yellow horn. The caterpillar pupates on the ground amongst the leaf litter. The newly emerged adult moth has wings covered in scales, but these drop off as the moth flies around, creating the clear wing.

OTHER SPECIES OF NOTE

Pandorus sphinx *Eumorpha pandorus*
This attractive hawkmoth is found in the eastern half of the United States and Canada. The upper wings are shades of brown and olive green, with pink streaks along the veins. The underwings are yellow-green and brown. This is a night-flying moth, appearing at dusk to feed. Adults feed from flowers including petunia (*Petunia hybrida*), and white campion (*Lychnis alba*). There is a single generation in the north, from June to August, and at least two in the south, from April to October. During the winter months this species remains in a dormant stage (diapause) as a pupa, in a subterranean chamber.

Elsa Sphinx *Sagenosoma elsa*
The Elsa Sphinx is a rare moth that is found from Utah to Mexico. There is a single generation from May to July. The adult moth has speckled brown and black forewings with black and white bands. The hindwings are creamy white with two black bands. The mature caterpillar is green with six diagonal white and black lines along the sides and a black horn on the terminal abdominal segment.

Bedstraw Hawkmoth

Hyles galii

The Bedstraw Hawkmoth is a night-flying species, which becomes active at dusk. However, they may be seen during the day. There is a single generation from May to August. The females lay up to five eggs on the upper surface of the food plant leaves. The caterpillar is dark green to brown with yellow spots and a pink-brown underside. The caterpillar drops to the ground from the food plant and pupates in loose cocoons in shallow burrows in the ground. The pupae overwinter and complete their life cycle the following spring. This is a migrant species and in some years large numbers fly north during the summer months.

> **Distribution**: Canada, United States, Mexico, Europe.
> **Habitat**: Meadows, edges of coniferous woodlands, gardens.
> **Food plant**: *Galium* sp. and *Epilobium* sp..
> **Wingspan**: 60–80mm (2¼–3⅛in).
> **Status**: Not listed.

Identification: Upper forewing dark olive green-brown, lighter brown along margin, and light brown band from tip to inner margin. Upper hindwing dark brown, paler submarginal band, red-orange spot or band near inner margin.

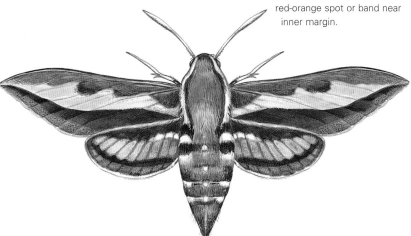

MISCELLANEOUS

The moths featured in these pages come from a number of families: the Hornet Moth, a type of clearwing moth (Sesiidae); the Urania moth of the Uraniidae, many of which are butterfly-like day-flying moths; the Leopard moth of the Miller moths (Cossidae); and the Peach Twig Borer, a Twirler moth (Gelechiidae), one of 650 species in North America, many of which are pests.

Hornet Moth

Sesia apiformis

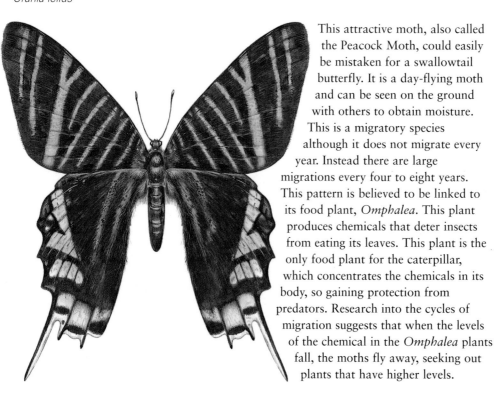

The Hornet Moth is easily confused with the true hornet. The mimicry gives the moth excellent protection; such that the moth is a similar size and has the characteristic jerky flight of the hornet. Close-up inspection reveals that the moth lacks the narrow waist and sting. It is also confused with the Lunar Hornet moth. The adults are seen in summer, and there is a single generation. They can be found resting on the trunks of its food plant, the black poplar. The females lay their eggs at the base of the tree. The caterpillars hatch and feed just under the bark near the ground. The caterpillars overwinter and continue their slow growth the following summer. They spend the second winter as a pupa and the adults emerge the following June. This moth is a serious pest of trees such as the aspen, poplar and willow. The caterpillars form extensive tunnels through the wood, weakening the tree at its base.

Distribution: North America, Europe, Asia.
Habitat: Forests, parks, hedgerows, golf courses.
Food plant: *Populus nigra*, *Salix* sp..
Wingspan: 33–48mm (1¼–1¾in).
Status: Not listed.

Identification: Wasp-like with clear wings. Thorax black with yellow, abdomen yellow and black segments.

Urania Moth

Urania leilus

This attractive moth, also called the Peacock Moth, could easily be mistaken for a swallowtail butterfly. It is a day-flying moth and can be seen on the ground with others to obtain moisture. This is a migratory species although it does not migrate every year. Instead there are large migrations every four to eight years. This pattern is believed to be linked to its food plant, *Omphalea*. This plant produces chemicals that deter insects from eating its leaves. This plant is the only food plant for the caterpillar, which concentrates the chemicals in its body, so gaining protection from predators. Research into the cycles of migration suggests that when the levels of the chemical in the *Omphalea* plants fall, the moths fly away, seeking out plants that have higher levels.

Distribution: South America.
Habitat: Tropical rainforest.
Food plant: *Omphalea* sp..
Wingspan: 90–100mm (3½–4in).
Status: Not listed.

Identification: Dark wings. Forewing has iridescent green and blue stripes and lines. Hindwing black with band of iridescent green and white scalloped margin. Long white tail edged in black.

Peach Twig Borer

Anarsia lineatella

Distribution: North America, Europe.
Habitat: Orchards.
Food plant: Fruit trees with stoned-fruits such as peach, apricot, plum, almond.
Wingspan: 11–14mm (4–5½in).
Status: Not listed.

This moth is a pest of orchards because of the caterpillars that feed on the leaves and fruits of trees especially stoned-fruits, such as plums and peaches. The adults fly from June to August. The female lays her eggs singly at the base of leaves. The caterpillars burrow through young shoots and fruits, all the way to the stone, and pupate at the base of the fruit or in a leaf. The caterpillars of the second generation overwinter under the bark of young shoots. They emerge in the spring and burrow into buds and shoots, causing them to wilt and die.

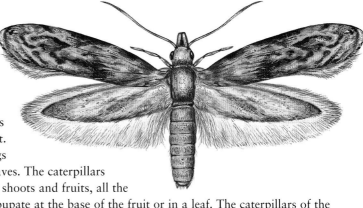

Identification: Very narrow wings. Forewings grey black or brown, with black stripes and single brown spot. Hindwings larger, grey with fringe. Two grey labial palps project forward from the head.

OTHER SPECIES OF NOTE

Urania sloanus
This butterfly-like day-flying moth is found in Jamaica. Its forewings are dark, with yellow and orange stripes. The hindwings have patches of yellow, orange, green and blue, and a jagged margin with long tails.

Purple Longhorn Moth *Adela bella*
This common micro-moth is found across eastern North America. They are day-flying moths. Typical of all long-horned moths, the antennae are exceptionally long, several times the length of the wings. They hold out their antennae in front of their body as they flutter around the food plants.

Pine Cone Borer *Eucosma bobana*
This is a pest of trees in southwestern United States, where the caterpillar burrows into the cone to eat the seeds. It is a small moth with red-brown forewings with a square dark patch on each wing. Females are larger than males.

Leopard Moth

Zeuzera pyrina

The Leopard moth is seen in June and July in woodlands, orchards and garden where it finds its food plants. There is a single generation. The night-flying adults rest on tree trunks during the day. The female moths lay their eggs singly on small shoots. The caterpillars hatch and burrow into branches. Their growth is slow but in their second year they move into larger branches and trunks, where they can weaken the tree. The caterpillars overwinter for a second time and then pupate in spring. Often there is just one caterpillar per tree.

Distribution: North America, North Africa, Europe, Middle East, Asia.
Habitat: Woods, parks, orchards and gardens.
Food plant: Various tree species including *Acer*, *Alnus*, *Betula*, *Fagus*, *Fraxinus*, *Malus*, *Prunus*, *Quercus*.
Wingspan: 35–60mm (1⅜–2¼in).
Status: Not listed.

Right: The lightly haired caterpillar is pale yellow with dark tubercles. Larvae bore into stems of shrubs and trees, especially apples, pears and plums, where they do much damage by eating the heartwood and killing the tree.

Identification: White wings with small black spots, thorax has black marks, abdomen bands of grey-black. Females larger than males.

DIRECTORY OF SOUTH ASIA AND AUSTRALASIA

This section covers the geographical areas known as the Oriental and the Australian region. The Oriental region is bounded on the north by the Himalayas and extends south through South and Southeast Asia. Much of the region experiences a tropical climate, with high temperatures for much of the year. The presence of tropical rainforest helps to boost the number of lepidopteran species, the region being second only to the Neotropics in diversity. In India, there are more than 1,500 species of butterflies, while tiny Singapore has more than 400 varieties. The Australian region extends from New Guinea, eastwards through Australia to Polynesia. New Guinea, being an overlap zone between the Oriental and Australian regions, is rich in lepidopterans, as is Australia, but elsewhere the diversity is much lower, partly due to oceanic isolation. New Zealand, for example, has fewer than 20 species of butterfly.

Above left and middle: Common Egg Fly (Hypolimnas bolina) caterpillar grazing on a leaf. Above right: Emerald Swallowtail butterfly (Papilio Palinurus). Right: Tree Nymph butterfly (Idea leuconoe).

PAPILIONIDAE

This region is home to some of the best-known and most beautiful of butterflies, the birdwings. Amongst their number is the largest of the butterflies, the Queen Alexandra birdwing (Ornithoptera alexandrae), the females of which have a wingspan of about 28cm (11in), and the Goliath Birdwing, the second largest. Sadly, many of the Papilionidae are under threat.

Common Clubtail

Atrophaneura coon

This is a widely distributed, but rare butterfly that occurs across south and Southeast Asia. It is a slow-flying butterfly found in forests where it visits flowers such as *Lantana* for nectar. It is poisonous, and the orange spots on the wing and the yellow abdomen serve as warnings to would-be predators, such as birds. The caterpillars take up the poison from the food plant, *Apama tomentosa*, a member of the Aristolochiaceae family, which is retained in the adult butterfly. There are eight subspecies.

Distribution: South Asia, Southeast Asia, south China.
Habitat: Forests.
Food plant: *Apama tomentosa*.
Wingspan: 90–120mm (3½–4¾in).
Status: Not listed, although some subspecies are threatened.

Identification: Upperwings dull black. Upper forewing long, narrow, with pale streaks and black veins, upper hindwing black with a blue sheen, elongated white spots divided by black veins, sub-margin row of white crescent-shaped spots, two marginal orange spots, long thin black tail. Undersides similar but paler. Yellow abdomen.

Ceylon Rose

Atrophaneura jophon

The beautiful Ceylon, or Sri Lankan, Rose is found only on the island of Sri Lanka. This butterfly is rarely seen, since it flies at dawn and late afternoon when the sun is low. It visits flowers in clearings and along paths, but for much of the time it remains hidden in the forest. The female butterflies lay their eggs on the underside of leaves of Aristolochiaceae. The caterpillars are purple-black with cream bands and red tubercles. The population size of the Ceylon Rose has fallen as a consequence of extensive deforestation on the island, together with collecting. Nowadays most of the butterflies survive in the Sinharajah Forest Reserve where they are protected.

Identification: Black and white wings with pink crescents on the scalloped hindwing. Females forewing wider with more white and larger spots on the hindwing. Abdomen black with red tip.

Distribution: Sri Lanka.
Habitat: Tropical Evergreen forest below 700m (2,300ft).
Food plant: Aristolochiaceae.
Wingspan: 10–13cm (4–5in).
Status: Threatened.

Rose Windmill

Atrophaneura latreillei

Distribution: Afghanistan, South Asia, southern China, Northern Vietnam.
Habitat: Forests.
Food plant: *Nepenthes* sp..
Wingspan: 11–13cm (4⅜–5¼in).
Status: Not listed.

Identification: Upperwings dull brown-black, upper forewing black streaks and veins. Upper hindwing has elongated white spots, submarginal orange crescents, tail with red tips. Underwings similar but paler. Body black and red. Sexes similar, although female slightly paler.

The Rose Windmill is seen mostly in South Asia, where it occurs in montane forests of altitudes of up to 3,000m (10,000ft). There is a single generation that flies from May to June. The female lays her eggs on pitcher plants of the genus *Nepenthes*. The caterpillar is purple-brown with a diagonal white band down the side of two abdominal segments. There are a number of purple tubercles with red tips. Many of the genus *Atrophaneura* are under threat from habitat loss and collection, but this species is not threatened. There are three subspecies, two of which are found in India. None of the subspecies is under threat.

OTHER SPECIES OF NOTE

White Head Batwing *Atrophaneura priapus*
This Windmill butterfly is found only on Java in Indonesia, where it occurs in forests from sea level to 2,000 metres (6,500ft). The wings are dull black with black streaks and veins, with a band of yellow across the hindwing. The head is white, which gives rise to its common name.

Atrophaneura luchti
This is another of the threatened species of Windmill butterflies. This species is endemic to Java, and as a result of deforestation and collection has recently been categorized as Vulnerable. Protection of the remaining populations is a conservation priority. Its biology and distribution are poorly known.

Great Windmill *Atrophaneura dasarada*
This beautiful woodland butterfly has a wingspan of up to 14cm (5½in), dark brown wings and a long and broad tail. There are white spots on the hindwing. It occurs across northern India, Bhutan and Myanmar into southeast China.

Common Rose

Pachliopta aristolochiae

The Common Rose belongs to the subgenus *Pachliopta* which is part of the genus *Atrophaneura*. This species is a common butterfly with widespread distribution across Asia. The warning colours on its wings and body indicate that it is poisonous. In addition, it produces a foul-smelling liquid if threatened. It is mimicked by a number of other butterfly species, including the Common Mormon (*Papilio polytes*). The butterfly is active from dawn to dusk, flying around the forest in search of nectar. At night it roosts with other butterflies on small branches. There are two generations in the northern parts of the range, but in the south, the butterfly is seen year-round. The females lay eggs on Aristolochiaceae plant leaves. The caterpillar is red-brown with a single white band and numerous red spines tipped with white. There are around 20 subspecies.

Distribution: South Asia, southeast Asia, South China.
Habitat: Lowland forest.
Food plant: *Aristolochia* sp..
Wingspan: 75–85mm (3–3¼in).
Status: Not listed.

Identification: Black wings, forewings have streaks and black veins, hindwings black with white and red spots.

Bhutan Glory

Bhutanitis lidderdalii

This spectacular butterfly is found in the Himalayas and mountainous regions of India and Southeast Asia, where it is seen flying over the tree tops. It has a slow, irregular flight pattern, staying high rather than descending to the ground. However, during rainy weather it rests on leaves with its forewings dropped down over the hindwings to disguise its bright colours. If disturbed, it flashes its wings to deter any predator. There are two generations a year, May to June and August to October. Although the butterfly is widely distributed, it has suffered from loss of habitat due to extensive deforestation and from over-collection, as it is a much-prized butterfly for collectors. There are four species in the genus *Bhutanitis*, and the other three species are identified on the Red List as being Vulnerable.

Distribution: Bhutan, India, southeast Asia.
Habitat: Forests to 3,000m (9,800ft).
Food plant: *Aristolochia* sp..
Wingspan: 90–100mm (3½–4in).
Status: Not listed.

Identification: Upperwings dull black with thin white lines crossing the wings. Upper hindwings patch of red, black and orange, three tails. Underwings similar. Thorax black with green sides, abdomen black with white lines.

Big Greasy

Cressida cressida

This butterfly has several common names, including Greasy Swallowtail, Clearwing and Mimicking Papilio. The newly emerged butterfly has white forewings, but the loose scales soon drop off, and the wings become transparent. The wings mimic other Australian Swallowtails, such as *Papilio amactus*. The butterflies are on the wing for much of the year, with peak numbers during the rainy season. The males patrol the breeding area, seeking females that fly closer to the ground in search of food plants. During mating the males produce a mating plug, called a sphragis, that they use to cover the female genital opening, thereby preventing other males from mating with her. The females lay their eggs singly on the leaves of the food plant. The caterpillar is dark brown with white spots, and is covered by many tubercles which are either brown or white.

Identification: Male forewing mostly transparent grey with black veins, black margin, two black spots. Hindwing black with white band, arc of up to five red spots. Body black, with red tip on abdomen. Female has wider wings that are partly transparent, pale brown with underwing pattern showing through.

Distribution: Indonesia, New Guinea, Australia.
Habitat: Forests.
Food plant: *Aristolochia* sp..
Wingspan: 80mm (3⅛in).
Status: Not listed.

Common Mime

Chilasa clytia

Distribution: South Asia, southeast Asia, southern China.
Habitat: Higher altitude forests.
Food plant: *Cinnamomum* sp. (wild cinnamon tree).
Wingspan: 10–12cm (4–4¾in).
Status: Not listed.

Identification: Light form: black wings with elongated creamy-white markings towards the body, and spots near the margin. HW yellow-orange spots along the margin. Thorax and abdomen black and white. Dark form: wings brown with white markings towards the margins, with a row of crescent-shaped spots along the margin of the HW.

The Common Mime belongs to the black-bodied swallowtails of the genus *Chilasa*. There are several forms across its range, and each form mimics a particular distasteful butterfly. For example, on the island of Sri Lanka there are two forms for each sex, a lighter and a darker form. The lighter form mimics the Blue Tiger (*Tirumala limniace*) while the darker form mimics the Crow (*Euploea* sp.). The Common Mime not only looks similar to its mimic, but copies its flight pattern too. The butterflies are found in open woodland, where they can fly low along the ground and mud-puddle. The pupa resembles a broken twig, and this provides effective camouflage and protection during this stage of the life cycle.

Below: The caterpillar is grey-brown and creamy white, with a red spot below each fleshy spine.

OTHER SPECIES OF NOTE

Chinese Three-tailed Swallowtail
Bhutanitis thaidina
This distinctive butterfly occurs in Tibet and is classified as Locally Rare. It has suffered from extensive deforestation of its mountain habitat. The butterfly is seen in June and July and there is one generation a year.

Dingy Swallowtail *Eleppone anactus*
This is an Australian species that is found around citrus trees; its occurrence on New Caledonia is due to either an introduction, or as vagrants. It is a mimic of distasteful species such as the Big Greasy swallowtail (*Cressida cressida*). The adults visit flowers for nectar, hovering in front of the flower in the same manner as a hummingbird. The males patrol hilltops and other elevated positions, looking for females. In recent years, the range of this species has increased with the planting of citrus trees. The eggs are large, light yellow, roughly spherical, and change to an orange colour when the larvae are almost ready to emerge. Females lay eggs on the new leaves of the host plant.

White Dragontail

Lamproptera curius

This is a butterfly of the tropical forests of Southeast Asia. The adult butterflies have a rapid flight, which creates a characteristic whirring sound. The long tail is used to steer and change direction, enabling the butterfly to dart this way and that, and even to stop in midair, in much the same way as does a dragonfly, hence its common name. The males are frequently seen near running water, such as streams and waterfalls. The females lay their eggs on the leaves of the food plant. Young caterpillars are black with yellow sides, but they become green with age, with black spots and three yellow lines along a few abdominal segments.

Identification: Wings dark brown with tapering white band across both wings. Forewing transparent outer half with black veins. Hindwing long, narrow tail with white tip, few white spots. Underwings brown with grey and white bands, and white spots.

Distribution: Southeast Asia.
Habitat: Tropical rainforest 1,000m (3,300ft) altitude.
Food plant: *Iligera* sp..
Wingspan: 50mm (2in).
Status: Not listed, but seen as Vulnerable in Malaya.

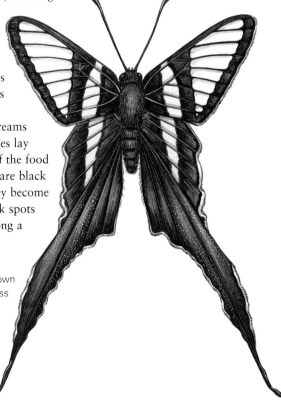

Tailed Jay

Graphium agamemnon

Identification:
Upperwings black with green markings across both wings. Underwings brown-black with pink flush. Females similar with a streak of green-white along dorsal margin of both upper- and underwings.

Distribution: India, Sri Lanka, southeast Asia.
Habitat: Forests, gardens, urban areas.
Food plant: *Polyalthia longifolia* (False Ashoka tree).
Wingspan: 60–70mm (2¼–2¾in).
Status: Not listed.

This common butterfly has several common names, including Green-Spotted Triangle, and Tailed Green Jay. The butterflies are seen all year but they are particularly abundant after the monsoon. They spend much of the time in the canopy but come to the ground in search of nectar flowers, such as *Lantana* and *Ixora* sp.. The life cycle is short, just four weeks, and there are as many as eight generations a year. The females lay their eggs on the underside of young leaves of the food plant. The mature caterpillar is green, with black spines and small black spots. Many Swallowtail species have experienced a decline in recent years, but the Tailed Jay has extended in recent years, due to the planting of its food plant, the False Ashoka, in gardens and urban landscaped areas.

Common Jay

Graphium doson

Identification: Upperwings black with pale blue, almost transparent broken band across wings, row of blue-green submarginal spots on both wings. Lower hindwing black with dark red centred bar. Female slightly longer tail, upper hindwing greenish streak on lower margin.

The Common Jay is another fast-flying species, the rapid beat of the wings makes it difficult to identify when in flight. This is an active butterfly that is always on the move, and rarely settles. It tends to stay in the canopy where it flies around searching for nectar-rich flowers, but comes down to find flowers such as *Lantana*. The butterflies fly all year, but they are particularly abundant during the wet season. The females lay their eggs singly on the underside of leaves. There are two forms of caterpillar, dark brown and bright green. Both have short spines on the fourth segment of the abdomen. The butterfly has become more common over the last few decades due to the increased planting of its food plants in gardens, such as the custard apple.

Distribution: Southeast Asia, India, Japan.
Habitat: Thick deciduous forest, semi-evergreen and evergreen forest.
Food plant: *Annona* sp., *Magnolia* sp..
Wingspan: 70–80mm (2¾–3⅛in).
Status: Not listed.

Right: The red marks on the underwing of this butterfly help to distinguish this species from other similar Graphium *sp. in the same habitat.*

Purple Mountain Emperor

Graphium weiskei

Distribution: Papua New Guinea.
Habitat: Forests.
Food plant: Unknown.
Wingspan: 70–80mm (2¾–3⅛in).
Status: Not listed.

Identification: Male forewing black with row of small green spots at margin and green and purple spots along the leading edge. Purple towards the body. Hindwing black scalloped margin and tail, green towards body, two central purple spots. Female brown with grey, green and black markings.

This striking Swallowtail with purple, green and black wings is found in the mountainous forests of Papua New Guinea and the surrounding islands, at altitudes of between 1,500–2,700m (5,000–8,800ft). It tends to stay within the canopy, so is not very often recorded. The best time to spot the butterfly is in the early morning, when it feeds on nectar. Since it spends much of its time in the canopy its life cycle is still to be discovered. Although the butterfly is collected, the fact that it spends much of the time high in the canopy makes it less vulnerable to collectors, and its forest habitat is relatively untouched.

OTHER SPECIES OF NOTE

Graphium codrus

Graphium codrus is found on islands from Sulawesi to New Guinea. There are more than 15 subspecies that vary in the colour of the band that crosses the forewing. The band can range in colour from lime green to yellow or blue green. In some subspecies the band is broken. The butterflies spend their time in the canopy, but come to the ground to feed on rotting fruits and for the males to mud-puddle.

Malayan Zebra *Graphium delesserti*

This Malaysian butterfly gets its common name from its striped appearance. The wings are creamy white with black patches and veins. There is a yellow spot on the hindwing. It is a mimic of the distasteful Danaids which it copies both in colour and flight pattern. Males are seen on the ground mud-puddling.

Blue Triangle

Graphium sarpendon

The Blue Triangle or Common Bluebottle is an active butterfly that darts quickly from flower to flower and is notoriously difficult to catch. The males descend to the ground to feed by puddles with other males. They also obtain moisture from animal droppings and animal remains. The female butterflies lay their eggs singly on the leaves of the food plant. The mature caterpillar is green, with a yellow band and short spines on the thorax and terminal segment. It tends to lie along the midrib of a leaf, its colour making it difficult to spot. If disturbed, they release a strong smell from their yellow osmeeria that pop up from behind their head. This species has proved itself to be very adaptable, and it has moved from a rainforest habitat into gardens and parks of cities as a result of the widespread planting of its food plants, in particular *Cinnamomum camphora* (Camphor Laurel).

Distribution: South and southeast Asia, New Guinea, Australia.
Habitat: Rainforest below 1,600m (5,200ft).
Food plant: Various including *Cinnamomum* sp., *Litsea* sp., (Indian laurel).
Wingspan: 55–80mm (2³⁄₁₆–3⅛in).
Status: Not listed.

Identification: Black with broad band of transparent blue-green across both wings. HW row of blue sub marginal spots, no tail.

Chimaera Birdwing

Ornithoptera chimaera

This Birdwing spends much of the time in the canopy, where small groups can be seen circling over the tree tops. However, it will fly lower in the canopy to visit nectar-rich flowers such as hibiscus. The female lays clusters of up to 20 eggs on the leaves of the food plant. Its numbers have declined as a result of deforestation and over-collecting for butterfly collections. As a result, the species is listed on Appendix II of CITES. Given the interest in specimens, there is considerable potential for local farmers to set up butterfly farms, to earn income and protect the wild populations. There are several subspecies, each found in different areas.

Distribution: Indonesia and New Guinea.
Habitat: Mountainous rainforest.
Food plant: *Aristolochia* sp..
Wingspan: 16–19cm (6¼–7½in).
Status: Not listed.

Identification: Male forewings black, with iridescent streaks of green and yellow. Hindwing mostly yellow with black margins and spots, green near margins. Body yellow and black abdomen. Females' upperwings brown and white, underwings yellow. Females larger than males.

Goliath Birdwing

Ornithoptera goliath

The Goliath Birdwing is the second largest butterfly in the world. It is a powerful flier that is seen high in the canopy of rainforest. The males chase the females over long distances before mating. Little is known about its life cycle. This species has suffered from over-collecting in the past and the loss of undisturbed, dense rainforest. However, there are now a number of butterfly farms that rear this butterfly, bringing income to remote villages. The villagers plant the nectar plants, which attract the adults. They then collect some of the pupae, and sell the adults under a permit system.

Identification: Male forewings black with iridescent green streaks, hindwings mostly yellow with green veins, black margin and three green spots. Female brown, with black, white and yellow markings; larger than the male.

Distribution: Indonesia, New Guinea.
Habitat: Rainforest.
Food plant: *Aristolochia* sp..
Wingspan: 20–22cm (8–9in).
Status: Vulnerable.

Left: Female wings are dark brown. The upperwing has a chain of pale spots, while the lower wing is brown and yellow, with dark brown spots.

Rothschild's Birdwing

Ornithoptera rothschildi

Distribution: New Guinea, especially Arfak Mountains
Habitat: Tropical rainforest, in particular at altitudes of 1,800–2,400m (5,900–7,900ft).
Food plant: *Pararistolchia* sp.
Wingspan: 150mm (6in).
Status: Vulnerable.

Identification: Forewing dark brown-black, with creamy white to green streaks. Hindwing yellow with black margin, black spots and small patch of green. Abdomen yellow. Female brown with creamy-white to grey spots.

This birdwing was named after the well-known lepidopterist Lord Walter Rothschild, who financed expeditions to New Guinea. The species was first discovered by Carl Brenders Pratt, and was then named by George Kenrick in 1911. The adults feed solely on nectar from flowers. Most male birdwings mud-puddle, but the males of this species obtain all their nutrients from flowers. The females lay clusters of up to 20 eggs on leaves of the food plant. The mature caterpillar is black, with spines and yellow horns. The pupa is black and yellow. The butterflies are found in remote, inaccessible mountains where there are forested slopes and deep ravines. These forests are not yet experiencing deforestation, so the butterfly habitat remains undisturbed.

OTHER SPECIES OF NOTE

Paradise Birdwing *Ornithoptera paradisea*
This beautiful birdwing, with its iridescent green, yellow and black wings, can be distinguished from similar birdwings by its unusually-shaped hindwing that has a small curved tail. The female looks very different, with brown-grey forewings, and hindwings that lack tails. The status of this butterfly is classed as Indeterminate.

Queen Victoria's Birdwing *Ornithoptera victoriae*
The hindwings have an unusual shape; they look as if they are wrinkled and have not expanded correctly. The male has iridescent green-and-black wings, with yellow-orange spots, while the female is larger, with black, yellow and white wings. This species is now protected due to over-collection.

Priam's Birdwing *Ornithoptera priamus*
This species has the widest distribution of any birdwing, being found in Australia, New Guinea and Indonesia. The males differ in wing colour, which varies from yellow and orange to blue and green. Although it is mostly found in rainforests, it does occur in other habitats.

Queen Alexandra's Birdwing

Ornithoptera alexandrae

The largest butterfly in the world, this species was named after the wife of King Edward VII by Lord Walter Rothschild. This amazing butterfly is found only in the rainforests in the Popondetta Valley in New Guinea, its restriction being due to the limited occurrence of its food plant, *Aristolochia dielsiana*. The males defend a territory against other butterflies and even against small birds. The females lay very few eggs, just 30 or so, on the food plant. The caterpillar is less fussy, and eats leaves of other *Aristolochia* sp.. The caterpillar is black, with red tubercles, and a cream band around the middle of the body. The pupa is black with yellow markings. The butterflies pupate in the early morning so that they can expand their large wings while the humidity is high. The butterfly is now Endangered. It is under threat from illegal poaching and from deforestation.

Distribution: New Guinea.
Habitat: Tropical rainforest.
Food plant: *Aristolochia dielsiana*.
Wingspan: 28cm (11in), possibly larger.
Status: Endangered.

Identification: Elongated forewing, male black with iridescent green and blue streaks, yellow abdomen. Female is larger, wings brown with white markings. Creamy yellow abdomen and red hairs on thorax.

Large Citrus
Papilio aegeus

The Large Citrus, or Orchard Swallowtail, is a common butterfly as it occurs in a variety of habitats, including gardens. This is partly due to the fact that it has a number of food plants, including lemons, Mexican orange blossom and others of the Rutaceae family. The slow-flying butterflies visit flowers for nectar. Females lay their eggs singly on the tops of leaves. The caterpillars feed on the leaves of the food plant, and may cause damage in orchards. The young caterpillars look like bird droppings, but they become green, with age. The caterpillars are green with yellow-white diagonal stripes which are edged in blue. When disturbed it displays its red osmeterium and releases a foul smell to deter would-be predators.

Identification: Male UFW black with creamy-white crescents, UHW black with white patch and red spot. Underwings less white, with more red patches, small blue crescents. Female has brown-black wings with white spot with brown veins on FW.

Distribution: Indonesia, New Guinea, eastern Australia.
Habitat: Orchards, gardens.
Food plant: *Citrus* sp., *Choisya* sp., *Fortunella* sp., *Poncirus* sp..
Wingspan: 10–12cm (4–4½ in).
Status: Not listed.

Common Mormon
Papilio polytes

This is a very common Swallowtail found widely across south and Southeast Asia, where it is seen in woodlands, gardens and parks. There are three forms of the female, occurring in different parts of the range. Each form mimics a particular butterfly, for example the form *stichius* mimics the Common Rose, while the form *romulus* mimics the Crimson Rose. The butterfly is seen all year, but it is particularly common during the wet season. The females lay their eggs on the surface of leaves of the food plant. The caterpillars become increasingly green with age. The underside is cream and brown, with a black-brown band around the fourth segment, two eyespots, oblique white and brown stripes along the side and red osmeteria. In the northern parts of the range, the pupae overwinter.

Identification: Black wings with white and red spots. Males UFW row of white spots, UHW band of elongate white spots, red crescents along margin. Females polymorphic, one form has black wings, with white spots and red crescents on the HW.

Distribution: South and southeast Asia, Japan.
Habitat: Woodlands, gardens and parks.
Food plant: Rutaceae.
Wingspan: 15cm (6in).
Status: Not listed.

Great Mormon

Papilio memnon

Distribution: India, through
southeast Asia to Japan.
Habitat: Open woodland to
2,000m (6,500ft), gardens.
Food plant: Rutaceae.
Wingspan: 15cm (6in).
Status: Not listed.

Identification: Males wings
black, dusted with blue with black
veins, single red patch under
leading edge. Underwings black
with red patch and red bases.
Females exist in three forms, one
of which has a tail.

-This is a common species that
occurs over a wide area and
for which there are at least 13
subspecies. The males and females
of this species look very different,
and the female is polymorphic as it
exists in three forms. The butterfly
inhabits wooded habitats up 2,000m
(6,500ft). The males are more
commonly seen in open areas, such
as clearings, but the females stay
under cover in more closely wooded
areas. The butterflies visit nectar-
rich flowers and the males mud-
puddle. The females lay their
eggs on the leaves of plants of
the Rutaceae family such as citrus trees. The caterpillar
looks very like that of the Common Mormon butterfly, and
is parasitized by wasps.

OTHER SPECIES OF NOTE

Fuscus Swallowtail *Papilio fuscus*
This relatively common butterfly is found in
northeast Australia in the drier rainforests and
monsoon vine forest in coastal lowlands. It is
particularly abundant in the wet season. The
females lay their eggs on plants of the Rutaceae.

Chinese Peacock *Papilio bianor*
This species has black wings with an iridescent
green sheen and red crescents on the hindwing.
It inhabits forests and gardens across China,
Korea, India and Myanmar. The females lay their
eggs on the plants of the Rutaceae.

Papilio agestor
This butterfly has brown to black wings with a
cream band, and blue and red spots towards the
base of the hindwing and a long tail. As well as
the colours, this butterfly mimics the flight and
resting position of the wings of *Danaus sita*. The
females lay eggs on the leaves of *Machilus* sp..

Common Lime Butterfly

Papilio demoleus

The Common Lime or Lemon Butterfly is
one of the most widely distributed and
common species of swallowtail. It is a fast-
flying species that is seen travelling low over
the ground, at heights of about one metre
(3 feet), looking for nectar-rich flowers. The
butterflies are seen all year round, but are
particularly abundant after the wet season.
There are several generations a year. The
females produce large numbers of eggs,
which they lay singly on the tops of leaves.
The caterpillars become
green with age. There
are regional variations
in appearance. In areas
where the caterpillars
feed on *Citrus* sp., the
mature caterpillars have
two eyespots and white
and brown diagonal
stripes on the side of the
body. In Australia, the
females tend to lay their
eggs on *Psoralea* sp., and
the resulting caterpillars
are green with two rows
of pink-orange spots edged
in black with scattered
black markings.

Distribution: South and
southeast Asia, southern
China, Japan, New Guinea,
Australia, Caribbean.
Habitat: Woodland, orchards,
grassland, gardens.
Food plant: Rutaceae,
especially citrus trees, also
Psoralea sp. (Fabaceae).
Wingspan: 80–100mm (3–4in).
Status: Not listed.

Identification: Black wings with
elongated white patches across
the middle of the wing and
marginal and submargin row
of white spots. HW
blue-red eyespot,
no tail.

Kaiser-i-Hind

Teinopalpus imperialis

The Kaiser-i-Hind or Emperor of India is much sought after by collectors. It is a strong flier found in high-altitude forest of the Himalayas. The males have territories which they defend against other males, chasing any intruder away. For much of the time, the butterflies rest high in the canopy, and they only visit the lower levels of the forest to find flowers or mud-puddle. There are one or two generations, April to May and May to July. The females lay their eggs on the underside of the food leaves. The caterpillars pupate and then overwinter. The butterfly is only found in restricted areas and over collection and deforestation has reduced its population to threatened levels.

Identification: Sexes different. Males forewing black covered with green scales, green patch towards the base, hindwing green with yellow-orange, black margin with green crescents, tail. Female larger, forewing shades of black, grey and green, with green base, hindwing black and grey, with yellow-orange patch, green base, submarginal green crescents and tails.

Distribution: Nepal, Bhutan, Indian Himalayas, Northern Myanmar, China.
Habitat: Dense forest in the Himalayas to 3,000m (9,800ft).
Food plant: *Magnolia campbelii, Teinopapus imperialis*.
Wingspan: 9–12cm (3½–4¾in).
Status: Near Threatened.

Cape York Birdwing

Ornithoptera priamus

Identification: Iridescent green and black wings. FW centre black with green streak either side, black margins. HW green with black veins, spots and margin. Underwings black with blue-green markings. Females larger, brown-black with creamy markings. Orange-yellow abdomen.

The Cape York Birdwing is also known as Priam's Birdwing, New Guinea Birdwing and the Northern Birdwing. The species was first described 200 years ago. Since that time about 18 subspecies have been identified, each geographically isolated. This includes four subspecies in Australia. They all differ in the patterns of green and black. The butterflies are seen year-round and there are several generations. They have a gliding flight pattern and are most active during the early morning and late afternoon, when the males are seen in the canopy. They rest in shady places near the ground. The females lay their eggs on *Aristolochia* species. The caterpillars are solitary and often pupate on the food plant. The caterpillars occur in two colour forms, light brown-grey or dark brown-black, dependent on the amount of sunlight they receive.

Distribution: Northern Australia and New Guinea.
Habitat: Lowland tropical rainforest.
Food plant: *Aristolochia* sp..
Wingspan: 12.5–15cm (5–6in).
Status: Not listed, but uncommon.

Right: The female has predominantly brown wings with white marks on the upper wing and yellow spots along the margin of the hindwing.

Golden Birdwing

Troides aeacus

Distribution: Northern India, Nepal, China, southeast Asia.
Habitat: Forest between 1,500–1,700m (5,000–5,500ft).
Food plant: *Aristolochia* sp..
Wingspan: 90–115mm (3½–4¼in).
Status: Vulnerable in some parts of the range.

Identification: Males upper forewing black with pale streaks. Upper hindwing black and orange-yellow, black veins, black scalloped border. The female is larger, dull black with orange on hindwing.

The Golden Birdwing has the most northerly range of any of the birdwing, as it extends into China. It is relatively common in some parts of its range, but rare in others, for example in Sumatra and China. The butterfly is found in forests where it tends to stay at heights of about 4–5m (13–16ft) in the canopy, only coming down to the ground to find flowers. The males defend their territory from other males. The females lay their eggs on birthwort. The caterpillars feed on the buds and leaves, and pupate on the food plant. The butterfly has lost large areas of its habitat due to deforestation, the main threat to its survival.

OTHER SPECIES OF NOTE

Golden Ornithoptera *Troides rhadamantus*
The Golden Ornithoptera is found in Indonesia and the Philippines where it lives in forests and gardens. The forewing is black with silvery streaks and black veins and the hindwing is black with an eye-catching yellow mark. The underside of the hindwing has more yellow. Although the butterfly has been collected, it is not threatened.

Troides hypo
This is a common species of birdwing that occurs in Sulawesi and the Moluccan Islands. It is the largest *Troides*, reaching 20cm (8in) in the female. The upperwings are black with streaks of silver-yellow while the hindwings are grey-black with a yellow band along the margin with a row of black spots and a scalloped black margin. The male has red on its abdomen; the basic colour of the female is dark brown with a yellow and black abdomen, it is larger than the male. This is a poisonous species.

Rajah Brooke's Birdwing

Trogonoptera brookiana

Discovered by naturalist Alfred Russell Wallace, this butterfly was named after Captain Brooke, the 'White Rajah' who ruled Sarawak, Borneo during the 19th century. Unusually, the female of this species is more eye-catching than the male, with its yellow and green wings. The butterflies are found in rainforest, close to streams with sandy banks and near hot springs. The butterflies are seen all year, but are more numerous during the dry season. Large numbers of up to 100 males gather to mud-puddle in the forest. The more secretive females stay within the forest. They lay up to 50 eggs, singly, on the leaves of the food plant. The mature caterpillar is grey-brown, with grey tubercles and red osmeterium. Unfortunately, the butterfly has been heavily collected in the past and is now threatened by extensive deforestation.

Distribution: Malaysia, Indonesia.
Habitat: Rainforest with hot springs and streams.
Food plant: *Aristolochia foveolata*.
Wingspan: 17cm (6½in).
Status: Not listed.

Identification: Males black wings, UFW has seven triangular green marks across wing, UFW central green patch. Females UFW black-brown with yellow-green zig-zag band, white streaks and tip, UHW black with green streaks and submarginal row of yellow crescents and white spots along margin. Head red, body black with red marks.

PIERIDAE

The Pieridae are well represented through the Oriental and Australian regions. One of the most common butterflies in South Asia is the Common Gull, which is a Pierid. A number of the Pierids are migrants, and this have a widespread distribution. Pierids are also well represented in mountain habitats, especially in the Himalayas, where the Jezebels are common.

Caper White

Belenois java

The Caper White varies in its appearance. There are two forms, a light one and a dark one that has more black and yellow-orange on the wing, especially the female. The reason for the difference is unclear, but it may be related to diet. The female lays large clusters of about 100 eggs on the leaves and stems of the food plant. The caterpillars hatch and stay together. They are voracious feeders and can completely defoliate a tree. The Caper White is a migratory species and, in years when conditions are favourable, large numbers of butterflies migrate south in spring. They migrate together, flying during the day and roosting together on trees and shrubs, before flying farther the next day. In some places, the numbers migrating are so large they are considered to be a plague. The females lay their eggs on any food plant they find on the route. In 1975, during a large migration through Adelaide, about 40,000 eggs were laid on one tree.

Distribution: Indonesia, New Guinea, Australia, New Caledonia, Fiji, Samoa.
Habitat: Woodland.
Food plant: Capparidaceae such as *Capparis* sp..
Wingspan: 55–60mm (2⅛–2¼in).
Status: Not listed.

Identification: Male UFW white, black at apex with white spots, single black spot centrally, UHW white with broad black margin enclosed white spots. LFW similar to UFW but white spots larger, LHW pattern of white and black with black veins, submarginal white spots with splashes of yellow. Female single black spot on UFW larger and merged with black border, UHW black bar and broader black margin.

Common Gull

Cepora nerissa

Distribution: India, Pakistan, Sri Lanka, Myanmar.
Habitat: Varied including grassland, meadow, forest, garden.
Food plant: Capparidaceae.
Wingspan: 40–65mm (1½–2½in).
Status: Not listed.

Identification: Forewing white with black veins and black margin, hindwing similar, less black. Lower forewing similar to upper wing, lower hindwing dark yellow. Veins outlined in green.

The Common Gull is one of the most common butterflies in South Asia. It is a strong flier and undertakes migrations. It is on the wing for much of the year in the more northerly areas, and from June to November in the rest. There are several generations. It can be seen in a variety of habitats including forest, grassland and gardens, and up to altitudes of about 2,400m (7,200ft) in the southern parts of its range. There are two forms of this butterfly, a wet-season form as described above and a dry-season one. In the dry-season form there is less black and the hindwings are a duller pale yellow. The caterpillars feed on plants of the Capparidaceae.

Striated Pearl White

Elodina parthia

Distribution: Queensland and New South Wales, Australia, New Guinea.
Habitat: Dry eucalyptus forests.
Food plant: *Capparis* sp..
Wingspan: 35–40mm (1⅜–1½in).
Status: Not listed.

Identification: Wet season: male white wings, upper forewing white with black apex, lower forewing cream white with orange patch, lower hindwing white with brown markings. Female upperwings pale yellow-white, upper forewing with black tip, upper hindwing faint black spots at ends of veins.

Like many species of Pierid, this butterfly has seasonal variations, a wet- and a dry-season form. The wet-season form, described left, occurs from October to April and is particularly abundant during January and February. The dry-season form is most common during May to September, and its underwings are mottled brown. There are several generations a year. The butterflies are slow, weak fliers and stay close to the ground. The females lay their eggs, singly, on leaves of *Capparis* sp.. The caterpillars are green with a white line along the back.

OTHER SPECIES OF NOTE

Cepora aspasia
This species of Pierid is seen in wooded habitats and along rivers near woodlands in Indonesia and the Philippines. Cream forewings with brown margins and veins, the hindwings are yellow-orange with brown margins. The adults visit flowers for nectar.

Hebomoia leucippe
This member of the genus *Hebomoia* has a completely orange forewing with black margins and veins, and an pale yellow hindwing. Like the Great Orange Tip, it is seen flying along rivers and forest edges.

Narrow-winged Pearl White *Elodina padusa*
This common butterfly is widespread across northern and eastern parts of Australia; where it is seen in a variety of habitats. The larval food plants are *Capparis canescens* and *C. mitchellii*. It is similar in appearance to *Pieris rapae* but it has a faster, more direct flight.

Great Orange Tip

Hebomoia glaucippe

The Great Orange Tip butterfly is the largest Pierid in Asia. It is a relatively common species of butterfly. This butterfly is a strong flier, and males may be spotted flying along river banks and tracks in rainforests, but they are seen less often than the female. There are two generations a year, one during the dry season, and the other in the wet season. There are slight differences in the appearance of butterfly. The females lay their eggs, singly, on plants of the Capparidaceae. The caterpillars are green with a brown and white line running along both sides. There are a number of subspecies that differ in the colour of the wings. *H. glaucippe roepstorffi* has orange-brown wing tips, while *H. glaucippe vossi* has yellow hindwings.

Distribution: India, Sri Lanka.
Habitat: Rainforest.
Food plant: Capparis sp..
Wingspan: 10cm (4in).
Status: Not listed.

Identification: Male upper forewing white-yellow, orange patch at apex bordered in black, black margins, upper hindwing white-yellow with small black spots along margin. Underwings white with brown mottling. Female similar but less orange.

Orange Albatross

Appias nero

The Orange Albatross is a stunning butterfly with deep orange wings, and surprisingly, this is the only species of butterfly that is completely orange. In freshly emerged specimens this is very vivid, but the colour fades to pale orange-yellow after a few days. Males have dark veins on the upperside forewings but are otherwise unmarked. Females have broad dark borders and a dark streak on the upperside. This is a forest species, and the males are more commonly seen than the females. The females tend to stay in the canopy, while the males descend to the ground to mud-puddle. These butterflies are swift fliers. The females lay their eggs on plants of the Capparidaceae.

Identification: Male forewings orange with dark veins, darker tip. Female forewings dull orange-brown with black border and black veins. Body yellow-grey. Underwings orange.

Distribution: India and southeast Asia.
Habitat: Forest.
Food plant: Capparidaceae.
Wingspan: 60mm (2¼in).
Status: Not listed.

Yellow Albatross

Appias paulina

The Yellow Albatross is found mostly in tropical rainforest where it can be spotted flying high and quickly above the ground. It is a migratory species, and in favourable years can be found further south and inland in Australia. There is a subspecies which is found in the north and east of Australia. The female lays a single green egg on the leaves of the food plants. The mature caterpillar is grey-green or yellow, with a single white dorsal stripe and many black dots. The pupa is pale yellow to white with black spikes and spots.

Above: The male Yellow Albatross is mainly white but with yellow hindwings on the underside.

Identification: Sexes different. Female, shown here, white wings with black margins, forewings have subapical white spots, underwings yellow to white with dark brown margins. Male white wings with black tips on forewing with subapical spots. Underwings similar with yellow hue.

Distribution: India, southeast Asia to Australia, Japan.
Habitat: Rainforest.
Food plant: Euphorbiaceae including *Alchornea ilicifolia* (Australian holly), *Drypetes deplanchei* (Yellow Tulip).
Wingspan: 50mm (2in).
Status: Not listed.

Yellow Migrant

Catopsilia scylla

Distribution: Thailand, Malaysia, Indonesia, Northern Australia.
Habitat: Forests, parks, gardens.
Food plant: *Cassia* sp..
Wingspan: 55–65mm (2–2½in).
Status: Not listed.

Identification: Male forewing white with black margin, hindwing chrome-yellow. Female larger, paler, with subapical black spots on upper forewing and triangular wedges on upper hindwing. Underwings orange with pale marks.

The Yellow Migrant is also known as the Orange Emigrant. As the name suggests, this is a migrant species. Occasionally it appears in areas beyond its normal range, including Sri Lanka. Butterflies of this genus have broad wings in bright colours, and the sexes are different. The butterfly flies rapidly along the ground at heights of 2–3m (7–10ft). It is usually seen in clearings in rainforest, in secondary rainforest and in surrounded open areas. The female lays her eggs singly on either side of food plant leaves. The caterpillar is green and smooth, with a white line along each side.

OTHER SPECIES OF NOTE

Common Migrant *Appias celestina*
This rainforest species is found in Indonesia and New Guinea, and appears as a migrant in the Cape York region of Australia. The males have blue-grey upperwings and yellow underwings with grey-brown margins. The female has white wings and thick black margins with white spots.

Spot Puffin *Appias pandione*
This relatively common butterfly is seen from February to May. The appearance of the butterfly varies during the year, with the dry-season form being less black that in those that occur during the wetter months. There are also a number of subspecies. Both sexes are fast fliers and they are difficult to approach. They inhabit forests in mountainous areas and are found to altitudes of 1,800m (6,000ft).

Lemon Migrant

Catopsilia pomona

Also known as the Common Migrant, this is a strong-flying, migrant butterfly that travels long distances. It can be found in Asia and parts of Australia, and its preferred habitat is clearings in rainforests and other open areas as well as gardens where people have planted ornamental plants with nectar-rich flowers. The female lays eggs in batches on leaves of *Cassia* species. The caterpillar is green, with a thin black and white line along the sides. in Australia this species occurs in two colour forms, one with black antennae and the other with pink antennae.

Distribution: India and Australia.
Habitat: Rainforests, parks, gardens.
Food plant: *Cassia* sp..
Wingspan: 80mm (3⅛in).
Status: Not listed.

Identification: Male UW pale white-yellow with stronger yellow towards body, black apex and thin black margin along leading edge. Underwings variable, white, yellow or green-white. Female UFW white-yellow wings, black spot, UHW series of black spots, underwings yellow or olive, with brown markings.

Common Wanderer

Pareronia valeria

Distribution: Southeast Asia.
Habitat: Forest.
Food plant: *Capparis* sp..
Wingspan: 80mm (3⅛in).
Status: Not listed.

As the name suggests this is a migrant species that occurs widely and in a variety of habitats, including forest. The males are seen visiting flowers for nectar, but the females are more secretive. They stay in the shady understorey where they seek the food plant, *Capparis* sp.. The female Common Wanderer is a mimic of the Glassy Tiger to reduce predation, both in colours and flight patterns. Another form of the female is known as the philomena form; this has blue wings with an orange streak along the inner margin, and mimics *Danaus aspasia*. There are numerous subspecies of this butterfly occurring through Southeast Asia.

Identification: Male wings pale blue with dark brown-black veins and thick margins. Underwings white with black-brown markings and veins. Female white rather than blue, with brown-black veins and margins, submarginal white spots.

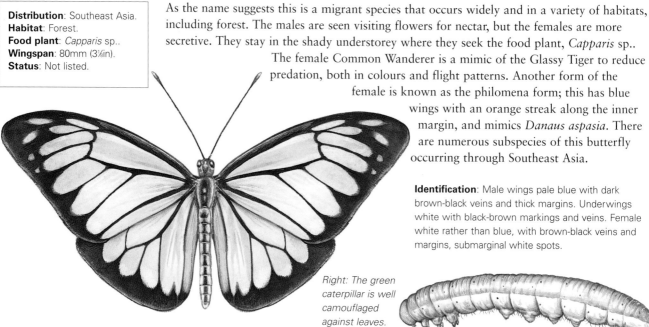

Right: The green caterpillar is well camouflaged against leaves.

Common Grass Yellow

Eurema hecabe

Distribution: South and southeast Asia, Australia.
Habitat: Garden, park, grassland, scrub, open forest.
Food plant: Fabaceae e.g. *Albizia* sp., *Leucaena* sp., *Senna* sp..
Wingspan: 40mm (1½in).
Status: Not listed.

Identification: Yellow wings, upper forewing has brown wavy margin. Underwings paler yellow with brown margins. Females larger but markings similar.

This widespread migrant butterfly is relatively common across its range, since it is found in a wide variety of habitats, from grassland and garden to open forest. The butterflies have a slow flight pattern, staying close to the ground, hence their name Common Grass Yellow. They feed on nectar from violets, such as the arrowhead violet. Despite their preference for grassy habitats, the females lay their eggs singly on plants of the Fabaceae. The young caterpillar is green and rests along the midrib of the leaves, making it very difficult to spot, but the older ones are green with a yellow line along the side, and the body is covered in short hairs. The pupa is found hanging from the stem of the food plant. About 18 subspecies occur in different parts of the range.

OTHER SPECIES OF NOTE

White Orange Tip *Ixias marianne*
The White Orange Tip is found in India and Sri Lanka. It has white wings with a large brown patch at the apex. There is a yellow-orange patch within the brown with brown spots. The underwings are yellow with pale markings. It favours grassland and scrub where the female lays her eggs on *Capparis* sp.. There is a dry- and wet-season generation. The dry-season butterflies have more obvious markings on the underwing. The characteristics vary according to the season in which the eggs are laid.

Ixias reinwardti
This Pierid is found on some of the islands of Indonesia, including Flores, Sumbawa and Alor. The forewings of the male are white with brown-black veins and margins, and an orange patch. The hindwings are white with brown margins. The female is browner and lacks the orange patch.

Bordered Sulphur

Eurema smilax

Distribution: Australia.
Habitat: Grassland.
Food plant: *Cassia* sp.,
Senna sp..
Wingspan: 30–35mm
(1³⁄₁₆–1³⁄₈in).
Status: Not listed.

Identification: Yellow wings.
Upper forewings have a black tip
and margin, upper hindwings
have a thin black margin.
Underwings are orange-yellow
with small dots.

The Bordered
Sulphur, or Small
Grass Yellow, is
a strong-flying
migrant species
which disperses
south to more
temperate habitats.
However, it is unable
to survive the winter in
these regions. It is found
across Australia and has
even been found on islands,
carried by winds. It often
accompanies the Caper White on its
migration, but not in such large numbers. The adults are seen throughout the year in
northern parts of its range, and in the southern areas it is seen in spring and late summer.
There are several generations a year. The caterpillar is green with a dark dorsal line and a
yellow lateral line along the body. The upper part of the body is covered in poison-tipped
hairs which contain an irritant to deter predators.

Yellow Orange Tip

Ixias pyrene

Distribution: India, Myanmar,
Thailand.
Habitat: Alpine to 900m
(3,000ft).
Food plant: *Capparis* sp..
Wingspan: 50mm (2in).
Status: Not listed.

The ground colour of the wings of this butterfly varies
considerably, as there are both dry- and wet-season forms
and several subspecies. The dry-season form is described
right. The wet season form has a large, more pronounced
black patch and the female has a pale yellow wing, rather
than white. The Yellow Orange Tip is found mostly in
mountainous regions, at altitudes of up to 900m (3,000ft).
There are several subspecies that occur through Myanmar,
Thailand and Peninsula Malaysia, where the butterfly is
found in coastal as well as mountainous habitats.

Identification: Male has yellow
upperwings, forewings have
black-brown patch at apex with
orange bar crossed with dark
veins. Female larger, upperwings
white with hint of yellow,
forewings have black patch at
apex enclosing white bar.

*Right: The
upperwings of
the female dry-
season form are
much paler than
the male.*

Common Jezebel

Delias eucharis

Identification: UFW white, thick black veins, narrow black margin. UHW white, narrow black veins, black margin. LHW white, narrow black veins, black margin, series of submarginal triangular-shaped red spots, yellow towards base.

The Common Jezebel is one of about 70 species of the genus *Delias* that occur through Asia and Australasia. This is a common species across its range, occurring in a variety of habitats including gardens and up to altitudes of 2,000m (6,500ft) in upland areas. In forests, it tends to stay high in the canopy, only descending to feed on nectar. The bright warning colours of its underwings are easily spotted by predators when it flies. This Jezebel is on the wing all year round, and the females lay their eggs in small clusters on the underside of leaves of its food plant. The caterpillars are gregarious at first, staying together in clusters on the plant, as they move from leaf to leaf. When disturbed, the caterpillar drops off the leaf and hangs by a silken thread. The butterfly is mimicked by the Painted Sawtooth Butterfly.

Distribution: India, southeast Asia, Australia.
Habitat: Forest, gardens, parks.
Food plant: Loranthaceae.
Wingspan: 80–90mm (3⅛–3½in).
Status: Not listed.

Below: The bright colours of the underwing are so precise that they look as if they have been painted on.

Hill Jezebel

Delias belladonna

Distribution: South Asia, China, southeast Asia.
Habitat: Forest and other habitats to 3,000m (10,000ft).
Food plant: Loranthaceae such as *Loranthus vestitus*.
Wingspan: 70–90mm (2¾–3½in).
Status: Not listed.

Identification: Upperwings brown-black, upper forewing diffuse white-grey streaks and dots, upper hindwing white streaks and dots, small yellow patch near dorsal margin and larger patch on inner margin, grey-white streak near body. Underwings black with orange-yellow spots.

The Hill Jezebel is a common, medium-sized Indian butterfly that occurs in the mountainous regions of South Asia, such as the Himalayas, and parts of Southeast Asia. The butterflies are seen from April, and they are attracted to nectar-rich flowers such as *Buddleia*. Large numbers can be seen on open ground near water and along forest edges. There are several generations a year. The caterpillars live in the shelter of silken webs on the food plant.

OTHER SPECIES OF NOTE

Red-banded Jezebel *Delias mysis*
This is a variable butterfly with many subspecies. Most have white wings with black tips to the forewings that enclose five white spots. They are nicknamed 'Union Jacks'.

Malayan Jezebel *Delias ninus*
The Malayan Jezebel is a common butterfly that is found throughout upland regions in Malaysia and parts of Indonesia, to altitudes of 900m (3,000ft). The butterfly has black forewings with streaks of grey and white, black veins and margin with yellow hindwings crossed by black veins, and with a black margin and red basal patch.

Orange Jezebel *Delias aruna*
The upper forewings of the male are orange with black apex and narrow margin, orange hindwing with a white streak along the inner margin and a narrow black margin. The female's upperwings are brown-black with a yellow-orange base and pale yellow spots on the forewing. Underwings of both sexes are brown, the male with a yellow streak on the lower forewing.

Spotted Jezebel

Delias aganippe

Distribution: Australia.
Habitat: Forests.
Food plant: *Exocarpus* sp.,
Santalum sp., *Amyema* sp..
Wingspan: 60–65mm
(2¼–2½in).
Status: Not listed.

*Below: The underwings
feature bright red and
yellow spots.*

The Spotted Jezebel, named after the particularly spotted underwings, is also known as the Wood White. It is one of the few Australian representatives of the genus *Delias*. The butterflies are found in forests, where they stay high in the canopy, occasionally descending to find nectar-producing flowers. The males are more secretive than the females. There are two generations a year. The females lay their eggs in clusters of leaves of the food plant. The mature caterpillar is black and covered by white spots from which white hairs emerge. The caterpillar is considered a pest by growers of Australian Sandalwood (*Santalum spicatum*), as the caterpillars, which are gregarious in the first stages, eat the leaves and reduce the growth of the plantation trees.

Identification: Male upperwings grey-white, black margin with grey-white spots, LFW black with grey-white patches and row of submarginal white-grey spots, LHW black, with creamy-yellow patches, row of submarginal red spots, edged in white, black margin. Female similar although upperwings more black.

Red Spot Jezebel

Delias descombesi

Distribution: South and
southeast Asia.
Habitat: Upland valleys.
Food plant: Loranthaceae.
Wingspan: 65–85mm
(2½–3¼in).
Status: Not listed.

This butterfly is common throughout its range and can occur in large numbers. It is seen in the warm valleys of the foothills of the Himalayas and other mountain chains, to altitudes of about 1,500m (5,000ft). It is on the wing from March to December. The adults visit flowers for nectar. There are a number of subspecies across the range which vary particularly in the colour of the upperwings, some are black and grey, others are brown and white. *Delias oraia* was once classified as a subspecies of *D. descombesi*, but is now a species in its own right.

Identification:
Male UFW white
black with grey
streaks, black
apex, margins
and veins, UHW
grey-white with
thin black margin.
LFW Black with
white-grey streaks,
LHW yellow with red patch
edged in black, marginal
white-grey spots between
the veins. Female UFW
black with grey-white
streaks and row of
submarginal white
spots, UHW grey with
thick black margin with
grey-white spots.
Underwings similar to male.

*Left: The
underwing
features a
bright red spot.*

BLUES, COPPERS, AZURES AND HAIRSTREAKS

The Lycaenidae is a diverse family of butterflies, particularly in Southeast Asia. However, few have a wide distribution because of their precise environmental requirements and their inability to cross barriers. In many cases they require a specific habitat, and are dependent on the presence of a particular species of ant to complete their life cycle. As a result, they are particularly vulnerable to environmental change.

Plane

Bindahara phocides

This butterfly is known as the Plane in Asia and as the Sword-tailed Flash in Australia. The males of this long-tailed butterfly are usually seen in shady places in the rainforests, where it flies quickly from leaf to leaf. However, the females are far more secretive and they spend much of their time in the canopy. The females lay their eggs on the fruits of the food plant. The caterpillars burrow inside the fruits to feed on seeds. When they are ready to pupate they burrow into the bark. There are a number of subspecies.

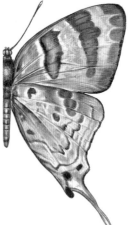

Below: The underwings of the male are pale brown with darker bands on the FW and thin lines on the HW.

Distribution: India, Sri Lanka, Myanmar. Indonesia, Australia.
Habitat: Rainforest.
Food plant: *Salacia chinensis*.
Wingspan: 30–40mm (1¼–1½in).
Status: Not listed.

Identification: Male brown-black wings, upper forewing chestnut-brown towards apex, upper hindwing brown to buff, patch of blue, very long yellow tail, lower forewing pale brown with chestnut bands, lower hindwing brown with lines and dark spots. Female brown wings, upper hindwing brown and white, no blue, with large black spot enclosed by white, tail black and white, underwings white with brown bands and spots.

Common Imperial

Cheritra freja

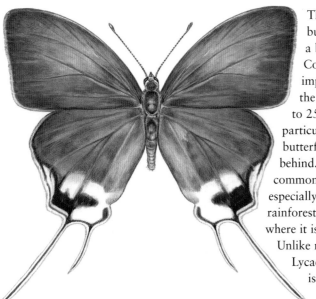

This is a small but attractive butterfly and, when fresh, it has a beautiful purple sheen. The Common Imperial has impressive tails. The longer of the two tails reaches lengths of up to 25mm (1in). The tails are particularly noticeable when the butterfly is in flight, as they trail behind. This species is relatively common over much of its range, especially Malaysia. It is found in rainforest, both lowland and upland, where it is seen flitting from leaf to leaf. Unlike many other species of the Lycaenidae, the Common Imperial is not associated with ants.

Distribution: India, Myanmar, Sri Lanka, Malaysia.
Habitat: Rainforest.
Food plant: *Xylia* sp., *Cinnamomum* sp..
Wingspan: 45–55mm (1¾–2⅛in).
Status: Not listed.

Identification: Male upperwings brown-purple, with two pairs white tails of unequal length. Underwings white with orange on the lower forewing and black marks and blue eyespots on the lower hindwing. Female upperwings dark brown.

Indian Sunbeam

Curetia thetis

Distribution: India, Myanmar, Sri Lanka and parts of southeast Asia.
Habitat: Low-level scrubland.
Food plant: *Derris* sp., *Heynia* sp., *Pongamia* sp..
Wingspan: 40–50mm (1½–2in).
Status: Not listed.

Identification: Males upper wings glossy red-orange, UFW edged in jagged black band that is broad at the apex, UHW thin black margin. Underwings silvery white, with dark lines and dots. Females brown upperwings with white-yellow patch on each wing.

The Indian Sunbeam gets its name from its brightly coloured wings. Although small, it is a powerful, fast-flying butterfly. The males have territories which they defend vigorously, chasing away all other butterflies. The females lay their eggs on a variety of plants from the Papilionaceae and Meliaceae families. The caterpillar is green with a dark green dorsal line and a series of short diagonal pale lines. It can evert two whip-like extensions from the end of its abdomen, which it swings around to deter would-be predators and parasitic wasps. This species is not associated with ants.

OTHER SPECIES OF NOTE

Cheritra orpheus
This stunning tailed butterfly is found in the Philippines. The upperwings are dark brown with bright orange veins. There are two tails, one particularly long and one short. The underwings are pale orange-brown, with black markings and a submarginal blue streak.

Common Oryx *Horaga onyx fruhstorferi*
The Common or Horaga Oryx is found across India and Southeast Asia. The butterfly has dark brown wings with streaks of iridescent purple-blue. The hindwings have three thin tails. The underwings are light brown with a white streak and thin white margin. There is a black eyespot close to the margin, by the tails.

Arhopala aurea
This brightly coloured butterfly is a powerful flier that is found in lowland rainforest areas of Malaya and Sumatra. The male has pointed forewings which are iridescent green with a hint of copper and blue scales towards the base. The hindwings are green with a broad dark border, and a very short tail. The female's wings are purple-blue and the forewing is more rounded.

Common Oakblue

Arhopala micale

Butterflies of the genus *Arhopala*, the Oakblues, are found in Asia and Australasia. The Common Oakblue is closely associated with ants, in this case green ants (*Oecophylla smaragdina*). The females lay their eggs singly on shoots of the food plant that is associated with the ants. The ants care for the caterpillars, and in return they milk them for honeydew. The caterpillar is green, with brown and yellow lines along the back, brown on the thorax and a yellow patch on segment six of the abdomen. The caterpillars feed on the leaves of the food plant, but as they mature, they are fed ant larvae by the nurse ants. When the caterpillar is not feeding, it rests inside a curled leaf at or near the entrance to the ants' nest.

Distribution: New Guinea, Australia.
Habitat: Lowland rainforest.
Food plant: *Buchanania* sp., *Cordia* sp., *Callophyllum* sp., *Terminalia* sp..
Wingspan: 40–50mm (1½–2in).
Status: Not listed.

Identification: Males upperwings iridescent blue with thin brown border, hindwings have a short black tail. Females upperwings blue with broad brown-black border. Underwings of both mottled brown with light and dark spots.

Blue Cornelian

Deudorix epirus

Distribution: Moluccas, New Guinea, Queensland Australia.
Habitat: Rainforest.
Food plant: *Harpullia ramiflora* (Australian Olive).
Wingspan: 30–40mm (1¼–1½in).
Status: Not listed.

The Blue Cornelian is also called the Epirus Blue and the Orange-lobed Flash. This is a secretive butterfly that is found within the rainforest. The males perch in the understorey and rarely fly, while the females flutter around in search of nectar flowers such as *Lantana*. The butterfly is on the wing for much of the year and there are several generations. The females lay their eggs on the fruits of the food plant, the Australian Olive. The caterpillars are rarely seen as they chew through the fruit to feed on the seeds inside.

Identification: Male forewing black with blue batch on inner margin, hindwing blue with two tails, one long, one short. Females have white patch on each forewing. Underwings of both sexes cream, with brown margin and brown bar across each wing.

Amaryllis Azure *Ogyris amaryllis*
The Amaryllis or Satin Azure is found across Australia. The male has dark blue wings, with a thick dark margin on the forewings and a thin scalloped margin on the hindwings. The females have a thicker brown margin on the wings. The underwings are a mottled brown and grey with spots of brown, white and red on the lower forewing.

Cornelian
Deudorix epijarbas
The species is found across Southeast Asia to Australia and the Philippines. The males have black-brown wings with a large orange patch. There is a long, thin tail on each hindwing. The females are brown. The underwings are brown with white streaks. The hindwings have a black spot surrounded by orange near the tail, and a black spot at the tip. The caterpillars feed on seeds of the food plant.

Eastern Large Bronze Azure *Ogyris halmaturia*
This attractive blue-purple butterfly is one of the largest Lycaenids and is an icon of south Australia. It is now rare as it has suffered from the loss of its habitat due to farming and urban spread, and is now restricted to a few colonies.

Small Brown Azure

Ogyris otanes

This species was once a common butterfly in southern Australia, where it was associated with mallee scrub. However, it is now in decline and is rare over much of its range, as a consequence of habitat loss. Its stronghold is on undisturbed grasslands of southern Australia, and is associated with sugar ants of the genus *Camponotus*. The male butterflies are active early in the day, when groups can be seen basking in the sun. They establish territories which they defend. The butterflies are slow fliers that stay a few metres above the ground. When they land, they are difficult to spot because of their cryptic underwing markings. The female lays her eggs in groups of up to four in the leaf litter at the base of the food plant. The caterpillar is white with black spiracles and a brown head. It feeds on leaves and bark as well as immature ant larvae. A pair of flaps on either side of the terminal segment are believed to emit a chemical to calm the ants.

Distribution: Southern Australia.
Habitat: Dry grassland, mallee scrub.
Food plant: *Choretrum* sp., *Leptomeria* sp..
Wingspan: 40mm (1½in).
Status: Not listed.

Identification: Males upperwings dark purple with bronze sheen and dark margins, hindwing scalloped margin. Females are similar colour with broad black margin and white patch near apex of the forewing. Underwings of both mottled shades of grey and brown with arc of black spots and two black and white spots on the lower forewing.

Dark Purple Azure

Ogyris abrota

Distribution: Southern Australia.
Habitat: Forest, especially Eucalyptus forest.
Food plant: Loranthaceae, especially *Muellerina eucalyptoides*.
Wingspan: 40mm (1½in).
Status: Not listed.

The Dark Purple Azure flies from April to October. They are active on sunny days, when the males patrol the tree-tops, and the females stay close to the food plants. There are two generations. The food plant is mistletoe, a parasitic plant that grows on trees such as *Banksia*, *Eucalyptus* and *Casuatina* trees. The females lay their eggs in small clusters on the bark of the host plant, so they are close to the food plant. The gregarious caterpillars are pink-brown, with a black dorsal line and markings. During the day they shelter under bark and emerge at night to feed on leaves. This species is associated with a number of ant species including the acrobat ant (*Crematogaster* sp.) and Argentine ants (*Linepithema humile*).

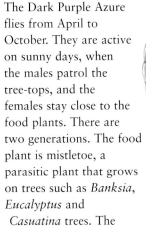

Identification: Male upperwings are purple with black margins. Female upperwings are brown with creamy white patch on each forewing. Underwings of both are mottled brown, grey and black. Males have a white crescent on the underside of the forewing, females have a cream mark.

Left: A distinctive creamy white spot is present on the female's upper forewing.

Sapphire Azure

Ogyris aenone

Distribution: Northeastern Australia.
Habitat: Mangrove swamps, dry open woodland.
Food plant: Mistletoes, *Lysiana* sp., *Amyema* sp..
Wingspan: 35–45mm (1⅜–1¾in).
Status: Not listed.

Identification: Male has metallic blue upperwings with broad black margin on the forewing and thin margin on hindwing, with a short tail. Females are larger with thick margins and dark veins. Underwings of both sexes are mottled brown and grey with black and orange spots on the lower forewing.

This blue butterfly is also known as the Cooktown Azure, as it occurs along the North Queensland coast. The food plant of the Sapphire Azure butterfly is mistletoe, and it is found in coastal swamps with paper-barks (*Meleleuca* sp.) and *Casuarina* woodland, both species that are parasitized by the mistletoe. The females lay their eggs on the bark of trees. The caterpillars shelter under bark during the day, and emerge at night to feed on the mistletoe. They are usually associated with black ants of the genus Iridomyrmex, which are found on mistletoes of the genus *Lysiana* and *Amyema*. However, in the northern part of the range, where there are other species of mistletoe, the helper ants are from the genus *Pheidole*.

Chequered Blue

Theclinesthes serpentata

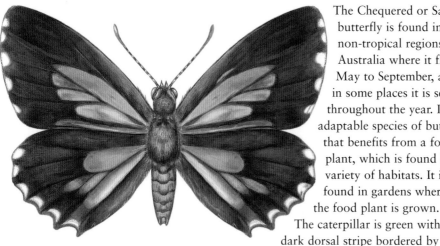

The Chequered or Salt Blue butterfly is found in the non-tropical regions of Australia where it flies from May to September, although in some places it is seen throughout the year. It is an adaptable species of butterfly that benefits from a food plant, which is found in a variety of habitats. It is also found in gardens where the food plant is grown. The caterpillar is green with a dark dorsal stripe bordered by yellow, and small white tubercles. These colours provide excellent camouflage on plants. It feeds on the leaves of the food plant, leaving the veins behind. It is attended by black ants. The pupa is small, pale green with brown markings, and is attached to plants.

Identification: Brown upperwings with blue-purple towards body, and chequered margins. Short tail. Underwings mottled shades of brown, grey and white.

Distribution: Australia.
Habitat: Various including grassland, gardens and parks.
Food plant: Chenopodiaceae e.g. *Atriplex* sp., *Chenopodium album*, *Einadia* sp., *Rhagodia crassifolia*.
Wingspan: 18–20mm (1⅟₁₆–¾in).
Status: Not listed.

Above: The body of the caterpillar is covered in tiny white tubercles.

Double-spotted Line Blue

Nacaduba biocellata

This common species is found across Australia and is particularly abundant inland. It is found in habitats with *Acacia*, where it gathers in large numbers during the flowering season of the Acacia trees. They are seen all year round, as the different species of Acacia flower at different times. In hot, dry places there is a mass emergence of several million butterflies after the rains – an amazing sight. The males emerge first and flutter around the acacia trees, just a few centimetres above the ground. Sometimes they establish territories around the tops of trees and wait for females. If there are many males, they tend to keep moving. The females lay their eggs singly on the flower buds of the food plant. The caterpillars feed on the flower buds and are attended by black ants of the genus *Iridomyrmex*. Usually the caterpillars pupate in the leaf litter, but pupae can be found on the leaves. If the rainy season is shorter than usual, the caterpillar stage is completed quickly but the caterpillars are small, and this results in smaller than average adults, so small, in fact, that they are among the smallest butterflies in the world.

Distribution: Australia, South Pacific.
Habitat: Woodland, scrub and other habitats with Acacia.
Food plant: *Acacia* sp..
Wingspan: 20mm (¾in).
Status: Not listed.

Identification: Males lilac-blue upperwings, darker blue to base, with thin black margins, females brown. Underwings of both sexes are pale yellow-brown, wavy light lines, two black spots under margin of the hindwing.

Below: The caterpillar varies in colour from green to orange and even pink, according to the part of the plant on which it feeds.

Common Dusky Blue

Candalides hyacinthina

Distribution: Australia, from Queensland to Victoria.
Habitat: Temperate woodland, dry woodland, heathlands and wherever the food plant grows as a scrambling parasitic vine.
Food plant: Lauraceae, e.g. *Cassytha* sp. (dodder laurel).
Wingspan: 40mm (1½in).
Status: Not listed.

Identification: Upperwings dull purple or metallic blue. Underwings pale brown-grey with arcs of dark spots and two black spots on each forewing.

There are different colour forms of the Common Dusky Blue, one form being purple-blue and the other a bright metallic blue. The purple form occurs in the temperate forests of the south, and the blue form in the dry mallee woodlands of the interior. When the range of the two forms overlap, a third form appears with a mix of purple and blue on the upperwings. These forms are believed to be the result of incomplete speciation as a result of geographical isolation. The purple form is seen from September to March, while the blue form flies from August to April. The adults are seen flying around the food plant, where the males establish territories on hilltops and other vantage points, which they defend against other butterflies. The females lay their pale green eggs singly on the buds and young shoots of the food plant. The caterpillars are green with orange patches on two segments, and are covered with short white hairs. The caterpillars rest during the day and emerge at night to feed.

OTHER SPECIES OF NOTE

Wattle Blue *Theclinesthes miskini*
This attractive blue butterfly is found across Australia, where it occurs in habitats with *Acacia* (wattle). It is a fast-flying butterfly with blue wings. The wings have brown margins, and there are a series of black spots surrounded by white along the margin of the hindwing, and a short tail. The underwings are orange-brown with a dark brown line and black spots along the margin. The winter form has darker underwings.

Green Hawaiian Blue *Udara blackburnii*
The Green Hawaiian Blue is one of just two species that are endemic to Hawaii. It is found in a variety of habitats, from coastal grasslands to alpine slopes. The upperwings are blue with black margins, while the undersides are bright green. It rests with its green underwings exposed, which makes it very difficult to spot. Its food plant is the *Acacia*.

Peacock Royal

Tajuria cippus

This fast-flying butterfly is found in forested areas up to about 2,000m (6,500ft) where they are seen flying around flowering shrubs with nectar-rich flowers. The female lays her eggs on plants of the genus *Dendrophthoe* and *Loranthus* genus, both of which are parasitic vines on trees. The caterpillar is dark brown with pink-grey patches. There are several subspecies that differ in colour patterns.

Distribution: South and southeast Asia.
Habitat: Scrubland.
Food plant: *Dendrophthoe* sp., *Loranthus* sp..
Wingspan: 35mm (1⅜in).
Status: Not listed.

Identification:
Male royal blue, with black borders on forewing, and blue-black lines on hindwing, with a spot and two tails on each wing, one long, one short. Female pale blue with thin black lines, orange and black eyespots by tail. Underwings of both silvery blue with thin black lines, orange and black eyespots on hindwing

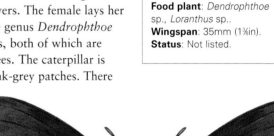

Moonlight Jewel

Hypochrysops delicia

Distribution: Eastern Australia.
Habitat: Woodland and scrub with *Acacia*.
Food plant: *Acacia* sp..
Wingspan: 30–40mm (1¼–1½ in).
Status: Not listed.

The butterflies of the genus of *Hypochrysops* are known as jewel butterflies because of the metallic silver and green markings that occur on the underwings. The butterflies are seen from September to April and there are two generations a year. The males fly during the late afternoon, and establish territories by flying around or perching on the topmost branches of *Acacia* trees where they await the females. The females lay their eggs in clusters of up to 40 on *Acacia* trees that have attendant ants. The caterpillar is brown and is covered with short brown hairs. The head is black, and there are black plates on the thorax and on the eighth abdominal segment.

Identification: Forewings pale with thick black margin and apex and iridescent blue sheen, hindwing bluer with series of orange spots along the scalloped margin. Underwings pale brown with silver sheen and rows of orange spots outlined in black or green. Female larger, with less blue.

OTHER SPECIES OF NOTE

Grand Imperial *Jacoona amrita*
The Grand Imperial is found across Southeast Asia. The male has iridescent blue upperwings with black margins, while the female is dark brown with black and white markings. The underwings are orange and creamy white, with black markings. It has extra long tails.

Southeast Asian Blue *Jamides alecto*
This common butterfly is found in rainforest across Southeast Asia. The upperwings are blue-white with a dark margin. The hindwing has a series of spots on the margin and a tail. The underwings are grey-brown with white lines, and an orange-and-black spot towards the tail.

Turquoise Jewel *Hypochrysops halyaetus*
The Turquoise or Western Jewel is found on coastal heath, sand dunes and *Banksia* woodland around Perth. The males are iridescent blue-green with dark borders while the females are blue-purple with brown and orange margins. The underwings are orange-brown with creamy markings and green spots. There is one generation that flies from July to December.

Yellow Jewel

Hypochrysops byzos

The Yellow Jewel is a highly variable species, in particular the females, which vary in the amount of orange on the wing and the colour of the underwing. The butterfly is on the wing from October to February. The females lay their rounded white eggs singly on the underside of leaves of the food plant. The caterpillar is flattened in shape, green with a pale dorsal line and dark markings, covered in short hairs. The caterpillars are active at night, feeding on the underside of leaves. They tend to align themselves with the midrib of a leaf so that they are perfectly camouflaged. During the day they shelter in a silken cocoon under the leaf. This species is not associated with ants.

Distribution: Australia; Queensland, New South Wales, Victoria.
Habitat: Grassland and scrub.
Food plant: Rhamnaceae, Sterculiaceae.
Wingspan: 30mm (1¼ in).
Status: Not listed.

Identification: Males metallic blue-purple, dark brown-black margins. Hindwing scalloped edge with two small spots. Females dark brown with orange blotch on each wing. Underwings of both pale brown with rows of orange bands outlined in metallic green.

Fringed Blue

Neolucia agricola

Distribution: Southern Australia.
Habitat: Heath.
Food plant: Fabaceae e.g. *Daviesia* sp., *Eutaxia* sp., *Pultenaea* sp..
Wingspan: 20mm (¾in).
Status: Not listed.

Identification: Upperwings dark brown with brown and white chequered fringe. Underwings pale brown with stripes of darker brown edged in black and white.

The Fringed Blue is on the wing from October to December, and there is a single generation. Females lay their eggs near the flower buds of the food plant, such as bush pea. The eggs overwinter and emerge the following spring. The caterpillar is either green or brown with a dark red-brown dorsal stripe that is bordered in pink and white. The head is brown and the body is covered in fine hairs. They are well camouflaged for feeding on flowers and flower buds. Sometimes the caterpillar is associated with ants of the genus *Iridomyrmex*. There are three races in Australia, which occur in different areas. The pupa is variable in colour, ranging from dark brown to shades of pink with darker spots.

Large Green-banded Blue

Danis danis

Distribution: New Guinea, Philippines, Queensland, Australia.
Habitat: Rainforest.
Food plant: *Connarus* sp., *Rourea* sp., *Derris* sp..
Wingspan: 30–40mm (1¼–1½in).
Status: Not listed.

Below: When feeding, the wings are raised, revealing the striking, slightly iridescent underwings.

The Large Green-banded Blue is a weak-flying butterfly that stays in the shady parts of the rainforest, under the protection of the canopy, although they may be seen resting on sunlit leaves. The butterflies visit flowers such as *Lantana* for nectar. In New Guinea the butterfly is seen for much of the year and there are several generations. Further south in Queensland there are two generations during the dry season; these are seen from May to July and October to November. The females lay their eggs on climbing vines like *Connarus* and *Derris*.

Identification: Sexes different. Male upperwings blue with large white patch, black margin. Females black with white patches, with blue hue to base of wing. Both have white underwings with broad black margin with metallic green streak. Hindwings have black spots in a green streak.

Grassland Copper

Lucia limbaria

This elusive butterfly was once common but has steadily declined due to habitat loss. It occurs in small colonies, which if not disturbed, survive for many years. It is seen from September to May. The female lays small clusters of eggs on the food plant and covers them with abdominal hairs. Interestingly, the female only lays her eggs in the presence of the helper ants. The caterpillars hatch and stay together, initially feeding on all parts of the food plant, especially the leaves. Then they separate and move into an ant nest. During the day the caterpillars rest below ground within the nest, and are tended by the ants. They emerge at night to feed, before returning to the same nest. Sometimes being accompanied by the ants. During the hot, dry season, the vegetation withers and the caterpillars have less to feed on. They rely on their fat store and shrink considerably in size. They survive until the next rainy season, when the food plant starts growing again. The caterpillars pupate underground in the nest, and the adults emerge up to two weeks later.

Right: The underwings are mottled brown, the female's wings being paler than those of the male.

Distribution: South and southeast Australia in areas where rainfall exceeds 25cm (10in).
Habitat: Grassland.
Food plant: *Oxalis* sp., especially *O. corniculata.*
Wingspan: 30mm (1¼in).
Status: Not listed.

Identification: Brown with chequered margin. Forewing large yellow patch and two black spots. Underwings are yellow-brown, with arcs of darker spots outlined in white.

Boulder Copper

Lycaena boldenarum

Distribution: New Zealand.
Habitat: River beds, tussock grassland, upland grassland.
Food plant: Polygonaceae incl. *Muehlenbeckia axillaris.*
Wingspan: 10mm (⅜in).
Status: Not listed.

Identification: Orange-copper wings with black markings, a hint of purple across the forewings sometimes visible. Submarginal black border, white margin, copper towards inner margin. Underwings in shades of white and grey, with submarginal row of black spots.

The sub genus *Antipodolycaena* is found only in New Zealand, where there are four species, all relatively common. The Boulder Copper is the smallest butterfly in New Zealand, with a wingspan of just one centimetre. It flies from October to April and is found along rivers and streams, on tussock grassland and above the tree line on open, rocky vegetation to 2,000m (6,500ft). The butterfly rests with its wings up, which provides perfect camouflage when it rests on boulders and gravel, hence its common name. The shades of grey, white and black vary according to the habitat. The butterflies fly only on sunny days, staying close to the ground. The males fly in a zigzag pattern, stopping to bask in the sun, feed or mate while the females fly more slowly, and in straighter lines between flowers. The females lay their eggs singly on the underside of the leaves and the stem of the food plant.

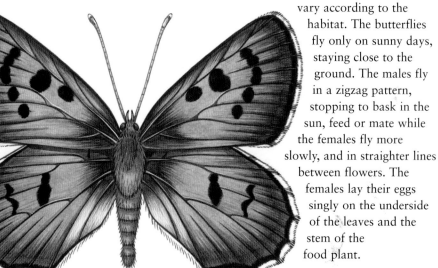

Silver Hairstreak *Chrysozephyrus syla*
The Silver Hairstreak is found at high altitudes of up to 3,400m (11,000ft) in the Himalayas of North West India, Pakistan and Afghanistan. The male is an iridescent golden green with a purple sheen and brown margins, and the female has pale blue forewings with a white bar and brown hindwings. Both have a silvery underwings with brown markings.

Amethyst Hairstreak *Jalmenus icilius*
The Amethyst Hairstreak has brown wings with a large patch of blue on each wing. The hindwings have two black spots and a stump of a tail. This Australian butterfly uses two food plants. The *Acacia* is its food plant in the southern parts of its range, while *Senna* sp. is the food plant in the north, even if an appropriate acacia tree is growing close by.

Silky Hairstreak
Pseudalmenus chlorinda

The Silky or Chlorinda Hairstreak is found in eastern Australia from New South Wales to Victoria and Tasmania, where it flies from September to December. There is one generation of butterflies a year. Their complicated life cycle involves black ants of the genus *Iridomyrex*, *Acacia* and *Eucalyptus* trees. The females lay their eggs on the food plant, *Acacia*. The caterpillars are attended by ants that protect them from parasitic wasps. The caterpillars move to pupate under the bark of a nearby eucalyptus tree. The butterfly has declined in recent years due to loss of habitat, and is classed either as Rare or Vulnerable. There are eight subspecies, which are also classed as Rare. Part of their vulnerability stems from the fact that whole populations can be dependent on one eucalyptus tree.

Distribution: East Australia.
Habitat: *Acacia* woodland with mature eucalyptus.
Food plant: *Acacia* sp..
Wingspan: 25–30mm (1–1¼in).
Status: Not listed.

Identification: Upperwings brown, UFW large, central orange spot, UHW small orange spot, chain of red spots and tail.

Common Imperial Blue
Jalmenus evagoras

Distribution: Australia.
Habitat: Woodland and scrub.
Food plant: *Acacia* sp..
Wingspan: 40mm (1½in).
Status: Not listed.

Identification: Upperwings iridescent blue with broad black margin, with a small black bar extending from the margin of the forewing, hindwing tail and two orange spots and thin white lines. Underwings creamy-brown with thin black lines, two orange-brown submarginal bands and patches, orange-red spots near tail.

The Common Imperial Blue is often seen gathered in numbers close to the food plant, *Acacia*. There are two generations a year, with the eggs of the second generation overwintering and hatching the following spring. The females lay their eggs in rows on the stems of the food plant. When the butterfly is resting, the tail, at the base of each wing, moves in the wind rather like an antenna. It is thought that this movement may deceive predators into attacking the tail rather than the butterfly's head. The young caterpillars are gregarious, feeding on leaves within a silken web. They seek out an ant trail which they follow in order to find older caterpillars and the attending black ants. The ants protect the larvae and pupae from predators. In return, the ants are rewarded by nectar from the bodies of larvae and pupae. The older caterpillar is flattened in shape and is dark green, with an orange dorsal line and spiky tubercles.

BROWNS, DANAIDS, FRITILLARIES AND NYMPHS

This varied family of butterflies is well represented in the Oriental and Australian regions. Species are brightly coloured, with angled and often indented wings. They have powerful flight, especially the Rajahs. Some species, such as the Plain Tiger (Danaus chrysippus), are particularly widespread.

Small Tortoiseshell

Aglais urticae

The Small Tortoiseshell is a common migrant species in many parts of the world, partly due to the abundance of its food plant, the nettle. There are usually two generations, although in the more northerly regions there is only one. Its abundance varies from year to year, and is believed to be linked to temperatures in spring and early summer that influence the adults and the abundance of parasitic wasps, the major predator of the caterpillars. The females lay their eggs on the undersides of nettle leaves. The caterpillars are gregarious, sheltering in a silk web. They are black with tiny white spots, black spines and two broken yellow spines along the sides. After the last moult they disperse and pupate. The adults of the second generation overwinter in buildings, shed and caves.

Distribution: Europe, across Asia to Pacific coast.
Habitat: Varied, from gardens, farmland and mountain.
Food plant: *Urtica* sp..
Wingspan: 45–65mm (1¾–2½ in).
Status: Not listed.

Identification: Orange-red wings with scalloped margins. Three black bars on leading edge of upper forewing, series of blue submarginal crescents on both wings, upper hindwing brown towards body. Underwings dark mottled pattern.

Book Butterfly

Cethosia biblis

The species name, *biblis*, means writing: this refers to the white 'V' shaped marks along the wing margins. However, the Book Butterfly has a wide range of common names, including the Choir, Malaysian Lacewing, Leopard Lacewing, and Batik Lacewing. It is believed that the elaborate lacy patterns in bright colours on the underside of the wings influenced the design of traditional Malay batik. The butterflies are seen flying for much of the year, often along forest edges, where they bask in the sun. The females lay their eggs on species of passion flower. The caterpillars are gregarious. They have poisonous spines, and this poison is retained by the adults, hence the bright warning colours of the wings.

Distribution: Nepal, India, Myanmar, Malaya, China.
Habitat: Forest edge.
Food plant: *Passifora* sp..
Wingspan: 55–65mm (2⅛–2½ in).
Status: Not listed.

Below: The underwing patterns may have been the inspiration behind traditional Asian batik.

Identification: Upperwings black and orange. UFW white stripe across wing, orange towards body, white 'V' shaped marks along margins. UHW mostly orange wing with black margin, white marks along margin, black spots on orange. Underwings ornate pattern of orange, red, white stripes edged in black, with white 'V' shapes along black margin.

Peacock

Inachis io

Distribution: Europe, Australia, across temperate Asia to Japan, absent from extreme southern Europe.
Habitat: Woodland edge and rides, hedgerows, gardens.
Food plant: *Urtica* sp..
Wingspan: 60mm (2¼ in).
Status: Not listed.

Identification: Easily recognized from the four red and blue eyespots or false eyes on the upperwings. Peacock eye on the hindwing blue-black centre and white halo. Eye on forewing blurred mix of yellow and blue. Underwings nearly black with black veins.

The magnificent Peacock butterfly is a strong flier found in a variety of habitats. Males establish territories, often along woodland edges and hedgerows. They chase off any intruders, including butterflies and other insects. The eyespots on the wings are for deterring predators. When threatened, the butterfly opens its wings to flash the false eyes. They also use sound. A scraping sound is made by opening and closing their wings so that the edges rasp against each other. Peacocks are long-lived butterflies. The summer generation over-winters in sheds, garages and hollow trees, and emerges in spring to lay eggs and die. The females lay their eggs in clusters on the underside of nettle leaves. The caterpillar is velvety black, with black forked spines and tiny white spots. The yellow-green pupa hangs from nettle stems, branches and tree trunks. This is a species that appears to be benefiting from global warming, as its range is expanding northwards, aided by the butterfly being able to colonize a range of habitats.

OTHER SPECIES OF NOTE

Plain Lacewing *Cethosia penthesilea*
This Lacewing is found in much the same habitat as the Book, and they can be seen together on flowers such as *Lantana*. The Plain Lacewing looks very similar to the Book, but it also has a white submarginal band on the underside of the hindwing.

Red Lacewing *Cethosia cydippe*
This is one of the larger Lacewings, reaching up to 10cm (4in) in wingspan. It is found in Australia, New Guinea and the Solomon Islands, where its food plant, *Passiflora* sp., occurs. It has orange and brown scalloped wings that have a prominent white bar across the forewings.

Indian Tortoiseshell *Aglais kaschmirensis*
Similar in appearance to the Small Tortoiseshell, this butterfly is found in a variety of habitats across Northern India and Bhutan. The food plant is the nettle (*Urtica* sp.).

Australian Leafwing

Doleschallia bisaltide australis

The Australian Leafwing has orange-brown upper wings, but when it rests it raises its wings up to reveal the mottled underwings. These resemble a dead leaf, so providing excellent camouflage. The butterfly is on the wing all year and there are several generations. The butterflies are particularly abundant just after the wet season. The female lays her eggs on plants of the Acanthaceae, such as *Asystasia gangetica*, and *Pseudoranthemum* sp.. The caterpillar is black with red markings, creamy white and blue spots and long black spines. The head bears two long branched spines. The caterpillar shelters during the day among leaf litter, and emerges at night to feed.

Distribution: Queensland, Australia.
Habitat: Lowland rainforest, eucalyptus forest, gardens.
Food plant: Acanthaceae, e.g. *Asystasia gangetica*, *Pseudoranthemum* sp..
Wingspan: 60–65mm (2¼–2½ in).
Status: Not listed.

Identification: Upperwings orange-brown, black margins, small white spots, small blunt tail. Underwings mottled shades of orange-brown with green and grey.

Meadow Argus

Junonia villida

Identification: Upperwings brown with orange and white markings towards the margins, one large, blue eyespot towards the margin of each forewing, two small eyespots on each hindwing. Lower forewing similar, but pale brown, lower hindwing mottled brown.

This common butterfly is seen from August to October. It is found in woodlands, parks and gardens where it can be seen resting on blades of grass or on the ground with wings open. The butterfly flies fast over the ground at heights of about 1m (3ft). It has a characteristic flight pattern of one or two fast beats and then a short glide. The males are territorial and chase other butterflies away. The female lays her green eggs singly on the food plant. The slow-moving caterpillars feed on a wide range of plants, including introduced species found in gardens. When not feeding, they shelter either under leaves or at the base of the food plant.

Distribution: New Guinea, Australia, New Zealand.
Habitat: Open woodland, grassland, parks, gardens.
Food plant: Various, including *Hygrophila* sp., *Scabiosa* sp., *Plantago* sp., *Verbena* sp..
Wingspan: 45–55mm (1¾–2⅛ in).
Status: Not listed.

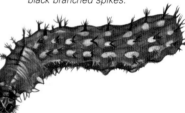

Below: The caterpillar is brown-black and covered with short black branched spikes.

Peacock Pansy

Junonia almana

Identification: Upperwings orange with black sub-marginal lines, UFW black bars on the leading edge, small eyespot, UHW large eyespot. Underwings pale orange-brown, black lines, white median band across both wings, eyespots on both wings.

These butterflies appear in a range of habitats including rice paddy fields, up to an altitude of 1,000 metres (3,300ft). It is on the wing all year round and there are several generations. There are two distinct seasonal forms; a wet-season form (described left) which is more abundant, and a dry-season form. The wet-season form deters predators by flashing the large eyespot on its upper hindwing. The dry-season form is tailed and its underwings are dark and leaf-like to provide camouflage, and lacks eyespots. The caterpillar is pale brown with black dorsal, sub-dorsal and lateral lines, a row of small spots below the lateral line, and short branched spines.

Distribution: South Asia, southeast Asia, Philippines.
Habitat: Various including farmland, forests, gardens.
Food plant: Acanthaceae e.g. *Asteracantha* sp., *Hygrophila* sp., *Vandellia* sp..
Wingspan: 65–70mm (2½–2¾ in).
Status: Not listed.

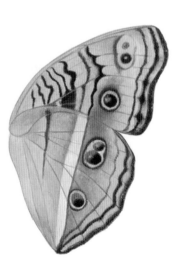

Right: The underwing of the wet-season form is crossed by several dark lines. There are several small eyespots.

Lemon Pansy

Junonia lemonias

Distribution: India, Pakistan, Myanmar, Sri Lanka.
Habitat: Various including forest and gardens, to altitudes of 2,400m (7,800ft).
Food plant: Acanthaceae.
Wingspan: 45–60mm (1¾–2¼ in).
Status: Not listed.

Identification: Forewings have large yellow patch with black margins, and small white spots near apex. Hindwings yellow with black margins, leading margin particularly broad with blue patch. Female larger, with more prominent eye-spots.

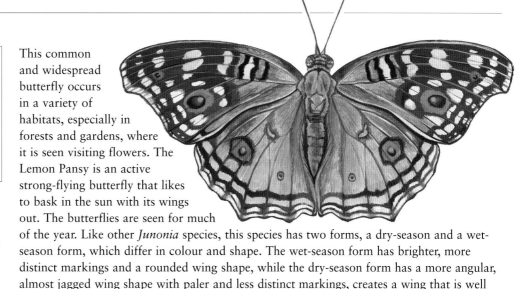

This common and widespread butterfly occurs in a variety of habitats, especially in forests and gardens, where it is seen visiting flowers. The Lemon Pansy is an active strong-flying butterfly that likes to bask in the sun with its wings out. The butterflies are seen for much of the year. Like other *Junonia* species, this species has two forms, a dry-season and a wet-season form, which differ in colour and shape. The wet-season form has brighter, more distinct markings and a rounded wing shape, while the dry-season form has a more angular, almost jagged wing shape with paler and less distinct markings, creates a wing that is well camouflaged among dead leaves. The male is territorial and chases off competitors. The female lays her green eggs singly on the leaves of the food plant. The caterpillar is blue-black, with a dark dorsal line and rows of short, dark spines. The caterpillar feeds on the underside of the leaf, and if disturbed it drops to the ground.

OTHER SPECIES OF NOTE

Blue Pansy *Junonia orithya*
The Blue Pansy or Blue Argus has a wide distribution, from Africa across southern Asia to Australia. It can be distinguished from the other Pansies by the large amount of blue on the upperwings. There is a pair of eyespots on the upper hindwings. It is seen all year round, and there are several generations.

Northern Argus *Junonia erigone*
This species has brown wings. The outer part of the wing is a darker brown, with an irregular row of creamy white spots and an eyespot with a blue centre. Two orange bars cross the wing nearer the body. The hindwings are brown, with a wavy orange line and a row of five small blue eyespots. The Northern Argus occurs in Indonesia, New Guinea and occasionally on the islands to the north of Australia.

Chocolate Pansy

Junonia hedonia

The Chocolate Pansy is also known as the Brown Pansy, Chocolate Soldier and the Chocolate Argus. The colour pattern of the wings varies with the seasons. The Chocolate Pansy is a slow-flying butterfly that lands frequently on grass and branches. At night it roosts with others in a head-down position on tree trunks. When its wings are raised, the pattern and shape of the wings resembles a dead leaf. The caterpillar becomes reddish brown with age, and has dorsal and lateral rows of short brown spines with a yellow base. There are numerous subspecies that occur across the range.

Distribution: Southeast Asia, New Guinea, Australia, New Zealand.
Habitat: Forest margins.
Food plant: *Hemigraphis* sp., *Justicia* sp., *Strobilanthes* sp..
Wingspan: 40–50 mm (1½–2in).
Status: Not listed.

Identification: Upperwings orange-brown. UFW hooked, dark brown lines, submarginal row of six small orange eyespots, UHW scalloped margin, two dark lines, series of six small orange eyespots. Underwings dark brown, purple tinge, with grey bands and pale eyespots.

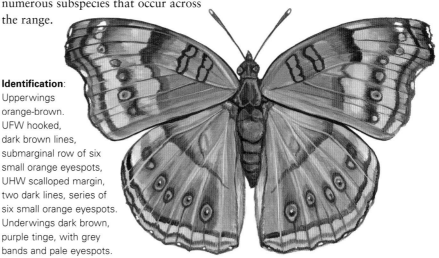

Australian Admiral

Vanessa itea

The Australian or Yellow Admiral is found in parts of Australasia. It is a strong flier and has spread from Australia across wide stretches of water to colonize Pacific islands as well as New Zealand. In New Zealand, it has a Maori name of Kahukowhai, which means 'yellow cloak'. In spring the newly emerged adults migrate south, often accompanying the Australian Painted Lady (*Vanessa kershawi*). This long-lived butterfly is on the wing during the summer months, when it is seen visiting flowers for nectar. It rests on vertical surfaces such as walls and tree trunks, with its head facing down.

There are several generations a year. The females lay their pale green eggs singly, or in pairs, on the upper surface of leaves. The caterpillar is brown, with a dark brown dorsal line and pale yellow lateral lines, and is covered in short, branched brown spines. The caterpillars of the last generation overwinter and pupate the following spring.

Distribution: Australia, New Zealand, Norfolk Islands.
Habitat: Gardens, scrub, grassland, waste land.
Food plant: *Urtica* sp., *Parietaria* sp..
Wingspan: 45–60mm (1¾–2¼ in).
Status: Not listed.

Identification: Upper forewing black with large central patch of yellow, creamy-white spots towards the apex, orange-red towards body. Upper hindwing dull red with black border, row of submarginal blue spots. Lower hindwing dark brown with irregular markings.

Australian Painted Lady

Vanessa kershawi

This strong-flying butterfly is a migrant species, moving south in spring in large numbers. The mass migration of 1889 was reported to be so large that the sky was darkened by the butterflies. Mass migrations have been seen in recent years, but the numbers are far smaller. There are several generations a year. The female lays her green eggs, singly, on the centre of leaves. The brown caterpillar has two yellow lateral lines and is covered in branched spines. It shelters during the day and emerges at night to feed. The Australian Painted Lady is very similar in appearance to the Painted Lady (*V. cardui*), and was once classified as a subspecies. *Vanessa kershawi* is distinguished by the blue-centred eyespots on the upper hindwings, which are not present on *V. cardui*. *V. cardui* does occur around Perth in Australia as a result of migration from Africa, but has been unable to extend its range.

Distribution: Australia, Christmas Island, New Zealand.
Habitat: Gardens, scrub, grassland, waste land.
Food plant: *Chrysocephalum* sp. *Helichrysum* sp., *Artemesia* sp..
Wingspan: 50–60mm (2–2¼ in).
Status: Not listed.

Identification: Upper forewings black with orange markings, brown towards body, four white spots near apex and white bar running from leading margin. Upper hindwings orange and brown with three or four submarginal blue eyespots. Lower forewings similar but pale, Lower hindwings mottled cream and brown, with faint eyespots.

New Zealand Red Admiral

Vanessa gonerilla

Distribution: New Zealand
Habitat: Varied, anywhere
the food plant occurs.
Food plant: *Urtica* sp..
Wingspan: 50–60mm
(2–2¼ in).
Status: Not listed.

Identification: Forewings black to
brown, with striking red bar and
an arc of white spots towards
apex. Hindwings brown, red bar
with pale blue dots edged in
black. Underwings similar pattern
on mottled brown, Lower
forewings have a red bar, black
patch with white markings and
blue ring.

This butterfly is
endemic to New
Zealand. Its Maori
name is 'kahukura',
which means 'red
cloak'. It is relatively
common throughout
New Zealand as its food
plant, nettles, is widely
distributed. It is a
strong-flying butterfly
that is seen during the
summer months, feeding
on nectar. These are long-
lived butterflies, surviving
several months. The females lay their
eggs singly on the young leaves of nettle plants. The caterpillars become more black with
age, developing hairs. They make a shelter by rolling the leaf into a tube. There are two
subspecies, one of which, *V. gonerilla ida*, occurs only on the Chatham Islands.

OTHER SPECIES OF NOTE
Orange Plane *Pantoporia consimilis*
The Orange Plane occurs in New Guinea
and Australia, where its larval food plant is
Lonchocarpus blackii, a vine that is found along
the edges of rainforests. The butterfly has black
wings, with two orange bands that cross
both wings and end with a single orange spot
near the apex of the forewing. The underwings
are similar but much paler.

Yellow-eyed Plane *Neptis praslini*
This butterfly has brown wings, with yellow
spots on the upper forewing and a yellow band
across the upper hindwing. It is a Batesian mimic
of the unpalatable Hamadryad butterfly. The
mature caterpillar is pale green, with a white
diagonal band along the side of the body and it is
covered in spines. Spines are present on the
head, thorax and on two of the abdominal
segments. Adults have a slow, gliding flight with
wings outspread, interspersed by one or two
rapid beats. Several generations are completed
a year.

The Common Sergeant

Pantoporia perius

The Common Sergeant was named by
British Army officers, who gave many
butterflies military-sounding names. This
species has previously been classified as
Athyma perius. It is a relatively common
butterfly across its range. It is found mostly
at lower elevations, but it is a powerful flier
and can be found up to 2,300m (7,500ft). It
prefers open habitats, where it can fly close
to the ground. It is constantly on the move,
only settling briefly on damp patches in
order to obtain moisture.

Distribution: India,
Himalayas, southeast Asia
Habitat: Open habitats
with the food plant.
Food plant: *Glochidion* sp.
(okra).
Wingspan: 60–70mm
(2¼–2¾ in).
Status: Not listed.

*Above: Caterpillars are yellow-green
with three rows of red spines.*

Identification:
Male upperwings
dark brown, series
of small white spots
along the margin, bands
of large white spots
across the middle of
each wing. Female brown
with white spots and
markings. Underwings
yellow-orange.

Purple Emperor

Apatura iris

Distribution: Europe (not Spain and Italy), across Asia to China and Korea.
Habitat: Broad-leaved woodland.
Food plant: *Salix* sp. (willow).
Wingspan: 70–90mm (2¾–3½ in).
Status: Not listed.

Identification: Male upperwings dark brown-black with iridescent purple-blue sheen. White spots on FW and white stripe on HW. Female dark-brown with white markings. Eyespot on both underwings.

The purple colour of the male is only visible from certain angles as it is due to the refraction of light from the surface of the scales and not from a pigment. The Purple Emperor is on the wing from June to August; however, it is a secretive butterfly that stays high in the canopy, where it feeds on aphid honeydew and tree sap. The males descend to the ground to obtain moisture from puddles and salts from dung. The females lay their bright green eggs on the upper leaves of its food plant. The caterpillar is bright green with tapered ends, diagonal yellow lines along the sides, tiny yellow dots, and two long horns tipped with red on its head. The caterpillars overwinter in the forks of tree branches and in buds, and resume their development the following spring. This attractive butterfly has experienced a decline due to loss of its woodland habitat. However, it appears to be expanding its range in Scandinavia and Russia.

Right: The underwings are mottled brown, with a distinctive eyespot on the forewing.

Black Rajah

Charaxes solon

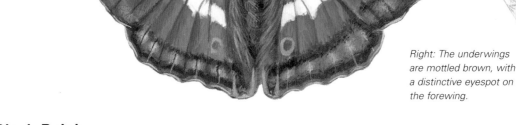

The Black Rajah is a strong-flying butterfly and is abundant wherever its food plant, the tamarind, grows. The dark underwing colours make the butterfly difficult to spot when at rest. It is frequently seen around trees such as *Cassia nodosa* and *Photinia japonica* that ooze sap from their bark. The butterflies are attracted to the sugary sap as well as the fermenting juice of rotting fruits, both on trees and on the ground. The males wait on hill tops or fly around in search of females. The caterpillar is dark green with yellow tubercles. The head has horns and red-tipped spines. They feed on the leaves of the tamarind tree.

Identification: Upperwings brown-black with yellow-white bands across both wings, breaking to spots near the apex of the FW. HW has a series of spots along margin, ending in large blue-green spot, two tails, longer in female. Underwings purple-grey to dark grey with black spots and lines, yellow spots along margin.

Distribution: South and southeast Asia.
Habitat: Up to 1,950m (6,400ft).
Food plant: Fabaceae e.g. *Tamarindus* sp..
Wingspan: 70–80mm (2¾–3⅛ in).
Status: Not listed.

Indian Leaf Butterfly

Kallima inachus

Distribution: South and southeast Asia to Japan.
Habitat: Rainforest.
Food plant: Acanthaceae e.g. *Strobilanthes* sp., Urticaceae *Girardinia* sp..
Wingspan: 8–12cm (3–4½ in).
Status: Not listed.

Identification: Both sexes blue upperwings. Upper forewings broad, curved with tip, orange band across wing, dark apex. Upper hindwings blue-grey with curved margin and tail. Underwings leaf-like with dark veins. Seasonal forms.

The Greek word 'kallima' means 'beautiful', and this description applies to this butterfly. However, its appearance is transformed when it closes its wings to reveal a pattern that mimics a dead leaf. This pattern, together with the shape of the curved wings, provides perfect camouflage when the butterfly settles beside dead leaves. There is a wet- and dry-season form of this butterfly, with the wet-season butterflies being darker. This rainforest butterfly is seen flying swiftly through the forest, where it favours the banks along streams. It comes to the ground to feed on the juices of rotting fruit.

OTHER SPECIES OF NOTE

Tailed Emperor *Polyura sempronius*
This is a mostly tropical species that has a large wingspan of up to 11cm (4⅜in). Its wings are black and cream with two long tails on each hindwing. The underwings are brown and cream, with orange markings.

Turquoise Emperor *Apaturina erminea*
This species occurs across the Moluccas and Solomon Islands to Australia. It has black wings with an iridescent blue-green patch towards the body, and a diagonal band of yellow-orange spots across the forewing with two white spots near the apex. There is a small eyespot on the hindwing. The underwings lack the iridescence.

Danaid Eggfly *Charaxes latona*
This Australian butterfly has orange and dark brown upperwings, and mottled brown-orange underwings with thin black lines. Each hindwing bears two short tails. The caterpillar is green with a pink patch on the dorsal surface of the first abdominal segment and black spots on the next three segments.

Clipper

Parthenos sylvia

This common and widespread species varies in appearance across its range. The background colour to the wings ranges from green in India, blue in Malaysia and brown to yellow in New Guinea and the Philippines. There are more than 20 subspecies. The name 'clipper' (a type of sailing ship) comes from the white sail-like patches on the wings. It is a forest species, where it is found high in the canopy. It has a powerful and fast flight. The caterpillars have a red-brown, cylindrical body with yellow-white lateral lines. There are long branched red-brown spines on segments three to twelve.

Distribution: South, southeast Asia, New Guinea.
Habitat: Rainforest margins.
Food plant: Cucurbitaceae, Passifloraceae e.g. *Adenia* sp., Menispermateae e.g. *Tinospora cordifolia*.
Wingspan: 10cm (4in).
Status: Not listed.

Identification: Upperwings variable in colour, from bright blue-green to brown. Distinctive band of glassy blue-white markings created by a lack of scales, UHW browner, with black zigzag lines and veins.

Cruiser

Vindula erota

Identification: Sexes different. Male upperwings orange, black lines and dots. UHW similar, with two small eyespots. Underwings mottled pattern of pale orange, grey and brown, LFW white patch. Female larger, paler orange to brown, UFW black margin with white spots and crescents, UHW black submarginal line, two small eyespots, tiny tail.

The Cruiser is a rainforest species. The females stay high in the rainforest canopy, but the males fly to the ground to feed on nectar from flowers such as *Lantana* and the juices of rotting fruits. There are two seasonal forms. The wet-season form is described left, while the dry-season male butterflies are smaller and paler and the underwings are red-brown with smaller markings. The dry-season females look very different, with a creamy white band across both wings. The females lay their eggs singly on the stems and tendrils of the food plant. The caterpillars are yellow, with two black bands and long branched spines. The head has two long, curved and branched spines. There are a number of subspecies across the range.

Distribution: New Guinea to Solomons, northeast Australia.
Habitat: Rainforest.
Food plant: *Hollrungia* sp., *Passiflora* sp..
Wingspan: 80mm (3⅛ in).
Status: Not listed.

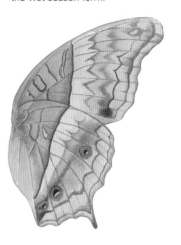

Below: The underwings of the male dry-season form are paler with smaller markings than on the wet-season form.

Archduke

Lexias dirtea

This butterfly is found across south and Southeast Asia, where it is found in forests. The Archduke is believed to be abundant in parts of its range. The brightly coloured males are often seen basking in the sun in forest glades. They fly along tracks and the edge of the forest, and defend territories. The females are more secretive, and their speckled appearance provides good camouflage in the shady forest glades. Both feed on the juice of rotting fruits and visit flowers for nectar. The Archduke is commonly confused with the similar *Lexias pardalis*, which has yellow tips to the antennae.

Distribution: India to the Philippines.
Habitat: Forests, uplands.
Food plant: *Garcinia laterifolia, Calophylum* sp..
Wingspan: 11–11.5cm (4⅜–4¾ in).
Status: Not listed.

Identification: Sexes different. Male upperwings are velvety black with metallic blue-green to violet margins on the fore- and hindwings. Females brown with bands of small creamy white-yellow spots. Black antennae.

Above: The female Archduke looks very different from the male, with a brown wing covered in small yellow spots.

Australian Lurcher

Yoma sabina

Distribution: Southeastern Asia, Northern Australia, New Guinea.
Habitat: Lowland rainforest, swampy areas within monsoon forest.
Food plant: Acanthaceae e.g. *Dipteracanthus bracteatus*, *Ruellia* sp..
Wingspan: 65–70mm (2½–2¾ in).
Status: Not listed.

Identification: Upperwings dark chocolate-brown with broad orange band across both wings. Males yellow spot in apex of forewing, females white spot. Forewing hooked shape, hindwing scalloped margin and short tail. Underwings mottled shades of brown, grey and green.

The Australian Lurcher is found only in the far north of Australia where it is relatively common, particularly during the wet season. The butterflies settle on leaves and open their wings to bask in the sun. When they rest with their wings up, they are difficult to spot among the foliage. The pattern on the underwings does vary during the year, to match the changes in vegetation. The butterflies are on the wing all year, and there are several generations. The females lay their eggs singly on the underside of leaves of the food plant. The black caterpillar has small dashes of orange and white along the sides, and is covered in black branched hairs. The caterpillars are voracious feeders and move from plant to plant, stripping the leaves. They descend to the ground to pupate.

OTHER SPECIES OF NOTE

The Glorious Begum *Prothoe calydonia*
This powerful butterfly has a wingspan of up to 12cm (4¾in) and is found in rainforest. The forewings are yellow with a black apex, while the blue hindwing has a black margin and short tail-like lobe. The underwings are a mottled pattern of orange, brown and black, with splashes of yellow and white. This butterfly may also be classified as *Agatasa calydonia*.

Large Yeoman *Cirrochroa aoris*
This large tropical butterfly has orange-brown wings and is found in India and Myanmar. The genus *Cirrochroa* contains more than 80 species which are found mostly in south and Southeast Asia.

Koh-i-Noor

Amathuxidia amythaon

This large, broad-winged rainforest butterfly occurs from India to Indonesia and in the Philippines. When it settles on the forest floor, it raises its wings to reveal the cryptic colouring of the lower wings. This provides perfect camouflage against the leaf litter. This species and others of its genus are crepuscular and are seen flying at dusk. Koh-i-Noor is the name given to one of the world's largest diamonds, which is believed to have been mined in southern India in the 12th century and is now part of the British Crown Jewels.

Distribution: India, southeast Asia, Philippines.
Habitat: Lowland rainforest, swampy areas within monsoon forest.
Food plant: Uncertain, but likely to be Acanthaceae.
Wingspan: 10–11cm (4–4⅜in).
Status: Not listed.

Identification: Males have distinctive iridescent blue band across brown-black wings. Broad wings with small tail-like lobe on HW. Females bright yellow-orange band across UFW, bright yellow HW, with small lobe-like tail. Lower wings pink-brown with four eyespots, and four or five dark-brown zigzag lines crossing both wings.

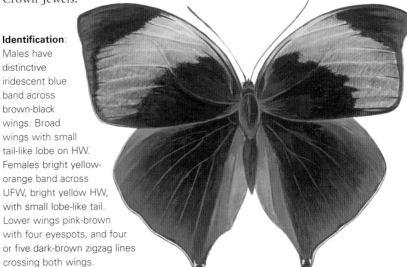

Grey Count

Tanaecia lepidea

Found in the lower Himalayas eastwards, from Almora, in the Western Ghats, central India, Bengal and into Assam and the Malay Peninsula, this is a rainforest species that prefers the low-lying wet evergreen forests. Here it feeds on juice from rotting fruit and tree sap. It is seen resting on leaves with its wings held out. The caterpillar is blue-green with four tubercles on segments three to 11, and pairs of yellow-tipped spines. There are several subspecies of the Grey Count that vary in appearance. The male is dark brown, with dark markings of transverse lines and an ash-grey band along the margin of the lower wing, while the female has a lighter brown colouring with a narrower grey band.

Distribution: India, Pakistan, Myanmar, Malaysia.
Habitat: Rainforest.
Food plant: *Melastoma* sp., *Careya* sp..
Wingspan: 65–80mm (2½–3⅛ in).
Status: Not listed.

Identification: Upperwings hooked, dark brown, pale, transverse markings at base of both wings. Male pale grey-brown marginal band across both wings, getting wider from forewing to hindwing. Lower forewing yellow-brown, lower hindwing pale brown with blue-grey markings near margin. Female grey band on upperwings darker, lower forewing yellow.

Diadem

Hypolimnas misippus

Identification: Male upperwings black with purple sheen, two white patches on forewing, one central white patch on hindwing. Scalloped margins. Females polymorphic; most common is yellow-orange upperwings, with black apex and white band, white spots on the forewing, and black margin on the hindwing.

The Diadem is also called the Danaid Eggfly, the Six-Continent and the Mimic. It is a widespread, and relatively common, species across the world. It was believed to have been introduced to the Americas from Africa by slave ships. As the name suggests, it is a mimic. The highly variable females are all mimics of the various forms of the African Monarch (*Danaus chrysippus*). In most places there are two generations a year, from April to May and from September to December. The black caterpillars have large white patches surrounded by purple rings and are covered in branched hairs.

Distribution: Australia, Pacific Islands, south Asia, southeast Asia, Africa, Caribbean, southern USA, South America.
Habitat: Open scrub and wasteland.
Food plant: Malvaceae, Acanthaceae, Convolvulaceae.
Wingspan: 55–70mm (2⅛–2¾ in).
Status: Not listed.

Right: The males all look the same, but there are four forms of the female. The wings are orange with black margins, with white patches and dots.

Blue-banded Eggfly

Hypolimnas alimena

Distribution: Indonesia, New Guinea, Queensland, Australia.
Habitat: Lowland rainforest, gardens.
Food plant: *Pseuderanthemum variabile*.
Wingspan: 65–70mm (2½–2¾ in).
Status: Not listed.

Identification: Male upperwings blue-black, with blue band across each wing, submarginal white spots, double row of marginal spots, scalloped margin to hindwing. Underwings brown with pale blue-white band across each wing, submarginal row of spots, white margin. Females extra row of spots on forewing, underwings similar to upperwings.

These butterflies are strong fliers, and they are seen in rainforest, flying from flower to flower, or resting with open wings on sunlit leaves. They also rest under a leaf with their wings closed, where they blend perfectly with the vegetation and are difficult to spot. The butterflies are seen all year round, and there are several generations. It is particularly numerous after the wet season. The females lay their eggs singly or in clusters on the leaves and flower buds of the food plant, which is found growing on the forest floor. The caterpillar is secretive, hiding in the leaf litter and under rocks during the day and emerging at night to feed. It moves quickly and eats voraciously. Frequently, the caterpillars exhaust their food supply and move away to find new sources.

OTHER SPECIES OF NOTE

Pearl Owl *Taenaris artemis*
This butterfly is found in New Guinea and across to the Cape York Peninsula of Australia. Like other members of the genus *Taenaris*, they have distinctive eyespots on their white hindwings. The females lay their eggs in large clusters on the fronds of coconut and *Pandanus* sp.. The young caterpillars are gregarious, but become solitary after the last moult. There are 17 or so subspecies that vary in the size of the eyespot.

Malayan Eggfly *Hypolimnas anomala*
This tropical butterfly is found from Malaysia to the tropical regions of Australia. It has predominantly brown wings which get paler towards the margins. The forewings have two rows of white spots along the margin.

Bordered Rustic

Cupha prosope

The Bordered Rustic is a forest butterfly that flies low over the ground, flitting between sunny patches where it settles on sunlit leaves. It open and closes its wings constantly, revealing the bright upperwings. The butterflies are seen all year, particularly during the wet season, and there are several generations. There are two seasonal forms, the wet-season form (described right) and the dry-season form, the underwings of which are pink-brown and lacks the black spots. The females lay their eggs on leaves of the food plant. However, females have been observed to lay their eggs on spider webs near the food plant, to gain protection for the egg. Once hatched, the caterpillars lower themselves down by silk threads on to the leaves.

Distribution: Queensland, Australia.
Habitat: Edge of rainforest and gallery forest, monsoon forest.
Food plant: *Scolopia braunii*, *Xylosma* sp..
Wingspan: 45–60mm (1¾–2¼ in).
Status: Not listed.

Identification: Brown-orange upperwings, broad black margin. Underwings pale brown with submarginal row of small black spots, small eyespot on lower forewing. Females slightly larger.

Common Silver Xenica

Oreixenica lathoniella

The Common Silver Xenica is seen from February to April, and there is a single generation. It prefers shady forest and tea-tree-dominated wetlands close to the coast, where there is an understorey of grass, its food plant. The butterflies stay close to the ground, flitting from one sunny spot to another. The females are often seen in the company of a large number of males. At night, groups roost together on grasses growing under trees. The females lay their pale green eggs singly on grasses. The caterpillars shelter during the day and emerge at night to feed. The mature caterpillar occurs in a range of colours from green to brown. There is a dark dorsal line edged in yellow, a yellow line along the sides and a number of pale sub-dorsal lines. The head and body are covered in short spines and there is a short, yellow, forked horn at the end of the abdomen.

Distribution: Australia.
Habitat: Damp forest and coastal grasslands with *Leptospermum lanigerum*.
Food plant: *Microlaena stipoides, Poa sp.*.
Wingspan: 45mm (1¾ in).
Status: Not listed, although classed as Vulnerable in south Australia.

Identification: Upperwings pale orange-yellow with darker patches, one eyespot on each wing. Hindwings larger than forewings. Underwings mottled shades of orange, brown and silver white with two eyespots.

Kershaw's Brown

Oreixenica kershawi

Distribution: Southeast Australia.
Habitat: Tea-tree and saw-sedge wetlands.
Food plant: Grasses, including *Poa* sp, *Tetrarrhena* sp..
Wingspan: 30mm (1¼ in).
Status: Not listed, but considered Vulnerable in parts of its range.

Identification: Upperwings brown with yellow patches. Upper forewing small eyespot near apex. Upper hindwing has large eyespot at base. The underwings have similar pattern but paler, two eyespots on the lower hindwing.

Kershaw's Brown Butterfly is on the wing from January to March, and there is a single generation a year. The males are seen basking in the sun with their wings open on tea-tree branches. The females stay close to the ground. They lay their small pale green eggs singly on leaves of the food plant, or on the ground close by. The older caterpillars vary in colour from green to brown, with a dark green dorsal line and pale yellow lateral lines, a few hairs and a forked tail tipped in pink. They feed on grasses at night, sheltering at the base of the food plant during the day. They pupate on the food plant, the spiky pupa hanging down from the leaf. This butterfly has declined in recent years due to the draining of its wetland habitats, where silky tea-tree and saw-sedge are found. The wetlands are now fragmented, and in some summers dry out and the grass die, causing the caterpillars to die too.

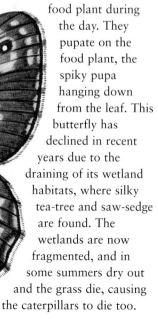

Sword Grass Brown

Tisiphone abeona

> **Distribution**: Southeastern Australia.
> **Habitat**: Saw grass wetlands.
> **Food plant**: *Gahnia* sp. (saw sedges).
> **Wingspan**: 60mm (2¼ in).
> **Status**: Not listed.

Identification: Brown wings. Upper forewings brown with yellow diagonal stripe, two eyespots, one large, one small. Upper hindwings brown, scalloped margin, two eyespots, one small and one large red and black eyespot encircling white spot. Underwings similar, two large eyespots on lower hindwings.

The Sword Grass Brown butterfly is on the wing from October to March, although the largest numbers are seen from November to February. There is either one or two generations. The female lays her large green eggs on the inside of young leaves where they are out of sight. The green caterpillars have very pale dorsal and lateral lines and are completely covered in long fine hairs that gives them a fuzzy appearance. The end of the abdomen is forked and tipped in pink. The young caterpillars feed all day, but the older ones shelter by day and feed at night. There are several subspecies that occur along the coast of southeast Australia. The butterfly is declining due to the loss of its habitat, the tall saw sedge wetland areas near the coast. The wetlands have been drained and cleared, fragmenting the butterfly's habitat.

OTHER SPECIES OF NOTE

Blue Baron *Euthalia phemius*
The Blue Baron occurs across Southeast Asia and southern China. The male has brown-blue upperwings and brown underwings. The female is larger and has dark brown upperwings, with a prominent white stripe across both the upper and lower forewings. The stunning caterpillars of the genus *Euthalia* have rows of long feathery spines along each side.

Helena Brown *Tisiphone helena*
This butterfly is found in Queensland, Australia. The wings are brown with a yellow band and an orange patch on the forewing. There are two dark eyespots on each of the wings, those on the hindwings being much larger. The females lay their bright green eggs singly on dead leaves found at the base of the food plant, saw sedge (*Gahnia* sp.).

Silky Owl

Taenaris catops

This butterfly is named after the owl-like eyespots on the upper hindwings. The butterflies are seen in the shady parts of the forest, flying low above the ground, looking for rotting fruits. They also feed on the sap of the cycad or sago palm. The sap contains a poison which is taken up by the butterfly, making it unpalatable to predators. At dusk they settle on plants where they roost, hanging from the underside of leaves. The mature caterpillar is black, with white and yellow lateral lines, black spiracles ringed in orange, and white hairs. The head bears horns with eight long, thin spines. The caterpillars are gregarious and stay together until after the final moult. They feed in a line starting at the tip of the leaf, and work their way to the base.

> **Distribution**: Papua New Guinea.
> **Habitat**: Rainforest, gardens.
> **Food plant**: *Caryota rumpha* (black palm), *Musa* sp. (banana), *Phaius tancarvilleae* (orchid).
> **Wingspan**: 8–10cm (3-4in).
> **Status**: Not listed.

Identification: Creamy-white wings and dark veins. Upper forewing black margin to leading edge, upper hindwing rounded shape, black margin and pale eyespot. Underwings similar but eyespots larger and more prominent with concentric circles of black and orange and central white dots. Female larger.

Common Brown

Heteronympha merope

Males flutter just above the ground, searching through the undergrowth for the more secretive females. When they land on the ground they raise their wings revealing the mottled brown coloured underwings, which provide good camouflage. The females lay their eggs singly on the leaves of the food plant. The caterpillars vary in colour, being green, grey or pale brown. They carry black or brown markings, including a broken mid-dorsal line and two lateral rows of spots. The whole body is covered in short hairs. The caterpillars shelter during the day on the ground near the food plant, and they emerge at night to feed on grass.

Distribution: Southern Australia, Tasmania.
Habitat: Open temperate woodland with grass.
Food plant: *Poa* sp..
Wingspan: 60–70mm (2¼–2¾ in).
Status: Not listed.

Identification: Male upperwings orange with brown markings and margins, eyespot on each wing, underwings pale orange with brown apex on LFW, LHW brown with zigzag lines and three eyespots. Female larger, upperwings orange, UFW brown towards apex, blue eyespot and three yellow patches, UHW brown margins with eyespot. Underwings similar, LFW grey apex, LHW mottled grey brown with zigzag lines.

Right: The wings of both sexes bear eyespots, but the female is larger and has a wider black margin on the forewing.

Banks' Brown Butterfly

Heteronympha banksii

The Banks' Brown Butterfly is on the wing from September through to March. The butterflies are active, flying from flower to flower in search of nectar. The males defend territories. The female lays her green eggs on grass leaves in autumn. The caterpillar is brown with darker brown spots, white tubercles and dark, waxy dorsal and lateral lines.

Distribution: Southern Australia.
Habitat: Upland grassland in ravines and on hillsides above 300m (1,000ft).
Food plant: Grasses and sedges *Carex* sp., *Gahnia* sp..
Wingspan: 40–50mm (1½–2in).
Status: Not listed.

There are two short horns on the head and two longer ones at the end of the abdomen. There are three subspecies. The caterpillar feeds by night and shelters at the base of the food plant during the day. It pupates on the food plant. The caterpillar eats various native and introduced grasses, while the butterfly drinks nectar from flowers. The butterflies are also attracted to fermenting fruit and gum seeping from tree wounds.

Identification: Upperwings black to dark brown with yellow-orange markings. Upper forewings have white spot near apex. Upper hindwings have an eyespot. Lower forewing similar to upperwing but paler, lower hindwing orange-yellow with bands of red and purple brown, small pale eyespots.

Common Evening Brown

Melanitis leda

Distribution: South Asia, southeast Asia, Australia.
Habitat: Grasslands, wetlands, rice paddies.
Food plant: Grasses including *Oryza* sp., *Andropogon* sp., *Cynodon* sp., *Imperata* sp..
Wingspan: 40mm (1½ in).
Status: Not listed.

Identification: Dry-season form (shown here): pale brown wings with eyespot on UHW. Underwings mottled grey with lines crossing wings. Wet-season form: brown wings. UFW hooked tip, orange crescent surrounding two white spots. HW scalloped margin, short tail and tiny white eyespot. Underwings brown with striated appearance and series of small submarginal eyespots.

This common butterfly is usually seen flying at dusk, close to the ground. When disturbed it flies a short distance and then falls to the ground, where it closes its wings. The shape and colour give the appearance of a dead leaf, providing perfect camouflage. The female lays her pale yellow eggs in small clusters on the underside of grass leaves. The caterpillar is bright green, with two long, brown, hairy horns on the head and two green horns on the tip of the abdomen. It is a gregarious caterpillar, with small groups feeding on leaves during the day. At night they settle on the underside of the grass leaves. The green pupa is found hanging from the food plant.

OTHER SPECIES OF NOTE

Bamboo Tree Brown *Lethe europa*
The Bamboo Tree Brown is found from India, across Southeast Asia, to southern China, where it occurs in large numbers during the wet season. The upperwings are dark brown, but the underwings are mottled shades of brown with a series of eyespots on the hindwing. The female is similar but has a white diagonal stripe across the upper forewings. Its food plant is the bamboo.

Yellow-barred Butterfly *Xanthotaenia busiris*
This brown butterfly is found in the rainforests of Southeast Asia, where it is seen flying in the undergrowth, searching for its food plant, *Calamus* sp.. The adults are frequently seen sipping the juice of rotting fruits. It takes its name from the yellow band across the forewing, which is clearly displayed when the adult rests with its wings raised.

Orange Bush Brown

Mycalesis terminus

These butterflies come to the ground to feed on the juice of rotting fruits. The females lay their yellow eggs in clusters on the underside of grass leaves. The caterpillars are brown with a faint dark brown dorsal line and diagonal markings, and forked dark brown horns on head and tail. The caterpillars feed on the leaf-tips of the grass plants, sheltering head-down near the base of the plant during the day and emerging to feed at night.

Distribution: New Guinea, Australia.
Habitat: Rainforest margins.
Food plant: Poaceae, e.g. *Imperata* sp., *Panicum maximum* and *Themeda triandra*.
Wingspan: 40mm (1½ in).
Status: Not listed.

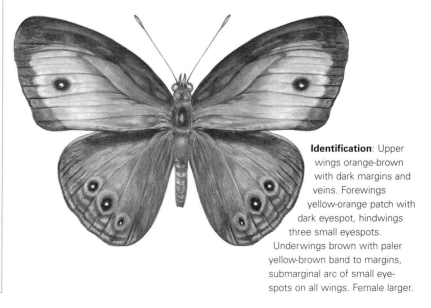

Identification: Upper wings orange-brown with dark margins and veins. Forewings yellow-orange patch with dark eyespot, hindwings three small eyespots. Underwings brown with paler yellow-brown band to margins, submarginal arc of small eyespots on all wings. Female larger.

Saturn

Zeuxidia amethystus

The Saturn is a medium-sized rainforest butterfly that is found in the shady understorey close to water, up to altitudes of 1,400m (4,500ft). The butterfly is on the wing from May to September. It is a relatively common species that is seen flying along tracks and paths in the early morning and late afternoon, as it prefers heavily shaded forested areas and generally flies no more than a few feet above the ground. The brown leaf-like underwings provide good camouflage against the leaf litter on the ground, where it can be found feeding on the juice of rotting fruits such as figs, papaya and guava. The caterpillar is green with short, dark hairs. The head is horned and it has a pale yellow collar band, with a forked process at the posterior. There are several subspecies that are found in the Philippines.

Distribution: Southeast Asia, Malaysia and Myanmar to the Philippines.
Habitat: Rainforests.
Food plant: Uncertain.
Wingspan: 11–13cm (4⅜–5in).
Status: Not listed.

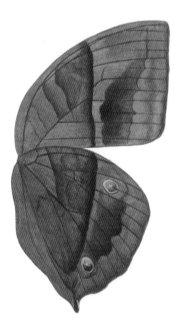

Identification: Male upperwings black with iridescent blue band across UFW and large blue patch on UHW. Small tail. Female black with yellow band and orange apex to hindwing.

Right: The male underwings are reddish-brown with small brown eyespots.

Northern Jungle Queen

Stichophthalma camadeva

The Northern Jungle Queen, as the name suggests, is found in thick forest, to 900m (3,000ft). This is a powerful flier that stays close to the ground or in clearings. It feeds on tree sap and rotting fruits on the ground. The underwings (shown here) provide camouflage when the butterfly lands and raises its wings. They are on the wing from June to August, and in some parts of the range there are two generations a year. Considered rare in some parts of its range, such as Sikkim.

Distribution: India, Pakistan, Myanmar.
Habitat: Forest.
Food plant: Palms and bamboo.
Wingspan: 12–13cm (4¾–5in).
Status: Not listed.

Identification: Underwings are green-brown with black lines near base, white band across both wings, row of brown spots with white centre between veins. Upper forewing pale blue, dark margins, upper hindwing dark blue to brown, white band below margin, blue veins.

Jungle Glory

Thaumantis diores

Distribution: India, Myanmar, North Thailand, China.
Habitat: Rainforest.
Food plant: Unknown.
Wingspan: 9.5–11.5cm (3¾–4½ in).
Status: Not listed.

Identification: Upperwings brown. Forewing iridescent blue band with silver gloss. Hindwing round patch of iridescent blue. Underwings rich brown crossed by yellow line, margins pale brown, small eyespot.

This rainforest butterfly is found from India through to Northern Thailand. It prefers swampy lowland forest, where it is found in shady places. During the day it rests on the leaf litter, where the pattern of its underwings provides excellent camouflage. If disturbed it flies away, flashing its blue upperwings before settling again. It feeds on rotting fruits on the ground. It is particularly active at dusk, when the dark colours of its wings make it difficult to spot. Due to the loss of its habitat, it is becoming rarer. There are several subspecies.

OTHER SPECIES OF NOTE

Ypthima baldus
This genus of brown butterflies occurs across Africa, Asia and Australia, and are characterized by brown wings with eyespots. *Ypthima baldus* is found across the Himalayas to Thailand, China, Korea and Japan. It is found in open forest, bamboo forest and grassland. Its food plants include *Poa* sp., *Digitaria* sp., and *Pogonatherum* sp.. Although this species is not considered endangered by the IUCN, it is considered locally rare in some parts of its range, notably Sikkim and along the borders of India and Myanmar.

Common Five Ring *Zethera incerta*
These butterflies are found in Sulawesi. The upperwings are white and grey-brown with dark veins. The underwings are grey-white with a yellow tinge, dark veins, eyespots and a strong black zigzag line around the margins.

Australian Fritillary

Argyreus hyperbius

Distribution: India, New Guinea, Korea, Japan, Australia.
Habitat: Coastal swamps.
Food plant: *Viola* sp..
Wingspan: 60–65mm (2¼–2½ in).
Status: Extremely high risk of extinction.

The Australian Fritillary or Laced Fritillary is found in open, swampy coastal habitats across eastern Australia. It is on the wing for much of the year in Australia, but only from April to November in the northern most parts of the range. The female lays her eggs, singly, on the leaves of the food plant. The young caterpillars remain on the food plant and feed at night. The older caterpillars feed during the day and shelter by night. The butterfly is suffering from widespread loss of its habitat and has been classed as at extremely high risk of extinction.

Below: The caterpillars are black with an orange dorsal line, and orange tubercles with short black spines.

Identification: Upperwings pale orange-brown with black spots and a marginal black band enclosing orange streaks. Underwings lower forewings pink-orange with black spots, pale brown apex with green-brown spots, lower hindwings pale brown with silver-and-black markings, green-brown spots, narrow silver-green marginal band.

Glasswing

Acraea andromacha

Identification: Forewing transparent, with brown-black bars on leading margin, hindwing creamy-white with black-brown spots, black-brown margin enclosing white spots. Body black with white spots.

The Glasswing, or Little Greasy, has a slow, gliding flight pattern, staying a few metres from the ground. This is a forest species. The Glasswing settles occasionally and visits flowers for nectar. It congregates at dusk to roost on the ends of dead branches. The butterflies are seen for much of the year, and there are several generations. Some years, when there is high humidity during the summer months, the Glasswing migrates south and inland to areas outside of its normal range, such as Victoria. Mostly, the females lay clusters of up to 200 eggs on the underside of leaves of *Passiflora* and *Hybanthus* species. The mature caterpillars are yellow-black with long black spines. They take up poisonous glycosides from the food plant, and these are retained in the adult. However, the common passion vine, *Passiflora edulis*, is toxic to the caterpillars.

Distribution: Northern Australia, New Guinea.
Habitat: Tropical and subtropical forest.
Food plant: *Passiflora* sp., *Hybanthus* sp..
Wingspan: 55–60mm (2⅛–2¼ in).
Status: Not listed.

Left: The pupa is creamy white, with yellow dots surrounded by a black ring located on each abdominal segment.

Below: The caterpillar is covered with branched black spines.

Common Crow

Euploea core

The Common Crow is found in a wide variety of habitats. It is, as its name suggests, a common butterfly. It is a migrant species that disperses north and south, for example into southern Australia, but the migrants do not form breeding populations. The butterfly is unpalatable and is mimicked by several other palatable and unpalatable species, for example the Common Mime (*Chilasa clytia*), and the Common Eggfly (*Hypolimnas bolina*). The butterfly is seen all year round, particularly after the wet season, and there are several generations. In many places the females do not breed during the dry season. Instead, they come together to overwinter in forest, and under rocks. The females lay their eggs singly on the underside of young leaves. The caterpillar is orange-brown with black bands edged with white. There are three pairs of long black horns behind the head and one pair on the tail. The caterpillars eat the leaves carefully, chewing through the veins first to restrict the flow of plant toxins into the leaf. As it grows it becomes more tolerant of the toxins and stores them in its body. There are numerous subspecies throughout the range.

Distribution: South India, southeast Asia, Australia.
Habitat: Many including rainforest, open forest, mountains to 2,500m (8,000ft), and gardens.
Food plant: Wide range including plants from Apocynaceae, Asclepiadaceae, Moraceae.
Wingspan: 80–90mm (3⅛–3½ in).
Status: Not listed.

Identification: Upperwings black-brown with series of large cream spots towards the margins and a row of small sub-marginal cream dots. Underwings similar pattern of brown with white spots, with smaller grey spots towards the body. Body brown with cream spots.

Black and White Tiger

Danaus affinis

Distribution: Southeast Asia, Solomon Islands, northeast Australia.
Habitat: Mangroves, tidal creeks.
Food plant: Asclepiadaceae e.g. *Cynanchum carnosum* (mangrove milkweed), *Tylophora* sp..
Wingspan: 60mm (2¼ in).
Status: Not listed.

Identification: Upperwings black with variable pattern of orange and white markings and spots. Underwings similar, but with orange markings on the lower hindwings.

This is a highly variable butterfly with more than 30 subspecies across its range, some of which are restricted to a single tropical island. The colours range from the typical white to orange. The butterfly is found in coastal regions. The female lays her pale yellow eggs singly, on the food plant, the mangrove milkweed. This is a climbing plant that is found on the edge of mangrove swamps and in tidal creeks. The caterpillars are dark blue, with yellow and white bands and spots, and three pairs of fleshy red and black filaments.

OTHER SPECIES OF NOTE

Parantica schenkii
This attractive butterfly is found in open habitats and along forest margins of the Solomon Islands and New Georgia. The male has pale yellow wings with black margins and veins. The females have white wings which are pale yellow towards the base and dark borders.

Chestnut Tiger *Danaus sita*
This butterfly, with its brightly coloured black and red brown wings, is found across South Asia, Southeast Asia and China. Large parts of the wing are transparent with a blue sheen. It is a slow-flying species occurring in forest glades. It feeds on a number of plants of the Asclepiaceae including *Cynanchum* sp. and *Tylophora* sp.. It may be classified as *Parantica sita*.

Hamadryad *Tellervo zoilus*
This black and white spotted butterfly is found in Australia and New Guinea, where it occurs in forests. Its food plants include *Aristolochia* sp. and *Parsonia* sp.. The caterpillar has a dark grey-black body with grey-white transverse lines and yellow to orange spots.

Plain Tiger

Danaus chrysippus

The Plain Tiger or Lesser Wanderer is also known as the African Monarch outside Asia. This is a common species seen all year round in scrub, coastal sand dunes and abandoned farmland, and other dry habitats in which its food plant can be found. There are several generations a year. The females lay their silver eggs singly on the underside of leaves. The caterpillars remain on the underside, feeding on the leaf from below. The caterpillar has a cylindrical body, with yellow spots and bands of black and white. It has three pairs of black filaments on segments three, six and 12. The butterfly has a tough exoskeleton and can survive predator attacks. It oozes a foul tasting liquid to deter enemies and will also feign death. It is mimicked by several butterflies including the Danaid Eggfly (*Hypolimnas misippus*), several Cethosia species and the Indian Fritillary (*Argyreus hyperbius*).

Distribution: Africa, southern Europe, across South Asia to Myanmar, Indonesia and China.
Habitat: Dry habitats such as coastal sand dune, abandoned farmland, dry grassland.
Food plant: *Calotropis gigantea* (common milkweed).
Wingspan: 60–80mm (2¼–3⅛ in).
Status: Not listed.

Identification: UFW orange brown with broad black margin around apex with white band or spots, UHW orange with black spots, narrow black margin with white spots. Another form has white HW. Male smaller and brighter.

SKIPPERS

Skippers are small butterflies characterized by their rapid, jerky flight. They have six functional legs, and antennae with a bent club end. Most have brown wings with orange, yellow or creamy-white markings. The greatest diversity of skippers occurs in the Neotropics, but there is a good representation of the family across this part of the world, with just under 230 species found in India and 125 in Australia.

Banana Skipper

Erionota thrax thrax

The Banana Skipper, as the name suggests, is found close to banana trees, where the caterpillars feed on the leaves. It is active at dawn and dusk. However, when it occurs in large numbers it is considered a pest because of the economic importance of banana plantations, where it can cause severe defoliation and reduced yields. A sign of infestation is the presence of rolled-up sections of leaves, which are shelters formed by the caterpillars. The caterpillars pupate within these shelters, where they defoliate the plants and reduce yields. The Banana Skipper is found across Southeast Asia and has spread eastwards to New Guinea. An extensive and successful biological control programme using a parasitic wasp (*Cotesia erionotae*) has prevented the skipper reaching Australia.

Distribution: South Asia, southeast Asia, New Guinea, China.
Habitat: Banana plantations.
Food plant: *Musa* sp..
Wingspan: 32–38mm (1¼–1⅜in).
Status: Not listed.

Below: The older caterpillars are covered in a white waxy powder that repels water, giving protection against drowning during heavy tropical downpours.

Identification: Brown wings. Upper forewing has large yellow spots. Distinctive large red eyes.

Halyzia Skipper

Mesodina halyzia

The Halyzia Skipper is also known as the Eastern Iris Skipper, after its food plant. These butterflies are seen from August to March and there are one or two generations. They fly low to the ground, and so favour open habitats. The males perch on stones and bare sand, and defend their territories during the afternoon. The female lays her eggs singly on the base of the food plant. The caterpillar is pale green with a covering of dusty white, and the head is black with white hairs. It feeds at dawn and dusk on the leaves of the flag iris. The rest of the time it shelters inside a leaf tent formed by joining leaves together with silk. It pupates in this shelter, head pointing down.

Distribution: Eastern Australia.
Habitat: Heathland, open eucalyptus woodland, grassland on sandy soils near the coast.
Food plant: *Patersonia* sp. (flag iris).
Wingspan: 30–33mm (1¼–1¾in)
Status: Not listed.

Identification: Dark brown wings. UFW white spots and white chequered border, LHW chequered border. LFW pale grey-brown, white patches, LHW grey-brown with darker patches outlined in black. Sexes have slightly different patterns of spots.

Praxedes Skipper

Trapezites praxedes

Distribution: Eastern Australia.
Habitat: Open woodland, coastal heathland.
Food plant: *Lomandra* sp. (mat rush).
Wingspan: 25–35mm (1–1⅜ in).
Status: Not listed.

The Praxedes Skipper or Southern Silver Ochre is found in coastal habitats in Eastern Australia. The butterflies are seen from September to March, when they are seen flying low to the ground over open vegetation. However, they will feed on eucalyptus flowers in the canopy. These butterflies are unusual as they make a humming noise as they fly. It is particularly loud when a group of males are chasing each other around. The females lay a single white egg on the base of a leaf stem. The caterpillar is red-brown with a pale dorsal line. The brown head bears white dots. The caterpillar shelters at the foot of the food plant and it is here that it pupates. It is red-brown and is covered in a white powder.

Identification: Upperwings dark brown with yellow patches on FW, single yellow patch on HW. LFW similar but paler. Male LHW brown with dark and light brown to yellow patches. Females brown with white spots outlined in dark brown.

Left: The male underwings are paler than the upperwings, and the hindwing lacks the yellow patches seen on the upperwing.

OTHER SPECIES OF NOTE

Coconut Skipper *Gangara thyris*
The Coconut Skipper has dark brown upperwings with pale yellow spots on the forewing. The underwings are pale brown with four blue-brown bands across the hindwing. The caterpillar is found on banana and palms. It is one of the larger Asiatic skippers and is found from South India across Southeast Asia to Indonesia, where it is seen around palm trees in forests at dawn and dusk.

Silver Spotted Ochre
Trapezites argenteoomatus
This common skipper is found in coastal heathland in Western Australia, where they are seen from June to October. The butterflies stay close to the ground, where they feed on flowers of *Senecio* and *Conostylis*. The females lay their eggs on *Acanthocarpus* sp..

Eliena Skipper

Trapezites eliena

The Eliena Skipper or Orange Ochre occurs down the eastern coast of Australia, where it is found in eucalyptus woodland and open woodland where there is an understorey of the food plant. It is on the wing all year in the northern parts of the range, but from October to March in the south. There are two generations a year. The males perch on high vantage points such as hilltops. The female lays her eggs singly at the base of the food plant. The caterpillar is green to green-pink with brown spots. It feeds on leaves and makes a tent shelter at the base of the food plant from leaves and silk. It pupates in this shelter. The pupa is brown with two black spots.

Distribution: Australia.
Habitat: Open woodland.
Food plant: *Lomandra* sp. (mat grass).
Wingspan: 30mm (1¼ in).
Status: Not listed.

Identification: Upperwings brown. UFW cream yellow to orange spots, UHW yellow-orange band, yellow margin. LFW red-brown, LHW red brown with white spots outlined in black.

Orange Swift

Parnara amalia

Identification: Brown wings. Upperwings chestnut brown with paler streaks and pale margins, series of tiny translucent spots. Underwings pale brown with similar streaks and margins.

The Orange or Hyaline Swift is a common Skipper in areas where cut grass and rice is found. The rice grows in swampy banks along water courses such as ditches, creeks and rivers. The Orange Swift is seen for much of the year, when it is often seen with the Grey Swift, flying quickly among the food plants. It is particularly abundant during the latter part of the wet season. Unusually, the mature caterpillar builds a shelter filled with a water-repellent substance, in which it pupates. This ensures that the pupal shelter floats should the water level rise or it is carried away by flood waters.

Distribution: New Guinea, Australia.
Habitat: Water courses with food plant.
Food plant: *Leersia hexandra* (cut grass), *Oryza* sp. (rice).
Wingspan: 25–30mm (1–1¼ in).
Status: Not listed.

Below: The green colours of the caterpillar provide camouflage on the food plant.

Dingy Dart

Suniana lascivia

Distribution: New Guinea, Australia.
Habitat: Open eucalyptus forest with grass understorey, coastal paperbark woodland, swamps.
Food plant: Grasses including *Imperata* sp., *Panicum* sp.
Wingspan: 25–30mm (1–1¼ in).
Status: Not listed.

The Dingy Dart is also known as the Dark Grass Dart, the Northern Dingy Dark and the Larrakia Dart. This butterfly is on the wing all year in the northern parts of its range, and from November to March in the more southerly parts. There are several generations a year. The butterflies fly slowly, staying close to the ground. The female lays a single cream egg with red markings on the leaves of the food plant. The mature caterpillar is pale green, with darker lateral lines and a brown head. It feeds on grasses at night and retreats into a leaf shelter during the day. There are several subspecies.

Identification:
Upperwings dark brown with narrow orange-yellow bands across both wings, more prominent in female.
Underwings pale brown, lower forewings darker brown patch toward body, and pale yellow streak. Males have black spot in middle of each upper forewing.

OTHER SPECIES OF NOTE

Doubleday's Skipper *Toxidia doubledayi*
This brown skipper has white spots on its forewings. It is found in coastal habitats along the east coast of Australia where the female lays her eggs on grasses such as *Poa* sp.. The pink-green caterpillar feeds at night and shelters during the day within a leaf shelter.

Decorated Ace *Thoressa decorata*
The Decorated Ace is found in wetlands along banks of streams and rivers of Southeast Asia. Although it is an uncommon species, it is locally abundant. This fast-flying species is on the wing from June to November. The males are seen more frequently as they perch on high branches watching for females and patrol a territory. The females are rarely seen as they are secretive and stay hidden in the scrub.

Alpine Sedge Skipper

Oreisplanus munionga

Distribution: Southern
Australia.
Habitat: Alpine and subalpine
woodland and grassland.
Food plant: *Carex* sp.,
Scirpus sp..
Wingspan: 25mm (1in).
Status: Not listed.

*Below: The underside of the
hindwings of both sexes
are yellow with black
markings.*

This species is also
known as the
Marrawah Skipper.
These skippers are
found in
mountainous regions
at altitudes of up to
1,060–1,600m
(3,200–5,250ft) where
they fly close to the
ground over alpine
meadows and open
woodland. They prefer
the damp areas and
swamps where the food plant
is found. It is on the wing from
December to March and there is one generation.
The female lays white eggs, singly on the underside of leaves
of the food plant. The caterpillar is green-grey with dark
dorsal lines and white lateral lines. The head is black with
brown markings. It feeds by night and shelters under a leaf-
tent during the day. There are two subspecies.

Identification: Male upperwings
brown with orange markings, pale
margin. Lower forewing brown
with pale orange-yellow markings,
lower hindwing pale yellow with
dark brown markings. Body dark
brown above and yellow and
black below. Female similar
but larger.

Regent Skipper

Euschemon rafflesia

Distribution: Northeastern
Australia.
Habitat: Forests.
Food plant: Monimaceae
e.g. *Tetrasynandra* sp..
Wingspan: 45–50 mm
(1¾–2in).
Status: Not listed.

Identification: Upperwings dark
brown with yellow spots.
Underwings are green with
yellow spots. Abdomen black and
yellow with a red tip.

*Below: The caterpillar reaches
about 5cm (2in) in length.*

This Skipper is unique in that the male has a primitive wing-coupling device consisting of
bristles at the base of the hindwing that link the fore- and hindwings together. This
arrangement is found in moths but not in any other butterfly. The butterflies are on the wing
for much of the year, and are usually seen in late afternoon and around dusk. The female
lays her eggs singly on the underside of the food plant leaves. The mature caterpillars are
green, with two dark sub-dorsal lines edged in white and white lateral lines. The head is
black and there are
two short yellow
horns on the
thorax. The
caterpillars feed at
night, and during
the day they shelter
under two leaves
stuck together with
silk. The mature
caterpillars cut out a
tent-like piece of leaf
under which they
pupate. There are two
subspecies.

MOTHS

Moths range in size from huge Atlas moths to the tiny micromoths. There are about 22,500 species of moth in Australia, the largest of which is the Hercules Silkmoth (Coscinocera hercules). Entomologists estimate that there are a further 10,000 species in India. However, in the rest of the region, especially in the remote tropical rainforests of Indonesia and New Guinea, there are few estimates of numbers of species.

Asota australis

Asota australis

Identification: UFW brown, patches of yellow, yellow veins, orange near base with tiny black dots, UHW yellow with thin brown margin. Hindwings similar pattern but paler. Thorax orange with black dots.

This moth is one of about 40 species of the genus *Asota* that are found in India, Sri Lanka, China, Japan, and through Southeast Asia to New Guinea and Australia. This is an Australian representative. The female lays a cluster of white eggs under leaves of the food plant, including fig species. The caterpillar, like other tiger moths, is very hairy. The caterpillars feed together at first but separate in the later stages. They pupate in a cocoon of matted larval hair. There are three subspecies.

Distribution: Australia, from Brisbane to Sydney, and southeast Asia.
Habitat: Coastal, casuarine woodland and scrub.
Food plant: *Ficus* sp..
Wingspan: 50mm (2in).
Status: Not listed.

Right: The underwings are the same in male and female.

Chinese Character

Digama marmorea

Distribution: Northern Australia, New Caledonia and Sulawesi.
Habitat: Scrub and woodland.
Food plant: *Carissa ovate* (currant bush).
Wingspan: 30mm (1¼in).
Status: Not listed.

Identification: Upper forewing grey with black speckles. Lower forewing yellow with a dark spot and grey tip. Underwings similar. Abdomen yellow with black spots along the dorsal line.

This common moth is found in northern Australia, and belongs to the Noctuidae family of moths, although the genus *Digama* was once classified in the Arctiidae. It is not to be confused with the Chinese Character moth found in Europe. Its cryptic colouring on the forewings provides excellent camouflage when resting on tree trunks. The caterpillar is grey, with a pale lateral line along each side. It feeds on the leaves of the currant bush, which is poisonous to other insects. There are several subspecies.

Scarce Hook Tip

Sabre harpagula

Distribution: Central and northern Europe, across Asia.
Habitat: Deciduous forests and steppe.
Food plant: *Tilia* sp..
Wingspan: 25–35mm (1–1¼in).
Status: Not listed.

Identification: Upper forewing has hooked apex, brown with dark brown-black spot along the margin. Upper hindwing brown with small dark spots. Underwing similar.

This moth belongs to the Drepanidae, and it occurs across Asia, from the United Kingdom, across Eurasia to the Far East. Although widespread, it is rare in many parts of its range. Its preferred habitat is deciduous forest. There are two generations of the Scarce Hook Tip moth a year, from May to June and August. The caterpillar has a pointed tail and, when resting, raises both its head and tail. It feeds on leaves of trees and shrubs, It pupates in a leaf shelter made by spinning leaves together with silk.

OTHER SPECIES OF NOTE

Asota orbona

This Australian moth has brown wings with two yellow patches, and orange veins on the upper forewings. The base of the forewing is orange with black dots. The hindwing is orange. The thorax and abdomen are orange with black dots.

Asota iodamia

This species of *Asota* has pale brown upper forewings with a circle of six black dots near the body. The hindwings are orange, with two black spots joined by arcs of smaller black dots across the middle. The abdomen is orange, with narrow black spots.

Coconut leaf miner *Agonoxena argaula*

This micromoth, as the name suggests, is found on coconuts, of which it is a pest. There are just four species in the genus *Agonexena*, and all are pests. Three are found on coconut palms, the fourth is a pest of the betel nut in Indonesia. The female moths lay their eggs on the leaves of the coconut palm. The caterpillars damage the leaves, although they are not usually present in sufficient numbers to do serious damage. Typically, the caterpillars burrow into the leaves, creating brown patches on the leaves as the leaf tissue is eaten.

Orange-spotted Tiger Moth

Ceryx guttulosa

This tiger moth is a mimic of a wasp and, as such, gains protection from would-be predators that mistake it for an insect that should be avoided. This moth is found across Southeast Asia, Papua New Guinea and Queensland, where it is found in woodlands and parks. It looks very similar to the closely related tiger moth, *Amata nigriceps*. The genus *Ceryx* is large, with representatives in Central and South Africa, across Asia to Australia.

Distribution: Australia, southeast Asia.
Habitat: Eucalyptus forest, woodland, gardens and parks.
Food plant: Unknown.
Wingspan: 50mm (2in).
Status: Not listed.

Identification: Black wings with five pale orange spots on each wing. The body is banded in orange and black, giving the appearance of a wasp.

Indian Moon Moth

Actias selene

Its beauty and large size make this Asian species of night-flying moth very popular with breeders. It is easy to raise as the caterpillars feed on easily obtained food plants such as apple, pear and hawthorn. In its natural habitat of forests, scrub and gardens, it feeds on a wide range of tree and shrub species. There are at least two generations a year, and in more southerly parts of its range there are continual generations with no diapause. Those found in more northerly regions can survive long periods of cold weather, but not freezing conditions. The eggs are white with dark mottling. The appearance of the caterpillar changes with the instars, early instars being mostly red, becoming apple-green in the third instar with brown head and legs and orange, spiny tubercles.

Identification: Males upper forewing pale green, almost translucent, becoming white near base, dark pink-red costal fascia, two submarginal dark lines, oblique pale yellow antemedial line, red-brown eyespot with pink margin. Upper hindwings similar with long pink-green swallowtail. Head, thorax and abdomen white, with pink band across thorax, pink antennae and legs. Female yellow antemedial line is paler and nearer to the base of the forewing and lacking in the hindwing, with less pink on the tail.

Distribution: South Asia, China, parts of southeast Asia.
Habitat: Forest, scrub, gardens.
Food plant: Varied, including *Coriaria* sp., *Hibiscus* sp., *Malus* sp., *Prunus* sp., *Pyrus* sp..
Wingspan: 8–12cm (3–4½in).
Status: Not listed.

Asiatic Atlas Moth

Attacus atlas

Distribution: South Asia, China, southeast Asia.
Habitat: Tropical and subtropical forests, scrub.
Food plant: *Citrus* sp.
Wingspan: 16–30cm (6–12in).
Status: Not listed.

Identification: Wings shades of brown, forewing triangular, with swept-back apex, submarginal lines in shades of yellow-brown, two transparent triangular eyespots with black margin. Hindwing similar. Body surprisingly small for size, hairy. Females larger and wings less tapered.

These are the giants of the moth world, with females having a wingspan of up to 30cm (12in) and a wing area of 400 square centimetres, larger than the White Witch Noctuid moth (*Thysania agrippina*) and the Birdwing butterflies (*Ornithoptera* sp.). Atlas moths may be named after the Greek Titan, but the name may also refer to the map-like wing patterns. The Chinese call them snake-heads after the shape of the wing apex. The adults, which live about two weeks, have no mouthparts and so rely on fat deposits within their body. The females lay their large, red-brown eggs on the underside of leaves. The caterpillars are pale blue-green, with spines covered in a white powdery substance. They are voracious feeders of leaves and can quickly defoliate a host tree. In India these moths are raised for their silk, although the cocoons are made from broken strands of silk, and not continuous ones as produced by the Silkmoth (*Bombyx* sp.).

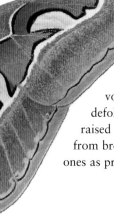

Imperial

Eacles imperialis

Distribution: Central, North and South America.
Habitat: Forests, scrub and gardens.
Food plant: *Acer* sp., *Liquidambar* sp., *Quercus* sp., *Pinus* sp..
Wingspan: 10–13cm (4–5in).
Status: Not listed.

This is a large, night-flying moth that is attracted to street lights. The adults are seen from June to August in the northern parts of the range, and April to October elsewhere. The adults have reduced mouthparts and so do not feed. There is one generation per year, and the female lays her eggs in clusters on the underside of leaves. Unusually, the first instar caterpillars wander off rather than start to feed. There are two colour forms within the caterpillars, an orange and black form and a yellow-green form. The body is covered in short white spines, with longer spines on the fore- and hind-segments. Although not classed as rare, this moth is in decline in parts of its range, especially in the northern part of its range, possibly as a consequence of habitat fragmentation.

Identification: Males have predominantly yellow wings with brown lines and spots, hairy body in yellow and brown. Several colour forms from yellow to pink-brown and purple-brown. Females larger, with more yellow.

OTHER SPECIES OF NOTE

White-stemmed Gum Moth *Chelepteryx collesi*
This moth is found on various gum and paperbark trees in southeast Australia. The wings are brown with bands of wavy yellow and grey. The male moth rears up when threatened, extending its forelegs and showing its underwings. This is likened to a spider about to strike. The caterpillar is black and grey, with yellow spots. The barbed hairs covering the caterpillar penetrate human skin and cause a painful rash.

Hercules Silkmoth *Coscinocera hercules*
The Hercules silkmoth is the largest moth in Australia, with female moths having a wingspan of up to 27cm (10½in). Only the male has a tail on each hindwing. The shape of the forewing is said to resemble a snake's head from the side with a black eye. This moth is found from New Guinea to Australia, occurring in tropical forests. The mature caterpillar is blue, with red spiracles and four horns on each segment. It feeds on leaves of numerous trees such as *Polyscias elegans* (celery wood) and *Prunus serotina* (black cherry).

Bee Hawk Moth

Cephonodes kingii

The name Bee Hawk comes from the moth's resemblance to bumble bees, both visually and in behaviour. These day-flying moths hover in front of flowers to sip nectar, and their rapid wing beats create a hum. The females lay their pale green eggs, singly, on the underside of leaves. The first instars are pale green, but later instars are green, grey and black with black lines, white warts on the head and posterior claspers, terminal horn and white spiracles edged in red. When threatened, the caterpillars arch back and regurgitate a foul-tasting liquid to deter predators. The caterpillars pupate in the soil.

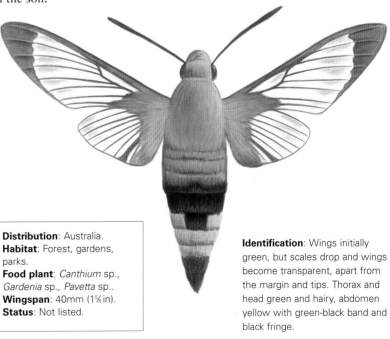

Distribution: Australia.
Habitat: Forest, gardens, parks.
Food plant: *Canthium* sp., *Gardenia* sp., *Pavetta* sp..
Wingspan: 40mm (1⅝in).
Status: Not listed.

Identification: Wings initially green, but scales drop and wings become transparent, apart from the margin and tips. Thorax and head green and hairy, abdomen yellow with green-black band and black fringe.

GLOSSARY

abdomen the third and hind body part of an insect

aestivate to become inactive or dormant during a period of adverse weather conditions

aggregations large groups

androconia patch of modified scales on the wing of a male from which pheromones are released

antenna(e) feeler on insect's head

arthropod invertebrate animal with a segmented body, exoskeleton and jointed appendages, belonging to the phylum Arthropoda

biodiversity the number of different species of animals and plant in a place

biological control using natural predators to control a pest species

biome a large area with a distinctive habitat, such as grassland or rainforest

camouflage colouring that blends with the background

captive breeding breeding of animals under controlled conditions, such as in a zoo or wildlife park

chemoreceptor a sensory receptor that is stimulated by the presence of certain types of chemical

chitin tough polysaccharide found in the exoskeleton of arthropods

chrysalis another name for insect pupa

CITES the Convention on International Trade in Endangered Species of Wild Fauna

clade a group of species that share a common ancestor

Above: The feathery antennae of the Giant Comet moth (Argema mittrei).

cocoon a silken case that surrounds and protects a pupa

coppicing traditional woodland management, in which trees are cut at ground level and allowed to regrow

critically endangered highest category of risk on the IUCN Red List, indicating that a species have, or will, decrease by 80% in three generations

crop part of the alimentary canal where food is stored prior to passing into the stomach

cryptic colouring that disguises appearance

defoliate to completely remove the leaves of a plant

deforestation the clearance of forest

diapause period of arrested development

dimorphic existing in two forms, for example dry and wet season forms

distribution the way individuals are spread over an area

DNA deoxyribose nucleic acid, the macromolecule found in the nucleus of cells that carries genetic information

ecdysone hormone involved in the moulting process

eclusion splitting of the pupal cuticle and the emergence of the adult

ectoderm outermost layer of cells, for example the epidermis

endangered at risk of being extinct, a category on the IUCN Red List

endemic native to a particular area

extinct no longer in existence, IUCN Red List category of not having been seen in the wild for 50 years

eye-spot distinctive spots on the wings of a butterfly or moth that resemble eyes

filiform thread-like

fogging a collection technique that involves releasing an insecticide in the canopy of a tree to bring down insects for study

frenulum row of bristles on the leading edge of the hindwing, to link fore- and hindwing together

gene pool the sum of all the genes in a population

global warming the process by which the average temperature of the Earth's surface is increasing

goblet cells large secretory cells

greenhouse gas a gas such as carbon dioxide that traps heat in the Earth's atmosphere

gregarious living in large groups

habitat the home, or environment, of an organism

haemocoel a series of spaces found in the bodies of invertebrates that have an open circulatory system

haemolymph the fluid that flows through the haemocoel

heterogametic of an organism that produces two types of gamete

honeydew the sugary liquid produced by insects such as aphids and other insects as they feed on plant sap

instar a developmental stage in the insect, each instar being the stage between moults

invagination an inward fold

iridescence the shimmering rainbow-like colours caused by the diffraction of light off the surface of scales

Below: At rest, an Ismenius Tiger (Heliconius ismenius) reveals its thorax and abdomen.

Below: Caterpillar of the Common Egg Fly (Hypolimnas bolina) chews using its mandibles.

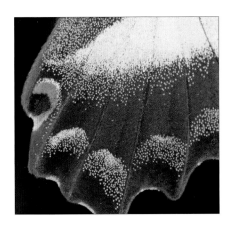

*Above: The iridescence of the wings of an Emerald Swallowtail (*Papilio palinurus).

larva the immature form of an animal that undergoes metamorphosis, called caterpillars in butterflies and moths

least concern the lowest category of risk in the IUCN Red List, evaluated as not under threat

logging the felling of trees

Malpighian tubule the excretory organ of an insect

mandible jaw

maxilla(e) paired mouthpart of an insect, used for chewing

metabolism the chemical processes of a living organism

metamorphosis a change in form; in lepidopterans the larval stage undergoes a complete transformation to become the adult form

migrant an insect that moves from one region to another and back again

migration a regular journey undertaken by animals such as butterflies, for example the migration of the Monarch (*Danaus plexippus*)

mimic an organism that resembles the colour, pattern, shape or behaviour of another

mimicry the process of copying the colour, pattern, shape or behaviour of another in order to benefit, for example, from reduced predation

morphology the study of shape and form

moult to shed a cuticle

mutation a change in the sequence of DNA in a gene or change in the structure of number of chromosomes

myrmecophily an association between ants and another organism

near-threatened a category of risk on the IUCN Red List, in which the species is not yet at sufficient risk to be classed as threatened, but could be in the future

obligate unable to live in any other way, for example, an obligate parasite cannot live without its host

oscelli (sing. oscellus) simple eyes

osmeterium brightly coloured, forked structure found on caterpillars of the Papilionidea, used for defence

palp appendage found near the mouth

parasitic living as a parasite, an organism that has a relationship with another called the host, and that does harm to that host

pectinate comb-like in appearance

pharynx part of the throat, behind the mouth

pheromone a chemical used for communication, such as for the male of a species to attract females

phylogeny evolutionary development of a species or group of species

pigment a coloured substance

polymorphic existing in several forms

proboscis tubular, sucking mouthparts

proleg fleshy outgrowth of the abdomen found on caterpillars, used for walking and gripping

pteridine pigment found in wings

pupa stage in the insect life cycle between larva and adult, during which the body of the insect undergoes change

scale tiny flat structures covering of the wing of lepidopterans

sclerite hard plates that form the exoskeleton and are bound to each other by membranes

segment a division of an animal's body

*Below: Close-up of the compound eye of the Emerald Swallowtail (*Papilio Palinurus).

*Above: The pupa of the Lime Swallowtail (*Papilio demoleus) *hangs from a branch.*

setae hairs found on caterpillars

sexual dimorphism a difference in appearance between males and females of the same species

speciation the process by which new species are formed

species a group of similar organisms that can interbreed

spermatheca sperm storage structure in the female

spinneret structure from which silk is released

spiracle respiratory opening on the body of an insect

substrate the surface or material on or from which an organism lives, grows, or obtains its nourishment.

tergum the name given to the dorsal sclerite of a segment

thorax the second body part of an insect, between the head and abdomen

tornus posterior part of the wing

tracheal system internal network of tubules that carry oxygen to the cells in the body of an insect

transect a path or line across a habitat, along which observations are made

tribe taxonomic category, ranking below family but above genus

tubercle outgrowths found on caterpillars, some are wart-like, others branched or horned

uric acid the insoluble, nitrogenous waste product of insects, reptiles and birds

urticating stinging

ventriculus part of the mid gut

vulnerable at risk of becoming extinct, category on the IUCN Red List, below the endangered category

INDEX

Below: Pararge aegeria.

Below: Hebomoia leucippe.

Above: Delias eucharis.

Below: Ixias pyrene.

Above: Eurema smilax.

Below: Erynnis tages.

Above: Danis danis.

Below: Phoebis philea.

Above: Nymphalis antiopa.

Below: Pseudalmenus chlorinda.

Above: Zeuxidia
amethystus.

Above: Lycaena phlaeus.

Below: Cethosia biblis.

Above: Callophrys avis.

*Below: Hamadryas
feronia.*

Above: Teinopalpus
imperialis.

Above: Zygaena ephialtes.

Below: Cephonodes
kingii.

Above: Pararge aegeria.

Above: Euschemon rafflesia.

PICTURE ACKNOWLEDGEMENTS

The Publishers would like to thank Robert Pickett at Papilio Photos for the specially commissioned photographs in this book.

Thanks also to the artists who provided the illustrations: Penny Brown, Peter Bull, Stuart Jackson-Carter, Felicity Cole, Joanne Glover, Jonathan Latimer, Carol Mullin, Fiona Osbaldstone and Denys Ovenden.

Additional photographs provided by the following agencies: The Nature Picture Library: 21 top, 22 top left, 22 top right, 26 top right, 30 top left, 34 top, 34 bottom left, bottom right, 35 top, 35 bottom left, 35 bottom middle, 35 bottom right, 37 top right, 40 top, 41 top right, 42 bottom, 43 bottom, 54 top left, 54 bottom, 55 bottom, 56 bottom, 57 top left, 58 bottom, 59 bottom, 63 bottom. Alamy: 40 bottom, 59 top, 64 bottom.

ABOUT THE AUTHOR

Sally Morgan MA, MSc, MI Biol, C. Biol, is a writer and photographer who studied biological sciences at the University of Cambridge, England. She has written more than 250 books covering a wide range of topics on natural history and the environment, for both adults and children. Her main interest is in food and farming, the natural world and environmental issues. She has visited many countries in search of the unusual and exotic to photograph. Sally owns an organic farm where she is carrying out several wildlife enhancement projects.